UHURU KENYATTA

PROMISES BROKEN

Joe Khamisi

Copyright © 2022, Jodey Book Publishers

All rights reserved. No part of this publication may be reproduced, stored in a retrieval system, or transmitted, in any form or by any means, electronic, mechanical, photocopying, recording or otherwise, without prior written permission from the publishers. Any person or persons who do any unauthorised act in relation to this publication may be liable to criminal prosecution and civil claims for damages.

Uhuru Kenyatta: Promises Broken
ISBN: 978-9966-192-134

Published by Jodey Book Publishers
E-mail: jodeybookpublishers@mail.com
Printed in Kenya.

To the Struggling Kenyans

AROUND the world, from the richest countries to the poorest, a dangerous new crop of leaders has sprung up. Unlike their totalitarian counterparts, these populists entered office through elections, but they show decidedly undemocratic proclivities. They propagate lies that become articles of faith among their followers. They sell themselves as noble and pure champions of the people, fighting against corrupt and greedy elites. They defy any constraints on their power and concentrate it in their own hands, launching frontal attack on institutions that sustain constitutional democracy, stacking the judiciary and the legislature, declaring war on the press, and scraping laws that check their authority

—Moses Naim,
A distinguished fellow at the Carnegie Endowment for International Peace and a renowned Syndicated Columnist, *Foreign Affairs*, March/April 2022.

CONTENTS

Acronyms & Abbreviations ix
Introduction xix

PART I: PEDIGREE 1
Chapter 1:   Kenyatta Brand 3
Chapter 2:   Kenyatta Business Empire 18

PART II: UHURU'S ENTRY INTO POLITICS 37
Chapter 3:   Project Uhuru 39
Chapter 4:   Minister for Finance 46
Chapter 5:   Second stab: Uhuru's Road to the Presidency 55

PART III: MR PRESIDENT 69
Chapter 6:   Uhuru's Reign: A New President 71
Chapter 7:   Dealing with terrorism 82
Chapter 8:   Violations of the law 95
Chapter 9:   Draconian Laws and Court Orders 119

PART IV: LOOTING 145
Chapter 10: Financial Wastage 147
Chapter 11: Corruption and Theft 169
Chapter 12: Scandals Galore 189
Chapter 13: Shame, Shame, Shame 204
Chapter 14: Uhuru, the "Discoverer" 226

PART V: THE INTRIGUES **249**
Chapter 15: Handshake, BBI Reggae and the Court-Shocker 251
Chapter 16: Uhuru Fallout with Ruto..272

PART VI: UHURU SUCCESSION **281**
Chapter 17: Ruto Betrayal 283
Chapter 18: Uhuru's Family Wealth: Innocent Inheritor?............289
Chapter 19: Kenyan Dynasties...299
Chapter 20: The Deep State 315

PART VII: THE SCRAMBLE.. **339**
Chapter 21: Who next?..341
Chapter 22: Uhuru's Scorecard 349
Chapter 23: The Last Word 375

Selected Bibliography 383
Index..397
Blurb..409

ACRONYMS & ABBREVIATIONS

ADC	– Aide-De-Camp
AFC	– Agricultural Finance Corporation
AfDB	– African Development Bank
AfriCog	– Africa Centre for Open Governance
AG	– Attorney General
AGPO	– Access to Government Procurement Opportunities
AGRF	– African Green Revolution Forum
AI	– Amnesty International
AIE	– Authority to Incur Expenses
AMCHAM	– American Chamber of Commerce
AMISON	– African Union Mission in Somalia
AMVTU	– Anti-Motor Vehicle Theft Unit
ANC	– African National Congress
ANC	– Amani National Congress
API	– Africa Policy Institute
APK	– Alliance Party of Kenya
ARA	– Assets Recovery Agency
ASTU	– Anti-Stock Theft Unit
ATPU	– Anti-Terrorism Police Unit
AU	– African Union
BAC	– Budget and Appropriations Committee
BBC	– British Broadcasting Corporation

BBI	– Building Bridges Initiative
BVI	– British Virgin Islands
CA(K)	– Communications Authority (of Kenya)
CAK	– Competition Authority of Kenya
CARICOM	– Caribbean Community
CAS	– Chief Administrative Secretary
CBD	– Central Business District
CBK	– Central Bank of Kenya
CBK	– Cooperative Bank of Kenya
CBRC	– China Bridges Railway Corporation
CCA	– Corporate Council of Africa
CCM	– Chama cha Mashinani
CEO	– Chief Executive Officer
CIA	– Central Intelligence Agency
CID	– Criminal Investigations Department
CIPEV	– Commission of Inquiry on Post-Election Violence
CJ	– Chief Justice
CKRC	– Constitution of Kenya Review Commission
CoB	– Controller of Budget
CoFEK	– Consumers Federation of Kenya
COMESA	– Common Market for Eastern and Southern Africa
CORD	– Coalition for Reforms and Democracy
COTU	– Central Organisation of Trade Unions
CRB	– Credit Reference Bureau
CS	– Cabinet Secretary
CSIS	– Centre for Strategic and International Studies
CT	– Computer Tomography
DC(s)	– District Commissioner(s)
DCI	– Directorate of Criminal Investigations
DFC	– Development Finance Corporation
DJ	– Disk Jockey

DO(s)	– District Officer(s)
DoD	– Department of Defence
DP	– Democratic Party (of Kenya)
DPP	– Director of Public Prosecutions
DRC	– Democratic Republic of Congo
EAC	– East African Community
EACC	– Ethics and Anti-Corruption Commission
EBS	– Elder of the Burning Spear
ECF	– Extended Credit Facility
ECK	– Electoral Commission of Kenya
ERF	– Emergency Response Fund
ERP	– Enterprise Resource Planning
EU	– European Union
FDA	– Food and Drug Administration
FKE	– Federation of Kenya Employers
FMSC	– First Mercantile Securities Corporation
FOCAC	– Forum on China-Africa Cooperation
Ford-Kenya	– Forum for the Restoration of Democracy-Kenya
FSD (Kenya)	– Financial Sector Deepening (Kenya)
GCA	– GEMA Cultural Association
GCG	– Grand Coalition Government
GDP	– Gross Domestic Product
GDR	– German Democratic Republic
GEMA	– Gikuyu Embu Meru Association
GF	– Global Fund
GNU	– Grand National Union
GSU	– General Service Unit
HRW	– Human Rights Watch

ICC	– International Criminal Court
ICDC	– Industrial and Commercial Development Corporation
ICFTU	– International Confederation of Free Trade Unions
ICIJ	– International Consortium of Investigative Journalists
ICJ	– International Court of Justice
ICPC	– International Centre for Policy and Conflict
ICT	– Information Communication Technology
ID	– National Identification
IDA	– International Development Association
IDP(s)	– Internally Displaced Person(s)
IEBC	– Independent Electoral and Boundaries Commission
IEDs	– Improvised Explosive Devices
IFMIS	– Integrated Financial Management Information System
IMF	– International Monetary Fund
IPI	– International Peace Institute
ISM	– Impact Standardisation Mark
JAP	– Jubilee Alliance Party
JBR	– Jumeirah Beach Residence
JKIA	– Jomo Kenyatta International Airport
JKUAT	– Jomo Kenyatta University of Agriculture and Technology
JSC	– Judicial Service Commission
JVA	– Joint Venture Agreement
KAA	– Kenya Airports Authority
KACC	– Kenya Anti-Corruption Commission
KADU	– Kenya African Democratic Union
KAF	– Kenya Air Force

KAM	– Kenya Association of Manufacturers
KANU	– Kenya African National Union
KAU	– Kenya African Union
KCA	– Kikuyu Central Association
KCAA	– Kenya Civil Aviation Authority
KCB	– Kenya Commercial Bank
KDF	– Kenya Defence Forces
KDOC	– Kenya Disaster Operation Centre
KEBS	– Kenya Bureau of Standards
KEG	– Kenya Editors Guild
KEMSA	– Kenya Medical Supplies Authority
Kenatco	– Kenya National Transport Company
KEPSA	– Kenya Private Sector Alliance
KETRACO	– Kenya Electricity Transmission Company
KFL	– Kenya Federation of Labour
KFS	– Kenya Forest Service
KICC	– Kenyatta International Convention Centre
KISA	– Kikuyu Independent Schools Association
KLA	– Kenya Land Alliance
KMC	– Kenya Meat Commission
KNCHR	– Kenya National Commission on Human Rights
KNH	– Kenyatta National Hospital
KNUT	– Kenya National Union of Teachers
KOT	– Kenyans on Twitter
KPA	– Kenya Ports Authority
KPLC	– Kenya Power and Lighting Limited
KPU	– Kenya Peoples' Union
KRA	– Kenya Revenue Authority
KRC	– Kenya Railways Corporation
KSEQIP	– Kenya Secondary Education Quality Improvement Project
KSh	– Kenya Shilling(s)
KTDC	– Kenya Trade Development Corporation

KTN	– Kenya Television Network
KUJ	– Kenya Union of Journalists
KWS	– Kenya Wildlife Service
LegCo	– Legislative Council
LGBT	– Lesbian, Gay, Bisexual, and Transgender
LSK	– Law Society of Kenya
M4M	– March 4th Movement
MCA(s)	– Member of County Assembly(s)
MFA	– Ministry of Foreign Affairs
MKF	– Mount Kenya Foundation
MoD	– Ministry of Defence
MoU	– Memorandum of Understanding
MP(s)	– Member(s) of Parliament
MRA	– Moral Re-Armament
MTRH	– Moi Teaching and Referral Hospital
MYWO	– Maendeleo ya Wanawake Organisation
NAD	– New African Development
NASA	– National Super Alliance
NCIC	– National Cohesion and Integration Commission
NCPB	– National Cereals and Produce Board
NDC	– National Delegates Conference
NDP	– National Development Party
NEC	– National Executive Committee
NEMA	– National Environment and Management Authority
NFD	– Northern Frontier District
NFK	– New Ford-Kenya
NG-CDF	– National Government-Constituency Development Fund
NGO(s)	– Non-Governmental Organisation(s)
NHIF	– National Hospital Insurance Fund

NIIMS	– National Integrated Identity Management Scheme
NIS	– National Intelligence Service
NLC	– National Land Commission
NMG	– Nation Media Group
NMS	– Nairobi Metropolitan Services
NPS	– National Police Service
NSAC	– National Security Advisory Committee
NSC	– National Security Council
NSE	– Nairobi Securities Exchange
NSSF	– National Social Security Fund
NSTF	– National Sugar Task Force
NTA	– National Taxpayers Association
NTV	– Nation Television
NYS	– National Youth Service
OACPS	– Organisation of African, Caribbean and Pacific States
OCS	– Officer Commanding [Police] Station
ODM	– Orange Democratic Movement
ODPP	– Office of the Deputy Director of Public Prosecutions
OKA	– One Kenya Alliance
PAC	– Public Accounts Committee
PEV	– Post-Election Violence
PIC	– Public Investments Committee
PM	– Prime Minister
PNU	– Party of National Unity
PPARB	– Public Procurement Administrative Review Board
PPDT	– Political Parties Disputes Tribunal
PPEs	– Personal Protective Equipment
PPG	– Pastoralists Parliamentary Group
PPOA	– Public Procurement Oversight Authority

PPP	– Public Private Partnership
PPRA	– Public Procurement Regulatory Authority
PS	– Permanent Secretary
PSC	– Public Service Commission
PSSS	– Public Service Superannuation Scheme
PWD	– Persons with Disability
QC	– Queens Counsel
RC	– Republican Congress
RML	– Relief and Mission Logistics Limited
RRT	– Rapid Reaction Team
RTP	– Restrictive Trade Practices
SALL	– Sameer Africa and Livestock Limited
SDA	– Seventh Day Adventist
SGR	– Standard Gauge Railway
SIS	– Secret Intelligence Service
SMEs	– Small and Medium Enterprises
SPLM/A	– Sudan People's Liberation Movement/Army
SRC	– Salaries and Remuneration Commission
TIFA	– Trends and Insights Africa
TIP	– The Independent Party
TJRC	– Truth, Justice, and Reconciliation Commission
TNA	– The National Alliance
UAE	– United Arab Emirates
UDA	– United Democratic Alliance
UDF	– United Democratic Forum
UK	– United Kingdom
UN	– United Nations
UNGA	– United Nations General Assembly

UNSC	– United Nations Security Council
UPK	– Unity Party of Kenya
URP	– United Republican Party
US$	– United States of America Dollar
USA	– United States of America
US-AID	– United States Agency for International Development
VAT	– Value Added Tax
VIP(s)	– Very Important Person(s)
VP	– Vice President
WB	– World Bank
WDM	– Wiper Democratic Movement
WHO	– World Health Organisation
WTO	– World Tourism Organisation
YK'92	– Youth for KANU 1992

INTRODUCTION

This book is about Uhuru Muigai Kenyatta, a man who, for ten years, was Kenya's fourth president. It is a narrative about his character, his ambitions, goals, successes, and failures. It synthesises Uhuru's life from the beginning and follows his path to adulthood. It analyses his political career and leadership, as well as his achievements and failures, both as a cabinet minister and president.

However, it is impossible to detach Uhuru the person and his administration, from the activities, omissions, and commissions, of the previous regimes. He inherited many of the problems left behind by his predecessors, but he also created some of his own. Thus, comparisons are inevitable. Mzee Kenyatta, President Moi, and President Kibaki, therefore, occupy some space in this narrative. Similarly, Uhuru's story would be incomplete and erroneous if it did not also delve into some key personalities surrounding his political and business life.

Uhuru's journey to the top involved many people. Among them were his biggest influencers such as his mentor Moi, his godfather Kibaki, and his uncle, George Kamau Muhoho. The latter guided him through puberty and into adulthood, later becoming one of his closest political advisers, pulling strings from inside the family. Moi and Kibaki, on the other hand, stood with him in his political quest even though Kibaki was his bitter competitor in the 2002 presidential run.

Also, in the mix of friends and foes who impacted Uhuru's life, and who could not be left out in this narrative are Raila Amolo Odinga, and William Samoei Ruto who, at different times, either supported his ambition or torpedoed his trajectory upwards. There are others too, like Musalia Mudavadi, whom Uhuru betrayed in 2013, and Kalonzo Musyoka, whose ambivalent position was sometimes difficult to discern. Musyoka was, periodically, one of Uhuru's biggest cheerleaders, even as he struggled to promote his own candidacy for the presidency.

When Uhuru was born, Mzee Kenyatta and Mama Ngina already had one child, Christine Wambui. Once out of detention, Mzee Kenyatta and Mama Ngina ensured their children lived in relative comfort and received the best education one could get in Kenya and abroad. They sheltered their children, yes, perhaps more than many parents, due to their status, but they also allowed them freedoms – as they grew up – to build relationships with others and to live as normal a life as possible.

Compared to many Kenyans, Uhuru's upbringing was not entirely an ordinary one. Unlike his father who had to struggle to get an education and eke a living from low-paying jobs, Uhuru's life was made up for him the minute he was born at Aga Khan Hospital in Nairobi. At the hospital to welcome the newborn baby was another famous and privileged man at the time, Jaramogi Oginga Odinga, who later became Kenya's first Vice President. Jaramogi too occupies a place in this narrative.

In his adulthood, Uhuru became an important keg in the Kenyatta mega business empire. Headed by Mama Ngina, the empire is managed by a coterie of siblings, the top among them Uhuru's younger brother, Muhoho, cousins, and nephews, who are assisted by a small group of advisers. The siblings, cousins, and nephews are also under scrutiny in this narrative. While Mama Ngina is the *de facto* Chairperson, Muhoho is the Chief Executive Officer of the empire.

But the Kenyatta Empire would not have prospered without the stewardship of the family patriarch, the late Mzee Kenyatta. It was Mzee, with the help of his surviving widow, who paved the way for Uhuru and other family members to find opportunities and exploit them for personal and family gain. Through Mzee Kenyatta and Mama Ngina, the family acquired numerous farms throughout the country, and built companies that today yield billions, if not trillions, of shillings yearly for the family.

When President Mzee Kenyatta died in 1978, he left behind a legacy of stability that "earned [him] a place in his country's affections unsurpassed in any African state."[1] But he also left behind a handful of unaddressed imperatives including poverty, illiteracy, corruption, tribalism, nepotism, economic inequalities, extra-judicial killings, and landlessness. These issues remained unresolved thirty-five years later as the fourth president, his son, Uhuru Muigai Kenyatta, took over the helm of government in 2013. And they remained so when Uhuru left State House in 2022.

Promises Broken is not an autobiography or a memoir, but a general study of a scion of one of Africa's most prominent and wealthiest families.

I hope you will find it enlightening, refreshing, and informative. *Karibu.*

---

[1] New African Development (NAD), March 1977, p. 211.

PART I
PEDIGREE

CHAPTER 1

Kenyatta Brand

Up until 1929, the Kenyatta brand, which propelled Uhuru Muigai Kenyatta to the presidency in 2013, did not exist. Jomo Kenyatta was the simple Kamau wa Muigai, a rustic boy from the bucolic Ng'enda village, in Kiambu County, with thick lips and slightly protruding teeth. He was renamed Johnstone Kamau at baptism in 1914. Later, while living in Narok, he adopted the surname, Kenyatta, which in the Maasai language means a beaded belt. The name stuck. Back in Nairobi, he became active in the Kikuyu Central Association (KCA), a semi-political, semi-cultural group. In 1929, KCA sent him to London to petition the British colonial government on land matters in central Kenya.

Johnstone (Jomo) Kenyatta stayed in England for only one year. He did not meet with his main target, the British Colonial Secretary for Colonies. But he did meet the Under-Secretary, Dr. Drummond Shiels. Kenyatta returned to Kenya briefly, only to return to England in May 1931. In 1932, he gave evidence before the Morris Carter Kenya Land Commission which the colonial government had appointed to investigate land disputes in Kenya, particularly in Kikuyuland. It was that commission that reaffirmed the continuation of the 'White Highlands" for the exclusive use of whites and the exclusion of Africans from the area. The British noticed Kenyatta's eloquence and knowledge of Kikuyu history and land rights and began to pay attention to what he said.

Jomo Kenyatta spent the next fifteen years studying, writing, and protesting alongside activists such as Peter Abrahams of South Africa, George Padmore of Trinidad-Tobago, and Kwame Nkrumah, who later led Ghana to independence in 1957. Kenyatta returned to Kenya for good in September 1946 and was met at the port of Mombasa by members of an affiliate KCA group, *Kiama gia Kunyamara* (the poor man's union), his first wife Grace Wahu, their 25-year-old son, Peter Muigai, and their eighteen-year-old daughter, Margaret Wambui.

In 1947, Jomo Kenyatta was elected president of the Kenya African Union (KAU). That is when he began the journey of building a political party to agitate for Kenya's independence from colonialists. He was a charismatic speaker who attracted large crowds wherever he went. He held meetings in Kikuyuland exhorting his people to work hard, avoid criminal activities, and shun prostitution. "If we use our hands, we shall be men; if we don't use them, we shall be worthless," he repeatedly told his people. But his efforts to mobilise the masses against colonialism were cut short when the British colonial government declared the state of emergency in 1952 and banned Mau Mau, an armed liberation movement of African freedom fighters.

In the pre-dawn hours of October 21, 1952, police raided his house at Ichaweri, Gatundu, about 47 km north of Nairobi. Authorities were confident of seizing him while still asleep. Instead, they found him fully dressed in his trademark leather lumber jacket and waiting derisively for their handcuffs. He held his hands out. "What took you so long, gentlemen?" He asked them tartly. [2] His arrest was masterfully planned and executed. He was taken to the airport and flown to Kapenguria where he was charged for managing Mau Mau.

With him in the dock were five other Kenyan leaders, all members of KAU: Bildad Kaggia, Kung'u Karumba, Fred Kubai, Paul Ngei, and Achieng Oneko. The group got the moniker the Kapenguria Six, Kapenguria being the town where the court sat. In

---

[2] Archer, Jules. African Firebrand: Kenyatta of Kenya, Julian Messner, 1969, p. 88.

April 1953 after a prolonged trial, Judge Ransley Thacker, convicted them. He ruled that the six were guilty of persuading Africans "to murder, burn, and commit atrocities...."[3] He sentenced them to seven years in prison each with hard labour.

The six prominent detainees served most of their sentence at Lokitaung, a desolate outpost of low hills and lava stone near Lake Turkana, close to the Kenya-Ethiopia border. Kenyatta called it a "prison in the wilderness."

After more than six years at Lokitaung, the detainees were transferred to Lodwar – a four-hour drive from Lokitaung and put under house arrest for two years. On April 11, 1961, the Kapenguria Six were again moved; this time to Maralal, 145 km away from Lodwar, to prepare for their release. Maralal was the administrative headquarters of what was then the Northern Frontier District (NFD).

Jomo Kenyatta's living quarters at Maralal consisted of a simple three-room dwelling with wooden seats, canvas pillows, metallic spring beds, and mattresses, made of sisal fibre. The house was in an area inhabited by poisonous snakes that dropped down from the roof beams and slithered across the floor in the dark.[4] In a letter to his friends in Europe, Kenyatta called life in Maralal "...one continuous monotony. Heat and dust shout their hallelujahs daily."[5] It was in that house and about that time that Uhuru was conceived. Ngina, who had not seen her husband since October 1952, had joined him there.

Although the detainees had more freedom at Maralal than in the previous camps, like being allowed to walk to the nearby shops, they were still under 24-hour guard by police constables. Early on the morning of August 15, 1961, police airplanes arrived at the dusty Maralal airstrip to pick up the Kapenguria Six for their final journey to freedom. Kenyatta's pregnant wife and daughters, Margaret, and Christine, were also present. They were flown to Nairobi from where they were driven to Gatundu for a tumultuous reception.

---

[3] Murray-Brown, Jeremy. Kenyatta. E. P. Dutton & Co., Inc., 1973, p. 320.
[4] Murray-Brown, Jeremy. Kenyatta. Uhuru & Dust, E. P. Dutton & Co., Inc., 1973, p. 355.
[5] Ibid.

Kenyatta was under house arrest for a week before he was formally freed on August 21. Their new house, built by the colonial government, stood almost at the same spot that his old house, destroyed by the colonialists upon his arrest, had stood. During his long absence, his three acres of land had been confiscated and given out. Still sitting in nearby bushes, however, was his rotting Hudson motor vehicle. Hudsons were popular cars among the African elite in the 1950s. Senior Chief Waruhiu wa Kung'u, an ally of the colonial government, who was assassinated on October 9, 1952, owned one.

After Mzee Kenyatta's return to Gatundu, Ngina concentrated on caring for her family in the best way she could. Kenyatta was a *muramati*, a family man,[6] who split his time between politics and his homestead in Gatundu.

Jomo Kenyatta became Prime Minister on June 1, 1963, when Kenya attained internal self-rule. Six months later, on December 12, 1963, the country gained full independence. On December 12, 1964, Kenya became a republic, and Kenyatta was sworn in as its first president.

An "intensely magnetic speaker with flamboyant, dramatic gestures,"[7] a "nationalist agitator, writer, teacher, and statesman,"[8] Kenyatta was already approximately 71 years old when he took over the reigns of power.

Jomo Kenyatta's 15-year-rule came to a sudden and shocking end on August 22, 1978, when he died at the coastal city of Mombasa. His death was the equivalent of an earthquake high on the Richter scale. Kenyans knew he was ailing from old-age complications, but they weren't prepared for his sudden demise. The death shook not only the country but the world. Kenyatta was a well-respected world figure. US President Jimmy Carter, in his message of condolence, described Mzee Kenyatta as "a giant in the African independence

---

[6] Angelo, Anais, *Becoming President: A Political Biography of Jomo Kenyatta (1958-1969)*, European University Institute, Department of History and Civilisation, a PhD Thesis, November 21, 2016, p. 73.
[7] Archer, Jules. *African Firebrand: Kenyatta of Kenya*, Julian Messner, 1960, p. 64.
[8] *Memory of the World Register: The Arrest and Mistrial of Jomo Kenyatta and Five Other Nationalists*, Ref. No. 2010/55 (Summer), p. 7.

struggle." Zambian President Kenneth Kaunda said Kenyatta was "one of the greatest leaders of men and a hero of nationalists."

NGINA MUHOHO

Ngina Muhoho was born in 1933 at Ngenda, a quaint village in Kiambu County, to colonial Chief Muhoho wa Gathecha and Anne Nyokabi Muhoho. She has two brothers: Paul Gathecha, an entrepreneur, and George Muhoho, a former Catholic priest who hung his vestments in 1976 to marry Jean Njeri Koinange from the rich and famous Koinange family. George Muhoho served as an MP, a cabinet minister, and the Managing Director of the Kenya Airports Authority (KPA). He was a key confidant of President Kibaki and played a pivotal role as one of the main campaign financiers of both Kibaki and Uhuru.

Little is known about Ngina's early years other than the fact that she was a religiously devout Catholic and went to church regularly. At her village home, she did what every other Kikuyu girl of her age did in a rural environment: fetch water and firewood and cook for the family.

Ngina was 17 years old when she was introduced to her future husband, Mzee Kenyatta. She was attending classes at the Kenya Teachers' Training College (KTTC) at Githunguri, an independent facility run by the Kikuyu Independent Schools Association (KISA). The college was established through donations solicited partly by Kenyatta via a letter addressed "To all members of the House of Mumbi whenever they may be." Kenyatta became the vice principal-cum-administrator of the institution serving under Peter Mbiyu Koinange, son of the pro-colonial Chief Koinange wa Mbiyu, one of the wealthiest and most powerful Gikuyu chiefs in colonial Kenya.[9] When Mbiyu Koinange left for England in May 1947, Kenyatta

---

[9] Koinange, Jeff. Collaborator and/or Nationalist? Koinange-wa-Mbiyu: Mau Mau's Misunderstood Leader, *Journal of African History*, Vol. 42, No. 3, 2001, p. 527.

assumed the leadership of the institution which, at the time, had 900 students.

The college was also a meeting place for pan-Africanists in the 1940s. Of the leading Africans who attended meetings at the college to discuss the future of the continent were Nkrumah, and Julius Nyerere, who later became the President of Tanzania. The trees they planted on the vast 54-acre compound in 1949 are still there.

By that time, Kenyatta had been married to two other women: Grace Wahu who bore two children, Peter Muigai and Margaret Wambui; and a British lady, Edna Clarke, who gave him a son, Peter Magana. After returning to Kenya from England, Kenyatta married Grace Wanjiku, daughter of Chief Koinange. Grace died while giving birth to their daughter, Jane "Jeni" Makena. Grace's brother was Peter Mbiyu Koinange, later to become Kenyatta's most trusted Cabinet Minister.

No real courtship is known to have occurred between Kenyatta and the young girl with short hair and long frocks. The marriage was a decision of the Muhoho family. For the Muhohos – Gathecha and Nyokabi – it was a great honour for them to give Ngina away to a man, age notwithstanding, who showed great promise of a good life ahead. Kenyatta was educated, tall, and presentable. He was 58 years old when he married Ngina in 1951. He was not rich but was financially comfortable by the African standards of the time. He exuded confidence, a polished gentleman indeed.

Even in those early days of his life, Kenyatta displayed class. He was "a big paunchy man, bearded, with slightly bloodshot eyes, a theatrically monstrous ebony elephant-headed walking stick, a gold-rimmed carnelian signet ring about the size of a napkin-ring, an outsize gold wrist-watch fastened to his hefty arm with a gold strap, dressed in European tweed jacket and flannel slacks – with as pleasant, ingratiating and wary a manner as you have ever met."[10]

---

[10] Murray-Brown, Jeremy. Kenyatta, E. P. Dutton & Co., Inc., 1973, pp. 268-269.

In the eyes of many Kikuyu, Kenyatta, "son of a tribal farmer, grandson of a rain-making magician,"[11] belonged to the elite class. Kenyatta was not at the same level with many ordinary Kikuyu of the time. At the Nairobi Municipal Council where he worked in the early 1920s, Kenyatta's daily work routine involved cycling from house to house reading water metres and measuring pipes. But he lived well, "a life of a dandy, a privilege few natives enjoyed."[12] At Githunguri College he was even more privileged. He lived in a large stone house with one of the most spectacular views in Kikuyuland.[13]

However, the colonial administration was not happy that Chief Muhoho had married off his daughter to Kenyatta, a man they viewed as a "troublemaker."[14] The colonialists unceremoniously relieved Chief Muhoho of his position and gave it to his brother, Kinyua Gathecha.

Apart from Grace Wahu, who was a small-scale farmer owning 5.5 acres of land at Dagoretti in Nairobi, and Edna Clarke, a simple teacher in rural Sandgate in England, Kenyatta's other two wives, Grace Wanjiku and Ngina Muhoho, were from exceedingly well-to-do families.

Uhuru Muigai Kenyatta

Uhuru Muigai Kenyatta was born in Nairobi on October 26, 1961, at a time of heightened social and political renaissance across Africa. Numerous African countries had already been freed from British, French, and Belgium colonialism. Those countries included

---

[11] Archer, Jules. African Firebrand: Kenyatta of Kenya, Julian Messner Publishers, p. 1.
[12] Angelo, Anais, Becoming President: A *Political Biography of Jomo Kenyatta (1958-1969)*, European University Institute, Department of History and Civilisation, a PhD Thesis, November 21, 2016, p. 6.
[13] Murray-Brown, Jeremy. Kenyatta, E. P. Dutton & Co., Inc., 1973, p. 268.
[14] *Preliminary Reaction to Government's Aggressive Campaign Against the Mau Mau*, The Consul General at Nairobi to the Department of State, Foreign Relations of the United States, 1952-1954, Africa and South Asia, Vol. XI, Part 1, No. 93, October 24, 1952.

Ghana, Guinea, Cameroon, Senegal, Togo, Mali, Madagascar, and Zaire (now the Democratic Republic of Congo, DRC). It was the year when the UN condemned apartheid in South Africa, and when the Berlin Wall was built dividing East and West Germany.

In colonial Kenya, the state of emergency that began in 1952 had ended in 1959, and the following year, Africans had begun talks with the British colonial government on the country's independence constitution.

In February 1961, the first "multi-party" elections in Kenya were held and the Kenya African National Union (KANU) led by James Gichuru emerged the winner, beating the Kenya African Democratic Union (KADU) of Ronald Ngala, by eight seats in parliament. The former got 19 seats and the latter 11 out of 53 seats in the Legislative Council (LegCo).

Uhuru is the second-born in a Mzee Kenyatta-Mama Ngina family of four children. Christine Wambui was born in 1953, at the height of the Mau Mau rebellion. She was eight years old when Uhuru was born. Kenyatta and Ngina were to get two more children, Anna Nyokabi, in 1963, and Muhoho Kenyatta, in 1965.

At six years, Uhuru was enrolled at St Mary's School in Nairobi, a Catholic institution favoured by the elite. It is situated in a leafy area in Westlands on the fringe of the city. Former President Daniel arap Moi's sons Gideon and Philip attended the school, as did former President Mwai Kibaki's sons, Tony, and David. St Mary's motto written in Latin as, *Bonitas, Disciplina, Scientia* (*Goodness, Discipline, Knowledge*), highlights the rigidity of moral standards at the institution which was founded by the Holy Ghost Fathers in 1939.

Uhuru spent twelve years at St Mary's School. During all those years, as a matter of course, Uhuru was driven to and from school in a Mercedes Benz 280E by a chauffeur in the company of bodyguards. Uhuru was an active child who relished riding his bicycle around their well-secured compound at Gatundu. At school, he was active in sports, and his favourite subject was history. That subject earned him an achievement award, presented to him by Vice President Mwai Kibaki.

As he grew older, still at St Mary's, Uhuru took to driving himself to school in a Mercedes Benz 190E, without a driving licence of course. Occasionally, he would sneak after school to meet his girlfriend, Margaret Gakuo, at their Karen home. Margaret is the daughter of the first African Managing Director of the Kenya Railways Corporation (KRC), Dr. Ephantus Njuguna Gakuo, and his German wife, Magdalena.

Uhuru completed his "A" level education at St Mary's School in 1978.[15] While waiting to join university, he worked briefly at the Kenya Commercial Bank (KCB) as a teller. The choice for his higher education was between England and the United States of America (USA). Before Mzee Kenyatta died, the issue as to where Uhuru would go for higher education had already been discussed and settled. Mzee Kenyatta had surprisingly opted for the USA.

The choice of USA was as mysterious as it was incomprehensible. Kenyatta was more attuned to the British educational system than the American model. He had no personal ties in the USA but had plenty of friends in the UK. He had spent one year studying English Language at the Quaker College in Selly Oak, Birmingham, England. He had worked at the School of Oriental and African Studies in London. He had spent a year at the London School of Economics and Political Science at the University of London as a post-graduate student. He was also an adherent of the Church of Scotland in England which had a mission and school at Thogoto, Kikuyu, a school he had earlier attended. Also, Kenyatta had close relatives in England in Edna, his estranged wife, and Peter Magana, his son, and Uhuru's half-brother.

In addition, while in detention, Kenyatta had regularly corresponded with two English people he was fond of: Dina Stock, a lecturer in England who by that time had moved to India, and Geoffrey Husbands, an insurance clerk in London. In his "Dear Friend" letters to Husbands, he shared their memories and anecdotes. "I very often think of you and recall in my mind the happy memory

---

[15] Mutwol, Abraham. Great Inspiring Lessons from Uhuru Muigai Kenyatta, Creative Minds Consultants, 2015.

of how we used to get together and how we used to have lively discussions on various topics," Kenyatta once wrote to Husbands.

Every year, Husbands sent Kenyatta a Christmas card. Kenyatta was also a member of the International African Friends of Abyssinia (Ethiopia), an organisation that had powerful pan-Africanists including two activists, Padmore, and C. L. R. James, also from Trinidad-Tobago. So, the Kenyan leader had a plethora of friends in England who could have assisted in securing educational places for his children at British institutions.

So why choose the USA? Was it because he loathed British colonialism so much? After all, it was the British colonialists who had incarcerated him. The British colonialists had associated him with Mau Mau, though colleagues in the struggle insisted "that Jomo Kenyatta was no Mau Mau and that he knew nothing about the movement."[16]

Yes, in a way, Kenyatta did hate British colonialists. His detestation was evident during a meeting of the Manchester Fabian Society in October 1938. Addressing the group, Kenyatta railed at the British colonial policy, calling it a form of "fascism."[17] He compared the treatment meted to East Africans by the British colonial government to the treatment of Jews in Nazi Germany. That was one of the most scathing attacks on colonialism in all the years Kenyatta had stayed in England.

The most reasonable assumption why Mzee Kenyatta chose the USA over England lay with a man called Thurgood Marshall. It is not out of the realm of possibility that it was the late black-American civil rights lawyer who persuaded Kenyatta to send his children to America. Marshall, a profoundly amiable person, was an ardent Jomo Kenyatta enthusiast. He had compulsively studied Kenyatta during the Mau Mau trial and had admired his gallantry and nationalism. He had a deep affection for Kenyatta.

---

[16] Angelo, Anais. Introduction in Power and the Presidency in Kenya: Jomo Kenyatta Years, African Studies, Cambridge University Press, pp. 1-37.
[17] Murray-Brown, Jeremy. Kenyatta, E. P. Dutton & Co., Inc., 1972, pp. 341-342.

In 1959, Tom Mboya visited the US on a lecture tour. During numerous events while there, he appeared with Marshall.[18] It was during the visit that Mboya invited the American lawyer to Kenya.

In January 1960, Marshall arrived in Nairobi and officially accepted the assignment of advising the African delegation to the 1960 Lancaster Constitutional Conference in London. Marshall's job was to draft the Bill of Rights. He did and presented the draft at the conference. It was at that conference that the colonial government supported the idea of majority rule in Kenya.

One of the most important sections in the bill was in the preamble: the principle of equality. That "All persons are equal before the law and are entitled without any discrimination or distinction of any kind – such as race, colour, sex, language, religion, political or other opinion, national or social origin, property, birth, or other status – to equal protection of the law."[19] That section was important because it protected the rights of minority whites and Asians. It opened the way for a peaceful change from white rule to black rule.

Marshall's next visit to Kenya was on July 11, 1963, after the country had attained internal self-rule. During the independence ceremonies which he attended in December 1963, Marshall was an "honoured guest" of Kenyatta. Nevertheless, even in those early years of Kenya's independence, the American was disappointed and abashed by what he read about Kenya. He saw a country in turmoil. KADU had been railroaded to disband and join KANU, making Kenya a *de facto* one-party state.

There were also serious disagreements between President Kenyatta and his Vice President Jaramogi Oginga Odinga, to the extent that in 1966, Odinga's faction of 29 MPs stormed out of KANU to form the Kenya Peoples' Union (KPU). Vice President Joseph Murumbi, a principled man of unblemished character who had

---

[18] "Tom Mboya, Key Questions for Awakening Africa," *New York Times*, June 28, 1959.
[19] Dudziak, Mary L. Thurgood Marshall's Bill of Rights for Kenya: Exporting American Dreams, Thurgood Marshall's African Journey, Oxford University Press, 2008.

replaced Jaramogi, stayed in government for only six months before resigning in 1967 to protest rampant corruption in government.

On July 5, 1969, Tom Mboya was gunned down in Nairobi by Nahashon Isaac Njenga Njoroge, a man he knew who had ties with people in government. And on October 27, 1969, Jaramogi was arrested. There were strong rumours that the government had a hand in Mboya's death. Marshall was disappointed. The Kenyan leaders were not enforcing his advice on the rule of law.

In short, the path Kenyatta was taking was worrying. He was moving towards a dictatorship. He had transferred regional powers to the central government, was suppressing political dissent, and prohibiting Jaramogi from competing in elections.[20] Kenyatta had also started "centralising corruption. To expand his powers, he pressured parliament to pass several constitutional amendments [and]...created a government completely loyal to his objectives, and a country fearful of offending him."[21] There were strong signs that democracy was fading, and human rights abuses were accelerating. Kenyatta was not a democrat but an autocrat who did not hide his inclinations,"[22] some said. That was not what Marshall had expected from Kenya. Despite all that, the American lawyer continued to admire the Kenyan leader – a staggering thought – and the two remained great friends.[23]

Marshall's final visit to Kenya was in 1978 following Kenyatta's death. He led a powerful delegation to the funeral of the Kenyan leader, consisting mainly of black American icons: Ambassador Andrew Young, the US Ambassador to Kenya, Wilbert Le Melle, Congressman Charles Diggs, and Assistant Secretary of State for African Affairs, George Moose.

---

[20] "About: Jomo Kenyatta." DBpedia.org., undated.
[21] Vaughan, Ashley E. Council on Undergraduate Research, Meredith College, 2021.
[22] Murunga, Godwin R. & Shadrack W. Nasongo. Kenya: The Struggle for Democracy, Godesria Books, p. 177
[23] Craig, Lori, Thurgood Marshall and Kenyan Independence, USC Gould School of Law, December 12, 2008.

Even after Mboya and Mzee's exit, Marshall kept in touch with Kenyan leaders until January 25, 1993, when he died of heart failure. Marshall left behind a monkey skin cloak gifted to him by Mzee Kenyatta. Today, that cloak drapes one of his old office chairs at his home. Given their close friendship, it is therefore easy to conclude that it was the black American who persuaded the Kenyan leader to opt for American education for his children with Mama Ngina.

That decision by Mzee Kenyatta to send his children to the US saw Christine Wambui attend Kutztown State College and LeHigh University in Pennsylvania, Uhuru Muigai, Amherst College in Massachusetts, Anna Nyokabi, North-western University in Illinois, and Muhoho Kenyatta, Williams College in Massachusetts. Jeni Wambui, Kenyatta's daughter with third wife Grace Wanjiku, attended Indiana University. Jeni's two children also studied in USA, Nana Gecaga, Cushing Academy in Massachusetts, and Soiya Gecaga, Phillips Academy, also in Massachusetts. Uhuru's cousins Ngengi Muigai and Beth Mugo, children of Kenyatta's only known brother, James Ngengi Muigai, graduated from Amherst and Goldey-Beacom College, respectively.

Formerly called Olio College, Amherst is a small American liberal arts institution near Boston, USA. Uhuru's life at Amherst was a mixture of everything good and everything not so good. Uhuru was 19 years old, living in a society where a person of his age could drink alcohol and visit night clubs without having to show an ID. Those who knew him at Amherst say that he loved night life and was quite a babbling imbiber of alcohol. He received money regularly from home, but he needed more, so he occasionally rented out space in his apartment during summer holidays. He also worked briefly at a fast-food joint, earning the minimum wage of US$3 per hour.

Uhuru was also a heavy smoker. However, testimonies also show the son of Jomo was a good student during his four years at Amherst. "Quiet, reserved, but an attentive student… shy but very kind… friendly but a little aloof," are some of the observations some students and professors at the college had of Uhuru in those days.[24]

Uhuru must have inherited some (only some) of his father's traits. At the Thogoto Church of Scotland Mission where the young Johnstone Kamau attended school, teachers described him as "a clever boy, playful, ambitious…. [but] lonely at home."[25] Others differed saying Kamau had "no marked intelligence or aptitude… His English [language skill] was poor and there was little opportunity of improving it with the missionaries; his ability to read and write appeared below average."[26]

But Jomo was from the village. He did not have the opportunity of attending an elite school at the age of six like his son. Thus, Kamau may have started badly at school, thanks to the critically undeveloped social and economic environment in Gatundu at the time, but the advanced education he received in England polished many of those early limitations. He became a fluent speaker and writer of the English language. He authored *Facing Mount Kenya*, an ethnography of his Kikuyu people published in 1938. He also wrote another book, *Suffering Without Bitterness* in 1966, and penned articles and letters which were published in England and Kenya.

Like his father who participated in several anti-colonial protests in London during the 1930s and 1940s, Uhuru too may have joined a protest at Amherst during his graduation year in 1985. That, however, could not be confirmed from any source. Members of the Black Union marched and temporarily took over the office of the university president, Peter Pouncey. The students protested and demonstrated for a whole week, demanding action against discrimination of black students. Their activism resulted in campus discussions on racism which eventually led to tangible changes at the institution. Records could not be found to confirm Uhuru's participation in that protest.

Uhuru returned to Kenya in 1986 with a BA degree in Economics and Political Science. He was 25 years old. Used to

---

[24] Some, Kipchumba. "Amherst College humbled Uhuru in spite of high life back home," *Daily Nation,* February 18, 2017.
[25] Arnold, Guy. Kenyatta and the Politics of Kenya, J. M. Dent & Sons, p. 15.
[26] Murray-Brown, Jeremy. Kenyatta, George Allen & Unwin Ltd., pp. 63-64.

independent living, he did not move to either of his parents' homes at Muthaiga or Gatundu. Instead, he rented a furnished apartment in a residential complex along Gitanga road near Valley Arcade in Nairobi. Only family members and known friends were allowed into the apartment. His mother, Mama Ngina, regularly came to check on his son. Another routine visitor was his cousin, Ngengi Muigai.

Uhuru registered a horticultural business, Wilham Kenya Limited, which dealt with the exportation of French beans. He sold the company after ten years. After that, he joined his family businesses on a full-time basis.

Uhuru married Margaret Gakuo on December 2, 1989, in a colourful wedding at which the guest speaker was President Moi. The couple has three children, Jomo, a businessman, Ngina, owner of The Green Experience restaurant in Kiambu, and Jaba, a fashion designer.

CHAPTER 2

Kenyatta Business Empire

Mzee Jomo Kenyatta loved the soil (read land). In the preface of his world-acclaimed book, *Facing Mount Kenya*, Kenyatta pays tribute to land, saying that it is "The key to the people's life; it secures for them that peaceful tillage of the soil which supplies their material needs and enables them to perform their magic and traditional ceremonies in undisturbed serenity, facing Mount Kenya," he says. Those remarks would have made more sense if that "peaceful tillage of the soil" was enjoyed by every living Kenyan. Unfortunately, it wasn't! Jomo Kenyatta was a self-obsessed individual known for self-aggrandisement and plunder.

Even the British government felt Mzee Kenyatta had become not only "increasingly autocratic," but "detached, and preoccupied with considerations of personal enrichment."[27] A confidential British correspondence claimed Kenyatta was obsessed largely with three things:

- Land or money for himself and or members of his family
- Land for his tribe

---

[27] Norris to Secretary of State, 'Kenya: Annual Review for 1970,' January 12, 1971, TNA FCO, 31/851/1 p. 182

- Appointments and promotions of the Kikuyu within the hierarchy.[28]

Mzee Kenyatta started dishing out land to chosen individuals, mainly family and political allies, around May 1964, barely six months after attainment of full independence. That confirmed that land politics, in particular land distribution, was the linchpin of political loyalties. People allied to the opposition such as Bildad Kaggia, one of the Kapenguria Six, got nothing.

To sanitise land grabbing for his family and associates, Kenyatta exempted himself from the Land Control Act of 1967 which required that "all land purchases must be scrutinised by a control board and that all such exemptions be published in the Kenya Gazette." With the exemption at hand, the Kenyattas "purchased" thousands of acres of land in different parts of the country especially in the Rift Valley and at the Coast. They included a 52,000-acre farm in Nakuru, a 20,000-acre farm in Bahati, 29,000 acres in Kahawa Sukari, a 10,000-acre farm in Naivasha, and Mama Ngina's farm in Rumuruti, among many pieces of lands spread all over the country.

By early 1970s, resentment and internal dissent against President Kenyatta had increased while his popularity had waned. Fearing retribution, Kenyans kept quiet and went on with their business in the mode of Kenyatta's words 'Suffering without bitterness."

One memorable event illustrating Kenyans' frustrations over land grabbing by the Kenyattas was in 1974. Kenyatta had gone to Nakuru to address a public meeting. After joyously and loudly bragging about his government's achievements in buying-out white settlers, he then boisterously asked in his booming *basso profundo* voice: "Who has the land now?" He expected the people to respond 'Us." Instead, a lone voice from the back shouted "You."[29] One could hear a pin drop. The venue went dead silent. Kenyatta balked, then continued speaking.

---

[28] Confidential. Antony Duff to the Right Honourable Sir Alex Douglas-Home, 18 October 1972, BNA, FCO 31/1191.
[29] Private and Confidential. Report on Kenya, September 1974, BNA, FCO 31/1707.

The Truth, Justice, and Reconciliation Commission (TJRC) report[30] indicates that between 1964 and 1966, one-sixth of land held by European settlers was cheaply sold to the Kenyatta family. His "regime was riddled with land grabbing," the report said, "which was perpetrated by him [Kenyatta] for his benefit and [that of] members of his family...."

JOMO THE LEGEND

Even before becoming Prime Minister, Mzee Jomo Kenyatta, as a detainee, was considered as the omnipotent father of the nation and "the sole repository for the memory of the struggle for independence."[31] He was the legend of omniscience and indispensability. That presumptuous symbolism and deification gave parliament the impetus to pass a motion in November 1963 that made it an offence to show disrespect, even in jest, to the person of the Prime Minister.[32] The motion gave Mzee Kenyatta a licence to pilfer national resources and everything else therein, believing it was his absolute right to arbitrarily dish out land to relatives and cronies.

In April 1968, Attorney General (AG) Charles Njonjo cemented that symbolism by characterising Kenyatta as "Our most cherished institution...our most beloved citizen."[33] Njonjo, son of a colonial Paramount Chief, Josiah Njonjo, a collaborator of British colonialists in pre-independence days, was Kenya's first AG and one of Mzee Kenyatta's right hand persons.

---

[30] The task of this commission was to investigate human rights abuses, historical injustices, illegal or irregular acquisition of land and misuse of political power from independence. It released its report in May 2013.

[31] Charton, Helene. Jomo Kenyatta and Kenyan Independence: The Twists and Turns of Memory, Vingtieme Siecle. Revue d'Histoire, vol. 118, Issue 2, 2013, pp. 45-59.

[32] Murray-Brown, Jeremy. Kenyatta, E. P. Dutton & Co., Inc., 1973.

[33] Independence without freedom: The legitimisation of repressive laws and practices in Kenya, A Kenya Human Rights Commission Report, February 1994, p. 19

Then there was the sheer fanaticism surrounding the president? "Mr. Kenyatta," said one strong supporter "was chosen by God to lead Kenya, just as Moses was chosen to take Israelites out of Egypt."[34] Kenyans honoured Kenyatta with the title *Mzee,* 'a wise old man,' because to them, Kenyatta was a "second god," a pompous terminology used by Oginga Odinga.[35]

In 1961, at Nyeri, Oginga described Kenyatta as a "demigod." On 14 December 1964 when he unveiled Kenyatta's statue outside Kenyatta International Convention Centre (KICC), Odinga likened Kenyatta to "second to God. He is God's masterpiece,"[36] Odinga said presumably with concealed distaste. Dispatches sent by the British High Commissioner in Kenya to London depicted Kenyatta as "a man whose dominating political personality was feared by Cabinet Ministers… a formidable personality, daunting nearly all his ministers and officials."[37]

GREED

Kenyatta's unflinching greed for material things was not new. In the 1940s, he collected a lot of money from donations meant for the construction of Githunguri Teachers' Training College. He used some of that money to build himself a nice house at the college and to purchase a Hudson car. But the school itself had little to show for all the money that had been collected. "Its main block never rose higher than one floor…." There were periodic demands for Kenyatta to publish accounts, but he and his subordinates consistently refused to do so. "Teachers went on strike for long-over-due wages; the [education] standards were never very high and soon declined still

---

[34] Archer, Jules. African Firebrand: Kenyatta of Kenya, Julian Messner, 1969, p. 131.
[35] Thomas, B. Donald & Nugent, Paul J. "Walter Martin, 'Friends visit Jomo Kenyatta at Maralal'," Quaker History 99, No. 1, 2010, pp. 35-36.
[36] Kenyatta's statue unveiled in Kenya, *The New York Times*, August 30, 2019.
[37] Confidential. Diplomatic Report No. 53/71, "Kenya: Annual Review for 1970," January 12, 1971, BNA, FCO 31/851.

further, and numbers [of students] fell away."[38] It is not clear what action the college management took to punish Kenyatta for that misdeed.

While Mzee Kenyatta publicly deplored corruption, he also surreptitiously participated in it. As president, Mzee was an avid wheat farmer at Rongai in Nakuru. Together with his Lands and Settlement Minister Jackson Angaine, they colluded to upgrade the quality of Kenyatta's wheat from grade three to grade one, thus ensuring a higher price for the commodity. The president insisted that his wheat be given the highest grade regardless of its quality and recommendations by agricultural officers. However, Agriculture Minister Jeremiah Nyagah, stood with his officers insisting that grading must be based on quality. He was overruled by Angaine who invoked the president's name, also known as, *orders from above*. Over-grading of wheat favoured big people and meant that small scale farmers received lower than justified grades to compensate for the shortfall.[39] That was corruption in its rawest form.

And of course, there was the debacle of Harambee donations collected for the Gatundu Hospital, which has been well documented by historians. The amounts collected for the project in the form of cheques were handed personally to Kenyatta with instructions that the space for the name of the drawer be left blank. No one would dare question what happened to the tens of thousands of shillings contributed by businessmen and wananchi over a period of several years.

In March 1969, for example, a Meru delegation visited Gatundu and contributed US$33,000 (KSh.3.6 million today) towards the Gatundu Hospital self-help project. The money went into Kenyatta's pockets. Overall, contributions to the project were rarely channelled towards the construction of the hospital.[40]

---

[38] Murray-Brown, Jeremy. Kenyatta, E. P. Dutton & Co., Inc., 1973, p. 268.

[39] Githuku, Nicholas Kariuki. Mau Mau Crucible of War: Statehood, National Identity, and Politics in Post-Colonial Kenya, Graduate Thesis, and Problem Reports, 5677, West Virginia University, 2014.

[40] Brief on memorandum by the Meru people for Sunday, March 23, 1969, KNA KA/6/22.

When Mzee Kenyatta died, the facility, commissioned in 1966, was in a pathetic condition, not commensurate with the contributions made. The facility became the Gatundu District Hospital. In 2007, plans to expand and modernise it were conceived, but it was not until August 2013 that President Uhuru launched its expansion costing KSh.800 million. In 2016, he commissioned it and the facility became a Level Four Hospital. In 2017, it was elevated to Level Five.

No one knows exactly how much land the Kenyattas have. A figure of half-a-million acres is often mentioned but that is just guess work. No exhaustive list exists. How that land and other assets are divided among family members is even more secretive. As some people say *secrets [too] are secret*. It was therefore understandable for the AG Githu Muigai, to tell the International Criminal Court (ICC) in July 2014, that Uhuru did not own any land in Kenya.[41] Muigai also refused to table financial records which could have revealed what the president owned. He was testifying in the case in which Uhuru and others were accused of involvement in the 2007 post election violence.

Uhuru was unequivocal once when he said that whatever he owned belonged to the family. But as the Pandora Papers would later disclose, Uhuru has a 100% stake in the property his 89-year-old mother owns. According to the documents, whatever Mama Ngina owns will go to Uhuru when she dies.

Knowing Taita Taveta as an area replete with precious stones including ruby and tsavorite, Mzee Kenyatta commandeered 30,000 acres at Tsavo National Park and renamed his portion Gicheha Farm. He used it for ranching. A member of his family took another 50,000 acres and used them for mining gems. The gems were sold locally and exported overseas.

The Gicheha Farm is in the same general area where Mama Ngina, and other influential personalities, dislodged two American geologists from a ruby mine that had a ruby reserve estimated at US$5 billion (KSh.500 billion). The mine was then handed over to

---

[41] Namaswa, Mark. "How corruption rings run Kenya": *This is Africa*, September 22, 2015.

a Greek-born millionaire resident farmer, George Criticos, who was Mama Ngina's partner at the Kenya Trade Development Corporation (KTDC).

Initially, the Kenyattas did not want to deny or confirm the ownership of the Gicheha Farm, but in 2013, Uhuru admitted with a semblance of composure that, "we own 30,000 acres in Taita Taveta."[42] However, Uhuru insisted that the land was acquired on a willing-buyer-willing-seller arrangement. "There is nothing to prove that my family [has] illegally acquired [that] land,"[43] he said. In 2019, under pressure from the squatters and leaders in Taita Taveta, the Kenyatta's agreed to donate 2,000 acres of their land to the squatters, a tiny fraction of what they owned.

Despite that big land grab mania, Uhuru's infrequent friend, Raila, do not think it is fair to blame Uhuru over his family's transgressions. "Uhuru Kenyatta," he said in February 2013, "was an innocent inheritor. He did not commit the original sin. Kenyans should sympathise with him." Raila is the same man who had always linked Uhuru to the misdeeds of the latter's parents.

Another top government official who acquired land in the same area is William Samoei Ruto, President Uhuru's deputy. Ruto received 2,500 acres from Basil Criticos, son of George Criticos, after he (Ruto) had helped the Criticos repay a loan they owed a financial institution. The transaction took place in 2008 when Ruto was the Minister for Agriculture in Kibaki's Grand Coalition Government.

THE REVERED MAMA NGINA

There is a good reason why Kenyans revere Mama Ngina. [She] "is not just the president's mother, she remains the first symbol of unity of motherhood for the Republic of Kenya,"[44] said one source. The cynical extremity of public perception of the Kenyattas is

---

[42] Wanambisi, Laban. *Capital News*, February 25, 2013.
[43] Wanambisi, Laban. "We own 30,000 acres in Taveta – Uhuru," *Capital News*, February 25, 2013.
[44] Mwalimu, Mandela. Mother of the nation, undated.

unprecedented, with many believing in Mama Ngina's untouchability. Another reason why Kenyans consider Mama Ngina off-limit from abuse is because they risk possible prosecution.

In 2015, blogger Abraham Mutai was arrested for linking Mama Ngina to poaching. The case was so sensitive that even the police officer handling the case balked at mentioning the former first lady's name. Instead, the officer booked Mutai for "belittling big people in government."[45]

Politicians allied to Deputy President William Ruto went beyond attacking Uhuru's policies and his developmental record. MP Oscar Sudi, for example, went after the person of Mama Ngina. Authorities considered his remarks too insolent and disgusting. But Sudi was quick to clarify: "I only said that all mothers should be respected. They [critics] are only saying I disrespected Mama Ngina but cannot say exactly how I did it. If it is about the use of the word "breasts," it is in the Bible, but these people do not read it [the Bible]," Sudi said when asked to clarify his taped remarks.

Author Rasna Warah seemed to agree with Sudi. "He [Sudi] merely stated that Uhuru Kenyatta should not believe that the breasts that he [Uhuru] suckled are better than the breasts that Sudi suckled…that all Kenyans are equal, and that Uhuru and his family should not believe that they are more important than the rest of Kenyans or that the country belongs to them."[46]

Sudi's remarks triggered demonstrations in the Central Kenya region. Some women in Kiambu even threatened to strip and expose their breasts, a sign of cursing in many ethnic communities, if Sudi did not apologise. Sudi did not, and the women did not follow up on their threat. However, Sudi was charged in court on two counts of hate speech. In February 2022, he was acquitted for lack of evidence.

In September 2020, MP Johanna Ng'eno, another close Ruto ally was arrested for saying something that State operatives considered offensive to Mama Ngina. What he said was that Kenya "does not

---

[45] Ombati, Cyrus. "CID release blogger Abraham Mutai arrested for belittling 'Big people' in government," The *Standard*, January 18, 2015.

[46] Warah, Rasna. "Let it never be said that Kenyans went to war over mammary glands," The *Elephant*, September 18, 2020.

belong to Uhuru Kenyatta. It does not belong to Jomo Kenyatta or Mama Ngina. Kenya belongs to the people." He then added, "This is not a country you can rule the way you want, and if you want to shoot us, do it. How many people did your father [Jomo Kenyatta] shoot and Kenya is still standing?" Ng'eno asked rhetorically.

Uhuru's supporters did not take the remarks kindly. They blasted Ng'eno for allegedly disrespecting and disparaging the former first lady. MP Gathoni Wamuchomba, in defending Kenyatta's widow tweeted on September 12, 2020, that "Mama Ngina is a symbol of unity in Kenya. An abuse to her is an abuse to all mothers in Kenya."[47] This was a rather fallacious argument.

Kirinyaga County governor, Anne Waiguru, also joined in by advising Ruto supporters to "direct their responses and attacks at fellow politicians,' not Mama Ngina. "As women, we demand civility and respect in general," she said.[48]

Kenyatta's family members and close allies also rallied around Mama Ngina. MP Paul Koinange, of the famous Koinange family and a distant relative of the Kenyattas, asked DP Ruto to apologise since the two [Ng'eno and Sudi] were his 'attack dogs.' Koinange refused to accept Ruto's apology in the social media. "DP Ruto should apologise to the president, his family, and the entire nation in person, not through Twitter," Koinange said. Of course, Ruto didn't.

A State House surrogate, Mutahi Ngunyi, claimed the attacks were intentional. "If William Ruto can INSULT his mother (Mama Ngina) while he is still the DP, whom will he INSULT if he becomes PRESIDENT? A man who INSULTS his MOTHER is rotten to the core and from the CORE," he tweeted with interspersed capital letters.

The most virulent response, however, came from none other than Mama Ngina's son, Uhuru. "If you happen to meet those idiots [Sudi and Ng'eno], tell them to go and insult their mothers and leave mine alone," Uhuru said in fury.

---

[47] "Waiguru accuses Dr Ruto of hypocrisy after allies' insults to the president," *Kenyan News.co.ke*, September 9, 2020.
[48] Anne Waiguru was to later defect to William Ruto's political camp.

There were other violators to the don't-disrespect-the-Kenyattas-rule. On 29 March 2021, a rapper Philip Okoyo known as Japesa claimed that he was arrested for making demeaning and unprintable comments on Uhuru in Instagram. He was protesting the resumption of curfew restriction during the Covid-19 pandemic. He was freed after posting cash bail.

Why the successive Kenyan heads of state are always paranoid about discussing their families is difficult to understand. As public figures, the Kenyattas are subject to scrutiny and criticism like any other private citizens. When in September 2021, MP Rigathi Gachagua, an ally of Deputy President Ruto told Uhuru to return the huge tracts of land his father "stole" from Kenyans, the president's men came with clenched fists. "We are sending a public message that we will not countenance his venturing into crossing this line of referring to the family of the late President Mzee Jomo Kenyatta," Raphael Tuju, the Jubilee Alliance Party Secretary General said, adding, "he must call his goons to order."

It was crystal clear that Uhuru did not have the forbearance and temperament of a tolerant leader. Take the case of Samuel Aboko Onkwami, a ward representative. On 30 April 2014, he found himself in trouble after calling Uhuru a "bhang smoker." "Those close to President Uhuru," he said publicly, "should advise him to stop smoking bhang." In normal circumstances, such remarks would have been considered spasmodic and hysterical, coming from a village politician. It was not so in this case. Onkwami was charged in court for uttering words "calculated to bring into contempt the lawful authority of the president." He was released on bond. By June 2022, the case was still pending in court.

In 2015, a 25-year-old university student, Ali Wadi Okengo, was jailed for two years for posting in the social media 'abusive' comments against the Kenyattas. The comments were against the Security Laws (Amendment) Act which was passed in parliament and signed into law by Uhuru. Okengo was convicted after pleading guilty and apologising to the president. He was imprisoned for two years on a hate speech charge.

In September 2017, opposition MP Paul Ongili popularly known as Babu Owino was charged with subversion, insulting the president, and incitement to violence, by calling the president the "son of a dog." The MP was released on bail. Eventually, the case fizzled away after Ongili's ODM party leader, Raila, intervened, thanks to the handshake arrangement with Uhuru.

The following month, October 2017, another MP, Gideon Mulyungi, was arrested for making references to Uhuru's manhood. "He is not a superman. What is he trying to show us?" He retorted. If he removed his trousers and I remove mine, you will realise that my manhood is bigger than his. He is not a special man." Mulyungi was charged with two counts of hate speech. The prosecution said the comment demeaned the president and incited ethnic animosity. He was released on bail.

But what shook Kenyans most were the unsavoury remarks made by a Kenyan in the diaspora, Ombori Monari, in March 2022. The extremely abusive and disrespectful remarks against Mama Ngina were in a video clip that trended in social media platforms. Many felt Monari went overboard in his reaction to what Mama Ngina had said a few days earlier about presidential succession. Apart from backing his son for supporting Raila and asking Kenyans to follow Uhuru, Mama Ngina had excoriated those in the political arena who insulted others.

"Those who are insulting others," she said, "are defined by how they were raised." Monari immediately fired back from his base in the US with vulgar vitriol directed at Mama Ngina, bordering on character assassination. A section of Kenyans was disgusted. Women in Nairobi demonstrated, and calls were made for Monari's extradition to face unspecified charges in Kenya. The pressure was strong enough for Monari to apologise publicly to the Kenyattas and to Kenyan women.

TASTELESS AND VULGAR

As ordinary Kenyans were hauled to court for making disparaging remarks about their leaders, top politicians, in reverse, insulted *wananchi* with abandon without risking penalty. Some of their insults referred to parts of the human anatomy that are taboo to mention in public.

Mzee Kenyatta was the most notorious of all the four presidents, when it came to usage of tasteless language. He was vulgar and crass. His Kiswahili speeches were spiced with words that pointed to the reproductive organ of women. When Idi Amin of Uganda in 1976 threatened to annex some parts of the Rift Valley and western Kenya, Kenyatta snapped back with some nasty unprintable words. There was a time when he roared at Odinga's supporters, *"Ku** za mama zenu."* Although the remarks were invariably met with crackling laughter from crowds, they were gross and impudent.

It appeared Uhuru stole from his father's playbook. MP Kimani Ngunjiri once complained that "he [Uhuru] called us the word "*Ku***" as his father used to do. He reached halfway and stopped."[49] The MP was referring to Uhuru's outburst during a meeting of Jubilee Alliance Party MPs at State House after the 2017 general elections.

The only president who was clean in language was Moi. He was too religious for common street jargon. On the other hand, Kibaki's speeches were full of interesting quips. And even when he used phrases that had a tinge of sarcasm such as *"Aaah, kwenda huko…mavi ya kuku,"* something about chicken poop, his delivery and countenance were of an old, friendly comedian, not of an urban gangster.

Mama's power and influence

If there is one individual who shaped and influenced Uhuru's public life, it was Mama Ngina. She was at the centre of every step Uhuru took as he climbed the political ladder to the highest office in the land. And she did that with utmost reticence. Mama Ngina backed her son for the presidency in 2002, supported his association with Ruto leading to the joint ticket in the 2013 presidential election,

---

[49] Maina, Anthony. "Uhuru nearly insulted us with the word ku** - Jubilee MP," *Pulse*, November 14, 2018.

influenced the 'handshake' between Uhuru and Raila in 2018, and fully endorsed Raila as successor to his son.

In turn, Uhuru was always the obedient son. Once in January 2020, he abandoned a church function in Nairobi to respond to an urgent family meeting convened by her mother at her Muthaiga residence in Nairobi.

Of the three first ladies who strolled the corridors and inner sanctums of State House before Uhuru's wife, Margaret Kenyatta, none was as secretive and furtive as Mama Ngina Kenyatta. Mama Ngina was suppressed and restrained. She avoided the media with zeal, choosing to appear in public only when accompanied by her husband or close family members. She was circumspect of people outside her orbit.

Neither was Mama Ngina an exhibitionist. She maintained elegance and gentility throughout the 15 years as first lady. She was a "symbol of power, exuding grace…,"[50] some said. She was a "kind and welcoming lady;"[51] "…media shy, wealthy, and a respected matriarch of the Kenyatta political and business dynasty,"[52] others asserted. She was reticent and unassuming especially around strangers and kept her family matters private.

Just like Mama Ngina, Uhuru's wife, Margaret, carried herself with bashful modesty. Margaret was self-effacing and polite. She was the first African first lady to add environmental sustainability issues in her work. She is the patron of the Hands Off Our Elephants (HOOE) and had participated in anti-poaching campaigns and illicit trade in wildlife products.[53] What an irony considering Mama Ngina's past role on matters of conservation. HOOE is managed by a non-governmental organization called Wildlife Direct. Margaret was

---

[50] Mwanza, Eddy. "Details of Mama Ngina's first interview," *Kenyans.co.ke*, September 8, 2020.

[51] Kariuki, G. G. The Illusions of Power: Reflections on Fifty Years in Kenya Politics, East African Publishers Ltd, 2001, p. 33.

[52] "Prince charming. Here are all President Uhuru's women," *The Standard*, undated.

[53] "Kenya's first lady takes the helm in the war on poachers," The *Guardian*, June 27, 2014.

also a consummate philanthropist during her term at State House. In 2014, she started the Beyond Zero campaign to raise funds for mobile health clinics. She ran marathons, made public appeals, and even travelled abroad, to promote her pet project. For that effort, the UN named her the 2014 Kenya Person of the Year.

Conversely, the third first lady, Lucy, was completely the opposite. She spent a large part of her stay in State House courting controversy. She shut down a drinking joint within the residence and threw out presidential advisers she suspected to be using the executive office for their own personal interests. By the time her term ended, she had slapped a journalist and quarreled with her husband over a sidekick. She had also roasted a vice president, in a needlessly offensive manner, for a slip of the tongue.

Mama Ngina's influence and power was evident even during Moi's era. In 1997, along with her brother, George Muhoho, Uhuru's cousin Ngengi Muigai, Njenga Karume, and a top civil servant, Isaiah Mathenge, Mama Ngina campaigned to revive the Gikuyu Embu Meru Association (GEMA). The association was established in 1971 with the support of Mzee Kenyatta. The revival effort by Mama Ngina and others had the backing of Mwai Kibaki, then leader of the Democratic Party, who contended that its reestablishment would strengthen democracy.

GEMA was one of the most powerful ethnic-based associations "with the potential to own Kenya from the ground up."[54] The association was established in 1971 with the support of Mzee Kenyatta. In fact, both Mzee Kenyatta and Mama Ngina became life members in March 1976. However, GEMA was disbanded by President Moi along with other ethnic associations on November 3, 1978, as part of a crackdown on opposition to his rule.

GEMA's dominating and inspiring influence in the Kikuyu, Meru, and Embu, communities, attracted large numbers of members. It ran a slew of businesses, but also supported political candidates allied to its cause. GEMA was also behind a plot to change the

---

[54] Chilungu, Simeon W. "Kenya- Recent developments and challenges," *Cultural Survival Quarterly Magazine*, September 1985.

constitution to prevent Moi from succeeding Kenyatta in 1978. The effort to revive GEMA failed. Moi's decision to "kill" ethnic-based associations had mortally wounded the organisation and attempts to revive it were devoid of merit; it was like flogging a dead horse.

Seeing no hope, Kikuyu, Meru, and Embu leaders opted to register the GEMA Cultural Association (GCA). Although the GCA is dedicated to promoting understanding among the Kenyan people, its focus is on preserving the Kikuyu heritage and customs.

In recent years, however, the GCA has also become a tool of propagating certain interests. For example, in 2020 it controversially endorsed Uhuru as the region's political leader, and in December 2019, GCA came out to support the Building Bridges Initiative (BBI) that was born out of the 'handshake' between Uhuru and Raila.

But there was another side of Mama Ngina. She played the Machiavellian card. She used "drive and ruthlessness" in exploiting her position to become extraordinarily rich very quickly. In doing so, she "endangered the stability of her husband's regime."[55] The whole Kenyatta administration was seen as corrupt and insensitive to the interests of the majority of Kenyans.

During the late 1960s and early 1970s, a key member of the Kenyatta family negotiated a private deal with some elements at a public institution. The deal was for the individual to supply milk and vegetables for students and staff at the institution. There was no competitive tendering on that arrangement. One writer called it "a food racket."[56]

Fishy as the deal was, corrupt elements at the college allowed the Kenyatta family member to supply excessively large quantities of vegetables to the extent that some of it rotted. A lot more money changed hands in that deal. Those in the college management who complained about the fraudulent deal were expelled. Assistant Minister Charles Rubia who was a member of the College Board was removed when he brought the matter to the attention of the

---

[55] *The Sunday Times*, London, August 17, 1975, p. 5.
[56] Githuku, Nicholas Kariuki, p. 269.

management board.[57] The dark arrangement, it was believed, continued for years.

* * *

In 1986, Mama Ngina and her daughter Christine, registered trustees of the Waunyomu, L. R. No 10901/36 and 10901/37, agreed to sell 82.36 hectares of the land to Mahira Housing Company for Sh5m. But a dispute arose. The first lady claimed the buyer paid only Sh500,000, leaving Sh450,000 unpaid. The company, on the other hand, insisted it had settled the amount in full. The company went ahead and subdivided the land into plots of 50ft by 80ft and allocated them to 1,600 of its members. Mama Ngina wanted the occupants to leave. The matter ended in court in 2001 where the buyer produced receipts to prove payment. The court, however, found the receipts were forgeries and sided with Mama Ngina.

Then there was the saga of the 500-acre coffee plantation in Thika which belonged to Ari and Romi Grammaticas. Mama Ngina forcefully acquired it in January 1977 and paid only KSh.200,000 for a property then valued at KSh.1 million. The Grammaticas, who also owned the Governor's Camp in Masai Mara, sued her. After Mama Ngina discovered that the Switzerland-based owner had hired the distinguished British lawyer, Sir Dingle Foot QC, to pursue the matter, she buckled and agreed to pay the difference. Sir Dingle was one of the high-powered lawyers who defended the Kapenguria Six for their alleged involvement in Mau Mau.

Mama Ngina was also mentioned adversely over a 140-acre coffee farm on the Ruaraka/Gatundu road. The farm belonged to the family of Suri A. Savani. The farm had a newly installed irrigation system and had mature trees ready for harvest. It was a very well organised and managed farm. Mama Ngina saw it and liked it.

Initially, the Savanis did not want to sell the property, but Mama Ngina exerted pressure. When the owner eventually acceded, a price of KSh.2 million was settled upon and the first lady agreed

---

[57] Ibid.

to pay. The problem was that the Savanis wanted cash upon transfer of the land ownership. Mama Ngina demanded to be allowed to pay in instalments. There was a stalemate. Eventually the Savanis, in an act of deepening discouragement, surrendered to pressure. It is not known if Mama Ngina paid them all the money due.

As if that was not enough, Mama Ngina became a defendant in a case in which Kenyatta's stepbrother, Peter Mungai Ngengi, petitioned the court in 2012 over the ownership of a three-and-half-acre piece of land grabbed by Mama Ngina and her immediate family at Ichaweri in Gatundu. Mungai sued her together with Uhuru, who were the administrators of the estate. Mungai claimed that he inherited the land from his father, Ngengi Kungu, Jomo Kenyatta's brother.

Mungai further claimed that the land was wrongfully allocated to the first family by the Ministry of Lands. The first family allegedly merged that piece with another to build their existing executive residence. The court ruled in favour of the Kenyattas, saying the petitioner did not submit any evidence to prove Mungai owned the land.

Because of her station, those who had grievances against Mama Ngina did not feel comfortable suing her. The impression was that she was protected by the government. Also, she had the wherewithal to employ top-notch lawyers to defend her in a court of law. That scared a lot of people.

Nevertheless, in 2019, one family took Mama Ngina to the Thika Environment and Land Court, claiming that the first lady had used corrupt land officials to grab their 1.5-acre of land in Gatundu. The family members, Lucy Njeri, Esther Nyokabi Njoroge, and Daniel Muiruri, alleged that the president's mother had used "intimidation and coercion" to take over their land, situated just in front of the gate of the Kenyatta residence. The three claimed that Mama Ngina manipulated records to show their mother, Virginia Wairimu Njoroge, was the registered owner of the land while the land, they claimed, allegedly belonged to their father, Dr. John Njoroge Muiruri, who had died interstate.

Further, the trio claimed that they did not know the land, Plot no. 1520/1521/1522, had been sold to a company known as

Southbrook Holdings until security officers showed up in 2018 and told them to move out to pave way for a police post. Already built on the plot were flats occupied by GSU personnel. The land was allegedly acquired by Southbrook Holdings at KSh.20 million against an order by Justice Lucy Gicheru. The order had restrained Mama Ngina from selling or transferring the property. By June 2022, the case was yet to be resolved.

Southbrook was registered in 2016 in Kenya with three individuals as directors. But the records show the ownership changed hands to unknown entities.

Also, Mama Ngina allowed more than 2,500 families to be evicted from land to give way for the expansion of Mama Ngina University in Mutomo, Gatundu South. The families had to go to court early in 2022 to fight for the 100 acres they said they had occupied for generations. They sued the National Lands Commission (NLC), Kenyatta University, Mama Ngina University College, Ministry of Education, and the Commission for University Education (CUE), to block the seizure of the land. On the land, they say, were graves of their loved ones. The mostly elderly group of men and women said that the land was legally acquired, and it was "unethical and dehumanising" that they were being forced to exhume the bodies of their dead for reburial elsewhere.

In defence, the AG, Paul Kihara Kariuki, said the government had acted within its constitutional right to acquire the land, compulsorily, for national good. The government action was not only shameful but preposterous. It should have generated public anger, but it didn't. In February 2022, the court agreed with the prosecution and dismissed the case. The matter did not end there, however. The families agreed to move but demanded KSh.16 million each in compensation from the NLC. In May, the matter was resolved. The NLC agreed to pay an average of KSh.10 million to each of the complainants.

In 2010, a retired doctor, Isaac Kirubi, sued the former first lady in the Nakuru High Court claiming Mama Ngina had grabbed his two plots located at the Nakuru CBD. Dr. Kirubi claimed the plots measuring 1.97 acres were forcibly transferred to Mama Ngina on May 7, 1974, by the then Commissioner of Lands, James Aloysius

O'Loughlin, on orders from President Jomo Kenyatta. According to Dr. Kirubi the act by the commissioner infringed his constitutional right to own property. He wanted the land given back to him.

Through her lawyer, William Kabaiku, Mama Ngina, asked the court to throw out the case because she claimed Dr. Kirubi could not prove the land belonged to him. In June 2014, High Court Judge Anyara Emukule agreed with Mzee Kenyatta's wife. He ruled that Dr. Kirubi had relinquished ownership of the land and had in fact been compensated for it. Moreover, he said, Dr. Kirubi had failed to show any proprietary interest on the property.

The question is: With all the things Mama Ngina allegedly did, how come Kenyans never publicly called her out? The answer is simple. They feared her. They also did not call Mama Ngina out because of respect.

Instead of criticising her, people simply grumbled behind the curtain. True, there was once a spattering of murmurs against Mama Ngina. But those murmurs – remote and distance - came out when people discovered that she was earning a monthly salary from the exchequer. The first lady was, and continues to receive, KSh.568,218 tax-free money, as a widow of the late Mzee Kenyatta. The payments began before Uhuru became president and were based on the Presidential Retirement Benefits Act of 3 January 2003. The Act allows the spouse of a retired president who dies in office to receive pension at 40% of the salary of the incumbent president. Some people saw the payment as a form of "corruption." Others thought she deserved it.

Mama Ngina's legacy is on the many roads and institutions named after her all over the country: Mama Ngina Street in Nairobi, Mama Ngina Children's Home, Mama Ngina University, Mama Ngina Waterfront Park, Mombasa, Mama Ngina Kenyatta Mixed High School, Mama Ngina Kenyatta Primary School Library, and many others.

She was not only heir to the Kenyattas' bounty but was an invisible co-president throughout Uhuru's rule.

PART II
UHURU'S ENTRY INTO POLITICS

CHAPTER 3

Project Uhuru

Growing up in the company of his famous father, Uhuru had tasted the good life of a politician: the attention, the opulence, and the wealth. Thus, in the 1990s, riding on the debate over whether Kenya should maintain a one-party state or move to multi-partyism, Uhuru and four children of prominent Kenyans, Peter Mboya, Francis Michuki, Alfred Getonga, and Argwings Kodhek, added their voice to the multi-party debate in the hope of attracting attention.

Enthusiastically convinced that they would be heard, they issued a statement asking President Moi for a meeting to discuss the matter. Moi did not reply. Instead, the *Kenya Times,* responded with alacrity, unleashing a scathing editorial that dismissed the group as "spoilt sons of privilege best advised to keep their mouths shut."[58] *Kenya Times* was owned by the then ruling party, the Kenya African National Union (KANU).

Shut their mouths they didn't. They were determined, so they directed their views to the obedient and duteous 1990 KANU Constitutional Review Commission under Vice President Prof. George Saitoti, which Moi had appointed to forestall the agitation for multi-partyism. The commission responded with derision and

---

[58] Ngotho, Kamau. Kenya: "The day Uhuru was thrown out of government building," *Daily Nation*, September 13, 2020.

condemnation to the young men. It could not understand why Uhuru, son of a former president, would espouse views supporting the opposition.

Many of those who appeared before the commission supported multi-partyism, but at the end, the body concluded that the single party system should remain. The issue of what system the country would choose was settled only after Moi finally succumbed to pressure and agreed to the change in December 1991.

On Christmas Day in 1991, Mwai Kibaki resigned from the government and KANU and formed the Democratic Party (DP) of Kenya. The new party immediately received the support of some key members of the Kenyatta family: Mama Ngina, her brother George Muhoho, and Uhuru's cousins, Ngengi Muigai and Beth Mugo.

In the meantime, Uhuru was being wooed by all the major political parties among them, Moi's ruling party, KANU, Jaramogi Odinga's Ford-Kenya, Kibaki's DP, and Kenneth Matiba's Ford-Asili They all wanted to have the "young Kenyatta in their corner."[59] Moi eventually got the upper hand and took Uhuru under his wing.

However, it was not until 1997 at the age of 36, that a resolute Uhuru plunged into serious politics. He contested and was elected unopposed as chairperson of the Gatundu KANU branch. That same year, he took a gamble on the Gatundu South parliamentary seat, believing it would be an easy ride given his family name. The seat was formerly held by his late father (1963 to 1978), and his cousin, Ngengi Muigai, (1979 to 1983). Uhuru's gamble flopped. He was trounced by a little-known neophyte politician, Moses Muihia, thus bringing shame to the Kenyatta brand.

After failing to clinch the Gatundu South parliamentary seat, Uhuru was ready to give up public life and return to his family businesses. However, President Moi appointed him chairman of the Kenya Tourism Board (KTB) in 1999.

The following year, Moi gave him additional responsibilities as chairman of a 15-member Disaster Emergency Response Committee.

---

[59] Ngotho, Kamau. "Uhuru waited under Moi's wings for years," *Daily Nation*, November 1, 2017.

It became obvious that the president was preparing Uhuru for a bigger role in government.

In October 2001, Moi nominated Uhuru to the National Assembly. That nomination was politically controversial. On the day of the appointment, President Moi, Uhuru, and nominated MP Mark Too, a Moi sycophant, had dined together. Moi had asked them to accompany him on a tour of Nyanza. It was before that tour that Moi forced Too to vacate his seat for Uhuru. The diminutive businessman, with a relishing sense of humour, did not go voluntarily as Kenyans were made to believe. He was coerced.

But Uhuru's version of the events that day is different. He talks of a telephone call from Moi. "Moi called me and said Mark Too had agreed to vacate his seat for me. I was confused but I just said it is okay," Uhuru told one gathering. "Moments later, Mark Too came to my house, and I eagerly asked him what [had] happened, because we were to try to convince the MP for Mombasa [constituency] to give up his seat. [At that time, the constituency officially known as Mvita was represented by Sharif Nassir, also a close Moi confidante]. But Too told me Mzee had arrived at a decision."[60] Whatever the version or events, that matter had been sorted out.

From there, Uhuru moved up with breathtaking speed. In November 2001, Moi appointed him Minister for Local Government. A *Daily Nation* editorial said the appointment was significant because "it has so many national tendrils, is traditionally a steppingstone to great heights."[61] Indeed, it was!

The same year, Moi unilaterally pushed KANU delegates to elect Uhuru as one of the four national vice chairmen of KANU. The others were Stephen Kalonzo Musyoka, Katana Ngala and Musalia Mudavadi.

After that, Moi implored party leaders to nominate Uhuru as KANU's presidential candidate. By that time, Moi had been in power

---

[60] Wanambisi, Laban. "How Mark Too kick-started my political career – Uhuru," *Capital News*, January 9, 2017.
[61] "Key role for Obure as Moi reshuffles cabinet," *The New Humanitarian*, November 21, 2001.

for about 24 years uninterrupted, and according to the constitution, he was not eligible to stand for another term.

At the back of his mind, Moi believed Mzee Kenyatta's legacy was enough to rekindle Uhuru's political career.[62] However, his choice of Uhuru to succeed him bypassing a half a dozen other more qualified candidates backfired, at least at the party level. It drew the wrathful pugnacity of a section of KANU leaders who beseeched him to follow the party's nomination process. Moi ignored them.

Kenyans were surprised at Uhuru's nomination. Jomo's son had no leadership qualities that made him fit for the presidency, other than being a Kenyatta. He had not yet experienced the rough and tumble of Kenya's divisive and combative politics. He was too young, and a novice best left to mature. Yet he was the chosen one.

In July 2002, Mama Ngina jumped into the political fray with a special appeal to Kenyans to elect her 41-year-old son. Her remarks were followed by Moi's unequivocal endorsement and a nod from Kikuyu elders. Another notable support came from Maendeleo ya Wanawake Organisation (MYWO) which was then led by Uhuru's sister, Margaret Wambui. With that development, Uhuru's mood was one of pure exaltation even though a swath of the population was not convinced he had the intestinal fortitude to lead.

Apart from the fact that he was a Kenyatta, few Kenyans knew much about Uhuru. "He's a mystery to us," Gichara Kibara, the Executive Director of the Kenya Centre for Governance and Development told the *New York Times*.

"We know he is the son of the first president, but nobody knows what he stands for," Smith Hempstone, the controversial US Ambassador to Kenya, said "… it doesn't bode too well,"[63] that little was known about Uhuru. "I may have met him in passing, but I don't remember him." Thus, at the beginning of his political career, Uhuru had an identity crisis, but that was not for long.

---

[62] Badejo, Babafemi A. *Raila Odinga: An Enigma in Kenyan Politics*, Yintab Books, 2006, p. 45.

[63] Lacey, Marc. "Heir to power and to Kenya's great name," *The New York Times*, October 15, 2002.

In defiance of Moi's wishes, top party stalwarts declared their own candidacies for the top job. Musalia Mudavadi, a KANU vice chairman, announced on July 27, 2002, that he would contest the seat. He was followed by Raila Odinga, KANU's Secretary General the next day. The other two KANU vice chairman Katana Ngala and Stephen Kalonzo Musyoka declared their interest on July 30, 2002, and Vice President George Saitoti on August 4, 2002, one day after resigning. The message was clear: they did not agree with Moi on Uhuru's nomination. But Moi took the gambit, determined to push candidate Uhuru to the finish line.

As some rebel leaders defected to candidate Mwai Kibaki's DP, Moi embarked on a country-wide tour to popularise Uhuru's debut in the presidential poll. Kibaki was then the Leader of Official Opposition. It was Raila's surprise declaration of "Kibaki Tosha" at a public meeting at Uhuru Park on October 14, 2002, that propelled Kibaki to the top of the coalition presidential card.

President Moi contended that Uhuru was the right candidate because "he is a person who can be guided." But one reason why Moi embraced Uhuru was because he wanted protection in retirement. Moi did not complain when Mzee Kenyatta went on a binge of assets collection. While Mzee 'ate' with a bucket, Moi was content with a small spoon. His hope was that Uhuru would return the favour and protect his ill-gotten riches accumulated since he was appointed Vice President by Mzee Kenyatta in 1967. It was all in line with the adage: 'scratch my back and I'll scratch yours.' During his tours, Moi poured bitter and biting ridicule on his discomfited opponents. Conversely, he spewed accolades on Uhuru.

But President Moi's time to leave office was nearing. On October 25, 2002, he dissolved parliament and announced December 27 as the date for the General Elections. His official 24-year rule ended on December 30, 2002, when he handed over power to Mwai Kibaki in a swearing-in ceremony and Uhuru Park.

The 71-year-old Mwai Kibaki and his NARC easily won, driving the 41-year-old Uhuru and KANU to the back benches. Uhuru could not launch a coherent campaign against the older and more experienced opponent. When Kibaki left his lecturing job at

Makerere University in 1960 to join KANU as an Executive Officer, Uhuru was not yet born. Thus, Kibaki was the more experienced one. In the 2002 elections, Kibaki got 62.20% of the vote while Uhuru got 31.32%. It was Uhuru's second major political defeat. However, it was a big win for democracy and a denunciation of Moi's repressive type of governance. Major political realignments were to follow.

Role in Anglo Leasing scandal

It was Uhuru as Leader of the Official Opposition and chairman of the Public Accounts Committee (PAC) in 2006, who presented a harrowing report in parliament naming those allegedly behind the mega Anglo Leasing scandal of the 1990s. The report was compiled after PAC members had travelled to London to gather evidence from the former ethics czar, John Githongo, who had resigned while on an overseas trip. George Kegoro, the Executive Director of the Open Society Initiative for Eastern Africa called Uhuru's investigation of the Anglo Leasing contracts "heroic."[64]

A total of 20 Anglo Leasing contracts worth KSh.55 billion were signed by some top Kenyan government officials and mysterious companies whose identities were unknown. The companies were to supply multifarious items of a security nature to government agencies including the police and the meteorological departments. Githongo named four Cabinet Ministers and identified Finance Minister David Mwiraria as the mastermind of the fraud. Also on his list were Vice President Moody Awori, Energy Minister Kiraitu Murungi, and Internal Security Minister Christopher Murungaru.

Several officials still in service and others who had retired were charged with conspiracy to defraud, abuse of power, breach of trust, disobedience of statutory duty, and fraudulent acquisition of public property.

---

[64] "Anglo Leasing: Uhuru had carried out heroic probe," *Nation*, May 3, 2014.

In September 2012, Permanent Secretary Sylvester Mwaliko was the first one – and the only one of the top officials – to be convicted. He was fined KSh.3 million or in default serves a three-year jail term.

In 2015, Uhuru as president, ordered the National Treasury to pay KSh.1.4 billion to two companies which had sued the Kenya government. The companies, the First Mercantile Securities Corporation (FMSC) and the Universal Satspace, had gone to court and secured a ruling requiring the Kenya government to pay for services and goods that were not delivered. The money represented the principal and accrued interest on the amount agreed after Nairobi terminated the contracts.

The FMSC was paid KSh.722 million for a contract involving telecommunication equipment, while Satspace received KSh.705 million for a contract involving supply of bandwidth spectrum. Uhuru defended himself from critics, saying he had to pay the monies to avoid the multiplication of interest after the government had exhausted all legal avenues of appeals.

CHAPTER 4

Minister for Finance

In the 2007 elections, Uhuru Kenyatta tactically opted not to run, leaving Mwai Kibaki of the Party of National Unity (PNU) to seek a second term in a contest with Raila Odinga of the Orange Democratic Movement (ODM). Uhuru's absence from the race and support for Mwai Kibaki consolidated the Kikuyu vote.

The elections were controversial. ODM accused the Kibaki side of rigging the polls, but the Centre for Strategic International Studies (CSIS) which audited the numbers said there had been irregularities and vote rigging on both sides.[65] Almost immediately after the results were announced, riots erupted. Protesters burned tires and hurled stones and other objects at anti-riot police personnel.

In ODM neighbourhoods, rioters robbed, and beat up people suspected to be Kibaki's supporters. The reverse happened in areas deemed to be inhabited by supporters of PNU. In less than three hours after the Electoral Commission of Kenya (ECK) announced the results on December 30, 2007, Kibaki was hastily sworn in at State House.

The disputed results were tight with Kibaki getting 46.42% of the vote against Raila's 44.07. On January 5, 2008, Kibaki announced he was ready to form a Government of National Unity, but Raila

---

[65] Background on the Post-Election Crisis in Kenya, CSIS, August 6, 2009.

and his supporters refused to participate. Three days later, Kibaki announced a 17-member cabinet.

In the meantime, Raila announced that he would be sworn-in at Uhuru Park as the 'people's president' and would form a parallel government. The government warned him that the action would amount to a coup d'état. Raila and ODM did not carry out the threat.

Violence continued for weeks. Over 1,300 people were killed, 600,000 displaced and properties worth million of shillings destroyed. The international community was stunned. The former UN Secretary General Kofi Annan arrived in Nairobi and helped broker a power-sharing deal between Kibaki and Raila. On February 28, a Grand Coalition Government was announced ending months of political stalemate.

In the January 8, 2008, Kibaki had appointed Uhuru Kenyatta as Minister for Local Government. It was a hastily put-up cabinet, amid crises. Uhuru held that position for only three months.

In April 2008, Uhuru was appointed deputy prime minister and minister for trade. Soon thereafter, in June 2008, a major scandal broke out involving the sale of the Grand Regency Hotel in Nairobi. Finance Minister Amos Kimunya was accused of selling the property to Libyan investors at a throw away price of US$45 million (KSh.5 billion). Analysts said it was worth US$115 million (KSh.13 billion). Cries of "Kimunya must go" rang out in parliament as MPs sought his resignation to pave way for investigations.

After days of insisting that, "I would rather die than resign," Kimunya bowed to the pressure, and on July 8, he quit. The lucky person to replace him at the finance ministry was none other than the son of Jomo. Unlike many of his predecessors, Uhuru did not have to follow a meandering trail to reach the pinnacle of one of the most sought-after government departments. His journey was like "a great express train, roaring, flashing, dashing headlong." Easy and smooth!

The Ministry of finance is a strategic department of government. The person chosen to the docket enjoys added privileges of renumeration as well as the honour of preparing and delivering the annual budget speech. The finance minister is in-charge of formulating and implementing macroeconomic policies involving expenditure and revenue and managing the public debt and all national financial obligations. The minister also mobilises domestic and external resources, prepare the annual Division of Revenue Bill and the County Allocation of Revenue Bill, and maintain bilateral and multilateral financial relations, among other duties.

Those were huge responsibilities on the shoulders of a greenhorn.

INTO THE DEEP SEA

It was a shaky start for Uhuru at the ministry of finance. He had no practical experience in the realm of finance. But he was received warmly in the financial circles. "I don't think it's a bad choice," said Robert Shaw, a Kenyan economist. "He has a reasonable grasp of fundamentals, and he is willing to listen." [66]

The public debt management report dated December 2012 for the period July 2011 to June 2012 was a mixed bag of mostly negatives. It showed that the public debt rose by 60% from KSh.870 billion in June 2008 to KSh.1.6 billion, representing 49.5% of GDP in June 2012.

The domestic component grew to KSh.859 million, equivalent of 26.2% of GDP. This meant that under Uhuru's watch, the ratio of the public debt to GDP had increased to 49.5% in nominal terms. The ratio of the external debt to multilateral and bilateral creditors had, however, declined from 50.9% to 46.1%, even though, there was an increase in domestic borrowing by 4.8% from 49.1% to 53.9%. Therefore, Uhuru's penchant for borrowing began when he was the minister of finance. It would later manifest itself on a grand scale when he became president of the republic.

There was additional mixed news for Uhuru on the economy. On taking over the ministry, he had predicted a GDP annual growth of 5% in 2010. Kenya did much better that year though and achieved

---

[66] Mwaura, Helen Nyambura & Andrew Cawthorne. "Kenyatta named as Kenya's finance minister," *Reuters,* January 23, 2009.

an 8.41% growth. Due to worldwide recession and increase in oil prices, however, growth declined to 6.12% in 2011 and collapsed further to 4.45% in 2012, the year Uhuru left the ministry.

One of Uhuru's first actions at the ministry was to order top government officials to discard their big cars for vehicles with an engine capacity of 1800cc or below. The move, he said, was to save taxpayers KSh.2.7 billion. Through the ministry of public works, the treasury bought 126 new 1800cc Passat vehicles to replace the 2996cc Mercedes Benz guzzlers. The government said the smaller cars were cheaper to run and maintain and each cost two thirds less than a Mercedes Benz.

Apart from criticisms of the Passat's per-unit-price of KSh.3.7 million, which some MPs said was above the market price, anti-corruption activists also questioned why the vehicles were sourced from a single dealer, the CMC Motors. "When every single vehicle is bought from one dealer…alarm bells start ringing,"[67] said Mwalimu Mati, founder and CEO of the internet-based organisation, Mars. Some lawmakers claimed that one of the CMC directors was Charles Njonjo, a former AG who could have influenced the deal through his high connections in government.

Early in July 2009, parliament summoned Uhuru to shade light on the matter. He insisted that the transaction, worth KSh.499.5 million, was done through a competitive tendering process. Njonjo, then a director of CMC Holdings, resigned from the CMC board in 2012 after forty years of service. He died on January 2, 2022.

The whole idea of officials surrendering their big vehicles for the smaller ones became contentious. Uhuru did not consult the malcontent users, mainly ministers, assistant ministers, and permanent secretaries, before purchasing the vehicles. He just announced the change and gave them a deadline to give up their luxury cars. Some complied but others, like immigration minister Otieno Kajwang, refused. "We are not school-children to be given

---

[67] Wadhams, Nick. "Kenya outrage after leaders ditch Mercedes," *TIME*, November 18, 2009.

uniforms in the form of Passats,"[68] he fumed. Kajwang declined to surrender his fleet. For Uhuru, the decision to dress down MPs was a political blunder as it diminished his clout in parliament and fuelled animosity with MPs. As for Uhuru, he led by example, and started using a VW Passat.

Then there was the question of what to do with the ditched Mercedes Benz vehicles. Many of the vehicles were in near excellent working condition. For several years, the vehicles gathered dust at a government yard. Then, the government decided to auction them. However, by the time the vehicles were auctioned in 2015, Uhuru was already president. He left the ministry on January 26, 2012, after the International Criminal Court (ICC) ruled that he was to face charges for crimes against humanity.

As it turned out, the sale of the vehicles was illegal. Officials had advertised the sale tender in only one publication instead of two as required by law. It was suspected that corrupt officials were colluding with cartels to dispose of the vehicles at grossly undervalued prices, pocketing the difference. A good example was that of a Nissan Patrol vehicle. It was worth over KSh.2 million but was sold for only KSh.145,000.

A Volkswagen Passat went for only KSh.32,000. The whole exercise was as odious as it was absurd. At the end, the government received KSh.170 million only from the sale of 488 cars. Although the Public Accounts Committee (PAC) recommended the prosecution of those involved in the insatiably greedy deals, nothing more was heard of the matter.

* * *

Uhuru was the minister for finance when Kenya adopted the Constitution of Kenya, 2010. Introduced in the new dispensation were a bicameral parliament, a devolved system of government, a tenured electoral commission, and a constitutional-tenured judiciary.

---

[68] Ibid.

With the addition of the 47 devolved governments, Uhuru had to readjust his budgets to ensure that 15% of government revenue went to the 47 counties established under the new constitution. Under the new constitution, the existing Provincial Administration (PA) was abolished and replaced by a new national government administrative system called the National Administration (NA).

The NA deploys an administrator to each administrative tier of government, absorbing district commissioners, district officers, chiefs and assistant chiefs.[69] There was therefore a need for a financial review to accommodate new appointments in counties, and budgets for senior officials posted there by the national government, including county commissioners.

Uhuru's tenure at the ministry of finance also saw a significant increase in infrastructure spending. For the fiscal year ending June 2011, Uhuru allocated KSh.182 billion or 18% of the government budget for railway, road, and energy improvements. He argued that the increase was meant to fast-track economic growth and open job opportunities for Kenyans.

Another crisis Uhuru had to deal with as finance minister was the teachers' strike in 2011. Two-hundred thousand teachers downed their chalks for a whole week demanding salary increase, better working conditions, and the hiring of more teachers. Uhuru agreed to the pay demand, the hiring of 5,000 more teachers, and the employment of 18,000 teachers, on permanent basis. The teachers' union called off the strike.

Uhuru is also credited for setting up a KSh.3.8 billion fund for Small and Medium Enterprises (SMEs) through an arrangement with three banks, the Cooperative Bank of Kenya (CBK), K-Rep, and Equity. Each bank received KSh.250 million from the government to lend to the businesses on favourable terms. The agreement stated that each bank would match each government shilling with five shillings to realise the KSh.3.8 billion ceiling. Eventually, the government

---

[69] Hassan, Mai. "Continuity Despite Change: Kenya's New Constitution and Executive Power," *Democratisation*, Vol. 22, No. 4, pp. 587-609.

released more funds into what came to be known as the Fund for Inclusion of Informal Sector.

As infrastructure spending grew, so did the public wage bill. Thus, there was a need to simultaneously cut government spending. Uhuru's drastic move to take big cars from the ministers was only one step. The other was to control the unending demands for higher pay by MPs.

In July 2010, Uhuru made enemies of his colleagues when he informed them that additional expenditure for their salary demands was not included in the 2010/2011 budget estimates. He explained that the government wanted to prioritise development projects and had no money for pay hikes for MPs.

The angry and notoriously profligate lawmakers argued that the increases were recommended by the Akilano Akiwumi Commission. The commission was formed by Kibaki in 2010 to investigate the legislators' pay and conditions of service and had approved changes in salaries and allowances for lawmakers.

The treasury remained adamant. "If they [MPs] want the money, let them tell us where it will come from because there was no provision in this year's budget,"[70] said a tough-talking Treasury official. But chances of Uhuru winning the battle with the determined MPs were slim. The MPs threatened to sink the budget if their demands were not met. The secretary general of the Central Organisation of Trade Unions (COTU), Francis Atwoli, called it "blackmail."

Eventually, the MPs got their way. They passed three bills to award themselves more money and pension benefits: the National Assembly Remuneration (Amendment) Bill 2010; the Parliament Pension (Amendment) Bill 2010; and the Income Tax (Amendment Bill) 2010. The increase translated to a 25% pay rise, raising their income from KSh.851,000 to KSh.1.1 million per month. In return, the MPs grudgingly agreed to pay taxes. A frustrated Uhuru had to find additional money elsewhere to pay the MPs, amid a storm of public indignation.

---

[70] "Uhuru blocks pay rise for MPs," *Insurance Newsnet*, July 5, 2010.

The finance minister was already in bad books of parliament after failing four times to appear before the budget committee. Legislators had wanted Uhuru to explain how his ministry had spent KSh.190 billion in 2009. The minister said he could not attend because he was busy with other national issues. Instead, he sent an official from his office to represent him. The MPs felt slighted. "This is not a matter of having a tight schedule," said a member of the committee, Ekwee Ethuro. "It is a matter of an Executive that does not appreciate parliament's probing; one that does not want to follow the law."[71]

In November 2010, Uhuru again earned the wrath of legislators when he failed to attend a meeting of the parliamentary energy committee. The MPs wanted the finance minister to explain the government's position on the rising fuel prices that were impacting the transport sector. Instead of showing up, Uhuru sent a letter stating that he was too busy and "did not have time for the House." Committee Chairman James Rege said Uhuru's absence at the committee amounted to contempt of the House and called upon parliament to reject all businesses tabled by Uhuru until he complied. He didn't.

The Energy Regulatory Commission had raised the price of super petrol by KSh. 2.75 to KSh. 120.50, and diesel by KSh. 2.77 to KSh. 110.94 per litre. The commission claimed the increases were due to a weak shilling, volatile economic performance, and erratic crude prices on the international market.

Those, however, were not the only issues Uhuru faced at the finance ministry. The anti-graft watchdog Mars Group detected a KSh.9.2 billion error in the 2008/2009 supplementary budget figures Uhuru had presented to parliament. Mars also found a discrepancy of KSh.163 million in the approved budget. In total, the non-governmental organisation (NGO) claimed, 200 budget line items involving 35 ministries had been inflated. The group further alleged that the ministry of finance had 'cooked' figures and shifted money

---

[71] "Uhuru no show for House Budget team," Nation, July 27, 2010.

from one vote to another to cover up a KSh.10.7 million difference identified in earlier estimates. That was a shattering blow to Uhuru.

The particularly notable error was detected when Uhuru asked parliament for an additional KSh.2.6 billion in the supplementary budget. After an audit of the figures by the parliamentary finance committee, the MPs were not satisfied and called for a parliamentary investigation. Uhuru quickly responded saying the difference was a "typing error." He assured Kenyans that the treasury had no intention of defrauding the public.

However, critics seized the moment and cried corruption. They pointed to a similar discrepancy during the Goldenberg scandal in the 1990s.[72] In the latest case, KSh.8.6 billion was found to have been included in a part payment of a loan to the United Kingdom. The loan did not exist. However, MP Simon Mbugua came to Uhuru's defence. He talked of a sinister plot to sabotage the finance minister, prompting the *Daily Nation*, to carry a story under the tendentious rubric: "Blunder or sabotage? Uhuru's new headache."[73] MP Maoka Maore cynically remarked: "Making mistakes is normal; the issue is what you do when you are found. If the minister has been sabotaged, what has he done about it?"[74] The explosive debate over the error ended only when Uhuru submitted reviewed estimates to the House.

Uhuru left the ministry of finance after 43 months, boasting about how transparent and open he had been while serving in government. Perhaps he could have performed better if it wasn't because of the 2007 election crisis, high global energy prices, the world financial crisis, and the worst drought period since independence.[75] Approximately 1.4 million people were affected by the 2008 drought that swept the north-eastern, eastern, and coastal parts of the country. In 2009, ten million people were at risk of starvation.

---

[72] The Goldenberg scandal erupted during Moi's rule but spilled over to Kibaki and Uhuru's regimes.
[73] "Blunder or sabotage? Uhuru's new headache," *Daily Nation*, May 25, 2009.
[74] Ibid.
[75] Roundtable with Kenya's Deputy Prime Minister and Minister for Finance, Uhuru Kenyatta, Africa Growth Initiative at Brookings, October 12, 2010.

CHAPTER 5

Second stab: Uhuru's Road to the Presidency

The story of how Uhuru Kenyatta, William Ruto, and other defendants found themselves at The Hague was epic. It started with the appointment of Justice Philip Waki, an appellate judge, to head a commission of inquiry into the cause of the 2007-2008 post-election violence in Kenya. The commission was to find out the people involved or those who had instigated the violence.

After listening to accounts from witnesses, the commission compiled a report and gave it to President Kibaki and Prime Minister Raila Odinga on October 15, 2008.[76] The report recommended that parliament should establish a special tribunal to try those suspected to have been involved in the mayhem. In the meantime, Justice Waki sent the names of the alleged suspects to Kofi Annan directly (in a sealed envelope). Annan had retired as secretary general of the UN and was delegated to handle the Kenya post-election crisis.

The commission recommended that should parliament fail to establish the tribunal Annan would forward the names to the International Criminal Court (ICC) for prosecution. Parliament failed to comply. In July 2009, Annan handed over the names to

---

[76] Nderitũ, Alice Wairimũ, *Kenya: Bridging Ethnic Divides: A Commissioner's Experience on Cohesion and Integration* (2018).

the International Criminal Court (ICC) prosecutor, Luis Moreno-Ocampo. In December 2010, Ocampo released names of six suspects to be prosecuted, among them Uhuru and William Ruto. "These were not just crimes against innocent Kenyans, but crimes against humanity as a whole," Ocampo said in a statement. He requested the ICC to issue summons to the suspects.

In March 2011, the ICC issued summons to the six individuals and asked them to appear in person before the ICC. Apart from Uhuru and Ruto, the others were the head of the civil service and secretary to the cabinet, Francis Muthaura, the suspended Minister for Industrialisation, Henry Kosgey, the former Police Commissioner, Major-General Hussein Ali, and a radio journalist, Joshua arap Sang. The suspects were charged with a variety of counts including crimes against humanity, murder, forcible transfer, rape, and persecution.

The ICC accused Uhuru and the others of orchestrating the violence that occurred before, during, and after the 2007 elections. Over 1,300 people died in the chaos that spread throughout the country. According to the US-based Centre for Strategic and International Studies (CSIS), an estimated 600,000 people were displaced, as supporters of President Kibaki's Party of National Unity (PNU) and of Raila's Orange Democratic Movement (ODM), fought over the disputed December 27, 2007, presidential election results.

Prosecutor Ocampo singled out Uhuru, then deputy prime minister and minister for finance, as a direct co-perpetrator of murder, rape, and forcible transfer of persons. The prosecutor further alleged that Uhuru had paid money to *Mungiki,* a quasi-religious sect with roots in Central Kenya, to murder followers of his rival, Raila Odinga. Ocampo's revelation threw Kenyans into a state of shock and disbelief.

One month after the ICC Pre-trial Chamber 11 issued summons to Uhuru and the others to appear before the court, the Kenyatta clan under its matriarch, Mama Ngina Kenyatta, congregated for prayers and reflection at their stately home in Gatundu, Kiambu County, 47 km from Nairobi. In attendance were close family members from both the Kenyatta and the Muhoho families. Mama Ngina's children and members of the extended family attended.

UHURU KENYATTA

The get-together of members of the inner circle of Kenya's richest and most powerful family was solemn and funereal. Mama Ngina – who was in pain from a knee injury – had not slept for days on end, worried about what would happen to her son, as the determined Ocampo pressed ahead with criminal charges against Uhuru. "I used to cry myself to sleep wondering how he would be jailed…,"[77] she recalled later. If convicted, Uhuru risked spending many years in a foreign jail.

On April 4, 2012, the day after the family meeting, Mama Ngina and her family attended a public prayer meeting at Gatundu Stadium. Religious leaders delivered sombre devotions asking the Almighty to protect Uhuru at The Hague trial. Mama Ngina said the ICC trial was not about justice but about settling political scores, calling it a "charade." The highlight of the meeting was a scene never seen before. In a gesture that unmasked a variety of conflicting and profound emotions, Mama Ngina asked Uhuru to stand up. She held him close to her face, placed her hands on his head and babbled prayers in Kikuyu.

She performed similar rituals on William Samoei Ruto, Uhuru's running mate in the 2013 elections. Mama Ngina's gesture was an inestimable honour for the man from the Rift Valley who had known Uhuru for over a decade. Both had been members of the ruling party KANU; Uhuru since 1990 and Ruto since 1992. Dozens of political leaders and thousands of bemoaning and bewailing people attended that superheated meeting beamed live on television. Speaker after speaker condemned the ICC and emotionally commiserated with Mama Ngina.

"How much can a wife and a mother bear?" Asked Uhuru's cousin Ngengi Muigai. "First it was her husband's tribulations from the British colonialists, and now it is her son from the same colonialists."[78]

It was a powerful scene. The atmosphere was melodramatic. Having spent five years in detention during the Mau Mau liberation

---

[77] Wambui, Mary. "Mama Ngina recounts her pain during Uhuru's ICC trial," *Nairobi News*, November 22, 2016.
[78] Ibid.

struggle, Mama Ngina knew what it meant to be deprived of freedom and to be separated from one's family. She also remembered how it felt when her husband was away for eight years as a prisoner of the colonial government. She wished nothing of the same for her son.

The March 4, 2013, general elections were about a year away. Campaigns were already in top gear. Uhuru was making his second attempt at the presidency. In 2002, he had lost to Mwai Kibaki.

Several things happened as the election date neared. On May 2, 2012, Musalia Mudavadi, who had been Raila's preferred choice for vice president in 2007, abandoned ODM to pursue his own presidential bid. Around that time, reports emerged that Uhuru was ready to abandon his quest for the top seat in favour of Mudavadi.

Uhuru and Ruto went to Mudavadi's residence in Nairobi to request him to make himself available for the presidential run. Why? Uhuru and Ruto were not sure about the outcome of the ICC trial. For Plan B, they believed Mudavadi was the best option. At their meeting, the trio even signed a Memorandum of Understanding (MoU), but the MoU lasted only two days. Uhuru tossed it out of the window following intense pressure from Mt. Kenya leaders. By doing that, Uhuru had badly betrayed Mudavadi, something the latter has never forgotten.

Another fear among Kikuyu leaders was that Kenyans may not support another Kikuyu candidate for president [Uhuru] immediately after Kibaki, a fellow Kikuyu. There was also concern about possible sanctions by western nations if Uhuru were to win.[79] If that happened, Kikuyu-owned businesses, which are dominant, would suffer the most. The Kikuyu leaders eventually ditched those concerns and allowed the "pair in mid-December to finalise the campaign strategy, under the eye-catching banner, 'Uhuru-Ruto.'"[80]

On May 21, 2012, Uhuru had left KANU to launch his own political party, The National Alliance (TNA). Uhuru had been the national chairman of KANU since 2005 when he defeated Nicholas

---

[79] *Daily Nation*, December 16, 2012.
[80] Wolf, Thomas P. International Justice vs Public Opinion? The ICC and Ethnic Polarisation in the 2013 Kenyan Election, *Journal of African Elections*, June 2013, p. 164.

Biwott in party elections. Many in the independence party felt his departure from KANU betrayed his father's legacy. Mzee Kenyatta had been a member of KANU for seventeen years from 1961 after his release from detention to 1978 when he died. Others thought Uhuru's move was meant to divert attention from the ICC trial. By establishing his own political vehicle away from the baggage of the ruling party, Uhuru's message was threefold: that he was his own man, that he feared not his arch opponent Raila, and that he was unstoppable, despite the ICC indictment.

Although Uhuru said his party would "work and even merge with other like-minded parties," he made it clear that TNA would "no longer settle for mediocrity and the barren promises made by the current [Kibaki] leadership." To distance himself from the old order, Uhuru chose a peer, Eugene Wamalwa, to introduce him at the TNA launch. That was seen as a generational shift from the "analogue technology to the digital technology."

The TNA chairman was a 28-year-old political novice, Johnstone Sakaja, and most of the other officials were youthful. The party colour was red, and the rallying call was "I believe." Wamalwa was still in government as minister for justice and constitutional affairs but harboured his own presidential ambitions via the New Ford-Kenya (NFK) party. He was also a member of the so-called G7, a group of leaders including Vice President Stephen Kalonzo Musyoka and William Ruto of the United Republican Party (URP), whose combined goal was to stop Raila Odinga from succeeding President Kibaki.

To flex his financial and political muscles, Uhuru held the TNA launch at two locations on the same venue: at the COMESA grounds where 3,000 people attended, and at the Kenyatta International Convention Centre (KICC) courtyard, where 15,000 people were present. The grounds were named COMESA in 1999 during a major exhibition by member countries of the Common Market for Eastern and Southern Africa (COMESA). Giant screens were also mounted in various parts of the country such as Mombasa, Kisumu, Kakamega, Nakuru, Eldoret, Nyeri, Bungoma, and Garissa, for people to follow the proceedings. The launch was transmitted live on TV, Facebook, and Twitter.

On December 2, 2012, Uhuru and Ruto – who had previously been in separate political camps: TNA and URP – joined hands. At a joint rally at Nakuru, they officially declared their candidacy as president and deputy president, respectively. Although the two had different susceptibilities, the rebirth of the Kikuyu/Kalenjin political alliance became the biggest threat to Raila's ODM and the wider Coalition for Reforms and Democracy (CORD) to which Raila was a principal member.

As Uhuru and Ruto were grappling with the ICC indictment, Raila escalated his criticisms of the two leaders. He told them to carry their own cross on the ICC debacle and to stop accusing him of being behind their woes. Uhuru hit back: "Raila was at the centre of the violence. He is the one who ignited the flames." At that point, Raila became a 'loose cannon.' He put Uhuru under siege, bombarding him and his family with accusations from all corners. He challenged him to declare his family's wealth, and pressed President Kibaki to release the Truth, Justice, and Reconciliation Commission (TJRC) report which contained details of the Kenyattas' land grabbing spree.

Raila's public meetings were always well-attended. His followers were exuberant and supercharged. Raila himself was fiery and unrelenting. "The son of a snake is a snake," he thundered during one frenzied rally at Uhuru Park in Nairobi in February 2013. Raila's attacks were directed not just to Uhuru but to the whole Kenyatta family.

Uhuru faced another hitch. Three weeks to the March 4, 2013, elections, four non-governmental organisations (NGOs) filed a case at the High Court seeking to bar the duo from contesting the elections because of integrity issues. The NGOs argued that "…any person committed to trial at the Hague-based ICC would not be able to properly carry out their duties of running the country, while the honour and integrity of the public office would also be damaged."[81]

---

[81] Eulich, Whitney. "Kenyan court clears Kenyatta for presidential bid, despite war crime charges," The *Christian Science Monitor,*" February 15, 2013.

However, a five-judge High Court bench dismissed the suit ruling that the two had already been duly cleared by the Independent Electoral and Boundaries Commission (IEBC), the body with the mandate to review and clear candidates for elective office. Stopping them from contesting, Presiding Judge Msagha Mbogholi ruled, would deny them their democratic rights enshrined in the constitution.

Moreover, the High Court said it did not have the "jurisdiction to deal with a question relating to the election of a president." That jurisdiction was with the Supreme Court. Moreover, Mbogholi said, the responsibility of electing leaders was in the hands of the people. "Limiting the people's rights would be inimical to the exercise of democratic right and freedom of its members." Thus, the matter ended there. Uhuru and Ruto were free to contest.

On February 11, 2013, all the eight presidential candidates met during a live television debate. Martha Karua, an active and aggressive former justice minister, was the only female candidate.

However, the focus was on the two long-time political enemies, Uhuru and Raila. The three-hour question-and-answer marathon session took place at Brookhouse School in Nairobi before a studio audience of 200 people. An estimated 15 million others watched the illuminating discussion on their television sets. The candidates fielded questions on corruption, land reforms, income disparities, tribalism, and governance.

Asked about his ability to rule post-ICC, Uhuru said his first task after winning would be to clear his name and ensure "the business of government continues and our manifesto and agenda for Kenya is implemented." Raila offered a refreshingly sarcastic rebuttal: "... running a government on Skype from the Hague would be tough to manage." He got an applause. "The job I seek," said Uhuru, "is going to be given by the people of Kenya... who full well know the personal issues I am confronted with."

It was during that debate that Uhuru, on prodding from Karua, admitted to owning 30,000 acres of land in Taita Taveta which he said was obtained legally. "I am keen for my honourable sister [Karua] to take me to this land I am alleged to own [illegally] so that I can start doing something about it," Uhuru said.

That first debate was followed by a second one. However, political pundits didn't think the debates changed any one's mind. Most Kenyans had already made up their minds on who to vote for. The Kikuyu were still going to vote for Uhuru and the Luo were still stuck with Raila.

New dispensation

The Kenya National Accord and Reconciliation Act which brokered the 2008 agreement between President Kibaki and ODM leader Raila Odinga led to the formation of the Independent Review Commission (IRC) which in turn, established the Interim Independent Electoral Commission (IIEC) in 2009. When a new constitution was passed in a referendum on August 4, 2010, a new body, the Independent Electoral and Boundaries Commission (IEBC) was established.

Apart from electing the traditional three representatives: a president, an MP, and a ward councillor (now MCA), voters in the 2013 elections had to, in addition, elect three more candidates: a governor, a senator, and a women's representative, totalling to six elected representatives.

Uhuru's Jubilee coalition invested heavily in media and publicity. The Star newspaper estimated that Uhuru had a budget of KSh.10 billion for his campaign.[82] Apart from hiring a slew of local and international strategists to promote its agenda, the coalition relied on the social media for most of its messaging, and adopted slogans such as *"Dunda na Uhuru"* (Dance with Uhuru), which were specially directed at young people.[83] Jubilee also targeted its marketing to specific groups such as pastoralists, small retail traders, and women.

---

[82] Mathenge, Oliver. "Kenya: Uhuru to spend Sh10 billion in campaign," *The Star*, January 7, 2013.

[83] Momanyi, Bernard. "Kenyatta's winning game," Refworld, March 30, 2013.

In addition, Jubilee flooded social media with Uhuru quotes and hired journalists and bloggers to spread party propaganda. Uhuru's campaign was rated as the most expensive in Kenyan history, although no figures were released to back that assertion. It was a "carefully crafted, strategically well-executed, and well-funded campaign."

Conversely, Raila's campaign was devoid of vigour and creativity. Its nomination process was disorderly, and Raila's manipulation of the process (including promotion of his siblings), angered CORD members and supporters alike."[84] Many votes were lost through those underhand shenanigans by party leaders.

THE WAY FORWARD AND THE BIG WIN

The 72-page Jubilee Coalition manifesto, *Transforming Kenya: Securing Kenya's Prosperity, 2013-2017*, set out three key pillars: unity, economy, and openness. Corruption, and how the new government planned to clean up the mess of graft featured in the last pillar. Through the manifesto, Jubilee pledged to introduce some of the "toughest anti-corruption legislation in the world."

"Corruption has been tolerated in Kenya for too long." "It is time to get tough on those who seek to use their positions of power for their own personal gain," the manifesto read.

On the other hand, CORD unveiled a 10-point agenda which included measures to enhance land reforms, provide universal healthcare, ensure food security, fight poverty, and create employment, among others. "This country will not be changed by hypocrites," Raila said proudly, "but by democrats." He said if elected, his government would take back all "stolen land." That was a clear reference to land allegedly acquired illegally by his principal opponents.

---

[84] *Kenya After Elections, International Crisis Group: Working to Prevent Conflict Worldwide*, Africa Briefing No. 94, May 15, 2013, p. 8.

There were fears that the elections could be marred by the same kind of irregularities in data transmission witnessed in 2007, thus triggering violence. There was also a general concern about the outcome of the ICC cases against both Uhuru and Ruto which had heightened ethnic divisions.

In 2012 and early 2013, inter-communal clashes left more than 477 people dead and nearly 118,000 displaced, according to the Human Rights Watch.[85] On the eve of the March 4 elections, President Kibaki made a last appeal for a peaceful election: "Let us send a clear message to the world, that our democracy has come of age," he said in a televised broadcast.

However, unlike the aftermath of the 2007 polls, the 2013 elections were relatively peaceful, thanks to institutional reforms and legal frameworks put in place by the 2010 constitution. Among them was an independent judiciary with a leadership determined to defend the constitution and live up to the expectations of the public.[86]

Eighty five percent of voters turned up at the polls. Like many previous contests, however, the 2013 polls were not without disputes. There were electoral malpractices that defied description, including vote rigging, bribery, and manipulation of the voter register. Even the electronic system which was relied upon to convey results from the regional tallying centres to the IEBC's national tallying centre collapsed. Officials were forced to resort to manual counting. That resulted in long lines at polling stations. In some polling stations, lines stretched to over one kilometre.

In short, mischief surrounded the elections almost everywhere in the country. Worse still was the heart-wrenching delay in announcing the winner. Rumours and conspiracy theories swirled, pointing to possible rigging of the elections by Jubilee coalition. The whole exercise was stigmatised as unfair and unfree. Thus, ODM's overpowering complaints of a nefarious scheme by the Jubilee coalition to deny Raila victory were not wholly insignificant. They

---

[85] "High Stakes: Political Violence and the 2013 Elections in Kenya," Human Rights Watch, February 7, 2013.
[86] "How Kenya delivered its peaceful general elections," ISS Today, March 20, 2013.

were valid. Tension was high. Security personnel were on standby everywhere to deal with any possible violence. Remembering what happened in 2007, many businesses closed shop.

On March 9, 2013, five days after the polling, IEBC finally declared the results. Uhuru, "a millionaire playboy,"[87] had won the elections with a clear margin of 50.07% to Raila's 43.3%. With that, Uhuru and Ruto earned "the dubious distinction of being the first ICC inductees in the world to jointly contest the presidency and win."[88]

A survey by Ipsos-Synovate immediately after the polls showed that Uhuru got votes from all over the country. He won more votes in some of Raila's strongholds such as Western Kenya and the Coast region. But Raila did not fare on well in Uhuru's Mt. Kenya region.

As Uhuru and Ruto savoured the moment of victory, CORD supporters took to the streets in Nairobi, Western Kenya, and Nyanza, to protest the results. Demonstrators engaged the police in running battles provoking officers to open fire. Numerous people were killed.

On March 16, Raila filed a suit in the Supreme Court challenging the results. He alleged manipulation of votes, claiming that the election result transmission system had been hacked, and that the presidential election was a sham. "He is not conceding," his senior advisor Salim Lone cried out, "because this election was flawed."

But on March 30, 2013 – two weeks after the petition was filed – the country's highest court made its much-awaited ruling. It unanimously rejected the petition and upheld Uhuru's win. Chief Justice Willy Mutunga who announced the court's unanimous decision ruled that the election had been free and fair. Raila conceded. "The court has now spoken," Raila said dejectedly with finality.

Uhuru was sworn into office without any incident on April 9, 2013. After getting an all-clear signal from the Supreme Court

---

[87] McConnell, Tristan. "Uhuru Kenyatta: from millionaire playboy to Kenyan president," AFP, August 4, 2017.
[88] Shilaho, Westen Kwatemba. Old Wines in New Skins: Kenya's 2013 Elections and the Triumph of the Ancien Regime, *Journal of African Elections*, Vol. 17, No. 2, 2013, pp. 103-104.

that Uhuru and Ruto were legitimately elected, thousands of people gathered at the Moi International Sports Complex, Kasarani to usher in the fourth president of the Republic of Kenya. Helped by his wife, Margaret, Uhuru held the Bible his father used when he was sworn-in as prime minister in 1963, and pledged to "diligently discharge my duties and functions of the Office of President..." Then with dignity and pomp, he received the symbolic sword of power from the outgoing President Kibaki.

Grim-looking foreign diplomats who had opposed the duo's candidature and election on account of the ICC indictment, sat embarrassingly at the podium next to exuberant African heads of state and other top officials representing presidents and prime ministers. Some of the envoys had thought Uhuru had not "a dog's chance" to win.[89]

Ugandan President Yoweri Museveni stirred the pot of disdain amongst foreign powers. Amid cheers from the large crowd, Museveni blasted western nations, calling them "opinionated and arrogant."

"They are now using it [ICC] to install leaders of their choice in Africa and to eliminate the ones they do not like...they have distorted the purpose of that institution.... Africans should reject the ICC 'blackmail.'" Museveni opined.

That sounded like music to the ears of Uhuru and Ruto. They felt vehemently exonerated. Uhuru's acceptance speech was welcomed with ululations. If Uhuru was angry about the position western nations had taken against him, he did not visibly show it. In his elaborate speech, Uhuru was firm and resolute, pledging to "uphold our international obligations, so long as these are founded on the well-established principles of mutual respect and reciprocity."

In his inaugural speech, Uhuru promised to build more schools, ensure food security, uphold peace and unity, establish a youth and women fund, support devolution, provide employment to the jobless youth, apply transparency in procurement of government stores, expand electricity generation, improve infrastructure, exploit natural resources to benefit all, enhance regional cooperation, diversify the

---

[89] "The return of President Kenyatta," *New African*, April 4, 2013.

economy, provide affordable medical care, abolish maternity fees, and provide free laptops to all primary school children. "We made a promise to our children, and we will keep it…," he said, enjoying the thrill of leadership.

Uhuru did not mention corruption, not even once, in his written speech despite the pledges made in the Jubilee coalition manifesto. Nevertheless, hope was in the air, so it seemed. What Kenyans wanted was a distinct paradigm shift. They wanted Uhuru to formulate a clear and comprehensive strategy to deal with cartels, 'tenderpreneurs,' and criminals, in the public and private sectors who were milking the country dry. They wanted him to continue to strengthen the economy with the same tempo and profound conviction as President Kibaki did during his ten-year period at the helm.

President Kibaki had set much higher standards of economic development than his predecessor. Kenyans wanted Uhuru to build on them. When Kibaki left, the economic growth stood at an impressive 7.1% compared to almost zero point in 2002 when he took over from President Moi. Although the wage bill of KSh.458 billion was dragging economic growth, the revenue collection performance at 24.3% of the GDP was strong. Income taxes were contributing 35% of the total revenue. That was not good enough, but there was a determination to improve collections. Overall growth was also affected following the 2008 post-election violence.

The Jubilee administration had its work cut out, but wananchi's expectations were exceedingly high. Kenyans wanted jobs, affordable healthcare, cheap quality housing, and a good education system. They were tired of empty premises.

Here was a duo that was young, educated, energised, and ready to go. Both had served as ministers in the previous governments of Presidents Moi and Kibaki. They were familiar with how the government operated. Both were political students of Moi, the self-styled "professor of politics." Both had strong grassroots support in their home base, the former in the Mt. Kenya region and the latter in the Rift Valley region. They were men of faith and had stable families. All vitals were in their favour.

PART III
MR PRESIDENT

CHAPTER 6

Uhuru's Reign: A New President

Kenyans did not know what to expect from President Uhuru and Deputy President Ruto. A lot of work awaited them. There was a cabinet to be formed, and promises to be fulfilled, many promises indeed, made over a period of more than two years of campaigning.

The first sign of trouble related to the inordinate delay in naming a cabinet. That was partially blamed on internal power struggles and the delay in vetting of candidates by the National Intelligence Service (NIS). As per the Constitution of Kenya, 2010, the new administration had a cap of 22 cabinet positions as opposed to the 44 portfolios of the previous government.

The long wait was worrying. Rumours circulating in the social media suggested a tussle between the two principals over who should be allocated what position in the new government. Ruto insisted on a 50/50 division of cabinet positions, some reports said, something Uhuru refused to accept. Ruto also opposed the inclusion of politicians in the government, demanding that only technocrats capable of "steering the development agenda" should be appointed. Uhuru disagreed.

Uhuru wanted in the Cabinet two of his political allies, Najib Balala and Charity Ngilu. Ruto suggested they should be given other positions outside the cabinet.[90] Eventually, Uhuru got his way. He however gave one condition to the prospective nominees: that they had to resign from all political positions and cease to engage in politics.

More drama followed. Twice the media were called to State House and both times the cabinet announcement was cancelled. Uhuru begged for more time to announce his line-up saying the duo wanted to appoint people with "the ability to deliver."

Finally, when the two appeared on the steps of State House on April 24, 2013, Uhuru announced names of only four cabinet secretaries (CSs): information communication technology, health, foreign affairs, and finance. Two days later, twelve more cabinet secretaries were named. Two more followed. Out of the lean cabinet of eighteen cabinet secretaries, six were women.

Uhuru tapped the private sector to boost delivery of service: former longserving CEO of Barclays Bank, Adan Mohamed was put in charge of industrialisation and enterprise development; Phyllis Kandie, formerly of the Standard Investment Bank, was given the ministry of East African affairs and labour; and Anne Waiguru who previously worked with Citigroup was tasked with devolution and planning.

For the key portfolios of finance and foreign affairs, Uhuru chose a fellow economist and former colleague at the Treasury, Henry Rotich, and a woman career diplomat, Amina Mohamed, respectively. "We are giving Kenyans the best brains that will enable us deliver our Jubilee manifesto and uplift the wellbeing of the nation," Uhuru boasted.

As expected, Uhuru's Kikuyu ethnic group and Ruto's Kalenjin community got the lion's share of the seats.

Standing on the steps of State House with matching ties and shirts rolled up to the elbow with no jackets, the self-styled "digital" team portrayed a picture of a middle-class working duo. Their perceived simplicity, however, contrasted sharply with their financial status. Uhuru and Ruto were among the richest individuals in Kenya.

---

[90] "Why Cabinet line-up was delayed," *Nation*, April 25, 2013.

Never had anyone entered State House with a billionaire's tag on his lapel like the Uhuru/Ruto duo.

Uhuru and Ruto faced the media on a pleasant sunny day, joking and laughing for the cameras. The thrill of leadership of the highest office in the land was painted all over their faces.

Settling down in State House, a building he knew well, Uhuru held his first cabinet meeting on June 6. The meeting was spiked with warnings, advice, and hard talk, for the new government officials: "You must take charge of your ministries, work as a team and get down to the business of serving the Kenyan people…As cabinet secretaries, you must be accessible to the public…You are responsible for your dockets, and staff who work in your ministries must deliver services to the people…We must deal with the agents of corruption and those who seek to enrich themselves at the expense of the country."[91]

After Uhuru's victory, the USA was "faced with an exquisite dilemma: how to deal with a popular figure accused of whipping up ethnic violence that rocked Kenya in 2007 and 2008."[92] On a trip to Africa in July 2009, US President Barack Obama had skipped the country – the land of his father, to avoid contacts with a man accused of crimes against humanity. That snub infuriated Kenyans. In a letter published in the *Daily Nation*, one Antoney Luvinzu, said Obama's slight "verges on snobbishness, not after the overwhelming goodwill he received from Kenyans of all walks of life in his emphatic quest for [US] presidency in 2008."

The American's late father, Barack Obama Snr., was a Kenyan and Obama had in August 2006 visited the country (as a senator) and had been warmly welcomed. In 2015, as president of the US, he again visited Kenya and held bilateral talks with Uhuru. That visit would be remembered for his critical remarks about corruption and gay rights which were not well received by government officials. In July 2018 after he had left office, Obama again visited his father's

---

[91] Kenya: Uhuru lays out agenda at first cabinet meet," Capital FM, June 6, 2013.
[92] Ritter, John. "America's 25 most awkward allies: How Obama has curried favour with a rogue gallery of tyrants and autocrats," *Politico Magazine*, March/April 2014.

village in Siaya, Kisumu. During that visit he praised both Uhuru and Raila for their 'handshake' and resolve to work together to avert future post-election crises.

The British High Commissioner, Christian Turner, had indicated earlier that the UK would keep its official contacts with Kenya to a minimum in view of the ICC trial of Kenyan leaders. Uhuru, who had hired a British PR firm, BTP Advisers, to offer strategic advice on his election campaign, blasted Turner, accusing him of "shadowy, suspicious, and rather animated involvement" in the 2013 presidential elections.

London however, viewed Uhuru's response to Turner's statement as being unusually harsh against an envoy of a former colonial power. London was also angered that a British PR company could have had a hand in drafting Uhuru's remarks. In Kenya, BTP's motto, "We deliver campaigns that change hearts and minds," worked.

Britain changed its course after Uhuru's win. In May 2013, it invited the Kenyan leader to London, and Uhuru, insatiably anxious of recognition, accepted. In Britain, Uhuru met Prime Minister David Cameron and participated in discussions on the volatile political situation in Somalia where terrorists were having a field day.

The US too made an about-turn and declared it would respect the will of the people.[93] "We... will continue to be a strong friend and ally of the Kenyan people," US Secretary of State John Kerry announced.

The hard work and ICC

The first two years of President Uhuru's regime brought unexpected challenges for the Jubilee government. Five months into the new government, disillusioned youths demonstrated in the streets to protest lack of jobs. The protests were organised by a little-known group calling itself March 4th Movement (M4M). The message to Uhuru was that Kenyans expected concrete results from

---

[93] Lough, Richard. "Analysis: Kenyatta's bid for Kenya presidency a diplomatic headache," *Reuters*, February 14, 2013.

his government, not empty rhetoric. The movement complained of lack of jobs and exorbitant food prices of basic food items such as maize and milk.

Media reports suggested that the M4M was using inflation as an excuse to incite the public into overthrowing the government the way demonstrators had forced President Mohamed Morsi of Egypt to lose trust and fall in an army coup on July 3, 2013. Reports said the organisation planned to collect 5.4 million signatures to force an amendment to the constitution to prevent Uhuru from serving a second term. The M4M-declared leader, Okiya Omtatah, was arrested and taken for interrogation. He was released without any charge being preferred against him. M4M was never heard of again.

Another crisis for the Jubilee coalition government was in the education and health sectors. Schools were temporarily shut down as teachers took to the streets, blaming the government for allocating KSh.15.37 billion to the school laptop project while denying them allowances and salary increases. About 280,000 members of the Kenya National Union of Teachers (KNUT) abandoned work in June 2013. The strike collapsed only after the government threatened to withhold their salaries.

Also, thousands of nurses who went on strike around the same time to demand better working conditions were sacked.

In the 2013 elections, internally displaced persons (IDPs) had voted overwhelmingly for Jubilee believing the new government would resettle them in safe places. That did not happen. Hundreds of IDP families, displaced during the 2007/2008 PEV mayhem and those evicted from Mau Forest in 2009, to pave way for the rehabilitation of the water catchment area, were still living in camps or as squatters under harsh conditions. For them, the alluring promise of prosperity under Jubilee did not materialise.

Similarly, little, or no significant steps were taken to fight corruption during those first two years of Uhuru's administration.

For every failure, there were a few but scattered cases of success for the Uhuru administration. One of the cases occurred in June 2013. In his inaugural speech, the president had announced free maternal care, which meant women were no longer to pay for maternal deliveries and other ante-natal services in public medical facilities.

Because of prohibitive costs of deliveries, many women, especially in rural areas, had resorted to giving birth at home largely under unhygienic conditions. The Kenya Demographic Health Survey reported that although 90% of the women received ante-natal care from clinics, only 43% of births took place in health facilities. The child mortality rate in home deliveries was high. Free maternal services were therefore aimed at reducing deaths.

However, a few months after the introduction of maternal care, things not anticipated happened. Pregnant women overwhelmed health facilities resulting in inefficiencies and neglect. Overstretched health workers could not cope with the sudden high increase of maternity cases. It got to a point where some women were delivering along corridors in health facilities because of lack of either nurses or beds. In one case in Nyeri, a woman went into labour, and because she was not attended to on time, her baby boy dropped to the floor at a health facility and died.

In the meantime, many of the Jubilee supporters were in a state of plausible deniability over the ICC accusations bedevilling Uhuru and his deputy. They felt the case had been politically motivated and meant to stop their leader from becoming president.

To fuel further confusion on the ICC matter, the Kenya envoy to the UN blasted the ICC saying the prosecution was "neither impartial nor independent." In a letter to the UN Security Council (UNSC), in early May 2013, the Kenyan ambassador, Macharia Kamau, said the trial threatened to destabilise the nation.

In an approach characterised by overreach and hubris, the envoy asked the UN Security Council to ensure "the immediate termination of the case."

"We are of the opinion that the UNSC must play its role and bring this matter to a halt, if the purpose for which the Rome Statute was negotiated, is to be achieved," Kamau wrote. No one knows who sanctioned the brief because Deputy President Ruto denounced it as not reflecting government policy.⁹⁴ Kamau's rather bizarre request was also condemned at the UN as unfounded and incorrect.

"It is a backdoor attempt to politicise the judicial processes of the [ICC] Court," Prosecutor Fatou Bensouda told the UNSC.

In June 2013, the ICC announced November 12 as the date for the status conference. That was to give more time for the defence lawyers to prepare their briefs.

At that point, the country was still deeply polarised on ethnic and political lines over the election outcome. ODM supporters were in a state of denial, refusing to accept the election results. The Jubilee coalition, on the other hand, was venting its frustrations on the ICC and demanding Kenya's complete withdrawal from the organisation. On September 5, 2013, Kenya MPs voted to suspend all links, cooperation, and assistance to the court. "Let us protect our citizens. Let us defend the sovereignty of the nation of Kenya," said Majority Leader Adan Duale.

Others advised President Uhuru to simply ignore the ICC summons and stay home. Uhuru made it clear that he preferred to remain in the country to deal with the terror group Al-Shabaab. The Westgate Mall in Nairobi had just been hit by Al-Shabaab militants. Thus, Kenya found itself in an exasperating circle of threats from Al-Shabaab. Some Jubilee acolytes warned Uhuru that absenting himself from the trial would violate the UN Rome Statute to which Kenya was a signatory. Others, mostly his critics in the opposition, rooted for his prosecution and conviction.

A top ODM official, Peter Anyang' Nyong'o, said Uhuru and the others had to face justice. Any failure to bring to justice perpetrators of the 2007/2008 post-election violence (PEV), he said, posed a grave danger to Kenya's internal peace and security. Uhuru's request to have the deliberations conducted via video link was rejected, and his request at the ICC to have the case terminated failed. The ICC also ruled against requests to have the case heard in East Africa as proposed by some of Uhuru's advisers.

---

⁹⁴ "Ruto denies bid to halt ICC trial," *Sunday Nation*, May 9, 2013.

The case was a complete distraction. "Nothing has been happening in government except the effort to derail the ICC,"[95] said James Gondi, a human rights activist.

Left with no option, Uhuru had to travel. On October 6, 2014, a constrained President Uhuru turned over executive powers to Deputy President Ruto whose own hearings at The Hague had not yet started. The brief handing-over ceremony was held at the Office of the President in downtown Nairobi.

A forlorn-looking Uhuru said he was handing over power because he did not want to put the sovereignty of more than 40 million Kenyans on trial. "Therefore, let it not be said that I am attending the status conference as the president of Kenya. Nothing in my position or my deeds as president warrants my being in court," he added.

That said, President Uhuru left in a small motorcade of cars without his aide-de-camp (ADC), signifying his new temporary status as a civilian. George Kegoro, the Executive Director of the Kenya chapter of the International Commission of Jurists (ICJ) praised Uhuru for that action. Gitobu Imanyara, a politician and lawyer, added: "If he had refused [to go to The Hague] it would have destroyed our economy. The economy would not have recovered during his tenure," he said.

Apart from its historical significance, the temporary vacation of the presidency underlined the unusually fluid state of political uncertainty at the time. No one had the prophetic vision to predict his fate at the ICC. Foreign nations which had opposed his candidacy because of the ICC trial were in a limbo. There was a modicum of truth in reports circulating in social media that some foreign nations, including the US, were edging for an election loss for Uhuru. The US Assistant Secretary of State for African Affairs Johnnie Carson had let out a cryptic message to Kenyan voters, days before the polls, saying "choices have consequences" hinting that electing ICC inductees could trigger adverse reaction from donor nations. But that was vain whining.

---

[95] McConnell, Tristan. "How Kenya took on the International Criminal Court," *The World*, March 25, 2014.

On October 7, Uhuru showed up at the VIP lounge at the Jomo Kenyatta International Airport (JKIA) – named after his father – dressed casually in jeans and a polo shirt. He was ready for the overnight journey to Amsterdam. His wife Margaret, and daughter Ngina, were the only family members travelling with him. Too distraught about the whole issue, Mama Ngina, chose to stay put. Three ministers and six MPs also tagged along. It was an irksome, painful, and depressing, experience for the first family.

The following day, the Kenyan leader stood before the ICC at The Hague for a status conference to discuss the merit (or lack thereof) of the charges against him. That appearance earned Uhuru the ignominy and misfortune of being the first sitting head of state to appear before the court since its establishment in 2002. Outside the court, Uhuru supporters demonstrated with placards and dances.

On being questioned by the prosecutor, Luis Ocampo, Uhuru flatly denied any links to the outlawed Mungiki sect which had been blamed for the post-election violence. Uhuru also denied he was aware of any plot to rig the 2007 elections. Instead, he blamed Raila Odinga for being the "leader" of the chaos that followed the polls. He said if Raila had gone to court instead of calling for mass action "violence would not have broken out."

Towards the end of November 2014, it became obvious that the charges could not stand. The evidence available was not enough to convict President Uhuru. The Kenya government refused to cooperate. In addition, several key prosecution witnesses withdrew their testimonies. There was also widespread witness-tampering. Indications were that the case was foredoomed to failure for the simple reason that it was the Kenya government and not the ICC that was controlling the evidence.

And it did! Uhuru's lawyer, Steve Kay, was ecstatic: "The case has failed, and it has failed in a way that means there is no prospect of it going further."[96] A thunderous ripple of applause could be heard from Jubilee coalition supporters all the way in Kenya as they

---

[96] "Kenyan President appeals for case to be dropped," Associated Press, October 8, 2014.

watched the trial on television. Kenya's *Daily Nation* reported that a Kikuyu language presenter at the Kenyatta-owned Kameme FM radio "sporadically broke into prayer while announcing the news."[97] Many of his supporters had all along viewed the case as a monstrous travesty of justice. Yet the victims had looked forward to justice, at last.

Charges dismissed

On December 5, 2014, the ICC prosecutor, Fatou Bensouda, dropped all charges against Uhuru, citing Kenya's refusal to provide vital evidentiary documents required by the court. Uhuru was free. A delirious triumphalism took hold in Jubilee strongholds. For Uhuru, it wasn't time to celebrate given the fact that cases facing his deputy and the others were yet to be resolved. However, Uhuru said he was "excited" and "relieved" by the court's decision.

After the collapse of Uhuru's case, it took two years for Ruto's charges of murder, deportation, and persecution, to be dismissed for lack of evidence. The prosecution complained about: "Serious tainting of the trial process by way of witness interference and political intimidation of witnesses."[98] The court did not acquit him. It left the case open should there be more evidence to prosecute him in future.

Ruto admitted later that the trial had been a "nightmare." Indeed, it had.

The other four defendants, on almost similar charges, Hussein Ali, Francis Muthaura, Henry Kosgey, and Joshua arap Sang, were also set free by the court at different times, for lack of evidence. Most of the witnesses relied on by the prosecution had either died, skipped court, changed, or recanted testimony, or had allegedly been coached to incriminate the suspects. The prosecution also talked of widespread witness intimidation including physical threats and

---

[97] "ICC Prosecutor Fatou Bensouda withdraws case against Uhuru Kenyatta," *Daily Nation*, December 5, 2014.

[98] "ICC: Kenya deputy president's case ends," Human Rights Watch, April 5, 2016.

bribery. In the case against Ruto and arap Sang, for example, 16 out of the 42 prosecution witnesses stopped cooperating with the court and refused to testify because of threats, intimidation, and fear of reprisals.[99]

On April 16, 2016, Uhuru led a huge thanksgiving rally at Nakuru in the Rift Valley accompanied by his deputy and a large contingent of Jubilee leaders. "I have repeatedly declared my innocence to the people of Kenya and the whole world," he thundered. "I repeat this even now." Uhuru added that he would not wish to see another Kenyan going through the same journey "…we went through. If we have an issue, the answer to it lies here."

The positive aspect of the ICC experience was that it helped Kenyan leaders to acknowledge that violence had consequences. That any future acts of incitement or participation in violence would not be tolerated by the ICC. Another lesson learnt was that more work needed to be done to deal with accountability and impunity issues.

The collapse of the case rendered a major blow to the ICC in efforts to prosecute serious human rights abuses. The African Union (AU) accused the ICC of bias against Africans. Until then, all cases brought before the court involved Africans, although human rights violations were prevalent elsewhere in the world.

The failure of the ICC to get conviction against the six Kenyans was also an indictment of the initial shoddy work of Prosecutor Luis Moreno Ocampo. He made the mistake of relying solely on witness testimony and evidence provided by governments than on forensics and other "evidence collected online."[100] At the end, though, it was the victims of the atrocities and their families who lost. Not a single person was held accountable. 'Thus, the court of last resort' failed to render justice to the victims of the 2007/2007 PEV in Kenya. With the ICC matter out of the way, and no further election challenges from the opposition, President Uhuru Muigai Kenyatta, was now free to proceed with the business of governing Kenya.

---

[99] Duerr, Benjamin. "Not guilty, not acquitted: Kenya ruling a major setback for ICC," IPI Global Observatory, April 11, 2016.
[100] Ibid.

CHAPTER 7

Dealing with terrorism

More trouble followed Jubilee in its first two years in office. There was a major terrorist attack at Westgate Shopping Mall in Nairobi on September 21, 2013. It was the biggest test of Uhuru's determination in the fight against terrorism. Only five months earlier at his inauguration, the new leader had committed himself to fighting terrorism and eradicating piracy. He had said the fight remained a central pillar of his government's policy on peace and security. Kenyans were confident the regime was prepared to meet the challenge of any serious terrorist attack. But was it?

The Al-Shabaab terrorists took a whole year to prepare for the attack. A clandestine group of militias posing as genuine businesspeople rented space at the modern mall complex outside the CBD. Gradually and meticulously, they moved weapons and supplies into the building even though there were at least 40 security officers manning the gates of the shopping mall.

The security routine at the mall was the same every day. Guards stopped cars, inspected vehicle interiors, trunks, and underneath, and used electronic wands to detect weapons and bombs.[101] They also frisked pedestrians and checked shoulder bags. How weapons

---

[101] McKenzie, David. "Kenya intelligence warned of Al-Shabaab threat before mall attack," *CNN*, September 30, 2013. Also see, Alexander Guy, "Kenyan mall shooting: 'They threw grenades like maize to chickens," The *Guardian*, September 21, 2013.

managed to pass through the heavily secured gates is hard to know. While running a bogus store at the mall, the terrorists, pretending to be genuine traders, gathered intelligence, acquainted themselves with the venue at large, and trained attackers on how to carry out the assault.

On the day of the attack, up to 1,000 shoppers were inside the building, unaware of what was to happen. On the upper parking deck, a film crew was recording *MasterChef Junior,* an American cooking competition programme. The multi-story Westgate Shopping Mall is in a leafy area of Westlands suburbs, and features expensive foreign brand shops, banks, restaurants and cafes, and an assortment of stores selling everything from children's toys to furniture.

CCTV footage showed the attackers enter the mall at 12.30 pm, armed with pistols and semi-automatic weapons. While two terrorists entered through the main entrance, two made their way up a ramp to the rear parking space. Then the worst happened. They opened fire on everyone on sight, creating a chaotic stampede. Those who could not escape recoiled in terror under counters and tables as the terrorists hunted them down for a kill.

The Westgate Mall attack revealed a massive intelligence failure by the National Intelligence Service (NIS). The agency had failed to track the movement of the attackers who had arrived in the capital from Somalia a few days earlier. It had also failed to pick up intelligence on the store rental by the terrorists, and the infiltration of weapons into the premises. The NIS claimed it did have that information which it passed on to the Inspector General of Police and the Criminal Investigations Department (CID) for follow-up. The Police denied the allegation.

Nevertheless, it was more than just an intelligence failure. There was also poor management of personnel and resources by government agencies. The mismanagement led to infighting between officers of different security agencies. The fissure between them was over who should oversee the operation. The absence of an efficacious organisation of security forces on site led to a badly botched operation.

To make it worse, cabinet secretaries were giving conflicting information about the unfolding events at the mall, signalling the nonchalant way in which the government was handling the operation. The official spokesperson tasked with providing updates on events at the Watergate Mall was not only inept but confused, and often relayed inaccurate information to the media. For example, the official kept referring to the terrorists as numbering between 10 and 15, yet CCTV had confirmed only four militias had entered the mall.

In another instance, Interior Minister Joseph Ole Lenku, declared that the smoke emanating from the building was caused by burning mattresses set on fire by the militants. The next day, he recanted that statement. It turned out that the flames had been ignited by rocket-propelled grenades fired inside the building by Kenyan troops.

At one time during the early hours of the attack, security personnel made the mistake of temporarily withdrawing from the mall. That gave the terrorists time to regroup and rearm. On top of that, the police failed to secure the perimeter area to stop people from leaving the compound, raising fears that some terrorists may have slipped out.

Moreover, when a contingent of the crack Flying Squad police unit arrived at the mall, it refused to move into the complex for lack of proper instructions. The prevailing hysterical confusion led police and army personnel to fire at each other, leaving one police officer dead. What emerged at the mall was a dispiriting picture of ineptitude on the part of security forces. If armed volunteers had not showed up to support the few police officers on site during the early stages of the attack, the number of fatalities would have been much higher than the 60 people killed.

In the rescue operation, a brave young man, Abdul Haji, who risked his own life to save some of those trapped in the building, became an international hero. One hundred and seventy people were injured. The commotion in the building was televised live by major international broadcasters, thus unmasking the government's apparent inability to deal with active terrorism.

A few months after the Westgate attack, Kenyans came to know of a bitter disagreement between the NIS, the Police, and the Kenya

Defence Forces (KDF), "over a security tender" that "could not be publicly revealed." So, it appears, greed and materialism took centre stage at a crucial time in the operation, when patriotism and gallantry, were of essence. After the deadly incident at Westgate, the NIS Director, Major General Michael Gichangi, resigned "on personal grounds" amid intense criticism of his department's response to the attack.

The Al-Shabaab assault was a well organised and executed operation. It was the first known incident where a terrorist organisation used Twitter as a tool in a deadly operation. The terrorists were not only communicating freely on Twitter but were also micro-blogging the attack as it unfolded. The popular platform may also have been used to monitor the placement of police and military personnel during the attack.[102] A recent report showed a growing reliance on social media by the terrorist group. Based on research carried out between 2020 and 2022, the London-based Institute for Strategic Dialogue (ISD), said Al-Shabaab had increased its use of alternative media especially Facebook to spread propaganda and recruit new members.

It took four days for security forces to search and wipe out the four Al-Shabaab attackers holed up in the premises. All the while, fear of other attacks loomed large in the country.

But there was an even darker side to the whole saga. According to a Council of Foreign Relations report dated October 9, 2020, the forensic investigation by Kenyan authorities was so sloppily done that it was impossible to determine how many terrorists took part in the attack. The bodies of the four terrorists accounted for were found in the mall while two militants were arrested and charged in a court of law for assisting the attackers. They were jailed for a total of 51 years.

A third suspect was not caught.

---

[102] Mair, David. Westgate: A Case Study: How Al-Shabaab Used Twitter During an Ongoing Attack, Conflict Terrorism, *Studies in Conflict and Terrorism*, Routledge, Vol. 40, No. 1, pp. 24-43.

Bloggers may also have contributed to the confusion surrounding the attack. Onlookers milling near the mall and elsewhere were taking photographs and posting tweets critical of the government's response to the attack. Some were even circulating information the government thought was sensitive and a security risk.

At one time, the Kenya Police asked a Twitter user to delete a post containing pictures of security helicopters "preparing to launch an attack on the mall." In another case, the Kenya Disaster Operation Centre (KDOC) asked a news channel not to air a story. "Please take that story down. It is misleading and bound to confuse." The KDOC asked media houses to exercise caution in airing or publishing stories on the operations at Westgate which were still sensitive.[103] There were an estimated 67,849 tweets exchanged during the four-day siege, according to one organisation.[104]

The military was also not happy with bloggers and journalists who tweeted and re-tweeted videos showing soldiers looting shops at the mall. The bloggers used the hash tags, #Westgate, WestgateMallAttack, #WestGateShoutout, among others, to spread their information. The army admitted the misbehaviour of its soldiers but threatened journalists with unspecified action if they continued to circulate videos of soldiers emerging with bags full of stolen goods. As commander-in-chief, Uhuru said nothing about the unbecoming behaviour of his troops.

On the third day out of the four-day siege at Westgate Mall, the police published a direct threat of prosecution to those sharing what it called "repugnant" information, saying they would be found and charged.[105] That was the harshest threat to the media by authorities during the attack. It underscored the authorities' frustration and anger over the twitter tirade. It is believed that the proliferation of Watergate hash tags pushed the government into enacting a cybercrime law a few months after that.

---

[103] Goldbert, T. Simon, Daniel L, Aharonson, D. Leykin, & B. Adini, *Twitter in the Cross Fire: The Use of social media in the Westgate Mall Terror Attack in Kenya*, Plos ONE, Vol. 9, No. 8, 2014.
[104] Ibid.
[105] Ibid.

When the siege was finally over, President Uhuru issued a statement that was more bluster than truth. "We confronted this evil without flinching, contained our deep grief and pain, and conquered it." Really?

The pain of the Westgate attack survivors, just like the pain of all the other terrorist victims, were never confronted, and the grief that affected families and relatives of the victims was never conquered. That speech exemplified how presidential speech writers got carried away with fancy words and descriptions and not fact. The government had made so many security blunders before that such hyperbolic statements made little sense to Kenyans; leave alone to victims and survivors of violence. The only relief was felt by the owners of Westgate, tenants, and individuals, who suffered material loss while in the building during the attack. An insurance company paid them KSh.5 billion in compensation.

The intensity of the Westgate attack evoked memories of the 1998 Al-Qaeda and the Egyptian Islamic Jihad terrorists' simultaneous attacks on the US embassies in Kenya and Tanzania that left hundreds of people dead.

Garissa attack

It seemed Kenya was a slow learner when it came to combating terrorism. Two years after the Westgate onslaught as a sense of pervasive insecurity rushed through the country, Garissa University in the north-eastern part of the country was attacked. With little security at the facility near the Somalia border, Al Shabaab terrorists sneaked into the campus one morning in April 2015 and fired indiscriminately at anyone on sight. One would have thought the government had learnt one or two lessons from the Westgate attack.

Once again, warnings by intelligence officials of an imminent invasion were ignored by the relevant agencies. Interior Minister Joseph Nkaiserry admitted that the government response was "poorly coordinated." Seven top policemen were suspended because of the blunders by law enforcement personnel. One-hundred-forty-seven people were killed, and seventy-nine others injured in that calamitous attack. Five hundred horror-stricken students escaped. It was the most serious terrorist invasion with the highest number of fatalities since the US Embassy bombing in Nairobi.

The fact that there were only two police officers guarding the Garissa University compound at a time when Al-Shabaab had accelerated their attacks on soft targets showed Kenya's lack of seriousness in deterring thugs from across the Somalia border. As Al-Shabaab brazen attacks increased, so did criticisms from Kenyans who felt that more needed to be done to quash terrorist incursions. "The people were trapped here for 13 hours," a member of the local community said, "Where was the government?"

Part of Al-Shabaab's existential attacks within Kenya lies in the systemic corruption at the border check points. Security personnel are bribed to allow small arms and light weapons to pass through from Somalia unperturbed. For example, the government could not explain how a large terrorist group with explosive devices managed to cross into Lamu County in September 2021 without detection. Luckily, the devices exploded and killed, not the local civilians, but all the 15 Al-Shabaab terrorists on board the vehicle. But the group had already planted some devices in disparate places in the county, their target being army and police personnel. The number of soldiers and police officers injured or killed by the Al-Shabaab in all the harrowing attacks is not publicly known, but it's believed to be in hundreds.

On July 6, 2014, terrorists attacked Gamba near Lamu, and left twenty-nine people dead. A week later, they raided Mpeketoni, also near Lamu. In that attack, they went door to door asking residents to declare their religious inclination. Sixty non-Muslims were killed. Instead of blaming the militant group, Uhuru pointed a finger at "local political networks," an unmistakable reference to Raila and his Cord coalition.[106] He blamed local leaders intent on dividing the country for the "well-planned, orchestrated, and politically motivated

---

[106] Hidalgo, Paul. Kenya Divided, Foreign Affairs, July 9, 2014.

violence. "This was not an Al-Shabaab terrorist attack," he said in a televised address.

The Kenya-Somalia border check points are also known for human trafficking and drug, charcoal, and sugar, smuggling. This stinging reproach has been documented by several NGOs including the Human Rights Watch (HRW). Fuelling the problem of terrorism further is the unrelenting radicalisation of young Kenyans into jihad, and the presence of large unverified Somalia nationals at refugee camps on the Kenyan side of the border. Militants posing as refugees have been nabbed within those camps.

In January 2019, another assault occurred at the upmarket Hotel DusitD2 in Nairobi, not too far from the Watergate Mall. Fifteen people were killed and more than 30 injured during that brazen attack as terrorists threw bombs at vehicles parked outside the hotel. One suicide bomber entered the lobby and blew himself up. At least four gunmen were involved in the raid which threw the city into another state of panic.

The frequency of Al-Shabaab attacks on Kenya has placed the country on a constant state of alert. Foreign missions in Kenya often post travel advisories warning their nationals about their safety in the country.

The terrorists' biggest demand has been for Kenya to withdraw its troops from Somalia. President Uhuru flatly rejected that demand. He repeatedly said that Kenyan troops would remain in Somalia until stability and peace were restored. "As I have stated before, our troops will continue being part of the African Union (AU) Mission in Somalia, AMISON, until such time that our objective has been achieved," Uhuru reiterated on December 3, 2019. And for being part of the AU-sponsored peace keeping troops there, Kenya has made unfathomable sacrifices.

Kenya entered southern Somalia in October 2011 to stop kidnappings and random attacks by Al-Shabaab in Kenya. Kenyan troops were later incorporated into AMISON. Immediately thereafter, sporadic incursion began. During a period of five weeks in September and October of that year, for example, Al-Shabaab carried out numerous terror attacks. They killed a British tourist and captured his wife. They abducted a French woman who later died in their captivity and captured two Spanish aid workers from the Dadaab refugee camp.

In April 2019, two Cuban doctors, Landy Rodriquez Hernandez, and Assel Correa, loaned to Kenya by the Cuban government, were kidnapped in Mandera, Kenya, by Al-Shabaab militants. They were held captive at an unknown location in Somalia for a year and half before their release in October 2020. The terrorists also made numerous attacks on facilities and vehicles.

The Al-Shabaab's main target is Kenya, but the terrorists also have their eyes trained on the US which it considers an enemy of Islam because of its ties with Israel. The presence of US troops on Kenyan soil is not a secret. On January 5, 2020, between 30 and 40 Somalia armed militias raided an American military base at Manda Bay, on the Kenyan coast, destroying a truck and six American surveillance planes. There was an hour-long gunfight. Part of the airfield was destroyed, and three Americans killed. The daring attack disconcerted and dismayed the US which rushed in 100 more troops to secure its base. In June 2021, President Biden wrote to US Congress to inform them of his intention to send special operations troops to Kenya to combat Al-Shabaab. He did not indicate the number of soldiers to be deployed.

Al-Shabaab, a branch of the bigger, more dangerous Al-Qaeda, continued menacing Kenya throughout Uhuru's term. Although analysts thought the group had been weakened because of increased crackdowns by both Kenya and the US soldiers, threats of attacks continued. Some of Al-Shabaab's commanders were killed during attacks by AMISON and US forces, or were murdered in internal feuds, giving the lie to the notion that the group had been weakened. Among the top Al-Shabaab fighters killed were Bashir Mohamed Mahamoud, aka Bashir Qoorgaab, and Yusuf Jiis, both high-ranking commanders, said to be responsible for a series of attacks throughout East Africa. They were killed in separate US air strikes inside Somalia in April 2020.

Though reputed for its enviable discipline, the Kenya military has also suffered a beating for its covert activities inside Somalia. Reports have circulated since 2011 linking KDF soldiers to illegal charcoal and sugar smuggling through the Somalia port of Kismayu. The Kenya government has dismissed the allegations as "absolute garbage."[107]

Kenya has also paid a hefty price for its presence in Somalia. Take, for example, the battle of El Adde. It took place on the morning of January 15, 2016. Al-Shabaab fighters overran an AMISON base manned by KDF soldiers, leaving behind heavy casualties. As is the practice, Kenya does not disclose soldiers killed in attacks, but Al-Shabaab claimed it killed 100 KDF soldiers and took away several others as hostages, as well as military vehicles, and weapons. Other sources suggested that more than 170 Kenyan soldiers were lost.[108] That was one of the worst military defeats KDF had suffered in Somalia. To the embarrassment of Nairobi authorities, the militants posted pictures of the fallen soldiers in the social media, together with their ID cards. They also dragged dead bodies of Kenyan soldiers along the streets of Mogadishu.

As if that was not enough, Al-Shabaab militants also produced a propaganda video showing the damage inflicted on the Kenyan troops in a blustering desire for maximum publicity. It also showed interviews with captured Kenyan soldiers. "The El Adde battle might therefore represent Al-Shabaab's deadliest attack on Kenyans, even surpassing the earlier massacre at Garissa University," said the International Peace Institute (IPI).

Kenyans got a glimpse of what transpired at El Adde when soon thereafter, wounded KDF soldiers began arriving in Nairobi. Two private jets transported the casualties back to Kenya on January 17, 2016. The government paraded some of the injured soldiers before cameras. The only details from the government on what happened on that day came from the chief of general staff, General Samson Mwathethe. He said the attackers used improvised explosive devices (IEDs) to breach the base defences. General Mwathethe refused to

---

[107] Blair, Edmund. "Kenyan forces accused of smuggling racket in Somalia, army denies," Reuters, November 12, 2015.
[108] "Why Kenya's defence forces fell at the battle of El Adde," *The Conversation*, October 29, 2020.

give an accurate figure of the casualties. He also denied Al-Shabaab claims that the terror group had taken prisoners of war.

President Uhuru, on the other hand, commissioned an internal review of AMISON after the attack, which concluded that its mandate was inadequate because it did not allow the African force "to completely destroy and annihilate the terrorist threat that is upon us." He called for a recalibration of the AMISON mandate. All in all, the El Adde attack was a demoralising moment for the KDF soldiers and Kenya at large.

The sad part of the war with Al-Shaabab is the issue of captured Kenyan soldiers held by Al-Shabaab. Although the government has admitted its men, and perhaps women, were hostages inside Somalia, it has not engaged Kenyans on how it plans to rescue them. This has left families of the captives in pain, especially after reports emerged in 2013 that some KDF soldiers had been executed.

Since the deployment of KDF troops in Somalia, Kenya has become a key recruitment centre for Al-Shabaab. Young, disillusioned Kenyans mysteriously disappeared only to surface in Somalia. The largely unemployed youths – including girls – were lured into the group by promises of financial rewards. Covert and invisible recruiters combed the country identifying the most vulnerable youths. Initially, the main regions where recruitment of women and girls took place were the coast and north-eastern regions, which have large Muslim populations. But in recent years, recruitment has expanded into other parts of the country, especially in Western Kenya.

Uhuru's peculiar reaction to frequent incursions by terrorists from Somalia was to build a wall along the 700-km border with the neighbouring country. Many laughed in ridicule when that announcement was made in 2015. Initially, the government could not decide whether the wall would go along the entire length of the border or a section of it. The government talked of a wall between the border towns of Bulla Hawa in Somalia and Mandera in Kenya.

The suggestion was archaic and totally bizarre. The KDF had projected that the whole length of the wall would cost KSh.8 billion, but after only 10 km, half of that amount had already been expended.

Apart from the question of cost, people wondered whether the wall would be effective at all in deterring incursions by criminal elements.

The original plan for that wall was for a concrete structure to be fitted with observation posts and electronic surveillance cameras. When making that decision, the Kenyan government did not consider the effects of separation of clans and families astride the border, and how such a wall could impact trade and commerce between the two countries. But the main question was: would the wall stop Al-Shabaab terrorists from crossing over and causing death and destruction on the Kenyan side? Or was Uhuru's decision a political ploy to silence critics because of his inability to meet the terrorism challenge?

At the beginning of the Jubilee administration, Al-Shabaab terror group was already in Kenya. Its members had infiltrated mosques and *madrassas* and had "pocketed" corrupt police officers manning borders.

A wall like the one US President Donald Trump started to build along the US/Mexico border, or the Israel West Bank barrier were not a deterrent to refugee incursions or terrorist attacks. There was speculation that the Kenya/Somalia wall was also meant to stop refugees from crossing over from Somalia to Dadaab camp in Garissa County. Kenya has for years tried to close the camp which houses more than 200,000 refugees.

In the meantime, work continued along the border, amid frequent incursions by terrorists and refusal by local communities to move away from the path of the proposed structure. Between 2016, when construction started, and 2019, only 10 km had been built. Up to that time, KSh.3.3 billion had been spent on building that stretch alone.

MPs were furious and demanded an explanation. Instead of a concrete structure, the project was scaled down to a barbed wire and chain-link fence. The government had nothing to say about that variance. The most astonishing part of this story is that there wasn't much public protest in Kenya to put the government on its defence.

Parliament suspended the project in March 2019 and demanded an investigation into the project because it suspected corruption. But

Uhuru remained mum on the fate of the wall, and nothing was said about the investigation by anyone in government.

As Uhuru prepared to leave office, what remained of the wall was an edifice of failure. Parts of the wall were vandalised, and terrorists were still entering Kenya through other porous border sections. And within the country citizens were still vulnerable to terrorist attacks.

CHAPTER 8

Violations of the law

Kenyan courts have come a long way since the autocratic days of President Moi. It was a common practice then for President Moi to order judges to make rulings that favoured his interests, the more reason Moi packed courts with expatriate judicial officers. Under an arrangement with the British government, several judges including chief justices were seconded to Kenya on contract because Moi considered them more loyal to the presidency than their Kenyan counterparts.[109]

The same happened during the reign of Jomo Kenyatta. As a rule, the expatriate judicial officers invariably toed the Executive's line. When, for example, Chief Justice Dennis Farell, reduced the sentence given to Bildad Kaggia, from one year to six months for holding an illegal political meeting in 1968, Kenyatta was exasperated. He immediately fired the expatriate judge.

Kaggia was part of the Kapenguria Six, but he quit KANU alongside Jaramogi Oginga Odinga, to form KPU. He became the party's vice president. From being a loyal follower of Mzee Kenyatta, Kaggia became one of Mzee Kenyatta's bitter rivals.

After removal, Justice Farell was replaced by the first African Chief Justice, Kitili Mwendwa, who lasted only three years. He too

---

[109] Africa Watch, Kenya. Taking Liberties, An African Watch Report, July 1991, p. 151.

was fired after he was linked to a plot to overthrow Mzee Kenyatta's government.

To survive the expatriate judicial officers had to be subservient to the Executive and to the person of the president. One former chief justice, Alan Robin Hancox, even went further and urged all lawyers and judges to "be loyal to the government and to the head of state."[110] Expatriate judges were easy to manipulate especially in politically sensitive cases. Moi used them to deny applications for bail, and to throw out challenges to the constitutionality of various changes to the law.[111] Things however changed as the judiciary, emboldened by the 2010 constitution, asserted its independence.

"Anyone who breaks the laws of the country will be dealt with firmly…. This is what [the] Government is for, and what it should be." That was Mzee Jomo Kenyatta, speaking on Independence Day, December 12, 1963. Over the years though, Kenyans have seen a pattern of leaders disobeying laws with impunity. This pattern of disobedience, disrespect, and abuse of law has been commonplace since independence.

Mzee Kenyatta did it so did presidents Moi, Kibaki, and Uhuru, though in varying degrees. Because law is dispensed with whenever it becomes convenient to do so, a culture of impunity emerges.[112] This has created a notion that politicians can do anything illegal and get away with it, forgetting that the law is the "bloodline of every nation."[113]

Kenya's Justice Isaac Lenaola is one of numerous Kenyan judicial officers who believe court orders must be obeyed "whether one agrees with them or not." In one court ruling, Justice Lenaola said: "If one does not agree with an order, then he ought to move the court to

---

[110] See M. M. Kioga, Chief Justice's Pronouncements: (Are they law of politics?), *Nairobi Law Monthly*, April/May 1990.

[111] Abdication of Responsibility: The Commonwealth and Human Rights, Human Rights Watch (Organisation), 1991, p. 23.

[112] Akech, Migai. *Abuse of Power and Corruption in Kenya:* Will the New Constitution Enhance Government Accountability? *Indiana Journal of Global Legal Studies*, Vol. 18, Issue 1, Winter 2011, pp. 343-344.

[113] Pickard, Carmel. Challenging Culture of Impunity in Kenya, Africa LII, March 6, 2019.

discharge the same. To blatantly ignore it and expect the court would turn its eyes away is to underestimate and belittle the purpose for which the courts were set up."[114]

Over time, the culture of impunity trickled down to not only government departments including ministries and law enforcement agencies, but also to parliament, the body that makes all laws in the country.

A case in point was the *Judicial Service Commission (JSC) vs Speaker of the National Assembly & another*. In 2013, Riungu Nicholas Mugambi, petitioned the court pleading for the removal of six commissioners of the JSC. A five-judge High Court bench ruled in 2014 that the commissioners shall not be removed from the office pending the hearing and determination of the petition or until further court orders.

In the judgement signed by Justice G. V. Odunga, the court further ruled to restrain the national assembly or the parliamentary departmental committee of justice and legal affairs from presenting or forwarding the petition to the president for execution. The court also issued an order restraining the president from removing the officials, pleading that by ignoring court orders, the respondents "would be sending wrong signals not only to the people of Kenya from whom they derive their authority, but to the whole world, that they do not believe in the rule of law."[115] The court annulled both the proceedings of the parliamentary committee and the resolution of the National Assembly.[116]

However, the national assembly ignored the order and sent the petition to the president anyway. Apart from abuse of law, the 'Mugambi petition' also tested the doctrine of the separation of powers between two of the three branches of government, the national assembly, and the judiciary. In this case, parliament should have obeyed the court order since defiance was not only a threat to the

---

[114] Kibet, Emanuel & Kimberly Wangeci. "A Perspective on the Doctrine of the Separation of Powers Based on the Response to Court Orders in Kenya," *Strathmore Law Review*, January 2016, p. 229.
[115] Ibid.
[116] Regeru, Njoroge & Company. "High Court rules Judiciary is not under Parliament's control," Lexology, July 1, 2014.

legitimacy of the constitution and the rule of law but a challenge to the credibility and status of the Judiciary. Justice Odunga reinstated the six JSC commissioners in December 2013 and suspended the tribunal appointed by President Uhuru.

GENDER BALANCE IGNORED

Uhuru and his officials were serial abusers of court orders. Look at this: a provision in the Constitution of Kenya, 2010, mandated that five years after the promulgation of the constitution, MPs would ensure that not more than two-thirds of members in elective and appointive positions were of the same gender.

Anchored in Article 27 (3) of the constitution, the provision states that, "Women and men have the right to equal treatment, including the right to equal opportunities in political, economic, cultural, and social spheres." Article 27 (8) requires the State to take policy, legislative, and other measures, including affirmative action programmes, to ensure that "not more than two-thirds of the members of elective or appointive bodies shall be of the same gender."

The Supreme Court, led by Chief Justice Willy Mutunga, had in December 2012, advised parliament to implement the rule by August 27, 2015. But parliament was unable to achieve that, either because of lack of quorum or lack of political good will by both parliament and the executive. The last time the amendments were tabled in parliament for debate by Majority Leader Aden Duale was in 2019. Only 174 MPs were present, far short of the two thirds majority (233 MPs) required to pass the changes. Similarly, Uhuru refused to comply with those constitutional provisions and many of his appointments failed to meet the criterion.

Parliament extended the deadline by one year. But still, attempts to pass amendments to the constitution to achieve the gender rule failed. The president made no effort to mobilise the MPs to do the right thing. The lack of political will at the top as well as in parliament was a further demonstration of how the men folk cared less about women interests.

Parliament was controlled by men; so were many other institutions. There were only 76 women (21.87%) in the 349-member national assembly. In contrast, the Senate met the gender requirement by having 21 female members (31%) in the 67-member senate chamber. Efforts by political parties to nominate more women to parliament did not help. Women MPs blamed their male colleagues for blocking efforts to pass the amendments. Uhuru made the situation worse by appointing more men than women to government and parastatal bodies. For instance, when he reconstituted his government in 2015, Uhuru appointed only five women instead of seven, in a cabinet of twenty members.

In September 2020, Chief Justice David Maraga advised the president to dissolve the national assembly for failure to pass the gender rule. He was frustrated that four court rulings directing parliament to act had been ignored since 2012. He blasted the MPs for their "lackadaisical attitude and conduct." CJ Maraga noted that although the action he was proposing was drastic and would cause inconvenience and even economic hardships, "there is no gain without pain," he added quoting an old saying.

Of course, Uhuru ignored the advice. He neither commented on CJ Maraga's remarks, which were widely applauded by women organisations, nor gave any explanation as why he would not act on the advice. Several petitions were filed all the way to the Supreme Court by various parties. One of the petitioners was the ubiquitous Okiya Omtatah who took the opposite view. He wanted a review of the advisory opinion issued by CJ Maraga. He asked the court to set the opinion aside to save parliament from dissolution as stipulated in the constitution.

A five-judge bench under the new Chief Justice Martha Koome ruled that since the petitioners were not party to the proceedings that led to the advisory opinion, they had no *locus standi* in the matter. The court dismissed Omtatah's petition.

Violations of court orders did not occur only during Uhuru's tenure. His predecessor, President Kibaki was also a serial disobeyer of the law. In 2005, Kibaki rubbished a directive stopping government officials from issuing title deeds to the Ogiek, a community in the

Rift Valley. The High Court in Nakuru had barred the commissioner of lands, the chief lands registrar, the principal registrar of titles, and the Rift Valley provincial commissioner, from giving out the document because of a pending dispute.

Kibaki instead went to Olenguruone and issued 12,000 titles, saying every Kenyan had an inalienable right to own property. "What the president did was wrong in law," Otiende Amolo, chairperson of the Kenya chapter of the International Commission of Jurists (ICJ), lamented.

In 2012, Kibaki again ignored a court order. He failed to gazette the chairperson and members of the National Land Commission (NLC) as ordered by the High Court. The officials were nominated by the president and the prime minister and confirmed by parliament on August 14, 2012, but in-fighting within the executive branch of government had delayed the gazettement of: Muhammad Swazuri, Dr. Tomiik Konyimbih, Silas Muriithi, Dr. Rose Musyoka, Dr. Samuel Torerei, Abigael Mbagaya, Emma Njogu, Clement Lenachuru, and Abdulkadir Khalif. Finally, on February 22, 2013, Kibaki succumbed to pressure and gazetted the officials.

The government ignores orders on Ogiek

Almost sixty years after independence, land continues to be a major issue of contention. Communities still fight over land and pasture, families kill each other to settle land disputes, and politicians use land distribution and settlement issues, to win votes. Experts say that land questions in Kenya are complex, multilayered, and highly politicised.

For example, the violence that followed the 2007 disputed presidential elections and left more than 1,000 people dead was partly blamed on land problems. Communities were forcefully uprooted from their lands. Those who resisted were murdered and their property destroyed. The Constitution of Kenya, 2010 and the National Land Commission (NLC) set up in 2012 have not helped much to bring equity in land distribution. Issues of historical injustices remain unresolved, and millions of Kenyans live as squatters.

The Ogiek, one of the smallest communities in the country, for example, still cry for their grabbed land at Mau Forest. The Ogiek are believed to be the indigenous owners of the Mau Forest. They were first uprooted from their ancestral land by British colonialists in the 1930s. They were bundled together in a small area of Mau Forest while the rest of their land was taken away.

In 1993, they were moved further to the edge of the forest by Kenyan land grabbers who cleared the forest and planted tea. Settlers were beaten up and their property burnt to force them to move out. The biggest grabber of them all was President Moi who used his portion of the land to build the Kiptagich Tea Factory, one of the biggest in the Rift Valley. The destruction led to the decline in rainfall and the drying up of wetlands and lakes. There has been massive felling of trees and burning of charcoal, and hundreds of square miles of the forest have either been destroyed or replanted with the fast-growing cypress and pine trees.[117]

In 2010, the Kibaki administration ordered the Ogiek to move out again from where they were at the edge of the forest to allow the rehabilitation of the forest. The Ogiek referred the matter to the African Court on Human and People's Rights established by African nations in 2006.

In 2017, the court issued its judgement, directing the Kenyan government to give back the land to the Ogiek. The court ruled that Kenya had violated seven articles of the African Charter on Human and People's Rights of which it is a signatory. The court upheld the Ogiek's rights to "own, use, and occupy" their ancestral lands.

Despite the ruling, however, the Uhuru government refused to comply. Currently scattered, the Ogiek are benumbed and powerless in the face of obstinate defiance by authorities. The Uhuru government blamed the community for the delay. It said the Ogiek had created numerous hurdles by filing cases and obtaining

---

[117] Kamadi, Geoffrey. "Who should care for the forests? In Kenya, the question sparks violence," *The Christian Science Monitor*, October 14, 2020.

injunctions against the government. Whatever the case, there was no reason why the Uhuru administration could not have moved with speed to implement the court ruling and grant the Ogiek people their rights. As they say, justice delayed is justice denied.

Jail for defiance

There were numerous other cases pertaining to public officers disobeying court orders during Uhuru's tenure, without being penalized. In 2017, for example, the defence principal secretary (PS), Saitoti Torome, was sentenced to six months in civil jail for contempt of court. He had failed to pay KSh.17.2 million for compensation as directed by a court, to a family that offered land to the government. Torome was sued in 2009 for disobeying court orders issued on May 30, 2006, to compensate Eunice Makori and Hellen Makone for their land. The court then ordered the official jailed for six months or pay a fine of KSh.500,000.

The principal secretary was not apprehended. When that did not happen, Justice Joseph Sergon, ordered the Inspector General of Police Joseph Boinnet, to appear in court and explain why he had not arrested the PS. Boinnet, however, told the court that he could not arrest Torome because of a "stay order" the official had filed in court. As it turned out, no such application had been made. Torome eventually released the money to Makori and Makone and avoided the jail term.

The military too are guilty

Just like parliament, government agencies, and officials, the military too stand accused of abusing lawful orders.

In 2019, more than 20,000 residents of Burat in Isiolo County were evicted from their land by the KDF despite a court order stopping their removal. The military's 78th Battalion forcefully took over the land for training purposes. Representatives of the affected people went to the Environment and Labour Relations Court and obtained orders stopping the KDF from evicting them. The matter was also investigated by the senate committee on lands. Notwithstanding all that, the KDF went ahead and occupied the land.

A few months earlier, the KDF had done the same thing to residents of Meru County. It evicted 7,500 families from Tigania East despite the existence of a court order to the contrary. It was obvious that the military believed it was above the law. But that is not the case. The armed forces just like any other public entity, is subject to the rule of law. Any refusal by the military to obey court orders is a violation of the law. Nothing was done to KDF or the officers who ignored the court orders.

The military may have used a provision in the constitution which allows compulsory acquisition of community land for public use. But even then, wouldn't it have been better and more sensible if the military had engaged the local people to explain that?

MILITARISATION OF GOVERNMENT

In early 2021, Uhuru transferred the Kenya Meat Commission (KMC), a firm under the Ministry of Agriculture, to the Kenya Defence Forces (KDF), and appointed Brigadier James Githanga as managing director. The move was not totally unusual. Uhuru had appointed other military men to state offices before. Major General Mohamed Abdalla Badi, for example, was the Director General of the Nairobi Metropolitan Services (NMS) tasked to oversee the capital city.

He had also given top parastatal jobs to almost all retired Chiefs of General Staff (CGSes). In November 2021, Uhuru gave the ministry of defence (MoD) the management of KEMSA, giving the military responsibility of procuring for and distributing all medical supplies to public health facilities.

Uhuru's unilateral decision to militarise the meat processor was, however, denigrated by politicians and challenged in the High Court by the Law Society of Kenya (LSK). In February 2021, Judge Anthony Mrima, ruled the transfer of KMC to KDF violated the constitution because it lacked public participation. "The decision is hereby quashed," the court ruled. As usual, Uhuru defied the court and went ahead with the transfer.

Since inception, the KMC has faced myriad problems ranging from bad management, political interference, obsolete machinery, and corruption. Those problems, plus loss of business with the European Union because of outbreaks of foot and mouth disease, brought down the meat processor. Even after the Kibaki administration pumped in KSh.400 million to revive the facility in 2006, the organisation continued to experience operational problems leading to a high turnover at the top.

Then there was theft and corruption. In 2016, KMC auditors discovered that a top commission official had withdrawn KSh.11.5 million from the parastatal's bank account. The money, taken between December 2012 and January 2013, was for procuring livestock for use by Kenya soldiers serving in Somalia, but it was allegedly diverted to personal use. The matter was referred to the EACC and Ibrahim Haji Isaak was charged. In 2020, the High Court ordered the EACC to recover the money plus interest from the defendant. Justice John Onyiego ruled Isaak "had dishonestly spent the money without proper accountability, hence an act of fraud and breach of public duty."

KMC was also taken to task in mid-2020 when it was found it had a whooping KSh.681 million in pending bills owed to suppliers, farmers, and statutory bodies and had KSh.514 million in liabilities. The firm was going down as fast as a speeding train. Its sales had dropped by 32% during the year ending June 2020 to KSh.126.6 million from KSh.188 million the previous year. There were also serious discrepancies in accounting to an extent that Auditor General Gathungu could not reconcile books due to lack of documentary evidence. Millions of shillings were also feared lost during the transition from the ministry of agriculture to the KDF. There was another problem. The Treasury gave KMC KSh.280 million in the 2019/2020 financial year for drought mitigation and factory modernisation. That money was not reflected in KMC's financial statements, leading to adverse speculation.

After the military took over KMC, there was a marked improvement in its operation. In less than two years of management by the KDF, most of the debts owed to livestock farmers had been settled. Farmers were motivated and had substantially increased their supply of livestock to KMC. The rundown machines KDF inherited from the old management were rehabilitated, making it possible to slaughter a total of 600 cattle in a 24-hour circle. In the first three quarters since taking over, KMC under the military made a profit of KSh. 150 million compared to KSh. 5 million before. Uhuru's decision to militarise KMC was therefore prudent. The KDF is the biggest customer of KMC products buying tens of thousands of kilograms of meat every year. It therefore made sense that KMC's biggest consumer should also be its manager.

Uhuru's critics, including human rights activists, and former minister Martha Karua, however, claimed militarisation of public enterprises was against the "spirit of the constitution." Karua made a prescient prediction that "Slowly, the military will run the government." Some senators, including the Deputy Majority Leader Fatuma Dullo, went further to describe Uhuru's move of including uniformed men into the public service as "an old trick" used by 'fraudsters' over the years to disinherit wealth belonging to the public.[118] But the government dismissed those accusations and innuendos as misguided.

A SLEUTH IN THE GAME

Defiance of the law was not a habit of the presidency alone. It pervaded in the entire executive branch of government. In November 2021, the head of the directorate of criminal investigations (DCI), George Kinoti, was sentenced to jail for four months for defying a court order. The court had directed him to return guns confiscated from a Nairobi businessman, Jimmy Wanjigi, during an investigation

---

[118] Mageka, Hillary. "Senators raise alarm over 'militarization' of public institutions," *The People Daily*, September 20, 2020.

in 2017. Wanjigi claimed the raid was done without a search warrant, so in 2019, he lodged a complaint in court.

In his judgement, Justice Chacha Mwita, ruled that the government had violated Wanjigi's rights by confiscating the firearms, consisting of four Glock pistols, one Smith & Weston pistol, a Mini Archer assault rifle fitted with a laser, an M4CQ assault rifle, and 646 bullets. "The actions of the respondents were unlawful and actuated by malice," Justice Mwita said. "The court grants orders that all firearms be returned to the plaintiff." But Kinoti refused to comply. He retorted that he would rather go to jail than return the weapons to Wanjigi.

In 2020, Wanjigi filed a contempt of court charge against George Kinoti. The case was heard by High Court Judge Antony Mrima. In November 2021, Mrima sentenced Kinoti to four months in jail and ordered him to report to Kamiti Maximum Security Prison within seven days to start his sentence. Mrima told the Inspector General of Police Hillary Mutyambai to arrest Kinoti if he failed to report to prison.

Instead of reporting to jail, Kinoti filed an application in court to stop the police boss from arresting him. He claimed the orders threatened his responsibilities to the community and that it would cause "unfathomable and irreparable damage to the office he holds." There followed weeks of tense moments for the police chief. Kinoti went to the Court of Appeal to ask for conservatory orders pending appeal. On April 1, 2022, the Court of Appeal suspended the four-month jail term imposed on Kinoti.

The open disobedience of court orders even by those who are supposed to enforce them is short-sighted and wrong. It markedly reduces Kenya's claim of being a law-abiding nation and makes the country look like a banana republic. It also trashes the 'no one is above the law,' notion which the constitution affirms.

In 2013, AG Paul Kihara Kariuki, and Interior Principal Secretary (PS) Karanja Kibicho, were ordered to pay Lucy Nduta Ng'ang'a KSh.5.3 million for a decree issued by a Mombasa court. That was to compensate her for the murder of her husband, Edward Ng'ang'a Kuria, by a police officer while driving along the Nairobi-Mombasa highway on September 24, 2009.

Despite the court ruling, the two public officials failed to comply with the order. In January 2021, Justice Eric Ogola, asked Kariuki and Kibicho to appear in court for mitigation before sentencing them for contempt of court. A lawyer from the AG's office said Lucy had not been paid because of some bureaucratic challenges. He further asked the court to strike out the names of the two officials from the suit, saying an attempt to charge them for contempt of court would embarrass them and disgrace the executive. In November, the government did comply and pay, and the case was closed.

HE BLUNDERED, SO THE MILITARY TOOK OVER

For almost three years (2017-2020), the governor of Nairobi was Mike Sonko, a demagogue known for bling, glitzy attire, and gold-coloured high-end vehicles. Though elected by the third largest number of votes of any candidate in the 2017 elections besides Uhuru and Raila, Sonko was not popular among the elites. They were not impressed, not only by his seemingly snobbish personality, but by his eccentric style of leadership.

There were endless squabbles between senior officers at City Hall. Polycarp Igathe, his able deputy, only lasted four months before resigning citing "lack of trust from his boss." The Speaker of the County Assembly Beatrice Elachi got so frustrated that she quit in a huff citing "threats to people's lives and their families." Overall, the elites felt Sonko was a bad example of a leader for a city as important as Nairobi.

Sonko was a populist and a man of inspiriting spectacle, but the Nairobi City County government he led was drowning in corruption and malfeasance. Garbage was not being collected, taps were dry most of the time, crime was widespread, and the once sparkling Nairobi River had become a dumping ground for foetuses. Sonko had permitted cartels and corruption to thrive. The city transport system was in shambles as *matatus* overran the city causing incessant jams. Sonko himself owned several flashy *matatus* plying between the city and the crowded eastlands suburbs of Nairobi.

Initially, Uhuru and Sonko were good friends. Sonko was Uhuru's furious defender during the ICC trial. However, that friendship ended when Sonko, an ex-jailbird, MP, and senator, riled at Uhuru for allegedly working to topple him. There followed a virulent exchange of words and insults before the two acrimoniously parted ways. Uhuru explained later that he broke ranks with Sonko because "he was always fighting people, chaos everywhere."

On March 18, 2020, Uhuru appointed Air Force Major General Mohamed Abdalla Badi as Director General of the newly created Nairobi Metropolitan Services (NMS) to share power with Sonko. The bling bling man was eventually impeached by the Senate on four charges of violating the constitution, abuse of office, misconduct, and crimes against national laws. He left office disgraced.

Uhuru liked Badi so much that he proposed a seat for him in the cabinet. That was the first time in Kenya's history that a military man, without a portfolio, had been proposed for a seat in the cabinet. But Uhuru's decision did not sit well with his critics. MP Alice Wahome petitioned the court saying that by allowing an 'outsider' to sit in the cabinet, Uhuru would be contravening the constitution. The High Court agreed and overturned Uhuru's decision. Justice Anthony Mrima declared the president's action "illegal and void."

Uhuru scores own goal

At the outbreak of Covid-19, President Uhuru announced night curfews meant to curb the spread of the pandemic. People had to be in their homes during certain times. Bars, restaurants, shops, and all businesses, had to shut down before the start of curfew.

But in July 2021, Uhuru broke his own rule. Clad in a military jacket, Uhuru went out and launched five hospitals in Nairobi at night, violating his own curfew instructions. He explained that launching the facilities during the day would have broken social distancing guidelines. For four hours, he drove within Nairobi, from Kangemi to Kawangware, to Mukuru kwa Reuben, to Tassia kwa Ndege, and to Mukuru kwa Njenga, commissioning health facilities.

In a way Uhuru led by example in disobeying Covid-19 rules that had been issued by his own administration. Moreover, what is more superior: the law or some guidelines set up by a team of technocrats?

Uhuru's defiance invited a flurry of nasty tweets. "President Uhuru Kenyatta should tomorrow be arraigned in a court of law for breaking curfew hours," wrote Miqdad Abdissalam. "Why is Kenyatta launching projects at night?" "Why is he defying curfew hours? He has no respect for his orders too, leave alone court orders?" Asked Ongomak.

Up until Uhuru rescinded a bunch of restrictions relating to Covid-19 pandemic in October 2021, the ministry of health under CS Mutahi Kagwe, had issued more than half a dozen directives. The directives asked leaders and the public to comply with lockdown orders and follow protocols at social gatherings such as at burials and in worship places. The restrictions were unequivocally resented and largely ignored by almost everyone including the person who issued them: Uhuru. The president and other political bigwigs held super-spreader rallies around the country exposing the public to the dangers of the deadly disease.

One of the biggest violators of the government order was Deputy President Ruto. He defiantly held countless meetings in churches, open fields, and in indoor facilities, to sell his 'bottom-up' economic model amid continuous warning from health officials about the dangers of Covid-19. Ironically, the people attending the meetings, most of them without masks, jostled and pushed each other without care, as the election fever rose. Ruto also hosted many large gatherings at his official residence, Karen, making a fool of government directives.

He was not alone. Once Raila Odinga felt threatened by DP Ruto's massive campaign engagements, he too jumped in. Raila was buoyed by support from the powerful and wealthy Mt. Kenya Foundation and Uhuru's tacit endorsement of his presidential ambition. He made repeated forays into Kikuyuland hoping to capture some of the approximately eight million votes in the region. He also held rallies in other parts of the country. Many of his listeners did not wear protective gear either.

Mutahi Kagwe, the health cabinet secretary, who was party to the directives, stood helplessly as transmission figures went up and more Kenyans succumbed to the Covid-19 pandemic. No government security agency dared to arrest and prosecute the offending leaders.

IMPUNITY RULES

Experts say impunity undermines the legitimacy of the state and the government and undercuts good governance.[119] The constitution of Kenya, 2010, brought hope of "clean, robust, and efficient institutions."[120] Kenyans expected a paradigm shift from the old system of self-aggrandisement and greed to a new era of functional accountability and transparency. Expectations were that impunity in the public sector would be a thing of the past.

Like its predecessors, the Uhuru administration experienced a high level of impunity in government institutions, among them the National Police Service (NPS), the IEBC, and even the judiciary. Prominent people who committed serious economic crimes were treated differently from *Wanjiku* (common citizen) who stole chicken.

Indeed, one report showed that the criminal justice system in Kenya favoured the rich and condemned the poor. A task force commissioned by the government in 2017 to review mandatory death sentence showed the justice system was defective, leading to a disproportionate number of poor or vulnerable people being handed the death penalty for crime they did not commit.

In a paper, published by the Penn State *Journal of Law and International Affairs*, Francesca R. Jensenius and Abby K. Wood, argue that *de facto* immunity from punishment run with "class status,

---

[119] Hebling, Jurg, Walter Kalin & Prosper Nobirabo. Access to Justice, Impunity, and Legal Pluralism in Kenya," *The Journal of Legal Pluralism and Unofficial Law*, Vol. 47, Issue 2, 2015, pp. 347-367.

[120] Maina, Wachira. "State capture: The institutionalisation of impunity in Kenya*,"* *The Elephant.*

kinship, wealth, ethnicity, or status as a political elite."[121] They further say that the extent to which elites avoid punishment when caught for criminal acts was closely related to corruption.

GETTING AWAY WITH 'MURDER'?

As captured in Chapter 11, billions of shillings from public coffers continued to vanish through illegal tendering, inflated bills, and sheer theft, yet perpetrators, mainly senior government officials or their accomplices, went scot free. Impunity was also practised daily in the urban transport sector where *matatus* and poorly maintained public vehicles violated traffic rules without care.

The yearly damning reports by the auditor general pointing to misuse of resources had become routine that many people have stopped paying attention to them. The huge infrastructure projects undertaken turned out to be a cash cow for some privileged individuals in government. A good example is the Nairobi Expressway. The government spent a staggering KSh.88 billion constructing the passageway only to realise, even before the official launch, that essential exit points were not incorporated into the original plans. Therefore, more billions of shillings were to be spent to re-design the expressway to make it easier for motorists to access and exit the CBD.

In some countries, a matter such as this would have called for an inquiry and possible prosecution of the culprits, but not so in Kenya! Based on expert opinion, therefore, President Uhuru's term ended with a dent on his legacy for failing to curb the menace of impunity.

Also, how can you explain an MP shooting a man and getting away unpunished by law? In 2020, a Nairobi politician shot and seriously injured a DJ in a nightclub in Nairobi. He was arrested, charged with attempted murder, and freed on bail. As the case continued in court, an out-of-court settlement proposal was tabled.

---

[121] Jensenius, Francesca R. & Abby K. Wood. Caught in the Act but not Punished: On Elite Rule of Law and Deterrence, *Penn State Journal of Law and International Affairs*, Vol. 4, No. 2, 2016, p. 687.

The victim, Felix Orinda, popularly known as DJ Evolve, even wrote a letter to court wanting to withdraw the case. He said he wanted to concentrate on his treatment and not on the case which, he said, was interfering with his healing process.

In March 2021, Senior Principal Magistrate Bernard Ochoi ruled that the victim's application "did not meet the threshold set to withdraw a criminal case." In December, however, the application was accepted, and the accused and the victim were allowed to agree on a private settlement. Following the agreement, the murder charge against the MP, Babu Owino, was dropped. Did the status of the shooter help in this case?

There was also the case of Moses Kuria, the MP of Uhuru's Gatundu South constituency. In May 2021, he admitted receiving a bribe of KSh.100,000 to support the appointment of a majority leader in the national assembly. In Kenya, bribery is criminal. By accepting guilt, Kuria should have been prosecuted and convicted. But the investigative agencies did nothing, and Kenyans took the matter as a happy joke. If it had been a *Wanjiku* (common citizen), instant justice would no doubt have been applied.

How about Miguna's case?

Nothing demonstrated the extent of political impunity in Uhuru's government than the forceful deportation of a Kenyan citizen, Miguna Miguna, in February 2018. Miguna, a garrulous self-styled revolutionary, was dragged screaming into a plane and sent out of the country.

A week earlier, Miguna had sworn in Raila Odinga as the 'people's president' at an emotionally charged rally at Uhuru Park in Nairobi. The event was to protest the 2017 presidential election results. Miguna, a Kenyan-born lawyer has dual citizenship; Kenyan and Canadian.

After the mock event, Miguna had urged Kenyans to take down Uhuru's portrait from their offices and buildings, arguing that Uhuru was an 'illegitimate' president. Three days later, a contingent of armed police officers descended on his home in Runda, Nairobi. They ransacked it and arrested him.

After being shifted from one police station to another, so that no one could figure out where he was, Miguna was eventually declared a non-citizen and his passport withdrawn. The government explained that Miguna 'had acted detrimentally to national security.' The government's hasty action was not only manifestly harsh and barbarous, but also morally wrong. Miguna was born in Kenya and had all the birth rights to live and work in the country without harassment.

Miguna's lawyers went to the High Court to seek legal redress. They argued that the government had violated the constitution by denying Miguna his rights. "People have suffered for this constitution," Lawyer John Khaminwa, emotionally told the court. "They have died. Families have broken up. We cannot have one or two people trying now to water down this constitution. We shall not have it." High Court Judge George Odunga ruled that top government officials were in contempt of court for failing to release Miguna. He fined the interior cabinet secretary and heads of police and immigration KSh.200,000 each for contempt of court. As expected, the state officials did not pay, and they were not penalised.

On June 6, 2021, a three-bench Court of Appeal declined to declare Miguna a prohibited immigrant and ruled that his deportation was illegal. It also declined to quash KSh.7.2 million in compensation awarded to Miguna for destruction of part of his house by the police. The court further ruled that the National Resistance Movement (NRM), which Miguna claimed to head, was not a criminal organisation. So, the court ordered the return of his passport and a safe passage into the country. The government again refused to comply.

Miguna was still in Canada as Uhuru prepared to leave office.

Uhuru made another blunder that took Kenyans back to Moi's repression era. Soon after Raila's sham inauguration, President Uhuru denied two opposition politicians, James Orengo and Jimmy Wanjigi, permission to travel to Zimbabwe to attend the funeral of opposition leader Morgan Tsvangirai.

The Department of Immigration confiscated their passports only hours after a court had ordered the documents returned to them. The government refused to honour the court order, and the two were left stranded at the airport. However, they were later allowed to travel after a delay of several hours.

NO RESPECT FOR THE POOR

Slum colonies started mushrooming in Nairobi soon after independence as people rushed to the city in search of jobs. Mzee Kenyatta, in a move to keep Nairobi free of shanties, exhorted people to stay in rural areas and farm. That appeal did not stop people from flocking into the city of bright lights in search of employment. Seeing the futility of the intended restrictions, the President allowed new arrivals from the countryside to put up shacks on vacant lots, so long as they were not too close to the town centre.[122]

On taking over office from Jomo Kenyatta, President Moi adopted a different approach from that of his predecessor. The core tenet of his approach was the characterisation of dwellers as 'illegal squatters.' Thus, Moi denied them access to infrastructure, including electricity, clean water, sanitation facilities, as well as schools, and health facilities.[123] That however did not deter the multiplication of slums. More cropped up all around the city centre and next to affluent neighbourhoods. So, the demolitions began.

On May 25, 1990, after the expiry of three months' notice, government bulldozers moved into Muoroto area near the city centre at the spot where the 'Machakos airport' bus station is located. Thousands of people were left homeless as Nairobi City Council workers razed down countless homes, destroying everything on sight. The *askaris* used brutal force to eject the tenants.

Later that year, it was the turn of Kibagare shanty village on the fringes of Loresho, a Nairobi high-class area. An estimated 30,000 people were displaced in the demolition exercise that angered many residents of the city. Cardinal Maurice Otunga of the Catholic

---

[122] Syagga, Paul, Mitullah Winnie, and Gitau K Sarah, Nairobi Situation Analysis: Consultative Report, Government of Kenya, and UN-Habitat, 2001, p. 33.
[123] Ibid., p. 34.

Church visited Kibagare and was shocked at the "ruthlessness" and "violence" meted on the dwellers.

The demolition of slums continued throughout President Moi's regime and extended to President Kibaki's government, and then to President Uhuru's administration. During Uhuru's term, there were demolitions in Kibera, Ruai, Westlands, Mukuru kwa Njenga, and in several other informal settlements.

In Kibera, thousands of shanties were destroyed in July 2018 throwing 400,000 dwellers out in the cold to make way for a new road aimed at ending traffic congestion in Nairobi. Also destroyed in a section of one of Kenya's largest slum colonies, were schools, churches, and businesses. To make it worse, the demolitions were carried out weeks before the end-of-term examinations, leaving pupils in a desperate situation.

In Kariobangi area of the city, President Uhuru's government knocked down homes belonging to more than 7,000 people in May 2020. The Nairobi City Water Sewerage Company claimed ownership of the land saying the dwellers were occupying it illegally. That was after razing down the Korogocho market which served one-hundred thousand people.

At Mukuru kwa Njenga, 40,000 people were rendered homeless in October and November 2021, as the government demolished slum structures to pave way for the Catherine Ndereba Road. In fact, Amnesty International (AI), talked of a humanitarian crisis, as women and children were left in the cold, their meagre properties ruined. There was one case of death in the area as bulldozers swept through the crowded neighbourhood on the Nairobi city parameters.

Within weeks, the whole area was reduced to rubble. The evicted had to build makeshift structures in other spaces away from the path of the roadway. Ironically, Catherine Ndereba, under whose name the road was causing so much pain, is a renowned long-distance runner and a philanthropist who loves people. It is doubtful she sanctioned the demolition. It was not until January 2022 – after thousands of people had spent Christmas in the cold - that the government stepped in to resettle the evictees.

The perverse decision by governments to demolish slums was invariably condemned not only by locals, but by NGOs who felt the poor were being punished to satisfy the rich's appetite for residential land. Uhuru was in the loop about what was happening given his grip on the Nairobi Metropolitan Services (NMS). Not a single leader raised a voice to condemn the government.

Due to high rates of unemployment and lack of business opportunities, Nairobi slum areas have become breeding grounds for crime, disease, and political dissent. Lack of regulated water sources has forced slum dwellers to buy water by the buckets. Slum residents also tap into power lines to make illegal connections and use plastics for toilets. In 2021, John Guda, safety, health, and environment manager, Kenya Power, announced that 345 people had been electrocuted in the country in the previous three years.[124]

As demolition of shanties was ongoing in other parts of the city, a slum was being created in Nairobi's industrial area; this time along the Ngong River. Greedy businessmen were using soil and debris to fill up the river and create plots which they then sold to slumlords. The slumlords then leased the plots to rich people who built huts for rent.

Apart from the damage to the environment, the encroachment also created health hazards because dwellers released raw waste into the river. In addition, the closure of the waterway risked floods along sections of the river.[125]

For decades, the city had experienced flooding during heavy rains caused by heavy pollution and blockages especially along the Nairobi River. As factories, households, and careless citizens continued to use the river as a dumping ground for faeces, aborted foetuses, medical, and industrial wastes, the waterway became an eye sore, smelly, and dirty.

The once clear water turned brown and in other places pitch black. The elegant, crested cranes so ubiquitous in the city during the early years after independence had long disappeared. The birds

---

[124] "345 people electrocuted in the last three years – Kenya Power," *KNA*, May 18, 2021.
[125] "Lords of waste in Lunga Lunga slums are killing crucial Ngong River," *Standard*, August 21, 2021.

were the "ecological illustration" of Nairobi, as a city of order, beauty, *haute couture*, and class.[126]

Residential and business structures were also being erected along the path of the Nairobi River and others and on riparian land in the city. Early in August 2018, excavators moved in, and within days, shopping malls, a coffee shop, a petrol station, and residential buildings, built along the waterways, had been brought down and left in a heap of rubbles. Owners were not warned about the impending destruction, raising questions about the motive behind the hasty action.

The National Environment and Management Authority (NEMA) explained that the buildings were illegal, and some were on wetlands and had to go. Yes, but there was also a matter of decency and empathy. Uhuru was emphatic: "We will continue to demolish properties constructed on riparian lands, equally punish officials who made approvals for those properties," he said in August 2018.

The destructions started following the formation of the Nairobi Regeneration Committee in April 2018. The goal of the committee – a noble one too – was to save the city from further decay. The clean-up was also intended to restore the old glory of the metropolis once dubbed the green city in the sun. Authorities set aside KSh.800 million to start the job of rehabilitating not only the river, but the transportation system, education, housing, health facilities, as well as public safety. There were plans to establish a rapid-transit bus system, and to improve parks, garbage collection system, and roads in the estates. Some of those plans were accomplished during Uhuru's term. Others like establishing an environment-friendly garbage collection and disposal system remained a challenge.

The target was to demolish four thousand buildings. By the end of 2018, one thousand had come down. The government used the *Environmental Management and Coordination Act* of 2015 to implement the programme. Suddenly, the demolition stopped. The excitement the programme had created at the onset dissipated. But

---

[126] Kabukuru, Wanjohi, "Mass Demolitions Mark Start of Nairobi Regeneration," *New African*, March 23, 2019.

buildings such as the Taj Mahal, the Ukay Centre, the South End Mall on Lang'ata road, and Shell Kileleshwa, were in rubbles. Neither the Nairobi County Governor nor NEMA, the custodian of riparian land, explained why the demolitions stopped abruptly.

On the overall, President Uhuru's decision was good because it fulfilled his commitment to pull down structures built on riparian land. But the government could not explain why the controversial Weston Hotel was spared. Was it because it belonged to Deputy President William Ruto? At the time, the acrimonious warfare between Uhuru and Ruto had not yet peaked. The Nairobi City County Governor, Mike Sonko, declared the hotel would not be torn down even though it was reportedly on riparian land. He did not give a clear explanation as to why the hotel was spared

There were protestations from some politicians and property owners whose structures were demolished. MP Stephen Manoti, who owned the South End Mall building, claimed he had all the required approvals including those issued by Nairobi City County and NEMA. But NEMA disowned the approvals. It said the mall was built atop the Mutuini-Ngong River on Lang'ata Road and the building had to be demolished.

Kiambu County Governor, Ferdinand Waititu, had a frightfully bizarre contribution to make on the matter: "If there are people who support the demolition, I am not one of them," he said in Kiswahili, "but if your building is close to a river, then you should move the river instead of demolishing the building." The remarks brought Kenyans down in chuckles.

Despite Uhuru's threat, what came to light was that not a single official in government who approved the illegally constructed structures on riparian land was arrested, prosecuted, and convicted.

While Nairobi Regeneration Committee has met part of its mandate of improving roads and increasing the number of health facilities in the city, especially in areas with low-income earners, it remained clueless about how to clean up Nairobi River, and how to deal with hundreds of dishevelled and menacing *chokoras* (street children) and homeless families lining city streets. Some of those people were believed to engage in robberies and other criminal activities.

CHAPTER 9

Draconian Laws and Court Orders

During his rule, Uhuru approved some opprobrious and retrogressive laws. Take, for example, two bills that were some of the most controversial: the Kenya Information and Communication (Amendment) Act, and the Computer and Cybercrimes Act. Both legislations had elements of repressing press freedom. They were described by critics as 'draconian.'

For example, the *Information and Communication (Amendment) Act, 2013,* empowers the government to investigate and prosecute computer and cybercrimes including individuals who publish false information. It also punishes people who abuse others via social media. The new law was heavily criticised with some saying the government had overstepped its mandate.

Uhuru first declined to sign the bill in November 2013, because, he said, some of its provisions went against the constitution. He sent it back to the national assembly with a 33-page memorandum of objection. Morris Odhiambo, the regional project director of Freedom House, an international democracy watchdog, said in a statement that by "criminalising the publication of 'false' information, the government has overstepped its bounds and become an arbiter of truth on the internet."

Under all conceivable circumstances, the law, passed by parliament on October 31, 2013, was not only draconian but a threat to the freedom of expression. It did not only contravene Article 34 of the constitution on media freedom, but it also institutionalised state interference in the media and instigated intimidation of journalists especially on matters of governance and corruption.[127] At the end, Uhuru ignored critics and signed the bill into law on December 16, 2013.

Another legislation that created heat inside and outside parliament was the *Computer and Cybercrimes Bill, 2017*, outlawing the abuse of people on social media. It was intended to protect the confidentiality of data and prevent unlawful use of computer systems.

The bill was passed by the national assembly on April 26, 2018 and came into effect on May 30, 2018. The legislation allows for investigation and prosecution of computer and cybercrimes including cyber-harassment and 'publication of false information.' What the bill does not provide are measures to deal with identity theft and solicitation of minors through computer systems. Nevertheless, anyone convicted of sharing "false" or 'fictitious' information is liable to a fine of KSh.5 million, two years in jail, or both.

The legislation was seen as a perverse move to curb incessant attacks on Uhuru and his family, and criticisms of the government on social media platforms. The attacks were usually driven by anonymous bloggers within the Kenyans on Twitter (KOT) community. The law was vigorously opposed by media houses and NGOs including Freedom House which argued that the law would criminalise free speech. It also claimed the legislation was intended to gag journalists and undermine freedom of speech. But the Cabinet Secretary for Information, Communication, and Technology, Joe Mucheru disagreed. He said the legislation was necessary because some people were misusing the technology by spreading false information and using it to bully others.

Then there was the *Prevention of Torture Act* signed by President Uhuru on April 13, 2017. While some Kenyans described the Act

---

[127] Kenya: One Year in Office for Uhuru Kenyatta and William Ruto, Kenya Human Rights Commission, *undated*.

as a "milestone" in torture prevention, others believed the legislation would give the government power to use torture especially by police during interrogation of suspects. According to human rights NGOs quoted in the Kenya 2020 Human Rights Report, "physical battery, bondage in painful positions, and electric shock, were the most common methods of torture used by [Kenyan] police."[128]

The NGOs had also gathered credible narratives where security forces were rounding up and torturing suspects while in extended detention. This was happening even though Kenya ratified the UN Convention against Torture and other Cruel and Inhuman or Degrading Treatment or Punishment in 1997. People expressed fears that the new legislation would give security operatives an official licence to carry out torture contrary to some sections of the Constitution of Kenya, 2010.[129]

In Kenya, police officers were rarely prosecuted for using torture on suspects. The UN Human Rights Council has consistently appealed to Kenya to punish those who commit the offence. It has also asked that victims of torture receive redress and rehabilitation. While Kenya has accepted this recommendation, it has done nothing to implement it.

Media meddling

During President Uhuru's administration, there were obvious signs of meddling with press freedom. In March 2018, eight independent columnists abruptly resigned en masse from the Nation Media Group (NMG) citing "loss of editorial independence." They protested government interference and loss of independence in the media. But the NMG management denied that the government had a role in the resignation of the writers. It affirmed that the Group adhered to "the principles of independence, fairness, and balance," as espoused in its editorial policy. However, one of its editors claimed the columnists had an "activist background, and the paper could not

---

[128] "Kenya 2019 Human Rights Report, Executive Summary."
[129] Kenya 2017 Human Rights Report.

support their positions."[130] The eight columnists were some of the best and brightest commentators at the NMG.

Muthoni Wanyeki was the Africa director of the Open Society Foundation; George Kegoro was the executive director of the Kenya Human Rights Commission (KHRC); Nic Cheeseman was professor of Democracy at the Birmingham University; Father Gabriel Dolan, Maina Kiai and Gabrielle Lynch, were well-known human rights crusaders; and Rasna Warah, and Kwamchetsi Makokha, were popular journalists.

Their departure came amid reports that the Kenyatta family planned to buy the NMG. The reports were quickly dismissed in a statement by the group's chairman, Wilfred Kiboro: "The Nation Media Group is not for sale!" He said with firmness.

If it had managed to buy NMG, the Kenyatta family would have significantly expanded its media interests. The family already owns Mediamax, which controls numerous radio stations, a TV station, and a newspaper.

TV STATIONS SHUT DOWN

Three television stations aired Raila Odinga's symbolic swearing-in as the "people's president" on January 30, 2018, in defiance of a government directive. In February 2018, Interior CS Fred Matiang'i ordered the stations shut down. A civil society activist, Okiya Omtatah, went to court to force the government to lift the ban.

The court suspended the shutdown for two weeks, ruling that it had to await a decision on the case challenging the suspension. When Omtatah tried to serve the court order to the licensing authority, the Communications Authority of Kenya (CAK), officials there refused to receive it. The person sent to deliver it was detained by people who identified themselves as Kenya police.

The case caught the attention of the UN, the US, and the European Union (EU), which all called on Uhuru to respect the

---

[130] Eight columnists explain why they have stopped writing for Nation Media Group," March 27, 2018.

court order and reopen the TV stations. Despite the appeals, Uhuru refused to lift the ban immediately and the stations remained off air for five days. The government accused the media of being complicit in a plot to subvert the government and spark violence.

Nepotism

The tendency of appointing relatives, cronies, and political allies, to senior government positions, is not new in Kenya. In fact, Uhuru himself was a beneficiary of that magnanimity when Moi nominated him to parliament in 2001. Like his predecessors who favoured their own, President Uhuru tended to appoint people largely from his ethnic community. He did that without any shame. After all, he was just following *nyayo* since the previous governments of Mzee Kenyatta, Moi, and Kibaki, did the same. The Founding Father and Kibaki prioritised Kikuyu in senior appointments while Moi loaded the government with Kalenjin, some of them semi-illiterate. In the Jubilee government, Uhuru, a Kikuyu, shared power with Ruto, a Kalenjin. So, there was no surprise that the two ethnic groups took the lion's share of appointments in the Jubilee government.

Early in 2022, murmurs of disapproval were heard in the social media when Kenyans learnt that Ruto's twenty-something daughter was Kenya's charge d' affaires in Poland. Many viewed that as a blatant example of gross nepotism. But then, one of Uhuru's nieces was then acting as the CEO of the Kenyatta International Convention Centre (KICC. That's what is called power-sharing.

Orders from above

The familiar phrase "orders from above," in the Kenyan context, simply means instructions from someone at the top, be it a senior police officer, a cabinet secretary, or the president. The phrase has been in the Kenyan lexicon since the early days of independence.

Whenever the minister for lands and settlement under Jomo Kenyatta wanted to grab land for a politician or a favoured individual, he would invoke the phrase 'orders from above' meaning it was a directive from the president.

The phrase became even more popular during President Moi's tenure. The orders were sometimes referred to as 'roadside declarations.' "Mzee [Moi] would dish out a road there, a hospital, a school, or a market, until it became almost impossible to fund the budget. That was President Moi for you,"[131] lamented former Provincial Commissioner Joseph Kaguthi.

For example, in 1995, Moi gave out 420 acres of the Kamiti gazetted forest land belonging to the Kenya Forest Service (KFS) to people displaced in the Rift Valley during the 1994 post-election violence. The land had been proclaimed a forest area which meant it was reserved and protected. Moi did not consult the KFS or the ministry of environment which oversees forests.

"The normal procedure is that when the president makes verbal orders, it is followed immediately by a written communication by the head of the public service. That did not happen," Ministry of Lands Cabinet Secretary Farida Karoney said. According to her, Moi's orders were therefore invalid. She was testifying before the parliamentary lands, environment, and natural resources committee. The issue also caused a prolonged battle between stakeholders: the KFS, the Kamiti Development Association, Muungano wa Kamiti Group, Kamiti Forest Squatters Association, and the Kamiti Anmer Development Welfare Group.

In 2018, the committee visited the area to investigate, and recommended that the land be de-gazetted and excised from the forest. However, Karoney insisted that the land remained public property notwithstanding Moi's roadside declaration which made it difficult to de-gazette it for settlement. Although allotment letters were issued to 1,400 people, only a few hundred people got title deeds. The matter has remained unresolved.

---

[131] Njoka, Lewis. "Roadside orders: Expensive burden that baffled many," *The People Daily*, February 7, 2020.

Kibaki was the only president who shunned roadside declarations. That was in fulfilment of his promise during his inauguration that the "era of roadside declarations is gone." Roadside declarations, says Professor Karuti Kanyinga, a renowned academician, were "implemented without data to inform their worth."[132] They could as well be described as 'decrees' so popular in authoritarian nations.

President Uhuru too was 'guilty' of making roadside declarations. In 2017, Uhuru made a roadside declaration ordering chiefs and sub-chiefs to issue letters to people wanting to acquire national identification (ID) cards. He said that would circumvent bureaucracy in the registration department.

"Chiefs and their assistants know these Kenyans more than anybody," he said. "There is no need of asking them to produce birth certificates before registration and issuance of IDs."

Since the registration of persons hinges on security, Uhuru's directive was out of order. There was no prior consultation with the cabinet secretary or the relevant security organs before Uhuru made that declaration.

In May 2018, a truck was intercepted in Kitengela, Kajiado County, carrying sack-fulls of charcoal deemed to be contraband. KFS officers who stopped the truck wanted to detain the driver for illegally trading in illegal charcoal. Before they could impound the truck, they received a phone call from an official who delivered 'orders from above.' The officers were forced to release the driver and the suspicious goods. No one knows who gave those orders and why they were given in the first place.

During a presidential event in Nakuru in 2019, a young man, Dennis Ngaruiya, threw Uhuru into a frenzy of laughter with a captivating poem. After that joyous event, Uhuru reportedly promised to build a house for Ngaruiya's mother, Damaris Wambui Kamau, as a gesture of gratitude.

A house was indeed built and offered to the family, but Damaris rejected it saying it was a 'joke of a gift.' She claimed she had been

---

[132] Karuti, Kanyinga. From Jomo to Uhuru: How roadside declarations replaced research as the basis for national Policies," *Daily Nation*, November 22, 2015.

promised a more 'decent house.' To add to the confusion, the Rift Valley Regional Commissioner Chimwaga Mongo announced that Uhuru did not make such promise. "The president had only offered to pay school fees for the young man," he said.

Did Uhuru offer the money for 'a decent house' but part of the money was stolen? Or was it a misunderstanding of words? What followed was an 'order from above' to reallocate the house to someone else.

* * *

In 2020, President Uhuru ordered the Ministry of Agriculture to increase the price of unprocessed rice from KSh.45 to KSh.85 per kilogramme in response to complaints from farmers. A Kenyan economist, David Ndii, immediately classified that order as a 'roadside declaration.' He averred that the ministry had no powers to set prices of products, thus the presidential order was "intriguing."[133]

Ndii had similar views about Uhuru's order to the Kenya Cooperative Creameries (KCC) to increase farm-gate price of milk. He wondered why Uhuru chose to "personally wade into the milk farmers' woes," linking it to what he called Uhuru "family's cartelisation of the processed milk industry." That was a direct reference to the Kenyattas who reportedly owned the biggest share of the milk processing sector.

It is obvious, therefore, that 'orders from above' is well and alive. So, when Deputy President Ruto said in January 2020, that the concept had disappeared after the promulgation of the 2010 constitution, he was not being truthful. "There are no more 'orders from above," he had said, adding, "All decisions must be in writing." He told civil servants to stop obeying presidential orders from above without written authorisation from the president. Yet Uhuru continued to give directions from wherever he was and whenever he felt.

---

[133] Ndii, David. "The era of roadside policy declarations is back," *Elephant*, February 20, 2020.

And then there is what writers call 'Accept and move on' a concept in which Kenyans are urged to forget both the bad and the good of the past. Presidential elections in Kenya have always been problematic. In 2017, when Raila lost to Uhuru in a disputed election, and his supporters took to the streets to protest, Jubilee stalwarts were quick to tell Raila to 'accept and move on' and wait for the next elections. Raila hit back saying some of his supporters had been killed, "Yet they have the audacity to come and advise us to forget and move on?"

"It [Accept and move on] is an ugly and dismissive phrase that tells people that regardless of the problems they may have with the officially declared outcome of an election, they should just suck it up and carry on."[134] The mantra is repeated until everything looks like a distant memory.[135] It appears Kenyans were being asked to accept excesses without question.

JUDICIARY RESPONSE

Uhuru's disobedience of court orders was invariably met by what seemed to be a revenge onslaught from the judiciary. Courts turned down numerous of Uhuru's executive orders as a demonstration of their opposition to the president's anti-judiciary and anti-constitution stance.

In 2019, Judge Hellen Wasilwa, of the Employment Labour Relations court, quashed the nomination of two appointees to the National Land Commission (NLC). A former minister, Esther Murugi, and a former MP, Tiya Galgalo, had already been vetted by a selection panel of parliament but were refused a seat in the commission after Wasilwa ruled that their appointment was "unconstitutional." The judge said that their nomination flouted the principles of appointments in the civil service. "In the circumstances,

---

[134] Gathara, Patrick. "No, America should not 'accept and move on,'" *Al Jazeera*, February 1, 2021.

[135] Odero, Norbert. "Accept and move on: The handshake's hollow cure for decades of communal loss and grief," The *Elephant*, March 8, 2019.

I find the said nomination invalid, null and void, and proceed to quash their nominations accordingly," Justice Wasilwa ruled.

However, a few months later, the two got their jobs back after the government won on appeal. The Court of Appeal ruled that since the two had already been nominated as NLC commissioners, proper methods of their removal should have been applied. The ruling seemed to suggest that the lower court had no jurisdiction over the matter.

In 2020, the Court of Appeal declared the contract between Kenya Railways Corporation (KRC) and the China Bridges Railway Corporation (CBRC) illegal. Judges Martha Koome (now Chief Justice), Gatembu Kairu, and Jamila Mohammed, declared the multi-billion-shilling contract illegal because it failed to adhere to procurement regulations. The court ruled that KRC violated the constitution and the provisions of the Public Procurement and Disposal Act, 2005, which mandated that public entities must acquire goods and services in a manner which was "fair, equitable, transparent, competitive and cost effective."

On May 11, 2020, the High Court stopped Uhuru from placing constitutional commissions and independent bodies under the control of the executive branch. The court ruled that placing the Judiciary Service Commission (JSC), the Public Service Commission (PSC), and the EACC, among others (39 in total) under the executive was illegal. Uhuru had mandated through an executive order, that the institutions be placed under the control of the AG and related cabinet secretaries. Constitutional experts said Uhuru's move violated the fundamental law and infringed on the independence of the commissions.

The Law Society of Kenya (LSK) had sued the AG and the Head of Public Service claiming Uhuru's action was illegal and unconstitutional. It said the order violated the doctrine of separation of powers and interfered with the institutional and structural independence of the judicial arm of government. Justice James Makau ruled that it was possible Uhuru had misused his power as president. Such an exercise, he said, had to be done through a referendum.

In mid-2019, Uhuru, perhaps in retaliation, defiantly refused to approve 41 judges recommended by JSC for appointment as judges of the High Court, the Court of Appeal, the Employment and Labour Relations Court, and the Environment and Lands Court. That was despite orders issued by two separate courts compelling him to officially appoint and swear-in the judges. It also followed a sweeping condemnation of the executive by Chief Justice David Maraga. But Uhuru insisted that he would not appoint judges "with questionable character." The AG, Kihara Kariuki, said the president's refusal was within the law, but neither Uhuru nor Kariuki provided evidence against the accused judges.

When he finally succumbed to pressure from the legal fraternity, Uhuru gazetted only 34 judges on June 3, 2021, and omitted six: Justices Joel Ngugi, Aggrey Muchelule, Weldon Korir, George Odunga, Judith Omange, and Evens Makori, "for failing to meet the required threshold." Critics excoriated him for "endeavouring to claw back some of the powers that were taken away [from the executive] by the 2010 constitution."[136]

In October 2021, the High Court ordered Uhuru to appoint the six judges within 14 days, failure of which the judges would be deemed to have been appointed and would be sworn in by the Chief Justice (CJ). The government went to the Court of Appeal which suspended the order from the High Court, pending a ruling on November 19. When that day came, the Court of Appeal barred the newly appointed CJ Martha Koome from swearing in the judges.

More confusion was injected into the matter when CJ Koome supported Uhuru on his stand to reject the six judges. She went to the appellant court to dispute the High Court decision, saying she didn't want to appoint and swear in the judges. As at the beginning of 2022, the six judges had not yet been sworn in.

But in a surprise about turn, Koome on June 20, 2022, called for the impeachment of the president for violating the constitution. What was perplexing was the timing of the call. Why did the chief

---

[136] Yusuf, Mohammed. "Kenya's judiciary puts executive on the spot over appointment of judges," *VOA*, June 8, 2020.

justice wait so long to make that proposal? And why didn't she initiate the impeachment move herself instead of passing on the matter to the Court of Appeal. It was clear that with two months to go before Uhuru left office, it would have been impossible to achieve the removal of the President. Moreover, parliament was not in session. It had adjourned indefinitely in readiness for the general elections. But even if parliament had been recalled, it would have been impossible to get the one-third support from MPs as required by the constitution. Although the following day Koome tried to walk back on her remarks, the chief justice's position on the matter had become as clear as day.

Relations between the executive and the judiciary worsened when on June 1, 2021, Uhuru lashed out at what he called "irresponsible rulings," by the judiciary. "From nullification of a presidential election in 2017 to an attempt to stop the will of the people as expressed through BBI, the judiciary has tested our constitutional limits," he told the Madaraka Day crowd in Kisumu.

Uhuru was clearly frustrated. He called judges "crooks." Interestingly, he did not condemn them when the Supreme Court ruled in his favour and dismissed petitions challenging the re-run elections of October 2017 which Raila boycotted. He was then jubilant and full of praise for them. Even his supporters were not happy with the BBI court ruling. They took to the streets to demand the resignation of the six Supreme Court judges who presided over the case. But the LSK and other civic bodies warned that Uhuru's overarching comments undermined the judiciary.

On June 8, 2020 – five months after his retirement, Justice Maraga could no longer take Uhuru's punches at the judiciary lying down, even though he was no longer in office. He held a television interview and lashed out at the president accusing him of grave constitutional violations. Maraga blamed Uhuru for disregarding court orders, failing to approve the appointment of new judges, and acting in a manner likely to suggest that the president's agenda was to diminish the stature of the judiciary. He added that members of the judiciary were prepared "to pay the ultimate price to protect the constitution and the rule of law." That was the harshest criticism of the executive anyone had made on matters to do with the judiciary's independence. Maraga, a devout Seventh Day Adventist (SDA), won worldwide acclaim for quashing the 2017 presidential elections.

There was another ruling that got under Uhuru's skin. In May 2021, the High Court trashed some government appointments Uhuru had made in June 2018. The president had nominated 128 people – some of them election losers – to public service positions in government and parastatals.

In a case filed by two NGOs, Katiba Institute, and the Africa Centre for Open Governance (AfriCog), the High Court said proper procedures were not followed in making the appointments. The court ruled further that the exercise was not transparent, and not competition-based, as stipulated in the constitution. Justices Jessie Lesit, Chacha Mwita, and Lucy Njuguna, said "Kenyans desired those appointments be made in an open, transparent, and inclusive manner, considering the marginalised and people with disabilities. Since the appointments did not comply with those principles, they were unconstitutional and invalid," the judges said.

Uhuru did not agree with the ruling and therefore did not nullify the appointments, another example of impunity and abuse of office by President Uhuru. But the appointment of chief administrative secretaries (CASs) – a step down from principal secretaries - was the first in which a large group of people were given positions at one go. It is doubtful that the president considered or even cared about the financial implication of such a unilateral decision.

POLICE BRUTALITY

The Kenya police inherited everything that was bad in the colonial police force. And just like in colonial times, people fear police officers in independent Kenya. They do not respect them. In all administrations, Kenyan leaders used law enforcement agencies as personal tools to enhance and maintain their interests. They used them for political reasons, to intimidate opponents, and to sustain the "big-man syndrome." There were many occasions where Presidents

Mzee Kenyatta, Moi, Kibaki, and Uhuru, used unlawful force to break up protests and political meetings of opponents.

Youths in slum areas also suffered from police brutality. Police consistently violated the National Police Service Act of 2011 by rounding up slum dwellers and subjecting them to torture and murder, mainly without any convincing reason. The Act says that the use of lethal force is only justified when used strictly in unavoidable situations to protect life. It also says that arbitrary or abusive use of force and firearms constitutes a criminal offence. But rarely are police officers prosecuted for engaging in unbecoming behaviour.

During the protests in Kisumu against the results of the August 2017 presidential election, six women were raped and 171 tortured reportedly by police, according to Governor Anyang Nyong'o. The Kenya National Commission on Human Rights (KNCHR) put the number of women molested before, during, and after the 2017 elections at 201. Fifty-four-point-five percent of those incidences were blamed on Kenyan security forces.

A local NGO released a shocking report indicating that at least 107 Kenyans were killed by police in 2019. Most of the fatalities were of young men between the ages of 18 and 35 residing in informal settlements.

One death that epitomised the extent of police brutality on innocent citizens was that of infant Samantha Pendo. The baby was in the arms of her mother in a slum area of Kisumu when police burst in and started shooting. That was on the night of August 10, 2017, as Uhuru opponents disputed the 2017 presidential election results. In trying to arrest troublemakers in the area, police broke into the house of Joseph Abaja, the father, and Lencer Achieng, the mother, and smashed Pendo's head with a club. The killing outraged the nation.

Later, an inquest was conducted, and a court ruled that the National Police Service (NPS) was liable for the death of the child even though no one police officer was blamed for the killing. Further investigations were ordered, but there was no prosecution in a court of law. President Uhuru did not say a word about the sensational killings, amid public disgust.

KILLING FIELDS

Tsavo National Park is one of the world's most renowned safari destinations. Once, it was a game hunting ground for the rich and famous from all over the world. In recent years, however, it has also become a graveyard of people mysteriously murdered in other places and dumped there. Interestingly, there have been no witnesses to the junking of the bodies.

The expansive park, known for its huge herds of elephants, joined Ngong Forest, outside Nairobi, Kabiruini Forest in Nyeri, Muguga Forest in Kiambu, Yala River in Nyanza, and some rivulets in some other parts of Central Kenya, as places of the dead.

On December 30, 2014, the badly mutilated body of Meshack Yebei was found at Tsavo National Park. Yebei had disappeared from his home in Eldoret a few days earlier with reports saying he had been abducted by unknown people. Yebei was one of those listed as witnesses in a case involving Deputy President Ruto and four others at The Hague on charges of crimes against humanity. It could not be determined whether Yebei's murder had any links to the case. When his body was found, his eyes had been gouged out, his tongue cut out, and his private parts mutilated. He also had a bullet wound on his head.[137]

In February 2020, two decomposing human bodies were found at Tsavo National Park by Kenya Wildlife Service (KWS) rangers. They were naked and had torture marks. In March 2020, four more human bodies surfaced in the park. Some of the victims had been strangled to death using ropes. Others had been suffocated using paper bags. At least one had been burnt by acid. They were all Somali. It was a coarse and grotesque scene.

In May 2020, another body of a murder victim was found in Tsavo. It was that of Cynthia Mwikali Mukio, who had gone missing after a visit to Machakos. Mukio, a former employee at Whitesands Beach Resort Hotel, was killed elsewhere and her body, eyes gouged and tongue missing, dumped at Maungu in Tsavo East.

---

[137] Mutiga, Murithi & David Smith. "Discovery of witness's mutilated body feeds accusations of state killings," *The Guardian*, January 5, 2015.

And then there is the Muguga Forest in Kiambu County. That is where the body of a top official of the Independent Electoral and Boundaries Commission (IEBC), Christopher Chege Msando, was found. He had gone missing on 2 August 2017. The next day, he was found dead, and nearby was the body of a 21-year-old medical student, Maryanne Carol Ndumbu. Msando was strangled. His body had serious injuries meaning, he was tortured before being killed. The day before his disappearance he had appeared on TV to assure the country of free, fair, and credible elections that year.

Victims of those brutal murders had little in common.

Ngong Forest has become so infamous when it comes to dead bodies that families of missing persons usually start their search there before scouting morgues. Bodies of people, some as young as two years and others as old as 50 years have been found in the thick, sprawling, Ngong Forest, located only 18 km from the capital Nairobi.

On March 15, 2021, the body of the National Lands Commission Deputy Communications Director, Jennifer Wambua, was discovered there. She had been sexually assaulted and strangled to death.

Two months later, a US-based businessperson, Bashir Mahmoud, was kidnapped as he drove out of a restaurant in one leafy neighbourhood in Nairobi. A few days later, his car was found burnt to ashes in Ngong Forest. His body was never found.

In January 2022, dozens of bodies of unknown individuals stuffed in gunny sacks were retrieved from Yala River.

Another graveyard is the area along the Naivasha-Mai Mahiu Road where almost two dozen bodies were discovered dumped, in 2021. Many of those killed, including journalist Gatonye Gathura, whose body was found in Kihoto estate, were strangled. There was evidence that the people were murdered elsewhere, and their remains disposed of there.

Some of the suspected extra-judicial killings were more brazen and open. In January 2011, officers from the Criminal Investigations Department (CID) confronted six people along Lang'ata road. They ordered the men to lie face down (*Laleni vizuri tuwamalize! Lie down properly so that we can finish you*), then pumped numerous bullets into their bodies. It was a direct, cold-blooded murder, a deliberate, calculated unprovoked shooting to death of suspects who had clearly surrendered.[138]

Human rights organisations have persistently pointed a finger at the Anti-Terrorism Police Unit (ATPU), a police squad known for extra-judicial killings, as the one behind the killings. The ATPU has been associated with murders of not only known jihadists but also people deemed to be "enemies" of the state.

The most notable political killings occurred before, during, and after, the 2007 presidential elections. The Commission of Inquiry on Post-Election Violence (CIPEV), known as the Waki Commission, which investigated police activities then, reported nine-hundred-sixty-two police shootings, 405 of which were fatal. Often, police were prone to panic especially during public demonstrations and used live bullets when other less lethal containment measures could have been adequate. The commission concluded that gunfire was the single most common cause of death and assumed most deaths were caused by police.

But it was during the reign of President Uhuru that random extra-judicial killings peaked as the terror group Al-Shabaab upped its attacks on soft targets. Muslim youths suspected to collaborate or sympathise with the Somalia-based terror group became the major targets of police murders. Al Jazeera TV in its expose "*Inside Kenya's Death Squad*," interviewed a number of alleged Kenyan law enforcement officials who admitted participating in killings "on instructions of outside forces." The officials did not however, name those forces. But their instructions were clear: "You kill first before you are killed."

Several police units were identified as being responsible for most of the murders examined here. First, it was the Anti-Motor Vehicle Theft Unit (AMVTU) which was established in 1995. The unit was rebranded the Flying Squad. In 2019, the Flying Squad was disbanded and replaced by the Sting Squad Headquarters (SS), an elite quick response unit.

---

[138] Kiai, Mugambi. Extrajudicial Killings in Kenya, Open Society Foundation, January 30, 2011.

Then, there is the Rapid Reaction Team (RRT), part of the GSU's Recce Company. A *Declassified UK* investigation revealed that RRT was "set up, equipped, trained, and is guided on tactical counter-terror operations by America's Central Intelligence Agency (CIA)." That was the commando unit that raided the house of a motor-cycle rider, Mohamed 'Modi' Mwatsumiro, at Ngombeni village in Kwale, in August 2019. Police claimed Mwatsumiro threw a grenade at the raiding party, but it failed to explode. He was shot and killed. Seven bullets had penetrated his body: two through his left elbow, one through the right forearm, two through his chest, and two others through his left upper jaw. Authorities claimed Mwatsumiro was part of the group that attacked DusitD2 hotel in Nairobi in January 2019.[139]

The RRT acts on intelligence collected by the CIA, the NIS, and the British Secret Intelligence Service (SIS), better known as M16. RRT specialises in eliminating Muslim radicals, hence its moniker, 'the elimination unit.' "It's the intelligence agencies identifying the threat, figuring a way out to mitigate the threat, figuring out that this is going to be a law enforcement and state [capture] or not [kill] and then dealing with it,"[140] a former deputy chief (operations) of the CIA's counter-terrorism Centre, Henry Crumpton, said.

The Recce squad company is one of the most feared security units in Kenya. Recce officers undergo rigorous training both locally and overseas to deal with all types of confrontations. Part of its duties is to guard the president. The other is to conduct high-risk attacks such as the terrorist assaults. Within it is the Sky Marshal Unit comprising of undercover officers on board flights to deal with air jacking or other criminal acts in the sky. Recce officers are well armed with high calibre assault weapons.

Other known units within the National Police Service (NPS) over the years included *Kwekwe* and *Alfa Romeo*. It is common for authorities to disband one killer unit only to replace it with another with a different name.

---

[139] Shabibi, Namir. "Revealed: The CIA and MI6's secret war in Kenya," *The Daily Maverick*, August 20, 2020.
[140] Ibid.

The most notorious unit of all, however, is the US-trained ATPU which has largely been responsible for killings of Muslim youths it thought supported Al-Shabaab. Its duties are listed as detecting, preventing, and investigating crime. But it specialises in counter-terrorism response. It has been involved in beatings of terrorist suspects, renditions, and disappearance of people especially Moslem activists suspected to have links with terror groups. The ATPU was particularly active during Uhuru's term in office, arresting and deporting elements thought to be a threat to Kenya's security.

The ATPU was singled out by several human rights organisations for carrying out the assassination of Sheikh Aboud Rogo, the Muslim chief cleric of Masjid Musa Mosque in Mombasa, in August 2012. He was one of the most controversial clerics in the region. His car was showered with bullets as he drove his wife to hospital along the Mombasa/Malindi road. The murder exhibited excruciating police cruelty and injustice against Muslim faithful. The person who took over from Rogo, Sheikh Ibrahim Omar, was gunned down in the same way in October 2013.

On April 1, 2014, Abubakar Shariff Ahmed alias Makaburi, another chief cleric at Masjid Musa Mosque, became the third senior Muslim religious leader to be killed by police. He was eliminated in daylight as he left the law courts inside the Shimo la Tewa Maximum Security Prison, on the outskirts of Mombasa. He was suspected to be an Al-Shabaab contact person and coordinator of attacks in Kenya. An officer attached to ATPU confirmed that Makaburi's murder was "planned in Nairobi by very top, high ranking police officers and government officials.... The Government did it,"[141] he said without blinking an eye.

It "was not a stand-alone case [but] a pattern of brutal tactics by an elite Anti-Terrorism Police Unit (ATPU) targeting men accused of being part of the jihadist group Al-Shabaab," said a 2021 media investigation report by journalists John-Allan Namu, Mohamed Ali, Sam Munia, and Kasim Mohamed. Suspects were shot dead

---

[141] Exclusive: Kenyan counter-terrorism police admit to extrajudicial killings," *Al Jazeera*, December 8, 2014.

in public places, abducted from vehicles and courtrooms, severely beaten during arrest, detained in isolated blocks, and denied contact with their families and access to lawyers.[142] The people at the top saw nothing wrong in dolling out death to terror suspects, civilians, and even children.[143] It was callous and a monstrous travesty of justice.

The unrelenting police killings raised a storm of public indignation to the point that on December 10, 2016, the Human Rights Watch (HRW) wrote officially to President Uhuru asking him to appoint a judicial commission of inquiry into human rights violations. The letter, signed by eight civil rights organisations, blamed security forces for escalating extra-judicial killings with the excuse of conducting counter-terrorism operations. The HRW singled out the Kenya Police, the Kenya Defence Forces, and the Kenya Wildlife Service, as perpetrators of human rights violations in the country.

On August 18, 2021, Abdulhakim Sagar was abducted from outside a mosque in Mombasa Old Town by people who identified themselves as police officers. Authorities could not explain Sagar's whereabouts. For weeks, relatives searched for him in morgues and police stations, but their efforts were futile. Sagar was released a month later just as mysteriously as he was abducted. There was no explanation from anyone as to the reasons for his capture.

Another mysterious abduction was that of Dr Abdiwahab Sheikh Abdisamad, a prominent expert on regional affairs. As a group of people watched, Dr Abdisamad was grabbed by four men as he walked along a street in Nairobi's CBD on September 8, 2021, hauled into a pick-up truck, and driven away. He briefly struggled to free himself from the hooded men but was overpowered. It was assumed that the abductors were police officers because one was carrying a pair of handcuffs.

Police neither denied nor confirmed if they were involved in Dr Abdisamad's abduction. There were also reports that the abduction

---

[142] Human Rights Watch, Summary Report, 2015.
[143] Odula, Tom. "In Kenya, Police Kill Suspects with near-Impunity," *Associated Press*, December 5, 2014.

could have been carried out by Somalia government agents angry at Dr Abdisamad's opposition to some elements in Somalia. Similarly, those reports could not be verified.

For almost two weeks, Abdisamad's whereabouts were unknown. On September 21, he was released. He refused to say who had captured him or where he had been held, for fear of another visit from his tormentors. Such disappearances left families and friends of victims in anguish and feeling hopeless. Sagar and Abdisamad were lucky. Most abductees never returned.

One of the lucky victims of police brutality was DP Ruto's digital manager, Dennis Itumbi. Itumbi was abducted, savagely beaten but survived the ordeal. He was abducted by unknown people, assaulted, before being dumped on the outskirts of Nairobi City. He crawled to a road and was identified by a *boda boda* (motorcycle) rider who took him to hospital.

No one knows who grabbed Itumbi as he came out of a barbershop in the city. While Ruto opponents celebrated the brutal attack, many fretted about the security of government critics. *Daily Nation* columnist, Macharia Gaitho, wrote that Itumbi's attack should worry Kenyans. "What Mr. Itumbi underwent must serve as a warning that political repression remains a clear and present danger; and a reminder that eternal vigilance remains the key to liberty."

The National Security Council (NSC), chaired by President Uhuru, and whose membership includes high-ranking government officials, is the only government body that approves high-level security operations like those narrated above. Members of the NSC, and indeed the president, must have known about police excesses. It is the duty of the NSC to ensure that the rule of law is respected and that government directives that are inconsistent with laid out regulations are not followed.[144] But the perpetual silence by senior government officers meant they condoned the killings.

---

[144] Sossin, Lorne. Commission of Inquiry into the Sponsorship Program and Advertising Activities, Defining Boundaries: The Constitutional Argument for Bureaucratic Independence and its Implications for the Accountability of the Public Service, 2006, p. 25/30.

Another sensational case of police brutality was that of lawyer Willie Kimani, his client Josephat Mwenda, and their taxi driver, Joseph Muiruri, in June 2016. Willie was a human rights defender. As the trio left a courthouse outside Nairobi city where Willie had gone to defend Mwenda on a case against a police officer, they were trailed by unknown people and kidnapped.

For a whole week their whereabouts were unknown. Their bodies were later found dumped in a river with the skulls broken. Four Administration Police officers, Fredrick Leliman, Stephen Cheburet, Silvia Wanjiku, and Leonard Mwangi were arrested on July 18, 2016, and charged with the murder.

Covid-19 Murders

On the first day of Covid-19-imposed curfew on March 29, 2020, eighteen-year-old Ibrahim Onyango was killed by police in Dandora while on his way home from collecting plastics for recycling. It was past the 7 pm curfew time. Police severely beat him. He died from injuries the following day. Ten people were killed by police in the first ten days of the curfew, according to the Human Rights Watch (HRW).

As a matter of routine, police used colonial-era laws such as the Public Order Act to arrest curfew violators. That was the same law used by Mzee Kenyatta and President Moi to restrict people from holding meetings and demonstrations.

Hussein Moyo, father of a 13-year-old boy, Yassin Hussein, who was a victim of police brutality on March 30, 2020, explains the general scenario applied by police past curfew hours: "The police arrive yelling…They beat and rob people; they also throw tear gas into our houses." In the case of Moyo, a bullet ripped through the boy's intestines as he stood on a balcony, killing him instantly.[145] The police had entered the neighbourhood to enforce curfew restrictions.

---

[145] "Kenyan President Apologies for Police Violence During Curfew," *Al Jazeera*, April 1, 2020.

The officer allegedly responsible for the killing, Duncan Ndiema, was arrested and charged with murder. He pleaded not guilty.

On March 31, 2020, Kenyans watched a video in horror as a police officer pumped bullets into the bodies of two youths in Eastleigh, Nairobi. The execution was conducted in broad daylight. Later, the same officer went to Mathare slums and killed two more youths in a comparable manner. Both incidents were videotaped by onlookers and posted on social media. No legal action was taken against the killer police officer.

Around the same time, a mysterious character identified as "Hessy wa Dandora" began posting pictures of people murdered by police. The pictures were so horrifying that many suspected it was the work of either a rogue police officer or an ex-service officer who was sending a message to criminals to watch out. Another video posted on social media showed two young men merrily dancing to reggae music. One of them displayed a gun. 'Hessy' responded with a chilling warning: "I will get you!" It didn't take long before the two lads were murdered. No one took responsibility.

On November 18, 2020, a 19-year-old, Alex, and a friend were walking home in Mathare slums. It was 10.30 pm, 30 minutes after the extended government-set Covid-19 curfew. Six police officers on patrol confronted them wanting to know where they were coming from and why they were breaking the curfew laws. The two said they were on their way home.

A notorious killer police officer known for his maniac ways fired ten bullets killing Alex instantly. His friend luckily survived the attack but was severely injured. Why did they kill Alex? Because he was a gangster, they claimed. His mother, Sarah Wangari, on her way to the shop came across Alex's body but police chased her away. An aggrieved Wangari denied that her son was a criminal.

President Uhuru later admitted that indeed, the police used excessive force to effect curfew restrictions, and apologised to Kenyans.

But Uhuru's apology meant nothing to the families of many victims, including the family of the two brothers who were killed by police for a curfew violation in August 2021. Benson Njiru Ndwiga,

22, and Emmanuel Mutura Ndwiga, 19, were arrested at Kianjokoma in Embu County for breaking the 10 pm curfew restrictions. They were never seen alive again. Their bodies were later found in the mortuary. Six police officers were indicted for that murder: Benson Mbuthia, Consolata Njeri, Martin Wanyama, Nicholas Sang, Lilian Cherono, and James Mwaniki.

Even though the Police Service is an independent entity, Kenyans expected the President to do something. Rarely did Uhuru speak on plans to combat crime, not even when presiding over graduation ceremonies of new police recruits. That left criminals feeling protected and the public wondering whether the president was even aware of what was going on in the country.

In 2018, in a move to streamline the Police Service, Uhuru enacted major reforms in the structure, command, control, and welfare of the National Police Service. The reforms followed a report of a task force chaired by Interior Cabinet Secretary Matiang'i. In the reforms, the Administration Police Service was integrated as general duty police officers under the command of the deputy inspector general of police. A unified police command of all police units from the regions to the patrol bases was also established. Better pay and improved housing for officers were also suggested. It had been expected that those reforms would instil more discipline and order in the Police Service. But that did not happen.

Numerous police officers have been arrested and charged with engaging in illegal activities, including bank robberies, burglaries, hiring out of government-issued weapons to criminals, and extortion. There have also been incidences where police officers helped colleagues to escape arrest.

In November 2018, EACC officers carried out a sting operation at Kabete. They offered a KSh.100,000 bribe in marked notes to two police officers to stop them from prosecuting a foreigner. The police officers took the bait. Once the anti-graft personnel had handcuffed the suspects, their colleagues from the Kabete Police Station appeared at the scene and fired several bullets at them. The culprits got away still handcuffed, and still carrying the trap money. The EACC did nothing and left empty-handed. Nothing was known of the fate of the police officers or the money.

In February 2021, ten police officers and four civilians were arrested on allegations of theft of government property, bribery, and robbery with violence. They were suspected of stealing 11 seamless pipes worth KSh.275,000 from a construction company. They were taken to court and charged.

There is also the absence of checks and balances when it comes to auditing police officers' work. The Internal Affairs Unit and the Independent Policing Oversight Authority (POA), whose responsibility is to provide civilian oversight, are "overwhelmed and dysfunctional." They ignore public complaints of police excesses and fail to provide civilian oversight over the work of the police.[146] There is also impunity and corruption which makes it difficult for victims to obtain justice. The National Coroners Service whose duty is to investigate the cause of any death caused by non-natural cause is, by all descriptions, moribund. There is also the ongoing problem of interference from the top, making it impossible for the two important bodies: the internal affairs unit and the POA to operate independently and to make sound, fair, and professional, judgements.

How did Kenya get to this stage? Blame it on colonialists? During the pre-independence era, police used tactics that were rough-and-ready at best and at times abusive....[147] Their operations were characterised by use of brute force to impose and maintain the colonial social order and exploitation.[148] They engaged in rape, sodomy, beatings, torture, and looting of property. All those evils are happening today.

If that is not enough, Kenyan police officers are also known to be belligerent. Take the example of one police officer in Kericho

---

[146] Kivoi, Douglas Lucas. "Why Violence is a Hallmark of Kenyan Policing. And What Needs to Change," *The Conversation,* June 5, 2020.

[147] Kyle, Keith. The Politics of the Independence of Kenya, MacMillan Press Ltd., 1999, p. 61.

[148] Gimode, Edwin. The Role of the Police in Kenya's Democratisation Process, in Kenya: The Struggle for Democracy, Godwin G. Murunga & Shadrack W. Nasongo, Godesria Book, 2007, p. 229.

who attacked a lady motorist on the New Year's Day in 2017. She shoved and hit the motorist in a fit of rage. Her callous handling of the civilian did not go well even with her seniors. She was suspended after people complained.

Even when the law gives them the option of police bonds, police officers revel in keeping suspects in their custody for as long as possible. Overall, they treat suspects with indignity. In 2012, a British national, Alexander Monson, caught smoking bhang, was found dead in a police cell in Diani. Four police officers were charged with manslaughter and sentenced to between 12 and 15 years in prison. The severe punishment was to send a message to others that courts would not tolerate misbehaviour in the force.

In colonial days, recruitment of police officers was based on loyalty to the crown not on merit. In fact, there was no formalised training. Today, people are hired not because they qualify but because they either bribe or know someone of influence in or outside the government. People in high places send relatives and friends to recruitment officers with chits and brown envelopes knowing well that such people lacked the necessary entry qualifications.

It is clear then that Kenya police inherited everything that was bad in the colonial police force. And just like in colonial times, people fear police officers in independent Kenya. They do not respect them.

PART IV
LOOTING

CHAPTER 10

Financial Wastage

In 2019, Kenyans faced a serious scarcity of money in circulation. Cash outside banks had reached KSh.157 billion which meant Kenyans were hoarding money at home instead of saving it in banks fearing looming economic shocks. Although the amount had dropped from the previous year, it was still substantial. Much of the money outside banks was held by individuals and by *chamas* in which members contributed regularly and alternately passed on the collections in a lump sum to one contributor after another, in turns. Forty-one percent of Kenyans use *chamas*, according to the Financial Sector Deepening Kenya (FSD Kenya), an independent trust. Then there are the money launderers and other crooks who hide millions of shillings in homes.

So, when Uhuru was told about the sharp decline of money in circulation, he called a meeting of senior government officials at State House to strategise on ways to stimulate the economy. During his brief remarks, Uhuru, in blithe sarcasm, asked: "Why are people 'broke' anyway? Why is it that there is no money in their pockets?" Officials were perplexed. Uhuru expected his 'subjects' to have cash because, he said, his government was spending billions of shillings in development projects. "That should put cash into people's pockets," he added.

What his audience should have told him – which they didn't - was that Kenyans were broke because a big chunk of their money was being squandered and stolen by corrupt government officials. The 2020 report of the office of the deputy director of public prosecutions (ODPP) showed public funds stolen through corrupt activities had increased from KSh.67.1 billion in 2017 to KSh.140.2 billion in 2019. They should also have told Uhuru that Kenyans didn't have money because of the high salaries paid to senior government officials, as well as MPs, Senators, and MCAs, and the exorbitant allowances they earn for all manner of activities.

For the record, KSh.253 billion was circulating outside the banking system as at December 2021, an all time high.

In 2014, President Uhuru declared war on the country's fast-growing public wage bill, saying the expenditure was "unsustainable and unacceptable." The number of government workers has been fluctuating over the years, so has been the wage bill. In 2021, the annual wage bill for the 884,600 government workers was KSh.526 billion, a drop of 12% from KSh.603 billion the previous year. However, Treasury officials predicted the amount will increase to KSh.550.7 billion by the year ending June 2023.

The wage bill was a major worry not only to the national government but also to the donor community. The high expenditure was partly attributed to the introduction of a bicameral parliament and a devolved system of government which created forty-seven counties. After the adoption of the 2010 constitution, the number of MPs went up from 222 to 349. There were also 67 posts of Senators and 1,450 positions of elected members of county sssemblies (MCAs). Seven-hundred-seventy-two posts of nominated MCAs were also created to meet the two-thirds gender rule.

The controller of budget alarmingly reported that parliament spent KSh.32 billion in non-essentials such as travel, conferences, and hospitality expenses in the 2018/2019 fiscal year. A whopping KSh.17.2 billion was spent on domestic and foreign trips by both elected and non-elected officials and KSh.9.8 billion on hospitality.

The president and his deputy alone gobbled KSh.704.4 million on local travel and KSh.196.6 million on foreign travel. Between July and December 2021, civil servants had spent KSh.6 billion on local trips alone, up from KSh.4.89 billion for the same period the previous year. The highest amount spent for local travel by government workers in a six-month period was KSh.5.6 billion in 2013.

In salaries, Uhuru earned KSh.1.2 million, his deputy KSh.1.1 million and cabinet secretaries KSh.800,000 each per month. In comparison, the Tanzania president earns KSh.400,000 per month, while the Ugandan president is paid KSh.110,000 per month, making Uhuru the highest paid leader in East Africa.

In March 2014, Uhuru announced a 20% salary cut for himself and his deputy and a 10% reduction in pay for cabinet secretaries and heads of parastatals. The government did not indicate whether the salary cuts had any effect, if any, on the cumulative wage bill.

As Uhuru worked to find a solution to the increased government recurrent expenditure, MPs were at it again. In 2018, they began paying themselves a monthly allowance of KSh.250,000 for 'accommodation and house allowance,' without approval from the Salaries and Remuneration Commission (SRC). The matter ended up in court. Both the High Court and the Court of Appeal dismissed the MPs arguments on the case filed by civil rights activist Okiya Omtatah and the SRC. The Court of Appeal ordered each legislator to refund KSh.6.5 million – pocketed between 2018 and December 2020 – to the exchequer.

About the same time when the court was making the decision to penalize the MPs, the SRC was proposing new salary increases for the legislators and speakers of the two houses of parliament. In the proposal, an MP's salary was to go up from KSh.621,250 to KSh.710,000 per month. Each MP was also to be given an additional KSh.88,750 per month, thus raising the parliamentary wage bill up to KSh.3.5 billion from KSh.3.1 billion.

It was also proposed that the sitting allowances for legislators would increase. Committee chairpersons were to earn KSh.15,000 per sitting up from KSh.10,000, their deputies KSh.12,000 up from KSh.8,000, and MPs KSh.7,500 up from KSh.5,000. The SRC also proposed to increase salaries for MCAs from KSh.259,875 to KSh.404,250 per month.

The SRC proposal did not touch civil servants' salaries ostensibly because the government did not have money due to "Covid-19, wage bill ratios, investment priorities and the financial constraints faced by the government," officials explained.[149] The proposal was subject to approval by the public.

As his tenure ended, Uhuru was assured of a KSh.72 million gratuity from the public coffers for the years he served as president.

HIGH WAGE BILL A THREAT

The former chairman of the Public Service Commission (PSC), Stephen Kirogo, now deceased, warned that Kenya's huge wage bill posed a major threat to the economy because it crowded out public investments, and made it impossible for the government to invest in development.[150]

In 2014, the country received US$2 billion (KSh.202 billion) after floating the Eurobond. The highly oversubscribed sovereign bond, according to President Uhuru, was a "vote of confidence" in Kenya. He said the funds would cut the government's local borrowing requirement and help the government reduce interest rates. Although the government said the money would go towards infrastructure development, questions lingered over how it was used.

"Nobody knows whose account the money ended up in or whether it came into Kenya at all," Opposition leader Raila told reporters during a feisty press conference in January 2016.

The government maintained that the Eurobond proceeds were safe. The reason why the money did not show in the budget that year, officials said, was because it was allocated for the 2015/2016 financial year. The EACC agreed with the government that there was no evidence that the money had been lost. However, the auditor general, in his 2015 report, called out the government for breaking

---

[149] Odhiambo, Moses. "SRC gives huge pay rise to MPs and county bosses," Star, December 15, 2021.
[150] Muchira, Njiraini. "Kenya moves to tame rising wage bill with three-year-contracts," *The East African*, June 25, 2019.

the law by banking the money in a special Eurobond account at the Central Bank of Kenya (CBK) instead of depositing it in the national Exchequer bank account.

As revenue from tax collections continued to fall behind estimates and projections by KRA, the government floated another Eurobond in 2018 to raise an additional KSh.200 billion. That issue was followed by another bond floated in 2019 which raised US$2.08 billion (KSh.228 billion). The money was earmarked for development projects, budget support, and the refinancing of US$750 million (KSh.82 billion) debt from the first Eurobond issue.

Kenya's fourth bond in 2021 raised US$1 billion (KSh.108 billion). The 12-year bond is to be repaid at an interest of 6.3%. Part of it was for settling maturing Chinese debts. Although the economy was struggling due to numerous factors, both local and international, Kenyan officials, including Deputy President Ruto, insisted the economy was sound.

Come, we go!

There was also a massive expenditure on travel. The habit of lawmakers traversing the world, sometimes without any meaningful reasons, existed since the Moi days. MPs routinely burrowed into the internet searching for conferences bearing the slightest relevance to their committee work. They would then contact conference organisers and canvass for formal invitations. They would then travel first class and earn allowances. It's as simple as that.

In 2021, there was a debate in the senate and a conversation in the social media as to why a group of senators travelled all the way to the USA to investigate the crash of Boeing 737 MAX 8 in Ethiopia. The accident on March 10, 2019, killed 157 people, among them 32 Kenyans. Members of the parliamentary legal affairs committee went to the Boeing headquarters in Seattle, Washington, to get answers about compensation for families of the crash victims.

Yet the information they sought could have been readily and easily obtained either via e-mail or from Ethiopian authorities. But the legislators spent millions of shillings on first class travel and came back with "zero findings and zero recommendations." Senator Enoch Wambua criticised his colleagues for wasting taxpayers' money.

That same week, the controller of budget, Margaret Nyakang'o, had reported that MPs and senators had spent KSh.703 million on foreign trips during the three months ending in June 2021.

There were 247 remunerative and facilitative allowances during Uhuru's reign up from 31 in 1999. Those allowances meant enormous amounts in disbursements. In addition, KSh.14.1 billion was spent on domestic and overseas travel by ministries and departments during the 2020/2021 fiscal year, notwithstanding the Covid-19 travel restrictions.

Though the amount was lower than the KSh.14.6 billion spent the previous year, it was nevertheless excessive, prompting the controller of budget to issue caution about high travel costs especially for foreign trips.

In 2013, Deputy President Ruto leased an executive jet to fly to Nigeria, Congo, Gabon, and Ghana, while on a presidential assignment. The Parliamentary Accounts Committee (PAC) under the chair of MP Ababu Namwamba questioned the circumstances under which the Bombardier 850 Challenger aircraft was hired and how much it cost the taxpayers. The auditor general told the PAC that the plane was hired on instructions from President Uhuru. And while Ruto's office claimed the hire cost KSh.18.6 million, media reports quoted a figure of KSh.100 million.

The Ethics and Anti-Corruption Commission (EACC) which investigated the matter said no money was lost since the trip was sanctioned by the president. It also claimed the estimate of KSh.100 million quoted by the media was exaggerated, and that only KSh.18.6 million was paid by the exchequer. Many Kenyans thought the government was imprudent and thoughtless in its use of public funds.

As for the counties, six jurisdictions, Bomet, Baringo, Nandi, Samburu, Uasin Gishu, and Nakuru, had the highest wage bills out of the 47 counties, surpassing the 35% limit set by the Public

Finance Management regulations of 2015. For example, Uasin Gishu collected KSh.7.9 billion but spent KSh.3.02 billion on salaries.

Proposals by an audit team in 2018 led by then Auditor General Edward Ouko to reduce public spending did not receive the support of the national government. The proposals included reducing the number of MPs, cutting-back on the number of counties, and putting a cap on the salaries of the president and MPs at KSh.500,000 and KSh.300,000, respectively. However, some of the recommended changes would have required a national referendum.

Moreover, as more workers reached the retirement age of 60 years, the pension expenditure automatically goes up. Pension costs rose from US$271 million (KSh.30 billion) during Uhuru's first year in office to almost US$1 billion (KSh.110 billion) in 2019/2020 fiscal year.

In 2022, the Treasury expected to spend KSh.146 billion for the 300,000 pensioners. At least 20,000 civil servants retire every year. On top of that, Kenya must pay more than KSh.100 million yearly to 277,000 British pensioners who served in the country during colonial times. It is anticipated that the payments would continue until 2050 when, it is expected, all the pensioners would no longer be alive.

Fund for Agenda Four

In June 2018, President Uhuru announced a mandatory housing levy for all employees to fund his Affordable Housing Scheme under his Big Four Agenda. The agenda was part of Uhuru's ambitious plan to provide 500,000 low-cost houses, ensure food security, provide universal and affordable healthcare, and boost manufacturing. The four pillars were intended to be finalised before the end of his tenure in 2022.

Uhuru's housing levy plan required employees to contribute 0.5%, later increased to 1.5%, of their monthly basic salary, provided the amount did not exceed KSh.5,000. Each employer was to match the contribution of the employee with an equal amount. Other employees could also make a voluntary contribution of KSh.2,000 per month to the scheme.

Employers were to remit the money to the National Housing Development Fund (NHDF) by the 9th of each succeeding month along with other payroll statutory deductions. The scheme was scheduled to start in May 2019, with private firms building the houses and selling them out to qualified individuals based on a lottery system.

The announcement immediately got a backlash from the Central Organisation of Trade Unions (COTU), the Federation of Kenya Employers (FKE), and the Consumers Federation of Kenya (CoFEK). The three bodies went to court claiming that the levy would be an added burden on workers and employers.

The protest against the mandatory levy was so loud and so contentious that Uhuru was forced to back down on the original order. In December 2019, he announced that the scheme would be voluntary and not forced to "ensure that the implementation of the programme was not derailed any further,"

The protests aside, Uhuru's levy dug out something even more revealing. Economist David Ndii claimed controversially that the levy stood to benefit at least four companies owned by the Kenyattas. "At least four Kenyatta family companies… stand to benefit directly from the affordable housing schemes," he claimed in a tweet in April 2019. Included in the tweet were names of the four companies that specialised in construction panels, low-cost housing technology, and wood products. There was no reaction from the Kenyattas on this revelation.

Equally worrying were fears of corruption. Similar programmes, including the National Hospital Insurance Fund (NHIF), have over the years, suffered from rampant graft perpetrated by senior government officials and private cartels. For example, in 2002, the NHIF started work on a multi-storey car park in Nairobi. The original cost of the project was KSh.910 million. By the time it was completed in 2008, the cost had increased to KSh.4 billion, a 337% increase.

The public accounts committee (PAC) suspected graft and asked the EACC to investigate, but no action appeared to have been taken against those responsible for the discrepancy. This is only one example of how member contributions could be misused in ventures such as the housing levy.

Covid-19 issues

On March 25, 2020, President Uhuru announced a 10-hour country-wide lockdown to contain the spread of the Covid-19 pandemic. The lockdown involved the closure of schools, a ban on political gatherings, and the cancellation of international flights. Only essential service workers were permitted to be out on the streets during the curfew hours of between 7 pm and 5 am. Kenyans who were caught outside their residency areas went into a panic. For example, Nairobi residents caught in Mombasa could not travel back and vice versa, and those who had gone visiting their rural homes could not return to their workplaces in cities and towns. It was total chaos.

Before Covid-19, Kenya's economy was "robust and resilient."[151] It was rated as "one of the fastest growing economies in Africa, with an annual average growth of 5.9% between 2010 and 2018."[152] However, in 2019, the economic growth dropped to 5.4%, though it was projected to reach 6.2% in the 2020/2021 financial year, according to Brookings Institution, the Washington-based research body. But instead, it grew by -0.1% in 2020.[153] However, that changed dramatically in 2021. Bloomberg reported that Kenya's

---

[151] Onsomu, Eldah, Boaz Munga, & Violet Nyabaro. « The Impact of Covid-19 on Industries Without Smokestacks in Kenya: The Case of Horticulture, ICT, and Tourism Sectors, Africa Growth Initiative, Brookings, July 2021.

[152] "Economic growth and trade," USAID, May 4, 2022.

[153] Onsomu, Eldar, Boaz Munga & Violet Nyabaro. The impact of Covid-19 on industries without smokestacks in Kenya: The case of horticulture, ICT, and tourism sectors, July 28, 2021.

economy expanded by 7.5% that year.[154] The expected growth of 9% in 2022 may be difficult to achieve in view of inflation caused partly by food shortages, the weakening of the shilling against the US dollar, and the Russia-Ukraine war.

Thousands of people lost jobs in sectors such as agriculture, trade, and service industries. Unemployment doubled to 10.4% in the second quarter of 2020. And even those still employed suffered reduced working hours and consequently, deflated incomes. This exacerbated food insecurity, and elevated pain and human suffering. According to the World Bank, Covid-19 pandemic increased poverty by four percentage points, meaning that an additional 2 million people were added to the poverty index.[155]

Amid Covid-19 something positive happened in 2020. Uhuru announced a raft of measures to mitigate the effects of the pandemic. He allocated KSh.8.5 billion to a fund for the elderly, orphans, and those with underlying health conditions. He also released an additional KSh.500 million to persons with disability (PWD) and directed the ministry of health to develop a welfare package for health workers. He also released KSh.5 billion to counties and launched a cash transfer programme for the most socio-economically vulnerable population including the disabled. Those were only a few of the measures he took to try to help and ease the effects of the Covid-19 pandemic.

The question is where did the money go? A Human Rights Watch (HRW) report entitled *"We are all Vulnerable Here: Kenya's Pandemic Cash Transfer Programme Riddled with Irregularities"* gave examples of qualified people in desperate need of food and shelter who applied for the funds but did not receive any. In a survey, the HRW report found that less than 5% of the targeted population received any funding, leaving 95% of vulnerable households in dire need of help. Some of the participants in the survey said that they went without food for up to four days and had rent arrears stretching up to nine months.

---

[154] Herbling, David. "War in Ukraine seen putting brakes on Kenya's strong recovery," May 5, 2022.

[155] "Navigating the pandemic," Kenya Economic Update, World Bank, November 2020.

UHURU KENYATTA

Most careless borrower?

Of all the presidents, Uhuru was the most careless borrower, burying the country into extreme debt obligations that will take generations to repay. He borrowed trillions of shillings from overseas lenders mainly China, to build highways, railways, dams, and even a level-six research and referral hospital at the Kabete Military Barracks.

He took more loans from international finance institutions such as the World Bank (WB), the International Monetary Fund (IMF), and the African Development Bank (AfDB). In the fiscal year 2021/2022, the WB led the pack of foreign creditors, contributing KSh.121.6 billion out of the country's KSh. 3.0 trillion budget.

In 2012, the year Uhuru left the finance ministry, Kenya's debt was only KSh.1.9 billion. After Uhuru became president, the country borrowed feverishly. In 2014, one year into his presidency, the total debt was KSh.2.4 trillion or 101% of the GDP ratio. Borrowing accelerated during Uhuru's second term as he raced to complete infrastructure projects under the Big 4 Agenda, before leaving office.

By June 2021, debt had grown to KSh.7.2 trillion. By September 2021, the public debt had increased to KSh.7.6 trillion, representing 68.1% of Kenya's debt-to-GDP ratio, way past the sustainable level of 55%. The total debt amount did not include KSh.29.2 billion from the IMF disbursed in December 2021, and a domestic debt of KSh.3.94 trillion. As his term ended, the total debt was hovering around KSh.8 trillion. The top external lender was China. Its loans to Kenya represented 67% of the total external debt.

In the year ending June 2022, however, Japan topped the list of bilateral lenders, with KSh.36.5 billion, followed by China KSh.22.7 billion, and France KSh.18.9 billion. Germany and Spain were the other leading lenders to Kenya.

Of the KSh.6.8 trillion borrowed over the past two decades, President Uhuru was responsible for 84% of the debt. In the first seven months of 2021 alone, the Uhuru administration took loans of KSh.293.5 billion from foreign sources. The amount of the total debt could be much higher than the KSh.7.2 trillion shown by the government, because of some discrepancies detected by the Auditor-General that showed a variance of KSh.30 billion in 2020 alone. Desperate for loans, Kenya even paid commitment fees for loans to Japanese, Chinese, and European banks that would guarantee future loans. Commitment fees are charged on borrowers for credit that has not been advanced and is a way of guaranteeing that a lender will keep the funds.[156]

Unfortunately, a good portion of what Uhuru borrowed and the grandiose projects he built were more for his legacy than for the good of the larger population of Kenyans. There was a burgeoning feeling too that Uhuru didn't care much about how the loans would be repaid. An Infotrak survey showed that 58% of Kenyans were opposed to Uhuru's borrowing spree.

On September 16, 2021, the Central Bank of Kenya (CBK) Governor Patrick Njoroge warned that the country could default in debt repayments in the next two years if the government failed to stop excessive borrowing. According to a debt sustainability analysis by the IMF, Kenya was "one step away from being categorised as a candidate for default."

Independent Kenya has never defaulted in debt repayment. But in 2021, Kenya sought and was granted by the IMF a loan repayment holiday for six months from January to June, involving KSh.80 billion. That was intended to give Kenya a breathing space to put its house in order.

There were also serious concerns about domestic borrowing from local commercial banks, non-banking institutions, such as pension funds, and insurance companies. By 2021, the government owed such entities KSh.3.7 trillion, pushing the private sector out of the debt market. That gave commercial banks a windfall of high interest rates of 66% compared to 34% for external loans.

The borrowing also increased commercial bank assets from KSh.4.46 trillion in December 2019 to KSh.5 trillion in 2020, according to government figures. Much of the borrowing was in the

---

[156] Mutua, John. "Kenya spends KSh.1.7 billion to secure foreign loans," *Business Daily*, September 17, 2021.

form of treasury bonds and treasury bills. Treasury projections showed that by the end of Uhuru's term in August 2022, Kenya would have accumulated an estimated KSh.13 trillion more in public debt.

The senate committee on finance and budget too sent signals that unchecked borrowing was a risk to banks and pension funds, even as it admitted that domestic borrowing was "critical for cash flow management." "While this [domestic borrowing] promotes a healthy financial system, it also indicates that risk exposure, in case of debt distress, would largely affect banks and pension funds," the committee said in a 2021 report.

Some of the borrowed money was used to plug a budget deficit which had skyrocketed to KSh.970 billion in the 2020-2021 fiscal year or 8.7% of the GDP from KSh.330 billion when Uhuru took office.[157]

In 2019, the debt ceiling approved by parliament was KSh.6 trillion. That same year, parliament raised it to KSh.9 trillion or 50% of the GDP. Despite Kenya's distressful economic situation, bilateral and multilateral sources, continued to advance loans to the country, adding to the trillions of shillings Kenya already owed. In June 2022, parliament increased the debt ceiling to KSh. 10 trillion.

The World Bank (WB), the International Fund for Agriculture Development, Saudi Arabia, City Group Global Markets Europe, the African Development Bank (AfDB), and Belgium, wired billions of shillings in loans to Kenya, even as the IMF proclaimed that the country was drifting towards a debt distress.

Early in 2022, the WB loaned Kenya KSh.85.5 billion for Covid-19 recovery. The WB loan was the second of two tranches started in 2020 under its Development Policy Operations (DPO) programme aimed at accelerating recovery from the Covid-19. Although the loan's total yearly interest was 3%, much lower than what commercial institutions charged, it was still a loan and Kenyans would have to repay it. In total, Kenya received KSh.371.8 billion of DPO funds during the past four years. It was as if multilateral organisations were working for the country's demise.

---

[157] Kenya's FY 2021/2022 budget review, Cytonn, June 20, 2021.

In 2021, France rebuffed Kenya's request for money to fund a railway line linking JKIA and Nairobi CBD. The KSh.16.3 billion deal for the construction of the five-kilometre connection between the airport and the SGR terminus at Syokimau was supposed to have been signed during Uhuru's visit to France on June 30, 2021, but that did not happen, and no reasons were given. In both cases, Kenyans rejoiced.

However, behind the expected deal, a tender war over the line construction was brewing between a consortium of French companies and Chinese entities. KRC officials had already lined up the French for the job which was to be financed by BPI France Assurance Export, but the Kenyan treasury smelt a rat and raised a red flag, thus stopping another possible corruption scandal.

However, Kenya and France did reach an agreement on a public-private partnership for the construction of the Nairobi-Nakuru-Mau summit highway. The 181-kilometre KSh.160 billion toll highway is part of the Northern Corridor used to transport passengers and goods from Mombasa to the neighbouring countries of Uganda, South Sudan, Burundi, and Rwanda. The highway is expected to be completed in 2025.

Borrow, borrow, borrow!

On April 26, 2019, while meeting President Uhuru in Beijing, President Xi Jinping of China found it necessary to point out that the two had met three times in less than a year. That observation was significant because it underscored the strategic significance and the high-level status of the Kenya-China relations.

Interestingly, almost all the visits to China by Uhuru were for purposes of borrowing money, coated as they were, under the disguise of 'bilateral cooperation.' Every time Uhuru left for China, Kenyans held their breath, hoping and praying that Beijing would reject overtures for more loans from their leader. Their prayers were heard, at least once, in April 2019, when China turned down a request for a US$3.6 billion (KSh.400 billion) loan to finance the

Naivasha-Kisumu Standard Gauge Railway (SGR) line. Instead, Uhuru got only KSh.40 million to revitalize the old gauge line from the Naivasha dry port to western Kenya. Kenyans were happy, but not entirely; "Even KSh.40 billion is a lot," one tweeted, "because we citizens are the ones who will pay."

There was a steep increase in loans from China during Uhuru's tenure. In 2014, China owed Kenya US$737 million (KSh.82 billion) in debt. By December 2020, the debt had ballooned to US$6.4 billion (KSh.700 billion) representing a 766% increase in just six years. The loans were in the form of cash, technology, and equipment, such as those used for the SGR. As the deadlines for the first debut repayment approached in 2021, Kenya panicked and entered a hurried deal in January 2021 for a six-month repayment holiday worth US$245 million (KSh.25 billion). The debut repayment was for a loan of US$1.48 billion (KSh.165 billion) from the Export-Import Bank of China (Exim Bank) used for the Nairobi-Naivasha SGR railway line.

Treasury officials also rushed to the Paris Club of creditors and obtained a service debt suspension of US$300 million until the end of June 2021. The Paris Club is a group of major creditors comprising of mainly European and north and southern American nations. But those were ephemeral measures to give Kenya a breathing space as it struggled to meet its obligations, not only to China, but also to multilateral organisations.

Two major Chinese loans became due in 2021. There was the US$7.7 million (KSh.860 million) for "economic and technical cooperation" commitment and US$1.6 billion (KSh.180 billion) for the Mombasa-Nairobi SGR. As at the end of the 2021-2022 fiscal year, the country's debt repayments to China had shot up to KSh.73.48 billion compared to KSh.31.25 billion in the financial year ending June 2021.

Finance Cabinet Secretary Yatani warned Kenyans to tighten their belts as the country went through the debt repayment crisis. International media referred to Kenya's situation as a diplomatic 'death trap' in which at least 12 other African countries were ensnared. At times, Kenya had to borrow money to pay Chinese loans.

But Uhuru, in an interview with CNN in November 2018, rejected insinuations that the Chinese connection was a 'death trap.' He said the media lacked an objective understanding of China's cooperation with developing Africa.

Because of Kenya's failure to meet its obligations on time, China in July 2021 froze further disbursements. The ban was lifted only after Kenya resumed repayments early in August with a KSh.82.7 billion payment to Exim Bank. There were also rumours that the Chinese were eyeing the port of Mombasa in case Kenya failed to honour its obligations. It is widely believed that the port was one of the assets used as collateral for the Chinese loans. It would be a major economic blow to Kenya if that happened given the strategic importance of the port as a gateway for the country and the landlocked countries in the region.

But debt servicing is invariably a costly affair. Out of every KSh.100, KSh.60 went to debt repayments. During the fiscal year beginning July 1, 2021, debt servicing costs reached about KSh1.17 trillion, an amount more than the government's proposed KSh.660 billion spending on development projects.

To meet the challenge of increased debt, the KRA conjured new ways of taxing Kenyans and businesses. In 2020, Uhuru assented to the Tax Law Amendment Act (No. 2) which introduced a minimum tax at the rate of 1% of the gross turnover, and a digital services tax at 1.5% of the transaction value. The tax was to be paid in four instalments by the 20th day of the fourth, sixth, ninth, and twelfth month, of the year of collection of the income.

Another system was introduced to generate automated VAT assessments through the iTax platform. The new law increased the corporate income tax rate from 25% to 30% and reinstated the VAT rate to 16% from 14%. The above measures were in addition to a 30% tax for salaried employees earning over KSh.32,233 per month introduced by Uhuru early in 2020. Those changes were intended to yield KSh.6.8 trillion in tax collections over the period 2021/2022 to 2023/2024. But it also meant individuals and businesses would shoulder a much higher tax burden.

Maliza uende

In his ten years in office, Uhuru relied almost exclusively on China for infrastructure development. He often boasted about the thousands of kilometres of roads his government had constructed, a total of 11,000 kilometres, he said, during the Madaraka Day celebrations in 2022. That was six times more than what Kibaki had built. In fact, he said, Jubilee government built more roads than all the previous administrations combined, including the British colonialists during their 123-year rule. But all that was achieved on borrowed money.

The bottom line is that relations between China and Kenya are hinged on loans. The common mantra in the social media by Kenyans worried about the debt trap during Uhuru's last year in office was *"Maliza uende,"* finish and go. Kenyans were ready to open a new chapter with Uhuru's departure. But it was not just the Chinese loans Kenyans were against. They were against all loans. One man who was behind the anti-loans' narrative, activist Mutemi wa Kiama, was arrested in July 2021 for publishing a poster with Uhuru's picture warning the world not to give Kenya any more loans.

"This is to notify the world at large that the person whose photograph and names appear above is not suitable for public office. He is therefore not authorised to act or transact on behalf of the citizens of the Republic of Kenya, and that the nation and the future generations shall not be held liable for any penalties of bad loans negotiated and/or borrowed by him," said the widely circulated poster. Kiama was released without charge only because of social media protests from indignant Kenyans.

Only a few days earlier, the IMF had loaned Kenya KSh.255 billion for Covid-19 support. That was in addition to US$739 million (KSh.80 billion) IMF had given the country a month earlier for a similar purpose. Under Uhuru, Kenya was reduced to a miserable beggar. Its ties with the world fell under the category of 'friends-with-benefits', the country constantly begging for more cash, which often ended in people's pockets.

China-funded projects in Kenya, like all others, too have been mired in corruption and improprieties. Chinese-sponsored projects are worth an estimated KSh.395 billion. At least three projects had cases of financial misappropriation including theft of funds and kickbacks. One was the project to supply computer tomography (CT) scanners to Kenyatta National Hospital (KNH), Moi Teaching and Referral Hospital (MTRH), and to 34 county hospitals. The parliamentary public accounts committee (PAC) found that the scanners were overpriced fourfold in a conspiracy involving officials in the Ministry of Health and Treasury. Officials paid KSh.227 million for each of the 37 scanners while the market price was no more than KSh.45 million. Suspicion arose when officials at the ministry of health abandoned what was a government-to-government arrangement and entered a private deal with a Chinese company, Neusoft Systems Company Limited. Some of the scanners were for use at the Chinese-built CT Scan Centre at KNH in Nairobi.

Some of the money obtained by the government from foreign and local sources was lost to what officials said were "persistent and disturbing" problems in accounting. According to the 2013/2014 auditor general's report, for example, 98.8% of the money spent by ministries could not be "clearly and lawfully" accounted for. Auditor General Edward Ouko reported in the 2015 report that because of accounting problems, a lot of taxpayers' monies were lost through theft, corruption, and dubious transactions. He gave an example of US$2 billion (KSh.220 billion) which was mysteriously transferred to an offshore account contrary to regulations. The owner of that offshore account was not identified, and no effort was made by any government agency to find him or her.

Some of the public money was lost to conspiracies. In 2017, more than KSh.4 billion disappeared from the Kenya Revenue Authority (KRA) in a highly organised plot. An international syndicate of electronic hackers in collusion with insiders was blamed for the fraud carried out by professional fraudsters. A 28-year-old Information Systems graduate from the University of Nairobi (UoN) and 15 other people, including two Americans, were arrested, and charged. In court, the prosecution revealed the existence of an international ring of crooks comprising foreigners, police officers, and KRA officials, and blamed it for hacking the KRA computers.

A further shock came in June 2022, when the auditor general, in her report for the fiscal year ending June 2021, revealed that KRA had failed to collect tax arrears amounting to a staggering KSh. 1.6 trillion.

In 2016, KSh.18 billion vanished from financial institutions through hacking. In one bank alone, KSh.400 million was skimmed off customer accounts. Were any big shots involved? If so, who were they? One cyber gang known as Forkbombo, which is led by a Kenyan was reportedly behind numerous hacking incidents in the East African region. Twelve individuals belonging to the group were arrested in Rwanda and sentenced to long prison terms.

It was revealed in the same year that corrupt officials at the Central Bank of Kenya (CBK) had colluded with rogue commercial bank officials in a fraudulent scheme that saw depositors at the Imperial Bank lose KSh.42 billion. Imperial Bank was one of numerous such politically correct institutions to run into serious financial problems in the wake of illegal activities involving CBK and other government officials.

Documents filed in court revealed that senior CBK officials connived with top executives at the bank to hide billions of shillings belonging to individuals and companies. In return, the corrupt CBK officials were rewarded with hefty loans by the bank. Most of the loans were not repaid. In 2021, the CBK ordered the bank liquidated. CBK Governor Patrick Njoroge was not implicated in the fraud, but one of his predecessors was named adversely as a beneficiary of the illegal perks.

The country's fiscal position was not improving with time. In June 2020, the government slashed 26% or KSh.45 billion of money going to public universities, from KSh.170 billion to KSh.127 billion. In the 2021/2022 budget, universities received only KSh.99 billion. By the end of 2021, the government's financial situation was so dire that the treasury had to borrow money to pay salaries and meet its commitments to counties. That exercise was against regulations which stipulate that borrowed money must be used only for developmental activities. But the government continued to borrow, yet the use of the money was not always clear.

In April 2021, the government borrowed KSh.25 billion through the IMF Extended Credit Facility (ECF) to finance development projects. The following month, it received another loan of KSh.1.29 billion from Belgium to build phase two of the Medical Waste Management Project. The loan was to be repaid in tranches for a period of five years. In 2021, it took the government only a few months to borrow KSh.293 billion from various sources, including the Saudi Fund for Development, the Arab Bank for Economic Development, and the CBC Banque SA of Belgium.

And, instead of channelling KSh.80 billion received from the IMF and KSh.70 billion from Eurobond proceeds to finance projects, the treasury diverted part of the money to salaries. Some of the Eurobond money intended for sanitation, irrigation, water, and ICT, among other infrastructural projects, went to recurrent expenditure.

Despite the financial difficulties facing the administration, Uhuru's Treasury went ahead and spent KSh.10.6 billion on the failed Building Bridges Initiative (BBI) meant to amend the constitution. The exercise was not cheap because the task force responsible for the initiative held dozens of meetings and retreats all over the country. Hotel accommodation and allowances consumed millions of shillings during the two-year-long exercise.

Uhuru also had no qualms about spending money on meetings. In October 2020 Uhuru, his entire cabinet, security, and support staff, flew in helicopters to Tsavo National Park, for a cabinet meeting. Although the meeting was held at the government owned KWS Training Centre in Manyani, the cost of private, police, and military planes plus allowances, was staggering for the two-day retreat.

Deputy President Ruto, who, only a few days earlier, had blasted the BBI, was among those present at Manyani. Even the main item on the agenda, which was *Huduma Namba* and BBI, did not justify the decision to hold the meeting away from its regular seat at State House. The retreat, held ahead of the expected release of the BBI report, gave Uhuru an opportunity to mobilise his troops behind the report. But why Tsavo?

"When Huduma Number was being rolled out with funfair, I refused to register. I had this feeling it was a novel scam by mandarins in the Office of the President to steal money and afterwards pretend that the exercise never occurred in the first place… few years later what is huduma?" Lawyer Ahmednasir Abdullahi posted in a Tweet on September 11, 2021. The tweet echoed what many Kenyans had in mind. Kenyans were skeptical of the card since its inception via the Huduma Bill, 2019.

Huduma Namba (HN) is a biometric digital identity system that was intended to be the "only source of truth" about a person's identity. Literally meaning 'service number,' HN was intended to replace the current ID, integrating such information as contact details, tax PIN number, passport and drivers' licence information, a person's profession, and fingerprints. Every person between the age of six and 45 was obliged to register for the card. Those who failed to do so were to be denied government services. The plan was to have the use of the existing IDs discontinued by December 12, 2021, and for them to be phased out completely by November 2030.

The proposed change from the ID to HN ran into headwinds as soon as it was launched. Non-governmental organisations (NGOs) opposed the plan to collect sensitive personal data without adequate data protection safeguards or laws. They filed a petition in the High Court wanting the initiative discontinued. They also wanted the court to suspend the implementation of the Kenya National Integrated Identity Management Scheme (KNIIMS) until the government resolved existing risks, including data breaches, exclusion, and discrimination. In January 2020, the High Court agreed with them, ruling that HN was unconstitutional in the absence of data protection safeguards. That was a big blow to officials who had expected to cash in on some of the approximately KSh.6 billion earmarked for the roll-out.

Then came the bombshell on October 14, 2021. The High Court declared its roll-out illegal. The court also said the HN conflicted with the Data Protection Act, a law which itself was irregularly passed by parliament because there was no public participation. The government appealed the decision. But a three-judge Court of Appeal bench, in a ruling in March 2022, denied the government its plea to continue issuing HN cards without an impact assessment on data protection. The AG felt the judges were biased against the State.

The ruling meant KSh.10.6 billion of taxpayers' money went down the drain with no tangible benefits to Wanjiku. Another KSh.1 billion had been set aside in 2021 for the second round of registration for Huduma numbers. But that had to be halted in the face of the court decision. By that time, 38 million Kenyans had registered for the card. Consequently, Treasury Cabinet Secretary Ukur Yatani, in a supplementary budget early in 2022, reduced by half the KSh.1 billion budget that had been reserved for HN registration. In addition, the universal use of HN was put into question when the IEBC rejected it as an identification document for voting during the 2022 elections.

By June 2022, the fate of *Huduma Namba* was still in limbo. The matter was pending at the Court of Appeal. An attempt by the government to pass another *Huduma Namba* law to replace of the original one was thwarted by the NGO Katiba Institute which went to court to stop it. Katiba Institute averred that the government was yet to comply with the court orders given by the High Court.

CHAPTER 11

Corruption and Theft

Throughout President Uhuru's reign, Kenyan newspapers were awash with headlines that touched on corruption involving Uhuru family members. Sample these: "Uhuru kin in KSh.5 billion health scandal" (*Saturday Nation*, October 29, 2016); "Raila: Uhuru Sister's Firm Listed in Disadvantaged Group" *Sunday Nation*, October 30, 2016; "Uhuru Sister, Cousin Were Paid KSh.200 million Health Cash" (*The Star*, October 29, 2016); and "Uhuru Kin Got Millions from NYS Diesel Deal" (*The Standard*, June 13, 2018)," among others.

Uhuru, it seems, was constantly under pressure on allegations of corruption facing some of his family members. "There is no going back in the war against corruption," he said when things got hot. "If there is evidence against anyone, including my brother, charge them." That was June 27, 2018, at the American Chamber of Commerce (AMCHAM) Economic Summit at the UN Gigiri complex in Nairobi. A few days earlier, his younger brother, Muhoho, had been named in the joint Parliamentary Agriculture and Trade Committees as having engaged in the illegal importation of contaminated sugar.

MP Cornelius Serem told the committee that a company allegedly owned by Uhuru's youngest sibling had brought in 180,000 metric tonnes of brown sugar suspected to be laced with mercury and copper. The allegation was as scalding as a hot iron. Never had

Muhoho, the *de facto* chief executive of the Kenyatta business empire, been mentioned publicly in a scandal.

The committee had invited Interior Cabinet Secretary Fred Matiang'i to give details of a major sugar scam that had reached parliament. Matiang'i did not attend, prompting Serem to suggest that the cabinet secretary's absence was because he feared being questioned about Muhoho's role in the illegal trade.

Matiang'i was one of Uhuru's most trusted officials who was given duties once handled by the deputy president. He was delegated officially through executive order No. 1 of 2019, to supervise and coordinate all government projects on behalf of the president.

It would have been embarrassing and tricky for him to be present to answer questions about the first family's involvement in corruption. "A company by the name Protech Investment Limited is owned by one of the strongest people in this country," Serem claimed in his submission, "and that could explain why Matiang'i is not here. He is afraid."

Matiang'i's Interior Principal Secretary Karanja Kibicho defended his (Matiang'i's) absence saying the cabinet secretary was attending the East African Community (EAC) Heads of State Summit. Matiang'i's absence did not stop Serem from advancing serious allegations against Uhuru's brother. He tabled a document listing forty-eight sugar importing companies compiled by the ministry of agriculture and alleged that one of the companies on the list was owned by Muhoho.

Media reports identified Muhoho Kenyatta and John Stuart Armitage, a long-time friend of the Kenyattas, as directors of the firm. Armitage was also said to be a director of some of the family's premier businesses including Brookside Dairy, Heritage Holdings, and Green Park Investments.[158]

Several MPs interjected to stop Serem from continuing with his allegations. "I don't want us to cast aspersions as to the people who import sugar," shot up MP Kanini Kega, a Jubilee Alliance Party stalwart. Turning to Serem, he said: "Don't go in that direction." But

---

[158] Mutai, Edwin. 'Muhoho Kenyatta in list of sugar importers," *Business Daily*, June 26, 2018.

Serem continued, saying he hoped that "this animal called corruption will not affect or inflict the future generation of this country. We are fighting it [corruption] to protect the future generations." It was clear the MP had ruffled the feathers of impunity.

Mwangi Kiunjuri, then cabinet secretary for agriculture who was in the room, also defended Muhoho. "He [Serem] thinks dragging in the name of the president, or his family members will intimidate and weaken the resolve we have in the fight against corruption. Even if he shouts from the rooftop, the war is on, and we will remain emboldened."

However, Kiunjuri failed to confirm or deny the company belonged to Muhoho. He nevertheless assured MPs that Protech Investments Limited had not imported any sugar into the country. The company had applied for a licence in 2011, he said, but that licence was not granted. Two years later, Uhuru sacked Kiunjuri without giving any reasons.

A few days earlier, Majority Leader Adan Duale had accused Matiang'i and Treasury Cabinet Secretary Henry Rotich of shielding the "real sugar barons' while going for chicken thieves."[159] A University of Nairobi lecturer, Samuel Nyandemo, went further and accused some MPs of taking bribes from sugar industry players to cover up the involvement of two cabinet secretaries in the illegal importation. "A sizeable number of those members of parliament that didn't want to take bribes have come out openly to say they saw bribes being received,"[160] he claimed.

Speaking at AMCHAM, a clearly enraged Uhuru made it clear that if his brother was involved in corruption, he should face the law. "I have remained quiet because I have full confidence in the agencies that we have to do their job. I have said, if he is guilty let the process continue," Uhuru said. No investigation was done, so there was no process of any kind to establish if the allegations were true or not. In any case, it was unlikely that any government agency would be brave enough to investigate anyone in the Kenyatta orbit.

---

[159] Achuka, Vincent. "Unease in Jubilee as graft war splits UhuRuto allies," *The Standard*, June 23, 2018.
[160] Krippahl, Cristina. "Kenya: A 'sweet' deal gone sour," *Deutsche Welle*, September 13, 2018.

Uhuru had more to say about corrupt deals touching on members of his family. On March 22, 2019, he said, "If you are corrupt, we will fight you. You can be my brother or my sister or my closest political ally, but if you are corrupt, we will fight you. I won't be clouded by ethnicity or status in my quest to leave behind a united nation, and I will continue championing for Kenya's unity."

A little over a year later, in September 2020, NTV ran an investigative piece titled: "*Covid-19 Millionaires: Corruption and Covid-19 Moving at the Same Pace.*" The bombshell documentary indicted a close relative of Uhuru as being among those involved in a corruption-related Covid-19 pandemic scandal.

The investigative piece exposed individuals and companies that benefited from tenders worth billions of shillings from the Kenya Medical Supplies Authority (KEMSA) to supply Covid-19 materials. KEMSA is the only government body in the country mandated to procure and supply medicines to hospitals and health facilities. The documentary claimed a company partly owned by Uhuru's niece got a KSh.84 million contract to supply 120,000 pieces of KN95 face masks at an inflated price of KSh.700 a piece. The company was among twelve firms awarded questionable contracts worth KSh.3 billion by KEMSA, an organisation with one of the most atrocious records of corruption.

Another company, owned by a prominent member of the Jubilee Alliance Party, was registered only a few weeks before the first Covid-19 case was reported in March 2020. The company was awarded a KSh.4 billion tender. The cost of most of the supplied items was inflated, according to information submitted to parliament. David Murathe, a Jubilee Alliance Party vice chairman denied before the parliamentary public investments committee (PIC) in April 2021, that he was involved in two companies, Kilig Limited and Entec Technologies, which reportedly had dealings with KEMSA. His only role, he said, was to guarantee the supply of 50,000 PPE kits provided by Entec to Kilig for delivery to KEMSA.

In the meantime, Uhuru's niece, Samantha Ngina Muthama, and Jane Nduta Kinyua, owners of Ziwala Ltd., blasted the NTV documentary claiming it contained unfounded allegations. They demanded an apology and retraction of the story by the station.

They said the programme was misleading, false, and malicious. It is unknown if the media house apologised.

The Covid-19 scandal was one of the most shameful corruption episodes during Uhuru's tenure. The country was at the peak of a deadly pandemic. More than 1,200 people had already died from Covid-19, among them thirty-two health workers, including ten specialist doctors. Healthcare unions were complaining about inadequate and substandard personal protective equipment (PPEs). Doctors and nurses were threatening to strike over "extremely difficult, draining, hazardous, and injurious, environment." As Covid-19 curfews took hold, medical workers going or leaving work after curfew hours were harassed, some arrested. All that triggered a shortage of personnel in public health facilities. The result was that hospitals started turning away patients.

Government officials, businesspeople, and greedy cartels did not spare multilateral organisations and individuals that came to help. World Bank, the International Monetary Fund (IMF), the World Health Organisation (WHO) and the Chinese Jack Ma Foundation, donated money and/or protective equipment to Kenya. IMF sent in KSh.78.3 billion, the World Bank KSh.108 billion plus another KSh.6.8 billion, the African Development Bank wired KSh.22.5 billion, the European Union KSh.7.5 billion, all totalling up to KSh.223.1 billion. Many of the donations went into individual people's pockets. The Jack Ma Foundation donated 25,000 pieces of testing kits, protective gear, masks, and medical equipment, which arrived in Nairobi on March 24, 2020.

Despite international support, Kenyans were still asked to pay exorbitant fees for Covid-19 tests. When vaccine donations arrived, unscrupulous traders, conspiring with officials, hijacked them and sold them on the black market. Moreover, lack of transparency and accountability in the use of loan money meant to mitigate the effects of Covid-19, made it difficult for "oversight bodies and civil society organisations to hold the government accountable," said the International Budget Partnership (IBP), an independent non-profit organisation. In 2016, KSh.160 million of donor money intended for vaccines for children was embezzled or could not be accounted for.

Covid-19 Emergency Response Fund

Furthermore, KSh.1.3 billion collected by a committee appointed by President Uhuru in March 2020 was found to have mysteriously disappeared. The money was collected by the Covid-19 Emergency Response Fund (ERF) through voluntary contributions to deal with emergency cases related to the pandemic. The donations were derived from multinational companies and development partners, the exchequer, voluntary civil servant salary cuts, and Kenyans of means.

Being a government-sponsored body registered under the public finance management regulations, any contributions made would have been recorded in treasury books, but they weren't. Instead, in June 2020, a top official of the Fund registered a private firm, the Kenya Covid-19 Emergency Fund Limited Company, which allegedly continued to receive donations from individuals and organisations. It could not be ascertained if the money was banked in the company's account. The Treasury Principal Secretary Julius Muia who was listed as the fund's administrator, told the parliamentary PAC early in 2022 that the treasury did not know the whereabouts of the money. Moreover, he never attended any of the Fund's meetings. It turned out that another official from the office of the president was appointed to handle administrative matters as secretary to the board.

The ERF is top-heavy with private sector bigwigs. It was supposed to be chaired by Matiang'i, but the Interior Cabinet Secretary, and the Chairman of the Council of Governors Wycliffe Oparanya, who were appointed by Uhuru, were excluded from its meetings. No one at the ERF could explain why that was so. This raised a red flag that something fishy was ongoing in the organisation. The auditor-general questioned the legality of the company.

In a bombshell revelation in February 2022 that shocked everyone, Solicitor General Kennedy Ogeto, told the PAC that because Uhuru did not officially appoint the ERF, the kitty had fallen into private hands. In his announcement, the president had not appointed the chairperson and secretary of the Fund in writing through a letter bearing the seal and signature of the presidency. That meant the funds did not belong to the public and that the taxpayers did not have a legitimate claim to them, that is, according to the solicitor general.

That perspective raised several questions: "Why didn't the president follow the legal procedures?" "Who are the owners of the private company, and, what happens to the KSh.338 million contributed to the fund by government entities?" The ERF fiasco appeared to be yet another scandal in Uhuru's government.

* * *

KEMSA was so rotten at the core that Uhuru had to take the unprecedented step of sending home 600 out of 900 employees to pave way for restructuring its management. Twenty-nine senior managers were also sent on a 45-day compulsory leave. What surprised many was that he replaced some of the outgoing staff – though on a temporary basis – with members of the equally disgraced NYS.

The reasons given for sending the employees home included lack of financial control, poor debt collection, warehousing and distribution hiccups, a supply chain crisis, and purchase of non-priority items. Nevertheless, the senior managers sued the Health Cabinet Secretary Mutahi Kagwe and other officials for contempt of court. In its ruling in November 2021, the Employment and Labour Relations Court stopped KEMSA from declaring the officials redundant or terminating their services, pending a court judgement. By June 2022, that judgement had not been rendered.

In June 2020, the IMF, unhappy about the situation, gave Kenya 24 hours to reveal the names of the so-called "Covid-19 millionaires" or risk censure. Embarrassed by the scandal, Uhuru ordered that a list of all the companies awarded tenders by KEMSA be published, but it was too little too late. What was the point of publishing the names if tenders had already been awarded and money dished out?

Three months later, KEMSA published the list on its website. Several of the contracts between KEMSA and suppliers were of newly registered companies, some with no experience at all in procurement of medical supplies. The agency was big on contracting. In 2020 alone, it had awarded 301 contracts to suppliers, up from 132 in 2019 and 57 in 2018. It was certainly a money maker for KEMSA officials and their cronies using bogus companies.

A special audit by the auditor general found that KEMSA officials used what is known as retrospective direct procurement method. That meant commitment letters were issued to suppliers before the procurement process was completed, and money was paid before deliveries were made. Yet KEMSA had no authority to use this method. The system is only allowed under circumstances such as urgency, when acquisition prices compare well with known prices, when the purpose is not to avoid competition, and only after appropriate approvals had been sought. In numerous occasions, approvals were not sought.

The EACC launched an investigation and several KEMSA officials, and private company executives suspected to have been involved were arrested and charged. The anti-corruption agency also froze KSh.19 billion that KEMSA was preparing to pay suppliers. Because KEMSA had bought excess materials and at exorbitant prices, the government was stuck with KSh.1.5 billion worth of dead stock. Some of it had long expired while some was no longer saleable.

In September 2021, the public investments committee (PIC), under the chairmanship of MP Abdulswamad Nassir, recommended the recovery of excess monies paid to one-hundred-and-two companies that allegedly supplied Covid-19 materials to KEMSA. PIC also recommended the prosecution of the KEMSA chief executive officer (CEO), the director of procurement, chairman of the board, and one additional member. The CEO was faulted for issuing commitment letters without seeking professional opinion from the head of procurement. In turn, the CEO implicated CS Kagwe in the scandal. He accused the CS of calling him and sending text messages on procurement related issues. The response from Kagwe was simple: "Carry your own cross!"

However, it was not proved if any of the officials were involved in criminal activities related to Covid-19 supplies. In the meantime, the government disbanded the KEMSA board of directors and appointed a new one under the chairpersonship of Mary Chao. A probe by the Public Procurement Regulatory Authority (PPRA) ordered by the Senate, found numerous anomalies. Wrong documents were used in the tender process, and no market surveys were done as provided by regulations to verify market prices. By June 2022, none of the officers charged had been prosecuted. The Director of Public Prosecutions Noordin Haji said no one had been charged because the EACC had failed to investigate the case.

As Uhuru's departure neared, another scandal at KEMSA broke out. The UN-supported Global Fund (GF) announced that 908,000 mosquito nets, 1.1 million condoms, and KSh.10 million worth of tuberculosis drugs, had mysteriously disappeared from the organisation's warehouse in Nairobi. The items were suspected to have found their way into the black market. The GF has been at the forefront in the fight against HIV/Aids, tuberculosis, and malaria, and has spent billions of shillings in aid to the country. In a report issued in March 2022, the Fund also warned of fake suppliers who were demanding KSh.1.66 billion from KEMSA for items that had not been supplied.

When Uhuru disbanded the KEMSA board, he did so to enhance efficiency, through better accounting and administrative practices. The latest revelations of theft and skulduggery at the organisation proved that more radical changes needed to be made, including the complete restructuring of KEMSA and the deployment of a more dedicated and corruption-free management team.

What was even more suspicious about the awarding of tenders to members of the Kenyatta family was that one of Uhuru's relatives was a board member of the Public Procurement Oversight Authority (PPOA). PPOA deals with complaints arising from conflict of interest and unfair competition in the awarding of tenders.

Allegations of malpractice among members of the Kenyatta family have persisted for years. In October 2016, two of Uhuru's kins were accused of having pocketed KSh.41 million in questionable payments from the taxpayers' kitty. The kins – a sister and a cousin – registered a limited company, and within two years, the firm had won at least five tenders worth KSh.270 million from KEMSA to supply emergency nutrition commodities for HIV/Aids patients. The tenders were issued by the ministry of health in November 2015.

Under the Access to Government Procurement Opportunities (AGPO), 30% of all government tenders must go to women, youth, and Persons with Disabilities (PWD). The said company was granted the tender under that arrangement which was seemingly questionable given the fact that the company did not meet the established criterion.

The managing director of a company called Sundales, Kathleen Kihanya, Uhuru's second cousin, explained that her company had followed the right procedures and legally transacted business with the government.

But ODM leader Raila Odinga did not buy that explanation. "This is President Uhuru's scandal, and he must deal with it as such. Uhuru Kenyatta should tell the country what he knows, when he knew, and what he did about it," he said angrily at a press conference. Kihanya accused Raila of casting doubt "on our integrity for unnecessary political mileage."[161] She called the allegations false and totally unacceptable. Even DP Ruto could not restrain himself from commenting on the scandal calling it "shameless."

Uhuru did not respond directly to those allegations, but he spoke angrily when asked by a reporter about corruption and the number of corruption cases pending in courts: "How many cases of corruption are in the courts of law? Do you expect me to set up a firing squad at Uhuru Park?" That caustic remark provoked a hash tag on social media: #Uhurutocorruptiontrain.

* * *

In the meantime, Finance Cabinet Secretary Henry Rotich supported the Kenyatta family on the AGPO tendering procedures. He saw nothing wrong in the way Uhuru's kins were awarded tenders. "We do not differentiate who in the three categories is disadvantaged. As it stands, all of them are disadvantaged and have a right to do business with government," he told a meeting in Nairobi.

No, Mr. Cabinet Secretary; the Kenyattas are not disadvantaged. A family with billions of shillings in investments, assets, and cash savings, within and without the country, cannot be disadvantaged. The disadvantaged are the more than 60% of poor Kenyans. The

---

[161] Kaberia, Judie. "Kathleen Kihanya Speaks Out on Health Ministry 'Scandal.'" *Capital News*, October 29, 2016.

disadvantaged are the millions of people in coast, north-eastern, and northern Kenya, who must go through perennial droughts and famines, with no water for their animals, and no health and education facilities for their children. The disadvantaged are the hawkers, jua kali artisans, construction workers, peasant farmers, the jobless and the homeless. The list is long.

An internal audit at the ministry of health showed that contracts worth KSh.515.7 million were issued illegally by the ministry of health. KSh.5 billion meant for maternity care could not be accounted for. Because of the corruption in the ministry, the US suspended aid to Kenya in May 2017, amounting to KSh.2.1 billion (US$21 million). It said that it was concerned about graft and weak accounting procedures at the ministry of health.

Further proof of cartels capitalising on the Covid-19 pandemic was the clandestine importation into Kenya of 75,000 doses of the highly controversial Sputnik V vaccines from Russia early in 2021. Neither the World Health Organisation (WHO), nor the US Food and Drug Administration (FDA), had positively reviewed the Sputnik V vaccine. Moreover, it was said, the research methods used by the Moscow-based Galameya National Centre of Epidemiology and Microbiology, were opaque, even though Russian officials said the vaccine's efficacy was greater than 90%.

The Kenya government could not decide whether the drug was safe for vaccinating its citizens even as the vaccine was being administered privately at KSh.7,000 per dose. It didn't take long before the government stopped private companies from importing Covid-19 vaccines. Still, authorities did not explain what happened to the Sputnik V doses that remained in the hands of private clinics and practitioners.

* * *

In July 2021, Auditor General Nancy Gathungu reported that KSh.6.8 million belonging to KICC could not be accounted for. She blamed the KICC management for spending the millions during a trip to Mauritius to receive an award honouring Kenya as Africa's leading meeting and conference destination. Twenty members of the KICC board went on that trip. The auditor general said that the money spent was exorbitant. The Managing Director of KICC Nana Gecaga is Uhuru's niece. As expected, the president said nothing about the matter.

But Kenyans did not remain quiet. "[Uhuru]... is the head of government with all machineries to fight graft, said J. M. Karuga, "but he just cannot do that. He cannot throw a stone in a house made of glass because he lives in one. He is the chief priest of corruption." "If you look closely,' said Bonizzio Abdallah, "it is Uhunye's [Uhuru's] family members in the name of cousins, brothers, sisters, and the large extended family, who have stolen these billions, so Uhuru should stop shooting his leg by telling us what we know."

KICC, a premier conference facility in the heart of Nairobi has been at the centre of corruption allegations for years. In 2016, a meeting of the World Tourism Organisation (WTO) almost aborted amid a major procurement scandal that led to the sacking of the Managing Director (not Gecaga). Almost KSh.2.6 billion of revenue could have been lost if the government had not moved in to ensure last minute delivery of equipment for the conference, including translation systems and headsets. It would have been a great embarrassment to the country too if the meeting had failed to meet the WHO expectations.

Queries emerged after it was discovered that the KICC management had allegedly single-sourced equipment and services on tenders worth KSh.1.9 billion. As the date of the conference approached, no equipment had been delivered. The conference was saved by a last-minute intervention by the ministry of tourism and the treasury. Kenya was the first African country to host the global conference which was attended by 3,000 world leaders and top executives in the hospitality industry.

That the KICC has been poorly managed over the years is not in contention. In 2021, the auditor general warned that KICC risked being auctioned for non-payment of debts amounting to KSh.1.3 billion. Despite reports in 2019 that EACC had launched an investigation into the financial improprieties at the convention, nothing much has happened. And when Gecaga was summoned by the parliamentary committee on sports, culture, and tourism, to explain, the meeting had to be cancelled because she showed up in "casual clothes" which the MPs objected to. The matter ended there.

The scandals enumerated above and touching on the Kenyattas were not the only ones that raised eyebrows. Months before President Uhuru began a second term in office in 2017, reports emerged that a company associated with one of his relatives had been awarded a KSh.1 billion tender to construct police houses in Machakos County.

The houses were to be sold to police officers at prices ranging from KSh.3 million for a three-bedroom house to KSh.8 million for a four-bedroom house. The mortgages were to be paid at 18% interest over a 20-year period. The tender would have remained concealed were it not for a slip of the tongue by a senior State House official in January 2017 who divulged the company's name. Investigations showed that the company was connected to one of Uhuru's relatives who had also been named in other scandals.

Uhuru spoke frequently about corruption. He pledged to have a clean government and even declared corruption a national security threat. He appointed a *Task Force on the Review of the Legal Policy and Institutional Framework for Fighting* corruption and nominated his AG, Githu Muigai, to chair it. The task force reported to Uhuru in October 2015. It offered specific recommendations on how to curb corruption especially in the devolved governments, and how to share information, intelligence, and data. It also recommended a pathway to investigations, prosecution, and disposal of corruption cases, including the dismissal of any official under investigation for corruption.

The following month, Uhuru ordered private companies doing business with the government to sign an approved business code of ethics at the Public Procurement Regulatory Authority (PPOA). Banks found to break anti-money laundering laws were to forfeit their licences, and their company directors held culpable for abetting money laundering. The code of conduct also mandated that companies failing to comply would be disqualified for a period of five years. The document is gathering dust on a shelf somewhere.

* * *

In 2015, Uhuru fired five cabinet secretaries over allegations of graft. Four years later, he sacked Rashid Echesa, the cabinet secretary for sports and heritage. Uhuru did not give any definite reasons for dismissing the youthful politician. He just issued a typically bureaucratic statement that "In accordance with Article 152 (5) of the constitution, as read together with Article 152 (1) (d) of the constitution, the appointment of Mr. Rashid Echesa Mohamed, as a cabinet secretary, has been vacated." That's it!

Over the years, Echesa relentlessly asked the president to explain the reason for his dismissal. "If I have stolen anything belonging to any person, let the president tell Kenyans." The president kept mum.

The move by President Uhuru to show seriousness in tackling corruption did not convince John Githongo, an ascetic-looking intellectual with the countenance of a university professor. In remarks to the *Guardian* newspaper on August 6, 2015, Githongo fired a broadside at Uhuru for allowing what he called the most permissive environment of corruption in Kenya's history. More eating, he said, was taking place under Uhuru than at any time since experts started measuring graft in the 1990s. In Uhuru's first budget as president in 2013/2014, only 1.2% of the KSh.1.07 trillion was correctly accounted for. KSh.60 billion could not be accounted for at all.[162]

In October 2016, during a weekly summit on governance and accountability in Nairobi, Uhuru threw up his hands in frustration over corruption. Instead of proposing aggressive solutions to tackle the matter, he continued to unwisely attack the judiciary for allegedly not supporting his efforts in combating graft. "I give a directive for action on corruption cases... and I am told you don't have the powers to do that. *What do you want me to do?*" He asked, as his listeners cowed in disbelief. He admitted that corruption was one issue that frustrated him most as president.

---

[162] Githongo, John. "Kenya's rampant corruption is eating away at the very fabric of democracy, The *Guardian,* August 6, 2015.

UHURU KENYATTA

SWEET SUGAR SCANDAL

In a country that was once self-sufficient in sugar production, the importation of the sweet commodity from as far as Brazil is by itself a scandal. That scandal becomes even more outrageous if the sugar brought in by cartels, greedy government officials, and politicians, is laced with mercury and copper, endangering the lives of potential consumers. But that is what has been happening in Kenya for decades even as sugar factories collapsed for lack of business and farmers were rendered jobless. One of the major sugar importation scandals in Kenya's history took place under the watch of President Uhuru.

The said scandal hit Kenya in 2018. One thousand sacks of sugar entered the country through the port of Mombasa. The point of departure was Brazil. Once in the country, the sugar was repackaged and relabelled to indicate the source as Zambia. Some estimates put the value of the commodity netted by police in warehouses in Eastleigh, Nairobi, at US$17.8 million, or about KSh.2 billion.[163] It was undoubtedly one of the biggest hauls of contraband sugar found at any one time in Kenya. More than a dozen people, including a senior official of the Kenya Bureau of Standards (KEBS), were arrested and charged in court.

It was clear from the beginning that officers at the Customs Department, the Kenya Revenue Authority (KRA), and KEBS, had connived with the importers to clear the goods through the port of entry. Such a big consignment could not have entered the country without the knowledge of those agencies. However, officials could not agree whether the sugar contained dangerous chemicals. The Trade Cabinet Secretary Adan Mohamed said it didn't. Interior Minister Fred Matiang'i said it did. KEBS said the consignment didn't contain mercury, but it did have copper and lead, ten times more than the level of lead recommended. But whatever the amount of dangerous

---

[163] Okoye, Uju. "Kenya's latest scandal reveals the bitter taste of corruption," *The Diplomatic Courier*, June 27, 2018.

chemicals in the sugar, the fact that it was allowed into the country at all was a cause for worry.

KEBS, which is one of the most corrupt government agencies, also paid little attention to bogus stickers on goods bearing its logo. There were even allegations that the parastatal had cooperated with an Indian company to manufacture the fake mark-of-quality stickers which could easily be duplicated.

The director of public prosecutions (DPP) said in 2018 that investigations had revealed that KEBS officials had conspired with directors of a Madras-based security company to supply sub-standard Impact Standardisation Mark (ISM) stamps worth KSh.882 million. Before that, KEBS used to issue the stamps to manufacturers in soft copies for printing and sticking on KEBS-certified products. But rampant corruption and application of stamps on non-certified goods pushed the agency to control the printing and improve its security features through physical and digital technology.

The sugar industry in Kenya has suffered years of losses due to cheap imported sugar. Millions of farmers and workers have been rendered jobless because of the collapse of, or reduced production in, several factories. Several of the giant sugar mills of yesteryears such as Miwani, Ramisi, Mumias, Nzoia, and Muhoroni factories, have either shut down or are on the brink of collapse due to mismanagement and inability to sustain the pressure from smuggled sugar. Out of 16 sugar factories, only 12 are operational, producing 56,800 tonnes of sugar annually. The Kenya Association of Manufacturers (KAM) blames the government for these woes, including smuggling, in the sugar sector.

There is also the problem of sugar cartels operating along the Kenya/Uganda border. The cartels smuggle the commodity in truckloads from the Kamuli and Kakira factories in Uganda. In Kenya, the contraband sugar, whose quality is not inspected by KEBS, is repackaged, and released into the market. The good news is that the revenue body, KRA, managed to recover more than KSh.20 million from prosecutions and alternative dispute resolution processes, in cases involving sugar smuggling along the Kenya/Uganda border. That is a small amount though compared to the KSh.100 million the government loses in taxes every year due to smuggling. Between 2018 and 2021, KRA seized more than 1.6 million kilograms of sugar valued at KSh.235 million and handled 198 cases of sugar smuggling through borders and the port of Mombasa.[164]

Uhuru had plenty of opportunities to deal with the cartels during his ten years in office, but he didn't. Instead, he issued a gazette notice in 2017 allowing the importation of duty-free sugar without restrictions on quality. That opened the door for sugar to come in from outside the Common Market for Eastern and Southern Africa (COMESA). That was a license for cartels to import sugar without minding quality, but it was also a death nail for the local sugar industry.

A report by the Kenya Anti-Corruption Commission (KACC) in 2010 identified corruption and mismanagement of factories in the Kenya Sugar Board (KSB) as two of the biggest impediments to the growth of the industry. But experts also say that whenever the government allowed the importation of the commodity to bridge a shortfall, importers flooded the market with more sugar than was authorised with the connivance of officials at the ministry of agriculture, KSB and KRA. On such occasions, local sugar piles up in factory stores, as distributors switch to the cheaper imported variety.

In November 2018, President Uhuru Kenyatta appointed the National Sugar Task Force (NSTF) to recommend ways of reviving the collapsed and struggling sugar companies. Two years later, the NSTF presented its report to Uhuru. The report showed that Kenya produced over 490,000 metric tonnes of sugar annually against a demand of about one million metric tonnes. The shortfall of over half a million metric tonnes must be met by imports of cheap sugar from outside the country.

Normally, Kenya imports 350,000 metric tonnes of sugar from within the EAC and COMESA regions. In 2021, the country planned to bring in 90,000 tonnes of sugar from Uganda and another

---

[164] Mburu, Peter. "Smuggling sours Kenya's sugar industry as KRA intercepts 198 rings in three years," *Nation*, February 7, 2022.

160,000 metric tonnes from elsewhere. That is where cartels and corrupt officials cash in.

The task force report noted that officials often made false declaration of value and amounts of imports, compromised consumer safety, and violated licensing regulations. One of its recommendations was a call for the privatisation of publicly owned sugar mills to enhance efficiency and root out corruption. It also wanted names of all sugar importers to be made public, something that had all along been shrouded in secrecy. Other than that, the report contained nothing new. Yet Kenya loses over KSh.9 billion in tax revenue yearly arising from black market and contraband sugar, according to KRA statistics, while local manufacturers lose KSh.4.2 billion annually too.

COULDN'T GET MORE BIZARRE THAN THIS

Hata mwizi huibiwa is a common Swahili saying which literary means, *even a con gets conned*! What happened to two of Kenya's richest men, Uhuru Kenyatta, and businessman Naushad Merali, is a tale of legends which few in government or business circles would want to talk about. It is an embarrassing story of naivety, shady deals, and possible corruption, featuring a sly con who became an instant millionaire by pretending to be President Uhuru.

A sleek manipulator whose career history reads like a book of success, Merali was a chief accountant at Ryce Motors in Nairobi in the early 1980s. He was promoted to chief manager, and a few years later, got loans and bought the company. From there on, his thirst for buying out failing companies peaked. He bought several subsidies of American companies including Firestone, Carbine Union, the First Bank of Chicago, and the Prudential Insurance Company. As his business expanded into telecommunications, public works, real estate and imports and exports, the shrewd businessman attracted influential investors including members of the Kenyatta and Moi families into his various enterprises.

Thus, Merali was a multi-billionaire when he received a call in early in 2019 from a man who identified himself as Uhuru Kenyatta, offering a sweet deal on a piece of land in Nairobi's Milimani suburb. The caller offered to sell the property to Merali, who was then on an overseas trip, for KSh.10 million. Without hesitating, the businessman agreed and ordered his finance director to immediately transfer the money to a bank account of one Reuben Mwangi.

It was after the money was credited that Merali's people discovered that the caller had not been Uhuru but a con artist mimicking the president's voice. 'Mwangi's' incessant calls for more money from the chairman of the NSE-listed Sameer Group of companies, led to the arrest of seven people: Duncan Ndichu, Joseph Waswa, Isaak Wanyekeche Wanyonyi, William Simiyu Mulala, David Likaja Kikuyu, Gilbert Kirunja, and Antony Wafula Simiyu. They were taken to court and charged with conspiracy to defraud and obtaining money by false pretence.

The puzzling twist about the transaction, however, was how easily Merali was tricked into parting with such a huge sum of money. It was assumed that because Merali talked to Uhuru regularly, he should have recognised the distorted voice. Lawyer Cliff Ombeta was categorical in court that the telephone number used by 'Mwangi' belonged to Uhuru.

"Why didn't Merali instruct a lawyer or a professional adviser to handle the payment instruction, and why didn't the finance director issue a cheque instead of cash?" asked an official of the Confederation of Consumers of Kenya (CoFEK). There was speculation that the money could have been a 'bribe' paid in exchange for some unknown state favours for Merali.

Top lawyers Paul Muite and Ahmednasir Abdullahi wanted Merali prosecuted for bribery. Activist Boniface Mwangi claimed in a Facebook blog that Merali "was paying a bribe to Uhuru for a tender and it is clearly something he has done for many years." Mwangi did not specify which tender, and so his claims could not be verified. Mwangi was a bitter critic of the Kenyatta's and repeatedly referred to Uhuru as "son of a thief" in reference to his father's land grabbing mania.[165]

---

[165] Mwangi, Boniface. "Son of a thief," *Facebook*, September 26, 2019.

Around the time of the con incident Merali, through one of his companies, had been lobbying for a multi-million-shilling deal to build 11,000 houses for the Kenya Defence Forces (KDF). The project was to be funded through the public private partnership (PPP) model. KDF was to inject KSh.1 billion in the construction project with the rest of the funds coming from private investors. The houses were then to be rented out for 15 years while the investors recouped their money.

Merali was said to have shares in a company that was bidding for the project. But that company was up against other big bidders including a consortium of three local companies, Zutari Kenya, Blink Studio, and North Wind Consulting, under the stewardship of Centum Real Estate Company. There were also four Chinese companies seeking to secure the contract. It is not known whether this was the tender Boniface Mwangi was referring to. It had also been alleged that Merali paid a bribe of KSh.500,000 to people masquerading as KDF officials to secure a KSh.1.05 billion deal for the supply of tyres to KDF. The allegation could not be confirmed.

The much-respected *Forbes* magazine had listed Merali as one of the richest individuals with an empire worth more than KSh.55 billion. His savvy, debonair, personality, had brought him close to all the Kenyan presidents. Apart from the Kenyattas, Merali was a business associate of Moi and Kibaki. His name featured prominently in the Kroll report which indicted Moi and his associates in mega corruption scandals. Kroll is an international risk consultancy firm. In 2001, Moi decorated Merali with a state commendation of Elder of the Burning Spear (EBS), the same time he honoured Uhuru and Raila with the Second-Class Elder of the Order of the Golden Heart of Kenya (EGH) commendation.

Before Kibaki's retirement, Merali donated 1,000 acres of land at Mweiga in Nyeri, where Kibaki's KSh.500 million residence stands. The farm was owned by a tea company of which Merali was chairman. One of the people with stakes in the company was the late President Moi. Merali also owned 5.6% shares in the Kenyatta-owned Commercial Bank of Africa (CBA) which merged with NIC to become NCBA.

CHAPTER 12

Scandals Galore

During the first two years of his rule, Uhuru had to contend with several major scandals involving financial misconduct in his government. His first tendrils of problems were at JKIA in May 2015. There he came face to face with an apron bus scandal. He had gone to the airport to open Terminal 2 built at a cost of KSh.1.7 billion. The plan was to elevate the passenger capacity to 2.5 million travellers per year.

Until Uhuru's visit, the airport had no buses to ferry disembarking passengers to terminals and vice versa. Travellers had to endure rains and chilly weather, and risk lives as they dodged vehicles and planes. So, in 2012, the Kenya Airports Authority (KAA) signed a KSh.1.1 billion contract with the Relief & Mission Logistics Ltd. (RML), to supply five buses, to ferry the passengers. Each bus was to have a capacity of 115 passengers.

What shocked Uhuru was the cost: KSh.2 million per month to operate and maintain one bus. "Why didn't you come for the NYS (National Youth Service) buses?" An exasperated Uhuru asked the KAA management officials. "I find it impossible to believe you have buses here costing KSh.10 million per month to run."

President Uhuru ordered the immediate arrest of those responsible and recovery of public funds involved. The hire arrangement was said to have been made against the advice of some top KAA officials who wanted the buses bought but leased to a third party to operate and maintain.

Under the arrangement, the winning bidder was also required to build supporting facilities such as a maintenance yard and a fuelling facility. The cost of the service was to be recovered through collection of fees and charges from 48 airlines using the service. However, it was discovered that KAA had not charged the airlines since the service began in November 2014, according to an audit report.

Consequently, the organisation was losing at least KSh. 14 million per month. KAA executives could not explain why money had not been collected from the airlines. Following the president's order, six KAA officials were interdicted. They were the then CEO Lucy Mbugua, finance manager John Thumbi, airport engineer Christopher Warutere, procurement manager Lilian Okidi, examination finance head, Martin Kamau, and company secretary Victor Arika. And in June 2015, the government suspended the lease agreement.

However, Uhuru's erratic "roadside" order and the lease cancellation that followed came back to haunt the country. In September 2021, RML presented a bill of KSh.934 million to KAA as concession fees and damages for the arbitrary cancellation of the tender after only seven months. The contract was for eight-years. KAA explained the cancellation was due to "necessity, convenience, and in the public interest." The company said it was a breach of contract. RML claimed it had not been paid despite having invested KSh.300 million in the

Because of similar blunders by Kenya government officials, taxpayers must pay billions of shillings to complainants and lawyers. In the 2020/2021 fiscal year alone, the government paid KSh.2.5 billion for legal services connected to bungled projects. That was an increase of KSh.1.2 billion from the amount paid out in the 2019/2020 fiscal year. Many of the cases related to the government breaching terms of contracts, compensation, general and/or exemplary damages. Early in March 2021, the parliamentary budget and appropriations committee (BAC) warned that soon, the Exchequer could part with at least KSh.1.2 trillion shillings in damages to companies and individuals unfairly treated by the State.

THE NYS MEGA SCANDALS

The catalogue of corruption cases under Uhuru could be as long as the Madaraka Express train. One of the biggest scandals during his reign, however, involved the NYS, a uniformed disciplined service.

Formed by Mzee Kenyatta in 1964, the NYS was meant to equip youths with essential and formative skills. After the promulgation of the 2010 constitution, NYS was put under the ministry of devolution and planning headed by Cabinet Secretary Anne Waiguru. That was the time the infamous scandal occurred.

The multi-million-shilling scandal washed away any pretensions that the Jubilee government was seriously committed to eradicating corruption. An estimated KSh.791 million was lost during what came to be known as the NYS Scandal One. It was a sophisticated operation involving NYS officials and private individuals to defraud taxpayers. They manipulated the government's Integrated Financial Management Information System (IFMIS) system by adding zeroes on all the transactions. That meant KSh.100 automatically became KSh.1,000 and so on. That resulted in a colossal loss of money.

IFMIS is an Oracle-based Enterprise Resource Planning (ERP) system used both at the national and county levels to enhance financial accountability and transparency. Through manipulation, the IFMIS became nothing but a conduit of fraudulent transactions.

The alleged participants in the scandal included businessman Benson Gethi, the alleged mastermind, and Josephine Kabura Irungu, the woman who admitted carting millions of shillings in gunny bags from one location to another. The name of Cabinet Secretary Devolution, Anne Waiguru, also featured in the case. Twenty-eight commercial banks were cited for handling the transactions.

Asked in court whether she had had any personal or business association with Kabura, Waiguru said she had "never met, seen, or interacted" with Kabura. But Kabura claimed the two were good friends. They met in 2012 when Kabura was working at a data processing company, she said. Kabura also claimed it was Waiguru who helped her register the companies used to apply for tenders and even instructed her to open bank accounts.

The drama which took place in the rooms of the Public Accounts Committee (PAC) and in courts, captivated Kenyans who were awe-struck that such vast amounts of money could be purloined in the presence of intelligence and security apparatuses. At one time, Kabura withdrew KSh.100 million from a bank, and stuffed sacks with between KSh.10 million and KSh.20 million each. She said she transported the money to a quarry in Ongata Rongai to pay workers. However, she could not provide payment receipts to the PAC to show the money was used for that purpose.

That case was still in court in June 2022.

NYS SCANDAL 11

In 2018, another KSh. 9 billion vanished into peoples' pockets in the NYS scandal 11. Big names trended in that scandal: Cabinet Secretary Waiguru, her Principal Secretary, Peter Mangiti, the NYS Director-General, Nelson Githinji, and his deputy, Adan Harakhe, the man who claimed his password to the IFMIS was stolen and used to manipulate the figures.

Fifty-four civil servants and individuals were arrested including the NYS director-general Richard Ndubai, and the permanent secretary youth ministry, Lilian Omollo. They were charged in October 2018, along with others, with forgery, money laundering, abuse of office, fraud, and obtaining money by false pretence. The case against Githinji was later withdrawn.

Further corrupt activities and decay were found at the agency by the auditor general in 2021. More than KSh.100 million was lost through inflated tenders and other malfeasance. The auditor general found that some suppliers were paid in full before approval which was contrary to the Public Finance Management (National Government) Regulations of 2015.

A good example was a sum of KSh.32 million which was paid to a supplier of woollen blankets, digital camouflage material, boots, and food items, one month before the tender was approved. The depressing and discouraging part of that scenario was that no procurement whatsoever was done. Also, there was an inventory of car tires worth KSh.255 at the NYS, but no records were found to show the items were there. And spares worth KSh.175.8 million purchased in the 2014/2015 financial year went unused and were therefore rendered obsolete.

The scandal at NYS gave the opposition an opportunity to jump on Cabinet Secretary Waiguru who was then close to Uhuru. The president had earlier issued a statement vowing to deal firmly with anyone caught "in the web of corruption." Opposition leader Raila wanted Waiguru to explain her role in the fraud and whether she knew a person by the name, Maria Blessing Nyambura Ng'ang'a. "What was the nature of your knowledge and interaction with the said person?" Raila asked in an affidavit. Ng'ang'a's name had featured on a list of directors of a company said to have pocketed KSh.40 million to supply powdered milk to NYS. Waiguru, who was once the director of IFMIS, head of the economic stimulus programme, and head of governance at the treasury, repeatedly denied any involvement in all dark deals at the ministry.

Investigators said five Kenyan banks, the Standard Chartered Bank Kenya, Equity Bank Kenya, KCB, Cooperative Bank of Kenya, and Diamond Trust Bank Kenya, were faulted by CBK for handling KSh.3.58 billion of the fraudulent money. CBK fined them a total of KSh.393 million for failing to report large transactions, a violation of Anti-Money Laundering/Combating the Financing of Terrorism (AML/CFT) regulations.

The Assets Recovery Agency (ARA) found KSh.10.5 million in eleven banks under the names of individuals and companies said to be associated with the accused. Some of the companies had only recently been registered before huge amounts of money were transferred into their accounts.

The case was ongoing as Uhuru left office.

NG-CDF

The National Government – Constituency Development Fund (NG-CDF) is among the most tainted parliamentary creations.

Since its inception in 2003, the CDF, whose objective was to devolve infrastructural development to the grassroots, has been dogged by theft, corruption, and all manner of rot. The fund was established to give MPs direct control of huge amounts of money for grass-roots development projects. Initially, 2.5% of the nation's total revenue collection was to go directly to constituencies. That figure was adjusted to 3.5% in the 2006-2007 fiscal year. That gives each MP about KSh.141 million per year.

But the more money was pumped into the constituency kitty the more of it was stolen or misused. In many constituencies, the revenue has served communities well. But in some, the CDF became another avenue for politicians to siphon money from the exchequer. Numerous MPs were unable to account for CDF money. There were a bountiful of cases of legislators flouting procurement regulations, inflating costs, and in some cases, stealing large amounts of money, through phony salary payments to non-existing workers.

In addition, MPs awarded contracts to relatives and friends and received kickbacks from suppliers. It was also discovered that MPs favoured relatives and friends for bursary funds, and channelled key projects to their areas of birth, denying development in areas of their opponents. The use of CDF for political patronage has led to lopsided development in most constituencies.

In Central Imenti constituency, for example, the CDF committee there claimed it disbursed KSh.27.4 million bursaries to students but could not shed light on how the recipients were chosen. Thus, the accuracy, completeness, and validity, of the bursaries, could not be ascertained. In Wajir West, KSh.26 million was said to have been disbursed to construct 54 school projects, but only 24 were completed. Rot was found in several other constituencies.

In August 2018, the Embakasi North constituency MP and eight others were charged for allegedly misappropriating KSh.39.8 million of CDF. MP James Mwangi Gakuya and his officials appeared before the Milimani Anti-Corruption Court to face counts of fraudulent acquisition of public property, conflict of interest, conspiracy to defraud, and wilful failure to adhere to procurement and disposal laws. All the accused pleaded not guilty to their various charges and were released on bail.

In 2020, the EACC announced it was investigating serving MPs over widespread allegations of malpractices over CDF billions of shillings. Vice Chairman Irene Keino said the commission was studying over 200 cases of misuse of funds. The investigation followed a damning report by the National Taxpayers Association (NTA) which talked of a "possibility that some legislators were either not in control [of CDF] or had become part of illegal schemes to siphon millions of shillings from public to private accounts." NTA estimated that KSh.242 million of KSh.1 billion allocated to 27 constituencies had been misused in ghost projects, incomplete, or abandoned projects. Some MPs stole and banked the money into their personal accounts.

The Auditor General Gathungu reported in her audit report that numerous buses purchased by legislators using CDF money could not be found and their logbooks could not be traced.

Among those questioned by the EACC for graft allegations relating to CDF was MP of Ol Kalou, David Kiaraho, in March 2020. The anti-graft organisation claimed KSh.120 million was involved in the suspected offence of fraud, conflict of interest, embezzlement, and misappropriation of public funds. He was questioned for four hours and let go.

In July 2020, MP Richard Onyonka of Kitutu Chache South was arrested for allegedly misusing CDF money. It was alleged in court in July 2020 that he used KSh.137 million of CDF money to buy sugar for distribution to internally displaced persons (IDPs) in his constituency in 2009. It was alleged that through the purchase, the government had lost KSh.18 million in value added tax (VAT). But Onyonka vehemently denied the allegations terming them "false." He said he did not buy the sugar since the fund was meant for development and not for business.

Another MP, Aisha Jumwa, was arrested in August 2020 for allegedly misappropriating KSh.19 million belonging to CDF. The director of public prosecutions (DPP), Noordin Haji, claimed that the MP used proxies to register several companies which were then awarded tenders worth KSh.57 million. The money was allegedly transmitted in cash to the legislator. However, out of the KSh.57 million said to have been misused, the DPP could only nail the MP on the KSh.19 million.

Jumwa was charged with numerous counts of corruption, conflict of interest, money laundering, forgery, and acquisition of proceeds of crime. She was charged together with six others, Wachu Omar Abdalla, Kennedy Otieno Onyango, Bernard Riba Kai, Sophia Saidi Charo, and Margaret Faith Kalume, all members of the Malindi constituency tender committee, and Robert Katana Wanje, a director of a private company. Multserve Contractors Limited. They pleaded not guilty. In April 2022, the trial magistrate postponed the case until after the 2022 general elections on August 9, to allow the MP concentrate on the polls.

On September 4, 2020, MP Jonah Mburu of Lari constituency was taken into custody by EACC detectives for allegedly misusing KSh.27 million of the CDF. Five others, Ayaan Mahadhi, accounts manager, Peter Mugo Mwangi, CDF chairman, Grace Muthoni Macharia, contractor, Francis Gachoka Kamuyu, clerk Lari constituency NG-CDF, and Paul Mucheru, were also arrested over contracts awarded for the constructions of schools, and for ICT hubs and sports activities. They were charged with abuse of office, conflict of interest, conspiracy to commit an offence of companies, dealing with suspect property, and acting without authorisation. Also charged was a company owned by Mburu, Pambazuko Distributors Limited. When Mburu appeared in court in September 2020, the court directed the legislator not to access the CDF offices and to surrender his passport.

Mischief in Counties

In 2015 alone, 20 out of the 47 counties were found to have embezzled public money, and nothing was done. Ten counties were identified in an EACC report as being the most corrupt: Wajir, Kitui, Kericho, Mombasa, Garissa, Marsabit, Lamu, Kilifi, Kakamega, and Nandi. Devolution brought resources to the grassroots, but it also brought bribery, nepotism, embezzlement, and mismanagement of taxpayers' money, to the local level. Since the beginning of devolution, numerous individuals have been arrested and charged in court throughout the country on a variety of charges including corruption, abuse of office, unlawful acquisition of public property, and conflict of interest.

Several governors including Zachary Okoth Obado of Migori, Mike Sonko of Nairobi, Ferdinand Waititu of Kiambu, and Moses Lenolkulal of Samburu, had disparate cases to answer in court.

In March 2019, Lenolkulal was arrested on allegations of abuse of office and conflict of interest leading to a loss of KSh.84.6 million from the public. He denied the charge. The EACC also wondered how Lenolkulal amassed wealth totalling KSh. 703.5 million in the years he had been governor. His salary since his election in February 2019 to March 2019 totalled KSh.43 million. His assets included buildings and luxury cars. Lenolkulal was the first public official to be ordered to step down by a court of law pending trial. High Court Judge Mumbi Ngugi ruled that the governor could only visit his office with the permission of the EACC. The EACC said it would no longer be business as usual for constitutional office holders facing criminal charges of corruption and economic crime.

A few months later it was the turn of Kiambu Governor Waititu. He faced a KSh.588 million fraud case involving an alleged personal benefit of millions of shillings in deals with numerous companies some of which he owned. He is charged along with his wife, Susan Wangari, and nine others. They all pleaded not guilty. In June 2022, the High Court froze 18 prime properties and high-end vehicles belonging to Waititu, pending the determination of the case.

In Kenya, corruption has turned into a family business. Several officials were prosecuted on graft charges along with spouses and family members. For Obado, it was his four children who were in the dock with him. The Obados and others found themselves in trouble over a query involving the loss of KSh.73 million belonging to the Migori County. They faced charges of gross misappropriation of public funds. The accused allegedly received kickbacks arising from work rendered to the county by several companies. The prosecution alleged that Obado used part of the money to pay tuition fees for his children. He also purchased two high-end vehicles and acquired a residential property in Nairobi. The accused denied all the charges. Obado too was barred from accessing his office awaiting the ruling of the court.

Separately, the EACC ordered the forfeiture of some properties belonging to Murang'a governor, Mwangi wa Iria, claiming the properties were obtained from proceeds of corruption. The EACC listed a 13-acre piece of land in Mweiga Thungare, Nyeri, and a house in Umoja Inner-Core in Nairobi, as those it wanted confiscated. In documents submitted to the anti-corruption court in Nairobi in January 2022, the agency claimed wa Iria received KSh.14 million through a media company from contracts worth KSh.542 million awarded to the company by the Murang'a County government. The company was owned by alleged associates of the county boss. The governor's wife, Jane Waigwe Kimani, was also mentioned in court as having handled the purchase of the Umoja house using part of the money. The EACC alleged that wa Iria "used his office to enrich himself." High Court Judge Esther Maina restrained wa Iria and Kimani from selling, leasing, developing, or subdividing the properties pending conclusion of the case.

In 2019, Sonko, the flamboyant Nairobi governor, was picked up by police on allegations of corruption involving KSh.357 million belonging to the county. The director of public prosecution, Noordin Haji, claimed Sonko forged documents, misappropriated county funds, and irregularly awarded tenders. His latest troubles, which he denied, followed a string of court cases over a span of several years.

He was previously accused of unlawful acquisition of public property and money laundering.

Sonko's predecessor, Evans Kidero, too faced corruption, and economic crimes charges, together with seven county officials.

Other governors charged in court during Uhuru's regime were Sospeter Ojaamong of Busia County who faced abuse of office and conspiracy to steal public funds related to services procured for a solid waste management system and Garissa Governor Ali Korane for issues relating to the KSh.233 million World Bank-funded Kenya Urban Support Programme (KUSP) project.

Another Governor in trouble for allegedly issuing a KSh.34.9 million tender award was Governor Muthomi Njuki of Tharaka Nithi. The tender was for the installation and commissioning of a solid waste incinerator. However, investigators claimed, the company that won the tender submitted fraudulent documents. Also charged alongside Njuki were county officials, Fridah Muthoni, Floridah Kiende, Lee Mwenda, Japhet Nkonge, Mike Murithi, Emily Mucheni, and Elosy Matti, among others. Two directors of Westomaxx Investment, Kenneth Ngai and Caroline Wambui were also indicted. The accused appeared in court in September 2020 to face 16 corruption-related charges. They pleaded not guilty.

THE 2017 ELECTION TENDER MATTERS

Al-Ghurair is a conglomerate operating in Europe, North America, the Middle East, and North Africa. It deals with among other things real estate, petrochemicals, and construction. In October 2016, the chairperson of the company, Majid Al-Ghurair, arrived in Nairobi and met Uhuru at State House. That meeting was so secretive that only Uhuru and closest allies were present. The meeting took place amid revelations that the government had awarded a multi-million-shilling tender to the Arab company.

Although the government and Al-Ghurair denied the meeting took place, the mystery behind the tender of 120 million ballot papers for the August 2017 elections became a matter of public debate. It was alleged that the Kenyatta family had an interest in the lucrative tender issued by the IEBC. Raila's coalition, then the National Super Alliance (NASA), claimed (without providing proof) that election ballot papers had already been printed even before the tender was awarded.

NASA did not stop there. In June 2017, after the tender had been issued, the alliance petitioned the High Court against the award. Raila alleged the deal was part of a conspiracy to rig the elections. His co-principal in NASA, Musalia Mudavadi, challenged Uhuru "to come clean on his family's links with the Dubai firm and state his interests in the contract." Uhuru didn't.

The IEBC chairman, Wafula Chebukati, defended the tender by giving reasons why the electoral body chose Al-Ghurair without subjecting the tender to competition: that the company had modern machines, with 50% of the machines reserved for the printing of ballot papers, had experienced, and qualified staff, and had a suitable emergency production, packaging, and delivery plan.

But the High Court nullified the award ruling that IEBC violated election regulations. In June 2017, IEBC again issued the tender to Al-Ghurair. NASA returned to court and the contract was again nullified. The Court ruled that the contract had not been sufficiently transparent. So, IEBC went to the Court of Appeal. On 20 July, the Court of Appeal overturned the High Court judgement and awarded the tender to Al-Ghurair.

As Uhuru vehemently condemned the opposition for allegedly trying to sabotage the elections, the Al-Ghurair company filed documents in court denying any links to Uhuru. It admitted that one of its top officials, Majid Saif Al-Ghurair, did meet with Uhuru, but only in his capacity as head of the Dubai Chamber of Commerce and not as a representative of the company. In its affidavit to court, the company said none of its staff or directors had ever been to State House or had ever met the president. It further denied any relationship whatsoever between Majid Saif Al-Ghurair and the Al-Ghurair Printing and Publishing Company, save for the name "Al-Ghurair".

However, NASA insisted the tender was influenced by Uhuru in collusion with some IEBC officials. NASA claimed the company's chief executive officer, Aziz Al-Ghurair, "is an intimate friend of the Kenyatta family and a frequent guest at the home of Muhoho Kenyatta." Uhuru's younger brother did not deny or confirm those allegations. However, Al-Ghurair refuted the reports. It said its website "does not state printing and publishing as part of its portfolio." That assertion was rubbished, however, when it emerged the company had been awarded a US$4.6 million (KSh.460 million) contract to print ballot papers for Malawi's May 21, 2019, elections. It was not only in Kenya where Al-Ghurair ran into trouble over ballot papers. Its credibility had also been questioned in Uganda and Zambia.

Promise unkept

Uhuru promised lifestyle audits of *all* government officials and their families, "including myself." The move was intended to catch public servants who had accumulated questionable wealth while in civil service. He said in June 2018 that, "all the governors and cabinet secretaries will be audited after the two of us [Uhuru and Ruto], before all other government officials are subjected to the same exercise."

A team of experts even drew rules to guide the process. The audit of all public officials did not happen. Only some procurement officers were audited. That was because of a vigorous pushback from some elected leaders over Uhuru's directive. Those allied to DP Ruto claimed the directive was a political witch hunt against Kalenjin leaders who opposed Uhuru's government. "It's mob justice," MP Nelson Koech lamented.

On the same month of October, Uhuru ordered lifestyle audits on the wealthy to check on those who under-reported incomes to evade taxes. That was not done and there are good reasons why. If such an audit was to be fair, then Uhuru's own family wealth would have to be scrutinised. No one knows whether all businesses owned by the Kenyattas pay taxes from profits they make. Obviously, Kenyans would be anxious to know the cumulative income from Kenyatta assets and the money rendered as taxes to KRA.

The SGR

One of the president's biggest and ambitious national projects was the Standard Gauge Railway (SGR) linking Mombasa and Nairobi. The project, initiated by President Kibaki, was to transform the three-metre gauge railway line into a standard gauge system. The Exim Bank of China was the main financier of the US$3.6 billion project, footing 90% of the cost. The rest was to come from Kenya. The SGR is part of China's "One Belt, One Road" initiative intended to improve land and maritime trade routes between China and Europe, Asia, and Africa.

Uhuru owned the project and proudly launched it after its completion on May 31, 2017. He called it a new chapter in the history of Kenya

Whether the railway line would succeed in transforming the country into: "an industrial, prosperous, and middle-income country," as Uhuru predicted, is difficult to say. But the SGR did improve passenger services between the two cities, shortening travel time from ten hours to a little more than four hours. It also provided an efficient and more reliable, albeit expensive, form of freighting goods to and from the port of Mombasa. For months, freight users shied away from using the line because of high costs of rail compared to road transport costs from Mombasa.[166]

The 480-km-SGR has been rated as "the most expensive infrastructure project implemented in Kenya since independence,"[167] averaging in cost to about US$5.6 million (KSh.610 million) per kilometre of track.[168]

Originally, it was to run between Mombasa to Nairobi and then to Kisumu on the shores of Lake Victoria. But in 2017, Uhuru ordered the line rerouted through Naivasha, a town in the Rift Valley,

---

[166] Shiundu, Alphonce. *Railway to Nowhere,* Development and Cooperation, December 22, 2019.

[167] Cope, Zak & Immanuel Ness. The Oxford Handbook of Economic Imperialism, Oxford University Press, 2022, p. 526.

[168] Kacungira, Nancy. "Will Kenya get value for money from its new railway? *BBC,* June 8, 2017.

90 kilometres northwest of Nairobi. The stretch between Nairobi and Naivasha was estimated to cost US$1.5 billion (KSh.165 billion). Uhuru launched the Nairobi to Naivasha railway line in September 2015 and it became operational in October 2019. Exim Bank paid 85% of that amount and Kenya 15%.

Uhuru's decision to change the route raised immediate protests from critics who dubbed the line "the railway to nowhere" because it passed through Duka Moja, a small sleepy trading centre on the Maai-Mahiu-Narok road where the railway line comes to an abrupt end." Duka Moja is 20 km beyond the last train station at Suswa, a cattle trading centre.[169] Freighters and economists considered the line to be not viable.

In June 2017, Raila, then presidential candidate of the NASA coalition, claimed the diversion was to benefit the Kenyatta family. He alleged that the land on which a proposed industrial freight park was to be built belonged to the Kenyattas. "We wanted this SGR to run to where there is a port and an international airport [that is, Kisumu], but Jubilee's greed has changed the entire thing," Raila lamented. The first family did not respond to any of Raila's allegations. In December 2021, KRC re-launched a train passenger service – using the old gauge - between Nairobi and Kisumu, after rehabilitation of the line at a cost of KSh.3.7 billion.

The immediate question among Kenyans is: What interests do the Kenyattas have at Naivasha?

---

[169] Ndii, David. "From game changer to railway to nowhere: The rise and fall of Lunatic Line 2.0," The *Elephant*, November 2, 2019.

CHAPTER 13

Shame, Shame, Shame

If there is one government parastatal that should be disbanded and/or reconstituted afresh due to rampant insider corruption, it is the Kenya Pipeline Company (KPC). The decay in the parastatal is beyond belief. Incorporated in September 1973, KPC was entrusted with the responsibility of transporting, storing, and delivering, petroleum products to consumers, through its pipelines and oil depot networks. But since its inception, the organisation has served as a tap-of-luxury for corrupt officials who have misused procurement regulations to siphon off billions of shillings belonging to the public.

Top management officials were in the habit of either inflating prices or conniving with construction and energy firms through illegal issuance of tenders and contracts. One of the biggest scandals affecting KPC was the Triton saga. It started during Kibaki's regime but cascaded into Uhuru's administration.

In October 2008, Triton Petroleum Limited, won a tender for oil amounting to 80,000 metric tonnes which was scheduled for delivery in December 2008. However, Triton was able to deliver only 56,000 metric tons, far too short of what was agreed in the Collateral Finance Agreement with KPC in 2004. But a computer system which was supposed to record the data failed. When the KPC management conducted an audit, it found that the oil which was supposed to be held in trust for financiers: the Kenya Commercial Bank, the PTA bank, the Glencore Energy UK Limited, the Emirates National Oil Corporation (ENOC) of Singapore, and Fortis Bank of France, had been released to Triton. KCB went to court and Triton was put under receivership while owing financiers KSh.7.6 billion.[170]

The man behind Triton, Yagnesh Devani, fled to England. In 2011, Kenya sent an extradition request to the UK to have Devani returned to Kenya to face at least 19 charges of fraud. By June 2022, however, Devani had still not been repatriated.

NHIF

The National Hospital Insurance Fund (NHIF) is steeped in so many scandals it's impossible to name them all. One glaring one during Uhuru's term involved the loss of KSh.10 billion through impersonation and fictitious claims perpetrated by public and private hospitals. The facilities colluded with corrupt NHIF officers to defraud the government by allowing one NHIF card issued to a specific individual to be used by multiple people at different facilities. Workers who had never received treatment were listed in returns, and in some cases, the government was charged double for services rendered. Some health facilities presented huge bills purporting to have carried out major surgeries when, in fact, the procedures were minor. One example is of "a small clinic the size of a kiosk" that was billing the NHIF KSh.15 million every month.[171] All its claims were deemed to be false.

In September 2021, the auditor general declared NHIF "broke" and said something had to be done to rectify the missteps at the health insurer. She noted a gap of KSh.3.6 billion between the KSh.23 billion earnings in the year ending in June 2018 and earnings ending June 2019. Kenyans who needed treatment especially after the outbreak of Covid-19 were frustrated by NHIF's inability to pay

---

[170] Analysis of the Triton oil scandal, AfriCog, July 2009.
[171] Ngetich, Jacob. « NHIF loses KSh.10 billion through fake claims from health facilities," The *Standard*, September 13, 2021.

for care. "With the current pandemic," said Raila during an NHIF membership drive in Mombasa in June 2021, "hundreds of Kenyans have died simply because they could not afford hospitalisation fees." He envisioned that the chance of a greater segment of the population dropping dead from illness was one infection away.

NSSF

The National Social Security Fund (NSSF) is another government body with serious problems of corruption. The conviction early in 2022 of people connected to NSSF, however, showed there was hope things could change. A case that had been in courts for almost 17 years was finally resolved, and four individuals were sent to jail and fined heavily for trying to defraud the Fund of KSh1.6 billion. The offences took place between 2006 and 2008.

A former investment manager at NSSF, Francis Zuriels Moturi, a former CEO of Discount Securities Limited (DSL), David Ndirangu Githaiga, and two officials of DSL, former finance director, Wilfred Munyoro Weru, and former investment manager, Isaac Nyakundi, were found guilty of several charges including irregularly trading in shares through the DSL, fraudulently making payments from public revenue, and fraudulent disposal of public property. The accused pretended to have purchased shares from the Nairobi Securities Exchange (NSE) but, in fact, they hadn't. Moturi was fined KSh.2.4 billion or serve 12 years in prison. Gichaiga, Mungoro, and Nyakundi, were fined KSh.803 million each or 12 years in prison. Magistrate Lawrence Mugambi fined DSL KSh.4 billion or risk its properties being auctioned. Two NSSF officials, James Akoya, and Mary Ndirangu, were set free for lack of evidence.

* * *

In November 2021, there were shocking revelations of how dozens of government health facilities were engaging in dubious transactions in collusion with teachers to defraud taxpayers of millions of shillings. At least three dozen hospitals were involved in defrauding an insurance company through false billings, falsification of days patients spent in hospitals, unnecessary prescriptions of drugs, overcharging, fake claims, and bribery. Minet Kenya, an insurance company, was forced to blacklist the offending hospitals. The amount of money lost through such illegality couldn't be determined, but it was believed to run into millions of shillings.

The chief executive of the government-run Teachers' Service Commission (TSC), Nancy Macharia, admitted malpractices existed but said it was only a tiny fraction of teachers who were involved, and that measures were being taken with the insurance company to eliminate the practice.

JAIL THE JAILERS

One would think that those who spend days and nights guarding thieves, murderers, rapists, and gangsters, would be as clean as a whistle, but revelations that the State Department for Correction Services paid KSh.1 billion to fictitious suppliers is a story that calls for jailing the jailers. Auditor General Nancy Gathungu disclosed that the department paid KSh.975.7 million to suppliers who were neither known nor contracted to supply goods and services to 129 prisons around the country. In addition, KSh.420 million was overpaid on pending bills. The payments were made between 2009 and 2018. Surprisingly, the fraud was discovered after almost a decade, raising questions as to why the malpractice at the department's headquarters was not discovered earlier to prevent losses. A few months before that, the prisons department had been cited by parliament for accumulating KSh.6.2 billion in pending bills.

The prisons department has a long record of corruption. Top officials collude with juniors to steal money from the sale of prison farm produce, prices of goods including prisoner rations are inflated, and warders who complain about not getting a share of corrupt proceeds, are transferred. On the other hand, jailers routinely receive bribes to allow into prisons prohibited goods such as drugs, phones, and foods. When businessmen Ketan Somaia and Kamlesh Pattni were in jail at Kamiti maximum security prison on fraud-related charges, they were catered from outside, slept in furnished private quarters, and allowed to receive daily newspapers. The two used their riches to ease their lives in prison while the rest of the prison population was sleeping on the floor with tattered blankets and eating unhealthy food.

Moreover, prisoners routinely use smuggled phones to manipulate citizens into paying money through fraudulent means. In a few cases, fights have erupted among prisoners over how to share the illegal yields. In one case at King'ong'o maximum security prison in Nyeri, a brutal encounter between prisoners Shem Kariuki and Peter Gachau over money led to the death of the former.

TURKANA DAM FIASCO

It was a matter of life or death for the starving people of Turkana. After decades of perennial droughts and dependency on aid, the government decided to invest in irrigation schemes in the Turkana County to provide water to the pastoralist communities. The job was left to the National Irrigation Board (NIB), a corruption-infested government parastatal, which had been involved in numerous corrupt deals in several projects elsewhere.

When officers of the Public Procurement Regulatory Authority (PPRA) visited Turkana in 2016 to assess the progress of the 15 irrigation schemes earmarked for the area, they found that some of the schemes had stalled. The government had pumped in KSh.953 million for the project, but there was not much to show. The ones that had been completed were not operating for several reasons including blockage of canals because of siltation. Some gabions had been swept away and canal walls had collapsed due to shoddy workmanship. The procurement process was undertaken irregularly. The tender committee breached regulations by approving contracts despite lack of quorum. Contract costs were also revised, all pointing to corrupt activities.

Despite the scandal, the county government of Turkana announced in February 2021 that it was proceeding with the construction of four more irrigation schemes. It also planned to revive all stalled irrigation projects in the county. Turkana in northern Kenya is one of the most vulnerable places in Kenya and suffers from frequent dry spells and food insecurity. The county's burden is exacerbated by an influx of refugees from neighbouring countries and a proliferation of small arms which are used in tribal conflicts. That makes insecurity a major problem in the area. Several international organisations including the UN Development Programme (UNDP) have teamed up with the government to assist in providing food and water during emergencies.

However, the problem of corruption relating to the fifteen dams was worrisome considering the many problems facing Turkana people. There was no indication that any serious investigation was carried out to determine whether corruption really occurred and if so, by whom. And more important, what action was taken.

The matter of the Kimwarer and Arror dams was still percolating as Uhuru served his last months in office. A former finance minister, Henry Rotich, a chief economist, Kennedy Nyakundi, a former Kerio Valley Development Authority executive, David Kimosop, and a former Managing Director of the National Environment Management Authority, Geoffrey Wahungu, were still attending court on corruption charges in 2022.

Other accused facing almost 30 counts of corruption were Jackson Kinyanjui, William Kipkemboi, Paul Kipkoech, Francis Chepkonga, and Titus Muriiithi. The main allegation was that in 2019, the individuals defrauded the government of KSh.63 billion through a contract for the construction of the dams without approval. Rotich was also charged with single sourcing a KSh.11 billion insurance cover for the dams, money which was paid even before work had begun.

The Treasury Principal Secretary, Kamau Thugge, was also among those initially charged, but his case was dropped after he became a state witness. The case was scheduled to continue in June 2022.

The prosecution claimed in court that the Italian company did not exist at the time the contract was signed and that it was not part of the tender bid documents. Moreover, prosecution said, the contract amount was inflated to benefit the accused. "We will prove that Rotich and his co-accused gave in to the corrupting influence of power, looted our coffers, and practiced corruption with impunity,"[172] a special prosecutor, Taib Ali Taib, said.

After receiving a technical committee report on the scandal in mid-2019, Uhuru cancelled the two projects. In the meantime, an Italian company mentioned in the scandal, CMC Di Ravenna, moved to the International Court of Arbitration at The Hague demanding a compensation of KSh.80 billion for work not done. If the court rules in favour of the company, Kenya could lose more than KSh.150 billion. As this was going on, auctioneers moved in and confiscated all the machinery belonging to the Italian firm, including trucks, water bowsers, tippers, and cranes, for auction.

GALANA

Corruption allegations also hit the Galana Irrigation Scheme in Tana River at the Kenya coast. An estimated KSh.10 billion was deemed lost through graft at the project, prompting the senate agriculture committee to ask Auditor General Gathungu in November 2020 to conduct a forensic audit. Galana was supervised by the NIB. The committee wanted the DCI and the DPP to investigate and conclude investigations and report findings.

The complaints centred on corruption and mismanagement of KSh.580 million which was issued by the government in May 2019 for bush clearance. It was alleged the work carried out was shoddy. The 10,000-acre project, officially known as the Galana-Kulalu Food Security Project, was part of Uhuru's Big 4 Agenda aimed at yielding KSh.1.2 billion in maize sales yearly. But until 2020, Galana was

---

[172] Ogemba, Paul. "Firm in dams scam seeks KSh.80 billion compensation," *The Standard*, November 24, 2021.

producing only 120,000 bags of 90 kg maize worth KSh.270 million due to the fact the full capacity had not been realised.

In February 2022, the project announced it had a stock of 20,000 fifty-kilogramme bags of maize in stores which it was ready to sell as it struggled to revamp its production. Still, equipment worth millions of shillings remained unused and any hopes of jobs and better standards of living for the local people was still a mirage. Finance for the project came from the Kenya government and the Israeli Bank Leumi which contributed KSh.6.35 billion.

Officials at the NIB were some of the earliest victims of Jubilee government's war on corruption. In 2016, Cabinet Secretary Eugene Wamalwa suspended the NIB board, the deputy general manager, Mary Chomba, and the procurement and supplies manager, Boaz Akello. Also suspended was the CEO, Daniel Barasa. Efforts by the cabinet secretary to have him reinstated on account that he had not been involved in the scandal went a cropper. The board said Barasa's suspension was in order and complied with regulations. However, in May 2016, the High Court stopped Wamalwa's disbandment of the board in a petition filed by activist Felix Mategei who termed the cabinet secretary's decision "unconstitutional and illegal." Justice George Odunga ruled that Wamalwa exceeded his powers in disbanding the board. Barasa also went to court to challenge his suspension saying because the board had not given notice for the special board meeting that ousted him, it had breached the law and had violated his terms of service. Barasa was reinstated but chose to resign.

There was another notable financial scandal at the NIB. KSh.20 billion went missing, according to the auditor general's report of 2015/2016. KSh.7.3 billion of that was meant for the Galana project. Some of the money was used or misused to lease 20,000 acres of land for five years from the Agricultural Development Corporation (ADC) when only 10,000 acres were required. The price of the land was also inflated. NIB paid KSh.3.6 billion in a deal that was worth only KSh.360 million. The board could not explain why they leased so much land nor why they paid so much to the ADC. At the same time, it was found, 21 irrigation schemes had stalled despite the government pumping in KSh.880 million.

As a result of the malfeasance at NIB, the government either postponed or scaled down some projects including phase two of the Lower Nyanza Irrigation Project and the Mwea Irrigation Project. The government also cut down the budget of NIB, revised contracts, and restricted tender committees from making unreasonable decisions.

LEADERS OF TOMORROW?

Kenyan leaders have always had big plans for the youth, at least on paper and speech. "You are leaders of tomorrow," politicians shout themselves hoarse. Yet, the playing field has not always favoured the youth. Conversely, older people, some well beyond their retirement age of sixty years, are the ones who continue to substantially benefit from jobs and economic opportunities.

There are those like the CEO of the Kenya National Chamber of Commerce and Industry, Samuel Matonda, who believe youths "shouldn't be leaders of tomorrow but leaders of today." Others like newscaster, Trevor Ombija, asked: The youth are the leaders of tomorrow, but are they prepared to lead? Those are the key questions.

Forty percent or thirty-five million young Kenyans between the ages of eighteen and thirty-five are unemployed, according to a 2020 Census report. But because they live in a country where elders dominate the state, political parties, and other instruments of power, young people are often rendered powerless.[173] They are used and misused for the benefit of political leaders by getting them to participate in unlawful demonstrations and violence. During election campaigns, it is the jobless youth who are ferried from trading centres and villages to meeting venues to create an aura of a candidate's popularity in exchange for money, sometimes as

---

[173] Maina, Grace. Opportunity or Treat: The Engagement of Youth in African Societies, *Africa Dialogue Monograph Series*, No. 1/2012, p. 58.

little as Ksh.500. That practice was rampant even during the 2022 presidential campaigns.

The empowerment of youths was probably what was in President Kibaki's mind in 2007 when he started the Youth Enterprise Development Fund (YEDF). The idea was to transform youth from "jobseekers to job creators and employers." Kibaki allocated KSh.1 million as a starting capital to be distributed to youths throughout the country. He also started an initiative called *Kazi kwa Vijana*, Jobs for Youth, to deal with the challenges of unemployment. To give youths access to government contracts, he ordered the easing of restrictions that stopped young people from competing equitably in industry and commerce.

From inception, the YEDF was managed and staffed by a relatively young group of professionals, some of them coming directly from university. There was a high expectation in the populace that such people would be diligent in serving their fellow compatriots with dedication and honesty. That did not happen. The organisation was infested with corruption and became an ATM machine for a few top executives of the organisation.

Signs of mismanagement and corruption emerged less than two years after its formation when YEDF money began to disappear. Large disbursements were made by YEDF to counties to help young people venture into business. The plan was for selected individuals or groups to get between KSh.100,000 and KSh.2 million each to start or improve their businesses. In many cases, the money did not reach the intended targets. Officials were pocketing the money. The officials registered private companies and used them as conduits for stolen money. Then they covered-up to mask the malfeasance. There was a case of some directors diverting KSh.65 million of YEDF money to personal use. All the cases were investigated by the EACC and the DCI, and several people were arrested and charged in court.

In 2009, the first CEO of YEDF, Umuro Wario, was suspended and then fired following revelations of financial, procurement, and recruitment, irregularities. The EACC eventually cleared Wario of wrongdoing and he was reinstated to his position.

When Wario's term ended, his place was taken over by Juma Mwatata Mwangala, who barely lasted a year. In 2013, he was hauled to court to face two counts of abuse of office. He was fined KSh.1 million for unprocedurally issuing a tender of KSh.200 million to Connete Technologies Limited for the supply of automated hatcheries. The transaction, the court was told, was made without approval from the YEDF board.

But that was just a small part of the problem because in 2015 a much bigger amount, KSh.180.9 million, was stolen from the fund in a web of collusion that ringed in YEDF executives, businessmen, and firms. The EACC and other government agencies investigated YEDF and discovered suspicious transfers of huge sums of money between February and April 2015. That led to the suspension of the chief executive officer, Catherine Namuye. Apparently, the board chairman, Bruce Odhiambo, an Uhuru appointee, was also in the loop. After the EACC investigations, the two were arrested in August 2016, along with two directors of Quorandum Limited, Mukuria Ngamau, and Doreen Ng'ang'a. Odhiambo had replaced Gor Semelang'o who was appointed by Kibaki in 2013 and fired by Uhuru in 2014.

Quorandum was supposed to supply YEDF with an Information Communication Technology (ICT) strategy, but it never did, even though the money was paid. The chief magistrate, Douglas Ogoti, was told that Ngamau used the proceeds of the deal to buy a house in the upmarket Lavington neighbourhood of Nairobi. The house was confiscated by the Assets Recovery Agency (ARA) in 2018. The rest of the suspected stolen money went to a law firm, individuals, and companies that were part of the conspiracy. They were not prosecuted.

Six years later in 2021, Ngamau was convicted and sentenced to thirteen years in jail or pay a fine of KSh.881 million for conspiring with YEDF senior officials to embezzle public funds, an economic crime. The court was told that he transferred part of the money, a little over KSh.59 million, to his company's account at Chase Bank. From there the money was moved to Standard Chartered Bank "to make further transactions and payments on various dates to third parties, including a payment of KSh.3.3 million to Bruce Dominic Odhiambo's account at Cooperative Bank, purportedly for supplies and consultancy services," said a report of the parliamentary investment committee (PIC). Ngamau was also ordered to pay KSh.180 million to YEDF as compensation. His co-director, Ng'anga, was acquitted.

Despite the financial shenanigans, the government kept on pumping more money in the organisation. In 2019-2021, YEDF received KSh. 470 million from the Treasury. That amount increased to KSh. 580 million in the 2021-2022 financial year. This was done even though the Fund had overspent KSh.1 billion of the revolving money meant for loans to youths.

NOT ALL IS WELL AT KAZI MTAANI

It was a noble idea when Uhuru rolled out the Kazi Mtaani programme in 2020 to cushion youths especially those in informal settlements. Tens of thousands of young people below the age of thirty years were to be hired for all manner of mundane work including garbage collection, unblocking of sewers, and general cleanliness of the environment. They were also to be trained on how to set up businesses, as well as on HIV prevention, counselling, and how to deal with mental health. The National Treasury set aside KSh.10 billion to kick off the programme.

With the allocation of KSh. 4.8 billion in the 2021-2022 financial year, the programme was further extended for an additional six months up to the end of 2022. However, Kazi Mtaani is an initiative plagued by serious problems of nepotism and bribery. Although officials at the State department of housing and urban development claimed the selection was based on experience, project requirements, and availability of projects in a particular area, the system of choosing candidates was far from being transparent.

Reports showed that local leaders including MPs, members of the county assembly (MCAs) and Nyumba Kumi elders, often demanded bribes from the youths. They also recruited relatives, supporters, and friends, bypassing genuine applicants. Some of the leaders even demanded a share of the daily salary paid to the youths which normally ranged from KSh.455 and KSh.505. Officials at the department of housing and urban development denied accusations of corruption and bribery.

Last November, 1.2 youths were registered for the programme. For the third phase, which began in June, only 55,608 young people were hired. The government cited lack of funds.

* * *

Uhuru blamed the opposition for 'politicising' corruption. However, corruption is by its practice political because many of those involved in corrupt activities are politicians or their allies in government. Name any scandal in Kenya, from the Goldenberg scandal to the KEMSA scam, and politicians will have a stake. The president blamed everyone else except himself, a stark display of presidential defeat and surrender. He fitted the definition of the Jewish mobster, Abraham Reles, of "a canary who could sing but couldn't fly!"[174]

The civil societies, like many people and organisations, were frustrated over Uhuru's inability to act more decisively against corruption. On November 4, 2016, NGOs sent a petition to the president with thirteen demands on corruption. They asked him to resign if he failed to implement them. They wanted the immediate dismissal of officials mentioned in corruption scandals, the freezing of all bank accounts holding corruptly obtained money, and the recovery of all stolen money. They also asked for measures to protect whistleblowers, and the release to the public of all wealth declaration forms of state and public officials. Uhuru ignored them.

While courts have ruled on a selective basis to freeze accounts of the corrupt, only a fraction of all monies obtained illegally have been recovered. It was nevertheless refreshing news from the EACC

---

[174] Reles, Abraham. The Canary Sang but Couldn't Fly: The Fatal Fall of Abe Reles, the Mobster Who Shattered Murder, Inc.'s Code of Silence, Union Square Press, April 2009.

in 2020 when it reported that KSh.11.3 billion in land, property, and cash, had been recovered from corrupt officials in the financial year 2019/2020. In 2021 and 2022, however, the EACC escalated its recovery programme and managed to recover property worth KSh.30 billion by April 2022.

In November 2021, the office of the director of public prosecutor (DPP) announced that funds stolen through corrupt deals had increased from KSh.67.1 billion in 2017 to KSh.140.2 billion in 2019. But there were still millions, and perhaps billions, of shillings hidden overseas and out of reach of government, that needed to be explained.

In 2018, Uhuru and his Swiss counterpart, Alain Berset, signed an agreement of cooperation aimed at recovering large amounts of money stashed in Swiss bank accounts. That was a move in the right direction. But there are monies in other European countries as well as in the Caribbean offshore banks that have not received government attention. The Bank for International Settlements (BIS) reported in March 2020 that US$3 billion, about KSh.339 billion shillings, had been transferred to offshore accounts between 1990 and 2010. It described the diversion as "appalling." "That kind of money," BIS said, "can build, for example, a power plant that generates electricity for an entire rural district."[175]

Nonetheless, Uhuru's hackneyed warnings, threats, and promises about fighting corruption were too many to attract Kenyans' attention anymore. And he made them with extraordinary vivacity. "We are going to deal ruthlessly with corruption, both real and perceived," he said at the 8th Presidential Roundtable Forum at State House in May 2018. On June 1, 2019, Uhuru repeated a similar chant in Narok, that the 'war against corruption is a war we are undertaking with no joy… [but] "I will not stop until the house we inherited from our forefathers has been swept clean." And in February 2020 while addressing the Marian Shrine in Nakuru, Uhuru asked for help from

---

[175] Himbara, David. "Kenya: Study reveals scale of foreign aid diversion offshore," The Africa Report, March 18, 2020.

Kenyans: "If each one of us play their roles effectively, I don't see the reason why we cannot tackle the challenges facing us."

In January 2021, Uhuru shocked Kenyans when he told a radio interviewer that KSh.2 billion per day [KSh.712 billion per year] was being stolen from the government through corruption. He failed to say who was stealing the money and what action he was taking to stop the steal. For a head of state to admit that money was being stolen and failing to act was baffling. "Uhuru barks but can't bite," said the African Centre for Open Governance (AfriCog), and that his approach was "largely tactical, too legalistic and prosecution driven, and will not yield the desired results."[176]

As a public outcry raged in social media over Uhuru's failure to prosecute robber barons, the government tried to walk back on the KSh.2 billion-per-day theft comments. Government Spokesman Cyrus Oguna said the president was misunderstood and explained the money was the cumulative number of losses over the years. But the damage had already been done.

But speaking during his last Madaraka Day celebrations on June 1, 2022, Uhuru appeared to acknowledge failure of his government's attempt to end graft. He instead asked Kenyans to elect leaders with credentials "to continue the clean-up [of corruption] we started."

The first big hooray

After years of empty talk about corruption, Uhuru got his first major conviction on a corruption case in June 2020. Businesswoman Grace Wakhungu and MP John Waluke became the first 'big fish' to be sentenced to long prison terms for fraud. Wakhungu, mother of a former cabinet minister, Judy Wakhungu, was sentenced to sixty-nine years in prison while Waluke got sixty-seven years, the stiffest sentences given by a Kenyan court at the time. The two, who were directors of a company called Erad Supplies & General Contracts Limited, were given an option of a hefty fine of KSh.707 million each.

---

[176] "Uhuru barks but can't bite, civil society says," AfriCog, May 24, 2019.

The two were found guilty of several counts of defrauding a government parastatal, the National Cereals and Produce Board (NCPB), of KSh.297 million in a maize deal. They were paid the money after presenting an invoice to the NCPB purporting to represent the cost of storing in a South African warehouse, 340,000 tonnes of maize, on transit to NCPB. As it turned out, the invoice was forged. Several law firms also benefited from the deal in the form of legal fees, but they were not charged. Three months after sentencing, Wakhungu and Waluke were freed on health grounds after paying a cash bail of KSh.20 million and KSh.10 million respectively. The successful prosecution of the businesswoman and legislator bolstered Uhuru's fight against corruption.

Another big win for high-level corruption came on September 16, 2021, when the former Sports Cabinet Secretary Hassan Wario was sentenced to six years in prison or a fine of KSh.3.6 million. He was charged on three counts of abuse of office. The offence was committed during the 2016 Rio Olympics which took place between August 5 and August 21, 2016. The anti-corruption chief magistrate, Elizabeth Juma, ruled that Wario took advantage of his position to include strangers in the Kenyan delegation to Brazil causing a loss of KSh.42 million. The travel costs and allowances of the three strangers were paid from public coffers, which was against government financial regulations. Wario, who was appointed an ambassador in 2018 in the middle of the Rio debacle paid the fine and was a free man within hours.

The head of mission to the games, Stephen Sio, received the stiffest sentence in the scandal: twelve years in prison or a fine of KSh.105 million. He pleaded not guilty to six counts of failing to comply with procedures of managing public funds. He was also charged with exaggerating the KSh.500 million Rio budget and by doing so occasioned a loss of taxpayers' money. Kenyans thought the sentences were too light and not commensurate with the offences. "What is the logic of this sentence vis-a-vis the crime committed," asked one Jacktone Mjumbe Ambuka, "because pilferage of public resources in Kenya is so endemic and catastrophic to the very livelihood of citizens? Prosecuting prominent Kenyans is problematic because they have the wherewithal to employ star lawyers and manipulate the course of justice.

The 2016 Rio Olympics had serious corruption and mismanagement problems, ranging from accreditation to accommodation. Team uniforms provided free by Nike, the sneaker manufacturer, were stolen. A Kenyan athlete was expelled from the games after testing positive for proscribed drugs. A top athletic official who arrived at the games without accreditation was sent home. Some athletes were abandoned and had to sleep in the slums of Rio de Janeiro. Team captain Welsely Korir publicly complained: "We did not sleep all night because of gunshots all night, mosquitoes everywhere."

When the Olympic team returned to Nairobi, Wario dissolved the National Olympic Committee of Kenya (NOCK) and set a task force to investigate the complaints. Committee officials took the matter to court and the dissolution was cancelled. Wario's task force team found the committee had bought 133 air tickets to Rio, the cost of which was inflated by KSh.88 million. Non-athletics officials, among them MPS and government officials, were included in the 175-member delegation without authority. They enjoyed free meals and allowances from the Olympics Committee even though they had received stipends from their various organisations. There were also four officials who did not travel but were nevertheless paid allowances amounting to KSh.761,000 each.

Half a dozen officials who had travelled to Brazil for the games were arrested and charged. Among them was the 78-year-old athletic icon, Kipchoge Keino. The legendary Keino was a two-time Olympic champion and a member of the IOC. He was not prosecuted. Others arrested were Patrick Kimathi, Stephen Kiptanui, Harun Komen, Ben Ekumbo, and Francis Kanyili.

The convictions validated Uhuru's seemingly tough posture on corruption. But that was only a minor achievement given the fact that dozens of corruption cases involving senior government officials had either collapsed in courts or were stuck in the judicial system for years. One big case which has been pending for years is that of top officials of the National Land Commission (NLC), among them its chairman, Mohammed Abdalla Swazuri. The case has been pending since August 2018 when Swazuri and 18 others were arrested for allegedly paying over KSh.100 million in compensation to individuals and entities. The payment was for land meant for the Southern Bypass and the Kipevu Terminal Link. Also arrested on allegations of fraud and abuse of office was the managing director of the Kenya Railways, Atanas Kariuki Maina. They all pleaded not guilty. By June 2022, the case of fraud, financial misconduct, money laundering, and abuse of office, among others, was still in court.

WHISTLEBLOWER IN CAMPUS

It had been known all along that corruption was rife in Kenya's public universities, but not to the extent of what transpired at the Maasai Mara University. The rot at the institution had been going on for years. However, it was only after *Citizen TV* ran an explosive expose titled the Mara Heist that the severity of the problem became public knowledge. The expose found that KSh.177 million was siphoned off by top university officials through illegal withdrawals. The money was taken between 2016 and 2019. The *Citizen TV* documentary relied on a witness account of a whistleblower, Spencer Sankale, a senior accountant at the institution, who described in detail how the officials withdrew money from numerous university accounts. Sankale was eventually sacked.

In August 2020, the DPP, Noordin Haji, ordered the arrest of Vice Chancellor Mary Walingo, the deputy vice chancellor for finance and planning, professor Simon Kasaine Ole Seno, the deputy vice chancellor for academic affairs, professor John Amadi Obere, the finance officer, Anaclet Biket Okumu, and driver Noor Hassan Abdi. The DPP noted that university officials failed to record the subject transactions/cheque withdrawals in the university's advanced accounting system perhaps "to hide the transactions from the university's financial records." The accused were charged under the Anti-Corruption and Economic Crimes Act before a court in Nakuru. They pleaded not guilty and were released on bond.

In 2019, the Kenya Universities Staff Union (KUSU) had raised an alarm over rising cases of corruption in institutions of higher learning. It particularly singled out Masinde Muliro University of Science and Technology, the Embu University, and the Jaramogi Oginga Odinga University of Science and Technology, as institutions with some of the highest number of financial misappropriation issues. There was also corruption in staff employment, student recruitment, and promotion of lecturers and professors

KARURA FOREST UNDER SIEGE, AGAIN?

Efforts to protect Karura Forest in Nairobi have been going on for years against unscrupulous developers wanting to grab the land for development. The late Nobel Peace Prize winner, Prof. Wangari Maathai, was at the forefront of those efforts. The 1,000-hectares Karura Forest is situated two kilometres north of downtown Nairobi. It is one of the last remaining indigenous forests providing a vital carbon sink for the city's industrial activity. It is also rich in different species of birds, colobus monkeys, and bats.

However, under Uhuru it appeared the conservationists' dreams of preserving Karura as an environmental paradise was again under threat. Firstly, the government sliced part of it to build the Northern By-Pass Road. And secondly, it issued illegal title deeds to developers to encroach the forest.[177] In 2015, influential real estate gurus holding illegally acquired title deeds showed up at the forest ready to put up commercial structures. One of them planned to construct a luxury hotel in the forest in a 25-acre block of land. The Green Belt Movement (GBM) fought with ferocity to block the planned development which it said violated the 2016-2020 Strategic Forest Management Plan developed jointly by KFS and FKF.

Things got thicker when MP Oscar Sudi, associated Uhuru's name to the Karura Forest saga. He alleged the President was one of the forest grabbers. However, Uhuru did not take that accusation

[177] Ibid.

lightly. At the annual Devolution Conference at Sagana State Lodge in 2019, he responded: "I heard someone say I stole somebody's property. I want to tell him to walk to the Directorate of Criminal Investigations (DCI) and report what I have stolen. There is no problem," he said.

An investigation by the EACC in 2014 found that all the land excised from the original Karura Forest "was illegally taken and sold by corrupt dealers with the connections to the ruling class." Uhuru never lent his voice to the continuing grabbing of Karura Forest, not when he was a minister in Moi's and Kibaki's governments, and not during his term as president.

IT SHINES, BUT IT ISN'T GOLD

Kenya and the UAE have always enjoyed good diplomatic relations. Sometimes, however, those relations have been rocky because of shady deals perpetrated by crafty businesspeople. A good example is when the Kenya government found itself at the centre of a gold scandal that sucked in the UAE ruler, Sheikh Mohammed Al Makhtoum. A Kenyan scammer had promised to deliver 23 tonnes of gold sourced from the Democratic Republic of Congo (DRC) to Emirati Ali Zandi, the ruler's nephew. The Emirati had paid a deposit of US$2.5 million (KSh.250 million) for the gold.

What happened next was a merry-go-round of lies between an individual masquerading as a senior Kenyan official and Zandi who was representing a gold trading company in Dubai called Zlivia. After a hiatus, Sheikh Makhtoum sent a protest note to Nairobi demanding the release of the gem which was reportedly held up at the customs warehouse. It turned out the gold story was a fraud. The gold did not exist which meant the Emirati was defrauded of his money.

In May 2019, the Kenya government launched an investigation of six people, one of them a senator. The legislator had flown to Dubai to convince Zandi of his capability to secure the release of the gold. In the meantime, another person masquerading as a cabinet secretary assured Zandi that he would find the mysterious gold. He demanded a payment which Zandi refused to give. Instead, Zandi flew to Nairobi, but the mission failed because relevant government officials refused to meet him. The matter took a final turn when Dubai officials declined to record a statement with the Kenya Police fearing further negative publicity. The matter died there.

NOT LEFT BEHIND

Despite Uhuru's reasons for appointing military officers to key positions, the record of the military was not always clean under his rule. Reports of improprieties in the armed forces including corruption, bribery, nepotism, and human rights abuses have circulated for years. The military is, just like in any other sector in Kenya, drowning in rot.

For instance, in 2014, the military and the then ministry of national security and the provincial administration, reported that they had transferred KSh.350 million to the National Intelligence Service (NIS). When Auditor General Edward Ouko checked with NIS, the money was nowhere to be seen. No evidence existed that the money even reached NIS.

Ouko determined that the transfer of the money which was made during the 2012-2013 financial year was illegal. When the auditors demanded reasons for the money transfer, the military said the payment had been authorised by the Treasury CS. Even if that was so, the transfer was illegal since monies allocated to one department cannot be transferred to another.

In 2015, according to Ouko, the ministry of defence (MoD) also refused to provide information to the Public Procurement Oversight Authority (PPOA) on purchases of military equipment worth KSh.4.6 billion. Some of that money, KSh.3.5 billion, bought military aircraft that were defective and could not fly.

The parliamentary public accounts committee (PAC) chaired by MP Opiyo Wandayi, demanded details of the purchase of seven aircraft from the Royal Jordanian Air Force in 2017. Although records showed the aircraft had been tested and cleared, the MoD found them to be inoperative. Wandayi wanted to be provided with minutes, names of tender committee members, and the list of government officials who were involved in the purchase. The MP should have known he was wasting his time. The MoD never listens to parliament; neither does it provide such information. The matter died a natural death.

In 2021, MoD failed to account for KSh.2 billion received from the African Union (AU) as reimbursement for troops serving in Somalia. There was also a case in which KSh.11.5 million was paid as a bribe to some officials to secure an arms deal. The officials were not identified, and the deal was not exposed.

In addition, there have been many reported cases of bribery during military recruitment. In May, three KDF officers were charged at Kahawa Garrisons with various corruption counts relating to recruitment into the service. Lieutenant Colonel Thomas Kiptum Poghisio, Corporal Tyren Ketah, and Gunner Anthony Kimeiwa Leboo, were accused of soliciting bribes from recruits.

Separately, Sergeant Andrew Muoki, appeared in court at the 78 Tank Battalion in Isiolo charged with soliciting KSh.480,000 from two recruits seeking to join KDF. Like his predecessors, Uhuru did not dare confront the armed forces over its malfeasance.

"Corruption," said Aly Khan Satchu, chief executive officer of Rich Management, "has created more holes in our security posture than Swiss cheese has holes." True, there were many holes in the procurement of military equipment that no one, including Uhuru, had the audacity to question.

CHAPTER 14

Uhuru, the "Discoverer"

"**U**huru Kenyatta, the greatest world explorer since Marco Polo and Ferdinand Magellan. He recently discovered a country called Kenya #UhuruinKenya." Muthui, a Kenyan, posted these words on twitter, on December 6, 2015.

In airline parlance, a person who travels a lot is called a frequent flier. In his ten years at the helm as the president of Kenya, Uhuru clocked more miles traversing the world than any other president since independence. He went east and west, explored the south, and conquered the north, all in search of "development" for Kenya. As columnist Macharia Gaitho said, Uhuru was always jet-lagged. As soon as he returned home "he grabs his pockets for [yet] another gruelling trip to the other side of the globe...."

Uhuru's overseas trips were so frequent that some Kenyans launched a website, *isuhuruinkenya.co.ke* in December 2015, to mock their leader. They gave their itinerant president sobriquets such as "airborne" and "visiting" president. That website did not last long though. It was quickly shut down on instructions from the government.

Take his visits to the wealthy Arab world, for example. In August 2013, just weeks after his election in March, Uhuru made his first visit to Dubai as president. He detoured there while on his way home from Russia and China where he had gone to negotiate a KSh.425 billion grant for various development projects. He spent three days in Dubai. Because it was during the month of Ramadhan, the visit did not achieve much. His planned visit to Riyadh, Saudi Arabia's capital, aborted, so he failed to meet with senior government officials.

At the end of 2013, Uhuru returned to the Arab world to attend the Africa-Arab Summit in Kuwait. He met with leaders of Qatar, Kuwait, Bahrain, Palestine, and Saudi Arabia. They discussed trade and investment, human trafficking, piracy, and terrorism. Uhuru also met with executives of the Kuwait Fund for Arab and Economic Development and begged for loans for the Wajir Hospital and schools in Nyanza. He also had private business discussions with investors.

In April 2014, Uhuru travelled to Qatar for a three-day state visit. Apart from meeting with leaders of that country, he also met members of the Qatar business community and Kenyans staying there. Four agreements for economic cooperation, and three Memoranda of Understanding (MoUs) on commerce and energy, were signed. That visit was reciprocated in April 2017 by the Emir of Qatar, His Highness Sheikh Tamin bin Hamad al-Thani, who arrived in Nairobi with a high-powered delegation for talks on strengthening cooperation between the two countries.

The Kenyan leader was again in the Middle East for four days in November 2014 for talks with rulers of Jordan and the UAE. Although the meeting reportedly centred on security matters, the two also discussed business interests. The visit became controversial after Kenyans back home discovered that Uhuru was in the UAE to watch the Formula One Grand Prix in Abu Dhabi. What angered Kenyans most was that in his absence, Al-Shabaab terrorists had crossed into Kenya and killed twenty-eight people in Mandera. The commander-in-chief was nowhere to provide leadership.

In April 2015, the peripatetic president was again on his way to the UAE when his Air Force plane was forced to turn around and return to Nairobi due to heavy fighting in Yemen. The civil war in Yemen started in 2014 pitying two groups which claim to be the official government of Yemen.

The plane was flying over the Ethiopian airspace when the decision to return home was made. The plan was for Uhuru to stop over in Dubai for an unspecified period, and then take a commercial flight to the USA to attend the Milken Institute Global Conference on health, education, and financial markets. Officials could not explain why Uhuru decided to take the long route to UAE instead of boarding a direct flight from Nairobi to Europe and over to the USA. After that visit aborted, the UAE Minister for Foreign Affairs Sheikh Abdullah bin Zayed visited Nairobi in June 2015, and met Kenyan high-ranking officials, including President Uhuru.

The "airborne" Kenyan leader was again off to Dubai in 2016 as a guest of the wealthy Al- Ghurair family at their residence in Burj Al Khalifa. It was during that meeting that a final decision appeared to have been made to give the Al-Ghurair Printing and Publishing Company the KSh.2.5 billion ballot printing tender for the 2017 elections.

In February 2022, President Uhuru made yet another visit to the UAE under the usual cover of "strengthening bilateral ties for the mutual benefit of the people of Kenya." Flying separately to the same destination the following day was Raila Odinga and a small entourage of his (Raila's) family and close advisers.

President Uhuru did officially meet with UAE leaders, but the congregation of top Kenyan leaders in Dubai meant only two things: begging for donations for Raila's presidential race, or as some tweeps speculated, "finalising a power sharing deal" between the ruling Jubilee Alliance Party, Raila's ODM, and the One Kenya Alliance (OKA), of Kalonzo Musyoka and Musalia Mudavadi. If there was such a plan, that arrangement did not materialise. OKA broke up, leaving Raila to team up with Kalonzo in the Azimio la Umoja One Kenya Coalition.

In May 2022, as the end of his term approached, Uhuru again flew to the UAE, this time to condole with the people there upon the death of their president, Sheikh Khalifa bin Zayed al Nahyan. He delivered a message of condolence to the new president, Sheikh Mohamed bin Zayed al Nahyan, at his presidential residence in Abu Dhabi.

The Arab world was not the only place Uhuru visited. Within the first two years of his term, his voracious appetite for travel took him on 43 overseas trips compared to his predecessor President Kibaki who clocked only 33 trips in ten years. Uhuru also visited Ethiopia, the UK, South Africa, Sudan, South Sudan, Uganda, Burundi, Nigeria, the Democratic Republic of Congo (DRC), Russia, China, Rwanda, Angola, Belgium, Turkey, Algeria, Japan, Namibia, Jordan, the United States of America (USA), Tanzania, Zambia, Italy, India, Malta, and France. President Uhuru visited some of those countries multiple times.

In comparison, Mzee Jomo Kenyatta as Kenya's leader, made only three overseas trips: to London as Prime Minister in September 1963 to finalise constitutional arrangements before full independence, and again in July 1964 to attend the Commonwealth Prime Ministers' Conference. From London he flew to Cairo, Egypt, to attend the African Leaders' Conference. His last visit outside the country was in 1969 when he visited his bosom friend Emperor Haile Selassie of Ethiopia.

President Moi did travel a lot overseas but his cumulative total trips in 24 years could not compare with Uhuru's trips in ten years.

* * *

"We are honoured @UKenyatta that you chose Kenya as your next travel destination, writer Francis Gaitho said via a social media platform on December 6, 2015. That was one of the many posts from Kenyans on Twitter (KOT) mocking Uhuru for his frequent overseas trips. The President had just returned home from France and Malta and was preparing to depart for Rwanda the same week. The previous week, he had been to South Africa for the Forum on China-Africa Cooperation (FOCAC).

At times, Uhuru used official trips as junkets for members of his family. In 2015, his critics slammed him for giving a relative a joyride to the climate change meeting in Paris, France. The relative had no official role in government and her interest in climate change was opaque. Including her in the Kenya delegation was wrong, they said, since a few weeks earlier, the National Treasury had announced austerity measures intended to reduce the country's ballooning budget deficit.

The previous year, 2014, another of the president's family members was seen in the Kenya delegation to the UN General Assembly. The image showing that relative and a nephew, Jomo Gecaga, Uhuru's Personal Secretary, sitting behind the president at the UN was implausible. It could not be confirmed however whether the individual was part of the official delegation. All that extravagant showmanship contrasted sharply with what President Uhuru had demonstrated to Kenyans while he was minister for finance. The old penny-pinch Minister Uhuru had apparently morphed into a thriftless President Uhuru.

By October 2019, after a six-day visit to Jamaica and Barbados in the Caribbean, Uhuru had clocked a total of 100 overseas trips. In June 2019, he had travelled to Canada to attend the Global Women Delivery Conference, and to Sudan to witness the formation of a transitional government there. "Basically, he has no time to sit down and deliver on the promises he made in the Jubilee Alliance Party manifesto," one analyst said. "So, of what importance does it bring to the nation? Can these foreign trips help reduce the wage bill of the nation?"[178] Another asked.

The presidential spokesman Manoah Esipisu's reaction to the humorous and sometimes quizzy expressions and exclamations from KOT was unsatisfactory. He said the visits were important for the development of the country. He gave the example of Uhuru's visit to South Africa to attend the FOCAC meeting. Esipisu explained that after talks with Chinese officials, Kenya had secured a loan of US$1.5 billion (KSh.165 billion) for the extension of the SGR from Nairobi to Naivasha.

China, according to Esipisu, had also agreed to give Kenya an additional KSh.4.5 billion for a state-of-the-art convention facility, and one-thousand new university scholarships for Kenyans to study in China. Esipisu dismissed criticisms about costs saying that cost "is really nothing compared to the results. These trips must continue because we cannot be the regional leader and shy away from taking up our role," he added. A coterie of officials, from Deputy President Ruto to Foreign Minister Amina Abdalla, also joined in the chorus of defending Uhuru's unending trips. No one knows what happened to the scholarships.

Kenyans had expected the government to save money allocated for foreign travel during the Covid-19 pandemic. But their expectations were far-fetched. At a time when the country had shut

---

[178] Mwangale, Alex. "Uhuru's frequent trips are a burden to the taxpayer," *The Saturday Standard*, March 9, 2016.

down for weeks on end, Uhuru's travel expenses still increased tenfold in a period of only three months ending in June 2020. What surprised even the controller of budget (CoB) was that Uhuru's diary did not show any travels during that period, raising questions about where the money went and who spent it.[179]

In mid-2021, after a pause caused by the Covid-19 travel restrictions, President Uhuru resumed his travels. In July, he went to London to sign security and economic agreements. From London, he headed to France for the Generation Equality Forum.

The same month, he travelled to Belgium to attend the Heads of State and Government of the Organisation of African, Caribbean and Pacific States (OACPS). Early in October, he went to Addis Ababa, Ethiopia, for the swearing-in of Prime Minister Abiy Ahmed for another five-year term. He then proceeded to Jamaica for the Conference of Heads of Government of the Caribbean Community (CARICOM) summit. In the Caribbean, the media showered him with brotherly praise, referring to him as "Mr. Big Man from Africa." It is possible he liked that definition.

His last visit to Europe was in February 2022, when he visited Belgium for a two-day summit of the 6th African (AU) – European Union (EU) leaders.

Uhuru was a spendthrift, either because he was born with a "silver spoon in his mouth," or perhaps money meant nothing to him. He travelled extensively and frequently without a care about the cost to the taxpayer. He took every invitation that came along and carried with him huge delegations of family, friends, and politically correct businesspeople. His travel budget was always overblown. That was against his own promise of March 2014, one year after taking office, that he would keep foreign trips to a minimum to reduce the public wage bill.

In 2019, President Uhuru was invited to Japan to attend the enthronement of emperor Naruhito. Instead of taking a commercial flight to Tokyo, he travelled in a private jet owned by a Dubai

---

[179] Mutua, John. "Uhuru office foreign trip costs up 10 times during flights ban," *Business Daily*, October 2, 2020.

company. The plane landed in Mombasa from Jaipur, India, on October 20, 2019, which was *Mashujaa Day*, a national holiday in Kenya. After the official celebrations marking Mashujaa day at Mama Ngina Waterfront, the president and his entourage drove to Moi International Airport and flew out.

The Airbus A318-112, with a capacity of 19 passengers, travelled to Almaty International Airport in Kazakhstan where it refuelled, and then proceeded to Tokyo. After the enthronement of the 59-year-old emperor, Uhuru flew back by way of Almaty and headed to the beach resort of Sochi, Russia, to attend the first Russia-Africa Summit, together with 50 other Heads of State and Government. Uhuru was accompanied on the journey by his wife, First Lady Margaret Kenyatta, top government officials, and businesspeople. He returned home on November 26, 2019.

No one, not even the relevant oversight committees in parliament questioned why the president chose an expensive private jet instead of a commercial flight. And no one dared to ask how much the trip cost the taxpayers. Reports indicated that the hire company might have charged upwards of KSh.1.5 million per hour, an excessive amount that could have been put to better use.

A commercial flight would have been much cheaper. If Kenya paid for the trip, it was a blatant display of financial impropriety by President Uhuru, bordering on gross abuse of office. If he had not been president enjoying immunity, he would have been prosecuted. He did emphasise that point in January 2022 when he said as president, he could not be prosecuted for performing presidential functions.[180]

The Uhuru jet issue was one of the many lamentable instances of profligacy on the part of government officials. In fact, that was not the first time a private jet hire by a senior government official had raised questions. There was the "hustler's jet" used in shuttle diplomacy immediately after Uhuru and his deputy were sworn in (see Chapter 6).

---

[180] Wambulwa, Annette. "I have absolute immunity, can't be sued – Uhuru," *Star*, January 19, 2022.

UHURU KENYATTA

FOREIGN RELATIONS

President Uhuru's major achievement in foreign relations came towards the end of his term. He successfully steered the country into occupying a seat in the UN Security Council after a hotly contested duel between Kenya and Djibouti. Thanks to fierce shuttle diplomacy by the president and his envoys and tacit support by the African Union (AU), Kenya won the seat in a second round of voting by 129 votes against Djibouti's 62.

Kenya was to occupy the seat for two years, along with the five permanent members, France, Russia, the USA, the UK, and China, and nine non-permanent members. It was an ecstatically happy return to the UN Security council for Kenya after 23 years, demonstrating the country's growing influence in the global arena. Kenya was a non-permanent member of the council twice before, in 1973 and 1997.

Kenya's entry into the Council did not only lift its global profile, but it also gave it an opportunity to play a leading role in peace and stability, more specifically in the eastern African region. It also gave Nairobi a chance to focus on climate change and sustainable development, two among the most debated issues in the world today.

Uhuru was a champion of climate change. During the COP26 World Leaders' Summit plenary session in Glasgow, Scotland, on November 1, 2021, Uhuru warned of a "global catastrophe" unless leaders shifted gear on climate change. In February 2022, he took over from South Africa's President Cyril Ramaphosa, as chairperson of the AU Climate Change Committee

Kenya's UN Security Council membership came at a time of heightened tension between Nairobi and Mogadishu over the twin problems of terrorism and the maritime border dispute in the Indian Ocean. Other African issues Kenya was expected to deal with in its new position included the Ethiopia-Tigray conflict, the leadership dispute in Sudan and South Sudan, and the showdown between Ethiopia and Egypt over the allocation of the waters of the Nile River.

But as Kenyan leaders were savouring the moment of joining the big league of nations, critics dismissed the notion advanced by some government officials that "Kenya will [now] have an opportunity to shape the global agenda and ensure our interests and the interests of Africa are heard and considered." Kenyan author, Rasna Warah, said Kenya's membership at the UN Security Council "might not amount to much as long as the UN's purse strings were controlled by a few rich and powerful countries...."[181] Thus, Kenya's hope of changing the world was unlikely to materialise in the big league of nations.

NOT MUCH HAS CHANGED

Changes in Kenya's foreign policy have been very nominal since the days of Mzee Jomo Kenyatta. The first president was unabashedly pro-western. And although he personally directed and controlled relations with other nations, he depended on the cabinet for advice. The day-to-day decisions were left to his foreign minister. The core of the foreign policy then, as it is now, was based on 'passive nonalignment,' that is, strengthening bilateral relations with all nations, economic development, tourism, and trade, with a focus on donor aid. With Uhuru at the helm, the element of loans was added to the matrix. In the early years of independence, there was what diplomats called 'Quiet diplomacy,' "a cautious and prudent approach to sub-regional, regional, and international affairs."[182]

Regionally, Kenya has always maintained a policy of 'good neighbourliness.' That policy has remained largely unchanged throughout the more than half a century of Kenya's existence. However, as Somalia became more belligerent and the Al-Shabaab group a menace, the foreign policy of both Kibaki and Uhuru on Somalia shifted to security along the borders of the two countries. Kenya's close cooperation with Britain and the USA helped to slow down incursions, but it did not stop terrorist attacks emanating from Somalia.

---

[181] Warah, Rasna. "Why winning a seat at the UN Security Council is nothing to write home about," The *Elephant*, July 2, 2020.
[182] Okumu, John J., Some Thoughts on Kenya's Foreign Policy, The African Review: *A Journal of African Politics Development and International Affairs,* Vol. 3, No. 2, 1973, pp. 263-290., p. 263.

In 2018, Kenya signed a border demarcation MoU with South Sudan and Uganda and began talks with Kampala on the dispute over the ownership of Migingo Island. A joint administration of the island on Lake Victoria was agreed upon.

The other touchy regional issue is the Ilemi Triangle which remains unresolved between Kenya and South Sudan. Unlike other borders, this frontier is unmarked. And for some reason, border lines on maps have been changing over the years, adding to the confusion. Although the late Colonel John de Mabior Garang, leader of the Sudan People's Liberation Movement/Army (SPLM/A), handed the Ilemi Triangle to Kenya "in return for logistical, medical, and moral support in the South Sudan civil war,"[183] the true ownership of the Triangle is still curiously in dispute. Colonel Garang was killed in a plane crash on July 30, 2005, as he flew home from (guessed it) Uganda!

Over the years, there have been frequent clashes over grazing lands along the common border between the Turkana community in Kenya and the Topossa community in South Sudan. Like his predecessors, President Uhuru did not seriously attempt to engage his counterparts on this issue, preferring to leave it as "an administrative convenience for the government of Kenya."[184] The Ilemi Triangle, comprising 13,000 square kilometres of territory, sits at the joint where Kenya, South Sudan, and Ethiopia boundaries meet. It stands out like a sore thumb in relations between Nairobi and Juba.

TENSE KENYA/SOMALIA RELATIONS

Relations between Nairobi and Mogadishu have been wavering between cordiality and unmeasured hostility. There have been diplomatic, trade, and border tussles, not to mention the maritime dispute which continues to hang on the necks of the two countries like the Sword of Damocles. The border dispute revolves around the

---

[183] Colins, Robert. The Ilemi Triangle, *Annales d'Ethiopie*, Vol. XX: 5-12, 2005, pp. 10-11.
[184] Ibid.

ownership of potential oil and gas deposits, some of it in Jubaland, a Somalia semi-autonomous state. The area is also rich in fish resources.

Somalia demanded that its maritime boundary run in the same direction as the south-easterly path of its land border. Kenya, on the other hand, wanted the boundary to take a 45-degree turn at the shoreline and run in a latitudinal direction, giving Kenya a much bigger share of the maritime area. Somalia took the matter to the International Court of Justice (ICJ) at The Hague, accusing Kenya of interfering in its maritime territory. Kenya wanted the issue settled out of court, but bilateral negotiations between the two states failed to settle the issue. So, the case went to court. And in a decision on October 12, 2021, a 14-judge bench of the ICJ ruled largely in favour of Somalia, denying Kenya several oil blocks.

As Mogadishu celebrated the decision and thanked Allah "for the fruit of the long struggle made by the Somalia people in preventing Kenya's desire to claim ownership of part of Somalia's sea," Kenya protested. Uhuru said Kenya would not surrender even an inch of its territory to Somalia or anyone else. With that decision, the two countries sank further into conflict. The warped relations between the two countries further became frazzled and fraught. Immediately after the court ruling, Kenya sent its Navy boats to patrol its territorial sea boundary to prevent possible aggression from Somalia. Mogadishu has warned Kenya to stay away from what it says is its territory.

KENYA/UK

Relations between Kenya and Britain have been described as "special"[185] because of their past colonial ties. More than any other country, Britain was Kenya's closest and most valued partner way before the latter's independence. Britain was Kenya's colonial 'master' for more than 70 years.

---

[185] Kamau, Michael Mubea. Kenya and Britain Diplomatic Relations, 1963-2017, Kenyatta University, November 2018.

But there have been challenges. One of them occurred in 2005 when President Kibaki "punctured" relations between the two countries by dropping the West as Kenya's favoured development partner in favour of China.[186] Kibaki's 'Look East Policy' followed a hiatus in relations with the US and Europe over matters of human rights violations and corruption. The 'Look East Policy' is also credited for increased trade and investments in infrastructure development in Kenya.

Also, the murder of a Kenyan girl in 2012 by a British soldier introduced a state of mistrust between Nairobi and London especially after Kenya insisted that the suspect be repatriated to face murder charges in Kenya. Twenty-one-year-old Agnes Wanjiru, a mother of one, was killed and her body dumped in a septic tank in March 2012. By that time, the suspect had already returned to Britain. After a diplomatic tussle between the two countries, London finally agreed to expatriate the man following talks between President Uhuru and the British Prime Minister, David Cameron in September 2015. By June 2022, however, the suspect had yet to be repatriated to Kenya. The Kenya government did not explain why.

The suspect was part of a rotating unit of 300 British soldiers training at Nanyuki, in Laikipia County, 198 km north of Nairobi. The British Army Training Unit (BATUK) is a permanent camp in Kenya that has existed since independence.

Then there was the controversy arising from a decision by London to put Kenya on the 'red' Covid-19 list in April 2021. Kenya, whose Covid-19 numbers of infections were not alarming at the time, was furious. Officials described the decision as "punitive... discriminatory, divisive, and exclusive in its character." The red alert translated to a ban on travellers arriving from Kenya, unless they were British or Irish nationals.

Travellers from Kenya into the UK were subjected to a mandatory quarantine in hotels for ten days. In retaliation, Kenya announced a travel ban of its own on all visitors arriving from UK airports, saying they would be quarantined for 14 days at a government facility at

---

[186] Ibid.

their own cost. The UK eventually lifted the ban but re-introduced it when Omicron (a variant of Covid-19) exploded. The UK scrapped the ban again in December 2021, prompting Kenya to follow suit.

Overall, though, diplomatic relations between the two countries have been relatively cordial and continue to grow.

Kenya/USA relations

Upon taking over the reigns of power, President Uhuru made it clear that his government would work with all its traditional partners in the west. But he also expressed interest to "look east," more specifically to China, as a continuation of Kibaki's Look East Policy. Instead of starting his overseas trips with Britain, its former colonial power, Uhuru instead went to China and Russia in August 2013 to sign bilateral agreements. The apparent shift wobbled the USA and Europe, Kenya's principal donor partners.

The *Washington Post* quoted analysts as saying that the visit highlighted the United States' "waning influence in a country vital to US interests."[187] Washington opened its embassy in Nairobi in 1964. However, Uhuru made it clear that he did not want to be drawn into "some proxy war" between the east and the west. "We don't want to be forced to choose. We want to work with everybody, and we think there is opportunity for everybody," Uhuru said.

Uhuru was the second Kenyan leader to meet three US presidents while in office: Presidents Barack Obama in July 2015, Donald Trump in August 2018, and Joe Biden in October 2021. That was a major plus in his efforts to consolidate diplomatic relations, investment opportunities, and security challenges, with the world's supper power. The only other Kenyan leader to visit White House thrice was President Moi. He met President Jimmy Carter in 1980, Ronald Reagan in March 1987, and George W. Bush in December 2002, days before leaving office.

---

[187] Raghavan, Sudarsan. "In snub to Washington, Kenyan president visits China, Russia in first official visit outside Africa," *Washington Post*, August 17, 2013.

But unlike Moi who was criticised in the USA media over human rights violations during his visit to Washington DC in 1987 and 2002, Uhuru's visits had less drama. The only black spot in Uhuru's visit to the White House to meet Biden was the Pandora Papers, the expose by the International Consortium of Investigative Journalists (ICIJ), linking him to offshore accounts.

The release of the papers coincided with President Uhuru's visit to the USA's capital. Many expected the international media to pounce on Uhuru during the joint press conference with Biden on October 14, 2021. But that did not happen. However, a section of the American media carried bold headlines on the matter: "Biden meets Kenyatta as Pandora Papers leak swirls around world leaders (The *Guardian,* October 14, 2021);" "Biden hosts Kenyan leader who is also facing family corruption claims (The *New York Post,* October 14, 2021);" and "Biden discusses 'transparency' with Kenya President (*Associated Press*, October 14, 2021)," among others.

Although the meeting with President Biden touched on bilateral relations, security and how to combat Al-Shabaab, trade, investment, and Covid-19, the two leaders also discussed financial transparency, given the rampant corruption and mismanagement of finances in Kenya. Details of their discussions were not revealed. But there was no indication Uhuru raised the issue of advisories with Biden or even his predecessor, Donald Trump, during their meeting in 2018. But the fact that Biden had nice words to say about the Kenyan leader – like calling him a "champion of democracy," and "You're doing a heck of a job," on defending peace, security, and democratic ideals in the region – put Uhuru in a class of his own in the eyes of America.

But the American public view of Kenya was evident in a background call between reporters and US administration official on the morning of the Biden-Uhuru meeting at the Oval Office on October 14, 2021. This is the verbatim of a question-and-answer session.

Reporter: The President [Biden] has said that anti-corruption is going to be a priority in his administration…. And I am sure you're aware, the recently released Pandora Papers show Mr. Kenyatta's family holding a lot of offshore wealth, and I am wondering if the President will be mentioning this at all and raising any sort of concerns about at least the appearance of what was revealed.

US Official: The President has taken note of President Kenyatta's statement that the Pandora Papers release will enhance financial transparency and openness around the globe. The United States, through various departments and agencies on the ground, at our embassy in Nairobi, has and will continue to build off our current efforts with Kenyans to bring additional transparency and accountability to domestic and international financial systems.

Reporter: The President of Kenya is a deeply corrupt guy. But I am wondering, is the President [Biden] concerned that he's giving this big platform to someone who is deeply corrupt like President Kenyatta?

Official: President Biden engages with a range of leaders in advancing, you know, his foreign policy priorities, foremost amongst which are absolutely to address and combat corruption.

While answering a question about Kenya-Ethiopia relations and the conflict in Ethiopia, the administration official said this: "Kenyatta is very much a senior elder – an elder statesman in the region, he is a leader. And we think that Kenya's voice is important – an important voice that resonates broadly in the region and hopefully with Prime Minister Abiy Ahmed Ali [of Ethiopia] as well."[188]

Another significant issue of disagreement between Kenya and the US relates to gay rights. During his visit to Nairobi in July 2015, President Obama, raised the issue with Uhuru. Obama pleaded with Kenya to respect gay rights and avoid passing laws that discriminated

---

[188] Background press call by senior administration officials on President Biden's meeting with President of the Republic of Kenya, The White House, via teleconference, October 14, 2021.

that segment of society. Uhuru, a devoted Catholic, did not buy that view. "For Kenyans," he said, "the issue of gay rights is really a non-issue. We want to focus on other issues that really are day-to-day issues for our people."

The west has for years coerced Kenyan leaders to accept homosexuality as a way of life. None of the first three Presidents, Mzee Kenyatta, Moi and Kibaki, succumbed to the pressure – sometimes given under threats of financial aid suspension. President Moi called homosexuality "a scourge that goes against Christian teachings and traditions." To the relief of many Kenyans, President Uhuru too resisted the push."[189] Deputy President Ruto also went on record saying that gay rights had no place in the Kenyan society.

Opposition to homosexuality has nevertheless not deterred the lesbian, gay, bisexual, and transgender (LGBT) community in Kenya from 'coming out' to assert its rights. The community has even gone to court to challenge laws that criminalise and discriminate against its members.

Strong USAID presence

The driving force behind the strong ties between Kenya and the USA is the US Agency for International Development (USAID). It has pumped trillions of shillings into health, agriculture, and infrastructure programmes in Kenya. Washington has also played a pivotal role in enhancing security, democracy, governance, and conflict resolution initiatives. It is estimated that the US contributes US$3 billion (KSh.300 trillion) to Kenya annually.[190] In 1980, the two countries signed an agreement permitting US military to use Kenyan sea and air bases in exchange for economic and military assistance.[191]

---

[189] World, Africa: "Moi condemns gays," *BBC News*, September 30, 1999.
[190] Custer, John & Sarina Patterson, AidData, June 17, 2020.
[191] Kenya – Foreign Relations, African Studies Centre, University of Pennsylvania, Vol. 3, Facts on File, p. 976.

The US is Kenya's fifth largest trading partner. In 2018, when Uhuru visited the US, several agreements were signed including one allowing Kenya Airways to launch direct flights between Nairobi and New York. Another pact was for America to supply US$232 million for the construction of the 100MW Kipeto Wind Energy Farm in Kajiado County. The plant, which is now fully operational, is part of the US Power Africa Initiative, meant to expand electricity to an increasing number of people in Sub-Saharan Africa.

The initiative was launched in Tanzania by President Obama during his Africa tour in 2013. It is aimed at supporting economic growth and development by increasing access to reliable, affordable, and sustainable power in Africa. The project is funded largely by the African Development Fund (ADF), by equity from BioThem Energy, a pan-African renewable energy platform, the Kenya's Craftskills Limited, and the US International Development Finance Corporation (IDFC). The Kipeto Farm provides electricity to an estimated 250,000 households in Kenya, a major contribution to Uhuru's Big 4 Agenda.[192]

Kenya and the US also signed a US$5 million letter of commitment to finance the expansion of Twiga Foods. The company uses technology to build food supply chains in food and retail distribution in Africa. In Kenya, Twiga Foods connects farmers with vendors for the latter to source the food and deliver it across the country. And in 2021, Uhuru witnessed the signing of a private-sector agreement seeking to expand trade and investments between the two countries. The agreement was signed between the Kenya Private Sector Alliance (KEPSA) and the Corporate Council of Africa (CCA), the largest umbrella body of American companies operating in Africa.

Apart from being a source of tourists for Kenya, America's presence is also notable in the number of firms represented in the country, especially in the sectors of technology, consumer services,

---

[192] Manufacturing, Food Security and Nutrition, Universal Health Coverage, and Affordable Housing.

banking, and finance. The two countries also collaborate on academic, cultural, and sports exchange programmes.

On security, the US has for many years assisted in professionalising Kenya's military forces. The US has helped in increasing its counterterrorism and border security capabilities, increasing maritime security awareness, and improving peacekeeping capabilities. The USA's presence in Somalia is part of that arrangement.

Despite those developments, Kenya and the US have also gone through numerous challenges over the years. One of the most frustrating aspects of the Kenya-US relations was Washington DC's frequent imposition of travel advisories for all manner of reasons. If it isn't for reasons of violent crimes such as armed carjacking, mugging, home invasion, and kidnapping, it is about Covid-19. America's "Do-not-travel-here-and-there" advisories were not only irritating but injurious to Kenya's tourism sector and hurtful to Kenya's global image.

In one dramatic instance, the American embassy in Nairobi closed for four days in 2013 because of "new and concrete information"[193] concerning terrorism threats, and "the appearance that Kenya is not doing enough to stop them."[194] Kenyan officials felt the closure was unnecessary. In May 2014, two bombs exploded at Gikomba market in Nairobi killing ten people. America joined Britain, France, and Australia, by issuing a travel advisory warning their nationals to avoid Kenya. Those who were already in the country were quickly evacuated. Twenty-five hotels at the Kenyan coast closed doors following that advisory and hundreds of employees were laid off.

In January 2022, as the US grappled with the fast-spreading Omicron virus with over 700,000 new Covid-19 cases, Washington announced a travel advisory against Kenya because of "high level" Covid-19 infections in the country. At that time, Nairobi was reporting only 1,600 new infections daily. It was difficult to understand the rational of that advisory.

---

[193] Maharaj, Davan. "Terror-related travel advisories harming tourism trade in Kenya," The *Baltimore Sun*, June 22, 2003.
[194] Ibid.

"The travel advisories are not helping," lamented Tourism Cabinet Secretary Najib Balala, adding, "some of them are political, some of them are not genuine."[195] Balala said the restrictions were adversely affecting Kenya's economy. Kenya has never retaliated by issuing similar advisories to its citizens living overseas, despite the many incidents of gun violence in the USA and even Europe. Eight thousand-one-hundred people were killed in gun violence in the USA in 2021, averaging 23 lost lives daily. Yet the 95,000 Kenyans living in the US were not advised by their government to avoid travel to or keep away from the country.

The US obsession with travel advisories did not stop even after the 2021 Presidents Uhuru-Biden meeting. Three days after arriving in Nairobi from his successful talks with the American president, the US announced a travel advisory for its citizens in Kenya and those planning to travel there. It warned American citizens to avoid areas near the Kenya-Somalia border and some areas at the coast which, it said were "prone to terrorism." In the advisory, the US Nairobi embassy also red-zoned several localities in Nairobi as no-go-zone areas, saying they were unsafe, and that Americans could be mugged or kidnapped.

In 2021, a stand-off in the health sector threatened to mar relations between Kenya and the USA. The impasse involved a large consignment of HIV/Aids medications donated by the USAID for supply to 1.2 million HIV-positive Kenyans. The consignment was held for weeks at Mombasa port because of a dispute over who was to distribute the drug: the government-run Kenya Medical Supplies Authority (KEMSA) or the US-based private company, Chemonics.

The reluctance by the US to have KEMSA distribute the medication was because of the organisation's credibility record. KEMSA had for a long time been mired in mega corruption scandals, the latest being the purchase of Covid-19 items (see Chapter 10). Illegal deals were made between KEMSA officials and dealers, leading to the loss of billions of shillings in fraud.

---

[195] Shimanyula, Andrew Wasike. "Kenya dismisses travel advisories, assures country safe," *AA News Broadcasting System* (HAS), October 7, 2021.

What added to the disagreements was Kenya's demand that the US pay KSh.90 million in importation tax for the drugs. Kenyan officials said the consignment was not tax exempt since, according to them, it was not a government-to-government donation. USAID had a five-year distribution contract with KEMSA, but that contract had lapsed. USAID then contracted the Global Health Supply Chain Programme-Procurement and Supply Management (GHSC-PSM) project which worked with Chemonics and other partners to procure HIV, malaria, and family planning, items for Kenya. So, in Kenya's view the US government did not directly import the commodity, hence the demand for importation tax.

As the various sides argued and stocks of anti-retroviral drugs ran "dangerously low," HIV-positive persons and sympathisers took to the streets to demand the release of the drugs. "Don't make us orphans," "Don't ration my ARV," read some of the placards the demonstrators carried. The drugs were eventually released, but the showdown was yet another example of the fragile nature of Kenya-US friendship.

Kenya/China ties

China was the fourth country – after Germany, Russia, and Ethiopia – to establish diplomatic relations with Kenya – on December 14, 1963, to be precise. The Chinese embassy in Nairobi is one of the most strategically located diplomatic missions in the city. It is situated across the fenced compound of the Ministry of Defence (MoD) and the military headquarters, at Hurlingham. Within the MoD compound are some of the most critical offices for the defence of the country, including the directorate of military intelligence, operations, and planning.

From their offices, Chinese diplomats can monitor the movement of people entering and leaving MoD and even eavesdrop on incoming and outgoing MoD communications. If there was one astounding mistake the Jomo Kenyatta government made at the diplomatic level was to offer the space to the communist nation, whose ideology – at that time - was anathema to Kenya's foreign policy thinking.

Also, the Chinese mission "is arguably the largest embassy in Africa both in terms of size and employees."[196] Apart from its offices next to MoD, China has satellite offices along Ngong Road and Kilimani Ring Road. Name plates on the premises identify them as offices of Chinese media agencies but that may be embellished truth. They could be dens of spies.

That Chinese diplomats routinely engage in espionage is not a secret. When in 2019, Kenyan detectives inspected boxes of equipment donated to the Kenyan parliament by China, they discovered electronic gadgets identified as bugging devices. The equipment included dozens of laptops, film projectors, and cameras. Kenyan officials speculated that the equipment was intended for monitoring debates in parliament with a particular focus on discussions on bilateral relations between the two countries. The officials were particularly concerned about a machine earmarked for installation in the Speaker's office which they suspected was a spying tool.

Chinese donations to Africa have been viewed with suspicion since it was revealed in 2018 that Beijing had bugged the headquarters of the African Union (AU) in Addis Ababa. Built by China over a span of five years, the headquarters featured hidden devices for monitoring events and telephone conversations. The captured material was then relayed to a server in China. The clandestine espionage operation was discovered when technicians detected unusually high volume of data being transmitted between midnight and 2 am at a time when the building was unoccupied. Officials of the Asian country denied bugging the building. Consequently, the AU replaced all the computers and removed the devices used in spying.

Altogether, China has built over 180 buildings for governments and 14 "sensitive intra-governmental telecommunication networks" in Africa, according to the Heritage Foundation, a US-based conservative think tank. Among them are residences of Heads of State, parliamentary offices, police and/or military headquarters.

---

[196] Mulati, Lilian Tunai., p. 737.

However, China dismissed the Heritage Foundation's report as nothing but "lies, illusions, and ideological bias."

Despite such potential security risks, the Uhuru administration accepted an offer from China to build a complex for Kenya, of the Ministry of Foreign Affairs (MFA), in Nairobi. In any country, the conduct of foreign policy is a highly sensitive and guarded affair. Handled badly, it can ruin ties and even cause war. That is why nations invariably use secure communication methods and diplomatic bags to convey information and correspondence to maximise security. To allow a foreign country, using foreign labour, to build a building in which Kenya's foreign policy is formulated is sheer lunacy. Kenya also accepted to use Chinese buses for its VIP guests. They too will mostly likely be bugged.

Before the bromance between President Uhuru and the Chinese President Xi Jinping, the Chinese population in Kenya was minuscule. The Chinese were largely in the service sector running restaurants and casinos. Today, the number of Chinese nationals has boomed. One estimate puts their number at 50,000.[197]

This enveloping presence of Chinese people in Kenya, and Africa as a whole, has raised concerns about the growing build-up of 'Sino imperialism,' only half a century after the exit of British colonialism. "We've had bad people before. The whites were bad, the Indians were worse, but the Chinese are worst of all,"[198] said one African official. Many cases of brutal attacks on locals by their Chinese employers have been reported. The Chinese ambassador to Kenya, Sun Baohong, in responding to allegations of assault on workers, said the assaults were "a little punishment."

The Chinese people "have created a small kingdom in which they run roughshod over Kenyan workers who say they are experiencing neo-colonialism, racism, and blatant discrimination...,"[199] one writer said. Others wondered whether Kenya had "unwittingly welcomed an

---

[197] "Corona Virus Update in Africa: Nigeria confirms first case, Kenya bans flights from China," *The Guardian,* February 28, 2020.

[198] Dok, Akol Nyok Akol & Bradley A. Thayer. "Takeover trap: Why imperialism China is invading Africa*," The National Interest,* July 10, 2019.

[199] Wafula, Paul. "Exclusive: Behind the SGR walls*," The Standard,* July 8, 2018.

influx of powerful foreigners who are shaping the country's future – while also bringing racist attitude with them."[200] After enduring more than 70 years of British colonialism, Kenya should not allow itself to be dominated by the Chinese using the money trap.

Moreover, 'China towns' are cropping up everywhere in cities, and buildings spotting Chinese characters are ubiquitous. The Chinese living in Kenya run motor garages, supermarkets, retail stalls, and food kiosks – businesses that previously were a preserve of Kenyans. Chinese signs compete with Kiswahili and English billboards especially at Chinese-built projects such as the SGR. Many workers in the railway system are Chinese and announcements in the trains are made in Mandarin and repeated in English. An attempt to erect Chinese signage along the Nairobi Expressway was thwarted by concerned Kenyans.

More than 70 large Chinese companies are operating in Kenya, many of them owned by the Chinese government. It is said that "China's growing economy is thirsty for sustainable supplies of mineral resources."[201] However, experts warn that if this is the only reason for China's involvement in the country, then this is likely to hurt Kenya in the long run because it will undermine the ability of local firms to exploit the same markets and resources.[202]

---

[200] Goldstein, Joseph. "Kenyans say Chinese investment brings racism and discrimination," *The New York Times,* October 15, 2018.

[201] Communication and Computer Ethics, "Work Ethic and Motivation," Stanford.edu.

[202] Mwengei, Kennedy. A Study on the Impact of China's Investments in Africa: The Case of Kenya, *Finance Management,* March 23, 2013.

PART IV
THE INTRIGUES

CHAPTER 15

Handshake, BBI Reggae and the Court-Shocker

After serving its first term, 2017 was quickly approaching where President Uhuru Kenyatta and his Deputy were required to seek a second term. As early as mid-2013, there had been talk about merging Uhuru's The National Party (TNA) and Ruto's United Republican Party (URP), in readiness for the upcoming polls. The proposed new party was to be called the Jubilee Alliance Party (JAP) and was to encompass at least ten other smaller parties.[203]

On September 10, 2016, Uhuru's TNA and Ruto's URP, and representatives of the small parties, met at Kasarani Indoor Arena and disbanded their parties to form the new alliance. Uhuru told thousands of jubilant delegates that the new party would embrace the whole country. "This party is not about Kenyatta or Ruto," he said. "We want every Kenyan to say this party is their home."

---

[203] The others were the Grand National Union (GNU), United Democratic Forum (UDF), Alliance Party of Kenya (APK), The Independent Party (TIP), New Ford-Kenya (NFK), Ford-People, Jubilee Alliance Party (JAP), Unity Party of Kenya (UPK), the Republican Congress (RC), and the Party of National Unity (PNU). However, PNU's gazette notice announcing its merger with Jubilee was declared invalid by the Political Parties Disputes Tribunal (PPDT).

Four months later, on January 31, 2017, five leaders: Raila, ODM; Kalonzo Musyoka, Wiper Democratic Movement (WDM); Moses Wetang'ula, Ford-Kenya; Musalia Mudavadi, Amani National Congress (ANC); and Isaac Ruto, Chama cha Mashinani (CCM), also met and announced the formation of the National Super Alliance (NASA). NASA was an expansion of the Coalition for Reforms and Democracy (CORD) – the coalition on whose ticket Raila had run with in 2013.

But there was a big problem for the new opposition alliance. Member parties could not agree on one individual to take on Uhuru. They haggled over the choice of the flag-bearer to the extent that they forgot how important it was to formulate a winning strategy.

While the Jubilee Alliance Party was busy refining their messaging, getting their organisational structures in place, and preparing a nation-wide strategy, the opposition was complaining about the new electoral laws, and planning country-wide protests. Its supporters held demonstrations in Nairobi and Kisumu demanding the resignation of top IEBC officials including the Chief Executive Ezra Chiloba. They alleged the officials were a party to electoral fraud in the 2013 elections. Numerous people were shot during the protests. A student in Kisumu and a 41-year-old man in Siaya were killed by the anti-riot police.

Unprepared as it was, NASA did not even have a website, a logo, or even a social media presence. [204] With the time running out without a presidential candidate, the alliance formed a 12-member committee in January 2017 to deliberate on the matter. Negotiations became even more difficult when Wiper Democratic Movement (WDM) leader, Kalonzo Musyoka, threatened to quit if he was not picked as the alliance's presidential candidate. However, eight members of the committee voted for Raila as flag bearer during its final meeting in April, prompting Kalonzo and Amani party leader Mudavadi to walk out.

On April 27, 2017, Raila was unveiled as the man to take on Uhuru during a public rally at Uhuru Park in Nairobi. For the

---

[204] Allison, Simon, ISS Today, February 6, 2017.

running mate, the party settled on Kalonzo Musyoka. The other parties were promised varying positions in the party hierarchy: Mudavadi was proposed as Prime Minister and CS in charge of government coordination; Wetang'ula, as Deputy Prime Minister and CS for economic sector coordination; and Isaac Ruto as Deputy Prime Minister and CS Social Works.

The stage was now set for the big battle. Six other candidates had declared interest in the presidency: Mohamed Dida, Ekuru Aukot, Cyrus Jirongo, Japhet Kaluyu, Michael Mwaura, and Joseph Nyagah.

Uhuru received his first big election boost in May when four political parties, Maendeleo Chap Chap of Machakos Governor Alfred Mutua, Narc-Kenya of Martha Karua, KANU of Gideon Moi, and the Economic Freedom Party (EFF) of Isaac Hassan Abey, endorsed him. A few days later, two more parties, the Democratic Party of Wilfred Machage, and the Labour Party of Ababu Namwamba, also announced support for Uhuru.

As an incumbent, Uhuru enjoyed the advantages of State resources and the benevolence of rich friends both locally and internationally. Using those resources, Jubilee hired the technological expertise of Cambridge Analytica, a controversial UK data analysis firm. According to an investigative report aired by Channel 4 in the UK in March 2018, a top Cambridge Analytica executive, Mark Turnbull, said the firm had "rebranded the entire party (Jubilee) twice [in 2013 and 2017], written their manifesto, done research, analysis, and messaging. I think we wrote all the speeches, and we stage-managed the whole thing – so just about every element of this candidate [Uhuru]."

The firm was later criticised for manipulating elections through fake news and disinformation, not only in Kenya, but in numerous other countries in Africa, including South Africa in 1994, and Nigeria in 2015.

The official campaign period officially started in Kenya on May 28, 2017. Uhuru's election platform was on his achievements during the first four years in office. He emphasised the construction of more roads and the introduction of maternal care. Both Jubilee and

NASA dwelt on economic issues as well, pegging them to the Kenya Vision 2030. The Vision sought to elevate Kenya to an upper-middle income country. NASA hammered the government on rising food prices and the alleged failure by the government to support farmers and provide agricultural markets. It also promised to solve historical land problems especially at the Coast and in the Rift Valley, which were contributors to periodic ethnic clashes. Each side promised great things for the people as they scrambled to appeal to the 19.6 million eligible voters.

Raila was confident of winning the elections even as he complained of rigging plans by Jubilee. "There are attempts to manipulate the results," he told an Al Jazeera interviewer on August 6, 2017, two days before the polls. "The only way Jubilee can win this election is by rigging."

But when the IEBC announced the election results on August 11, Uhuru had secured 54.27% of the ballots against Raila's 44.74%. Because Uhuru had received more than 50% of the votes, a second round of voting was not required. As expected, Raila disputed the results and took the matter to the Supreme Court for determination. In his petition, he listed numerous complaints against the electoral body. He said, for example, that the IEBC IT system had been hacked to manipulate the results. He claimed hackers had entered the database, created errors, and introduced algorithms that tampered with the results. The commission denied the accusations, saying the system was secure.

Apart from that, the elections were also fraught with other misfortunes including the mysterious murder of an IEBC official, Christopher Msando, only days before the polls, and the huff resignation of an election commissioner, Roselyn Akombe.

On September 1, 2017, the Supreme Court issued its verdict, and Kenyans were stunned. The court declared the polls 'invalid, null and void' and said they had been manipulated to ensure victory for Uhuru. Chief Justice David Maraga ordered fresh elections within 60 days. While Raila rejoiced, Uhuru was furious. He called judges of the Supreme Court "crooks." He said, "We shall revisit this thing," without elaborating.

Kenyans were looking forward to the second round of elections. Surprisingly on October 10, Raila announced he was withdrawing from the October 26 rerun, saying those elections would not be credible. His demands for electoral reforms were ignored. Among other things, he had asked that all the suppliers of equipment used to transmit election results be replaced. Raila had expected that his withdrawal would force a postponement of the polls pending reforms, but that did not happen. Uhuru said he was ready for the rerun. On the day of the election, many of Raila's supporters stayed away. The result was a 98.25% win for Uhuru. Raila's cast votes were only 0.96%. Uhuru was back on the saddle for five more years.

Uhuru-Ruto's second term started at a high note. At the swearing-in ceremony at the Moi International Sports Centre, Kasarani, on November 28, 2017, Uhuru articulated his vision for a better Kenya, including providing quality healthcare services, decent housing, creating jobs, and boosting agriculture. But he also talked of uniting the country, divided by politics and ethnicity.

Ruto stood by his boss. From his newly refurbished offices across the Office of the President in downtown Nairobi, the Deputy President executed his duties diligently and obediently. He was not only a breath away from the presidency but the president-in-waiting. Uhuru had made a public commitment to support Ruto after his term ended. But soon, subtle hints emerged to suggest that Uhuru was not, after all, that enthusiastic to endorse his deputy as his successor.

The biggest of all the hints came with the event that took place in early in 2018. It did not only come as a surprise to most Kenyans, but it altered completely the political dynamics in the country, propelling oppositionist Raila to the centre-stage of governance and presidential succession, and relegating Ruto – at least by the face of it - to a third tier on the Executive line-up.

Uhuru and Raila appeared on the steps of the office of the president in Nairobi, Harambee House, on March 9, shook hands, and declared a rapprochement.

Some saw the new friendship between the two as a betrayal of Ruto. It was as a bizarre a moment as it was chilling. One writer called it "the most consequential political moment in recent Kenyan history."[205] The Kenyan population was taken by surprise. A BBC news headline on April 9, 2018, said it all: "The handshake that left millions of Kenyans confused."

That event on a bright mid-Saturday morning, as the two wore radiant smiles of brotherly bond, came to be known as the "Handshake." Almost two months later, on 31 May 2018, the two appeared together at the Kenya National Prayer Breakfast at Safari Park Hotel, Nairobi, in a dramatic show of unity. In front of political, religious, and business leaders, they apologised to each other and pledged henceforth to work together. The two leaders then embarked on countrywide tours to display their newfound unity and commissioning development projects.

With the new political dynamics at play, Raila stopped criticising the government, and became a magnate that lured high-ranking government officials to his offices at Upper Hill in Nairobi. The officials including cabinet secretaries lined up to pay homage to a man, who only a few months earlier, had been considered a pariah.

Similarly, Uhuru avoided any mention of Ruto's name in his succession plan. In December 2018, Uhuru told Kenyans to "judge the potential [presidential] candidates [to succeed him] on the basis of their policies," rather than their political parties and where they came from. That was another hint that Uhuru was not committed to supporting Ruto for the top position.

Uhuru had hoped that the 'handshake' would magically unite Kenyans and end the ethnic polarisation emanating from the 2017 elections. Instead, the détente created unexpected obstacles and inextricable difficulties in the newly formed Jubilee Alliance Party. The party organs, from the parliamentary group (PG) to the national executive committee (NEC), were divided.

Then there was the meeting of Uhuru's allies at Naivasha in late October. A total of 70 MPs from the Mount Kenya region held a two-day meeting to discuss how the region could "capitalise on

---

[205] d Lang'at, Patrick. "What Exactly is BBI? An A-Z breakdown of Kenya's handshake initiative and why you should care," Vox, November 30, 2020.

the remaining years of the Uhuru administration."[206] Although the agenda had included matters of presidential succession, that topic was reportedly dropped following "pressure from State House and notable splits within the group."

It did not escape the attention of observers, however, that the meeting was taking place two weeks after Ruto allied MPs walked out of Uhuru's public function at Bomet University College in the Rift Valley. Seven MPs stormed out of the event to commission a new tuition block. Reports said they did so to protest being sidelined from speaking at the event. But other sources hinted that they were miffed by Uhuru's silence on the issue of Ruto taking over from him. Uhuru supporters smelt blackmail.[207]

Another blow to the Uhuru-Ruto relationship came when the president announced the appointment of Raila as the AU high representative for infrastructure development on Mashujaa Day on December 20. Apparently, Uhuru had received the appointment letter from the AU Commission chairperson, Moussa Faki Mahamat, and seized the day to make the announcement public. That was rather unusual. It's doubtful the AU expected the announcement to be made during a public rally.

After the 'handshake," it was like a whole row of dominoes had tottered. The leadership of NASA was thrown into disarray. Coalition leaders, Kalonzo Musyoka, Musalia Mudavadi, and Moses Wetang'ula, were astounded. They had not been informed in advance. Amid quite incredible confusion and accusations of "selling out," Raila summoned the ODM's decision making organ, the central management committee, to explain the new dispensation and assure the party that all was well.

The Standard captured the mood on its headline: 'A Handshake that Shook the Whole Country.'[208] The shock came partly because the meetings leading to the peace gesture were held in secret. Raila

---

[206] "Legislators meet in Naivasha to seek ways of reaping maximum benefits from Kenyatta's reign," The *Standard*, October 30, 2018.
[207] Odhiambo, Morris. Political Intrigue Surrounds Presidential Succession Plans in Kenya, Freedom House, December 20, 2018.
[208] A Handshake that Shook the Whole Country, *The Standard*, March 10, 2020.

alluded to the involvement of a team of elders he called "counsels of wisdom" as having participated in the negotiations. Media reports indicated that Raila's wife, Ida Odinga, the former first First Lady, Mama Ngina Kenyatta, and the director of National Intelligence Service (NIS), Philip Kameru, had played a key role in the realisation of the handshake.[209]

The strategy was for the handshake to happen before the arrival of the United States Secretary of State Rex Tillerson, who was due in Nairobi that day. That was to avoid any speculation that the handshake was influenced by the west. When Tillerson arrived two hours after the historical event, he expressed USA's support for the new cooperation between the two past nemeses. The US also warned it would sanction anyone opposed to the reconciliation effort.

In the final analysis, Raila saw rapprochement with Uhuru as the best way of rekindling his dwindling political fortunes. His previous aggressive attempts for leadership had failed. Now, he wanted to use the few arrows left in his quiver for a last-ditch attempt to ascend to the top. But he needed a ladder. And that ladder was, conveniently, President Uhuru, who was ready to be the propeller and chief overseer of Raila's plans. Henceforth, Raila talked of Uhuru and Jubilee achievements in reverential terms.

Raila Odinga's sudden shift from being President Uhuru Kenyatta's fierce critic to an underling of a man, 17 years younger, was nevertheless shrilly rejected by many of his supporters. He "has betrayed his integrity. He has betrayed us, and we are not happy," supporter Jack Omondi told *Deutsch Welle* radio of Germany. "Baba [Raila] must be very careful with this thing called handshake," said MP Babu Owino, one of his vocal supporters, adding, "We can't be duped twice." *The Standard* headlined a question: "Has Raila been outfoxed through the handshake?"[210]

A New York-based economist, Kennedy Chesoli, called the handshake a "poisoned chalice," and Raila as a man who forsook his

---

[209] Wanjama, Paul. "Raila speaks on "Counsels of Wisdom" – The elders who planned the handshake," *Kenyans.co.ke,* December 16, 2018.

[210] Nyaringo, Joseph Lister. "Has Raila been outfoxed by the handshake? *Standard,* April 20, 2019.

"Canaan-bound supporters by returning to Egypt to dine with the Pharaoh and other tormentors of his people." This was in reference to the biblical story of Moses and how he led Israelites to the Promised Land, Canaan. The fable had been used widely during the campaigns.

While some Kenyans were angry and surprised, others saw an opportunity for a flash of humour: *"It is handshake's turn to eat its own people,"* said Jonah Cheruiyot on Twitter. Among those unhappy about the new dispensation was Raila's closest adviser, Senator James Orengo, citing underlying implications of the move. Orengo claimed the 'handshake' was a manifestation of Uhuru's overt grand strategy to sabotage Raila's 2022 presidential ambition. Others saw it as signalling the end of opposition politics in Kenya. "NASA is now dead," Peter Kagwanja, the CEO of the Africa Policy Institute (API) and *Sunday Nation* columnist predicted, adding, "And its epitaph written."[211]

In the days that followed the handshake, President Uhuru and Raila were at pain to explain the motive of the now famous handshake. However, the answer came a few months later when they cobbled an arrangement, they called the Building Bridges Initiative (BBI). The BBI was created by a 14-member steering committee or task force formed by Uhuru on January 3, 2020. Its purpose was to explore the nine issues the two leaders [Uhuru and Raila] claimed were necessary to unify the nation. The idea was born out of the culture of violence often accompanying elections. The task force was to investigate issues of ethnic antagonism, corruption, strengthening of devolution, safety, and security. The task force toured the country and listened to views from Kenyans on a variety of issues.

On October 21, 2020, the committee, chaired by Senator Yusuf Haji, presented its report to the two BBI principals at Kisii State Lodge, amid reports that the document had been doctored. The claim was made by a member of the task force, Major John Seii, who opined that some of the proposals in the report were "totally strange" to them [members of the task force] and had never featured

---

[211] Herbling, David. "Raila Odinga leaves Kenyan opposition reeling with decision to bury the hatchet," *The Business Day*, March 12, 2018.

in their discussions. Seii further claimed that three days before the Kisii State Lodge meeting, Raila and Interior Principal Secretary, Karanja Kibicho, had allegedly pressured members of the task force to sign the report without giving them an opportunity to review the document.

Nevertheless, four days later, 4,700 delegates from across the country gathered at Bomas of Kenya in Nairobi for the formal endorsement of the BBI report. The main recommendation of the BBI report was a slew of constitutional changes. The task force report recommended the creation of the offices of a prime minister (PM) and two deputy prime ministers. The PM was to be appointed by the president and the latter to be chosen from among cabinet secretaries. Apart from supervising the functions of ministers, the prime minister was to be the Leader of Government Business in the National Assembly. Also in the arrangement was the position of Leader of Official Opposition which existed in the pre-Constitution of Kenya, 2010, but was scrapped because Kenyans chose a presidential system of government.

The BBI report proposals also provided for the office of the judiciary ombudsman to be appointed by the president with powers to reprimand judicial officials and reject complaints before they reached the Judicial Service Commission (JSC).

In addition to the proposed executive positions, an additional 70 parliamentary constituencies were to be established to bring the number of legislators to 448. The number of Kenyan lawmakers had increased exponentially over the years. During the 9th Parliament (between 2003 and 2007), the national assembly had only 222 MPs (210 elected and 12 nominated). After the promulgation of the constitution of Kenya, 2010, the number almost doubled to 418 – 350 MPs and 67 senators.

However, to implement the proposed changes, they had to amend the Constitution of Kenya, 2010. So, the BBI organisers went round the country collecting signatures from people in support of a constitutional amendment through a referendum. A bill was drafted and tabled in parliament. Uhuru said the amendments to the constitution of Kenya, 2010, were imperative, for national unity and for Kenya to progress further. But critics claimed BBI was a ploy to create executive jobs for the political elite both at the executive level and in parliament. "It is tantamount to abuse of office and state power," Ndung'u Wainaina, the executive director of the International Centre for Policy and Conflict, asserted, saying it is "undermining rules of democracy and subverting the constitution."[212]

Uhuru and Raila planned a charm offensive to try to convince MPs, county governors, and members of county assemblies (MCAs) to support the proposed bill. What they didn't know was that the leaders and other groups wanted "something" in exchange for their support. For example, the Pastoralists Parliamentary Group (PPG) wanted a stop on the BBI bill until their demand of land rights, and others, were accommodated in the legislation.

The governors on their part demanded higher perks including retirement benefits, while MCAs wanted 30% of the money allocated to their counties to be given to their electoral areas (wards) before they could support the bill. President Uhuru pleaded with leaders not to politicise the initiative. He said BBI was "about 50 million Kenyans and not any specific individual." But observers noted that it was Uhuru and Raila who had politicised the exercise. For example, nine of the fourteen task force members and two co-chairpersons were allies of either Kenyatta or Raila. The premise, therefore, was that the process was skewed towards the interests of the two leaders.[213] And moreover, the process was being midwifed through political institutions. If passed by MCAs and both the Senate and the National Assembly, the legislation was to lead to a referendum to take place before the 2022 elections.

Raila Odinga was the most hyperkinetic enthusiast of the BBI. As soon as the initiative was formalised, he gleefully went out to promote it. He started with a meeting with the Kikuyu Council of Elders in Ruaka, led by its chairman, Wachira Kiago, and then moved to western Kenya, the Coast, and the other regions to popularise the

---

[212] Wainaina, Ndung'u. "No, Uhuru Kenyatta, you can't change constitution while in office," *The Star*, December 5, 2019.
[213] Mbugua, Patrick. K. "Why BBI will not promote peace or prevent violence," *Elephant*, November 20, 2020.

initiative. Although many Kenyans had not read the BBI document, they were clear-eyed about its main intention: to create more seats for the elite. As Raila went round, people flooded social media platforms with posts urging him and Uhuru to abandon the BBI crusade and forsake the envisaged referendum.

In July 2021, a poll by Trends and Insights Africa (TIFA) showed that only 19% of Kenyans would vote "Yes" in a referendum intended to amend the Constitution of Kenya, 2010. But Raila was not a man to give up. He likened BBI to 'reggae' and said, "Nobody can stop reggae," in reference Lucky Dube's popular song, "Nobody *Can Stop Reggae.*"

But reggae did stop in early March 2020 when the Covid-19 pandemic exploded. The government banned all public gatherings, including BBI activities. In essence, Covid-19 ruined the entire initiative, albeit temporarily. In a cheery response, Raila asserted that the BBI reggae was only on "half-time" and would resume after the pandemic.

Meanwhile, Deputy President Ruto, who was flip-flopping on BBI – opposing it in rallies but supporting it privately with conditions – was holding meetings of his own in disparate parts of the country without any regard to the pandemic. He made inroads into Uhuru's generally impenetrable Mt. Kenya region with his "wheelbarrow" message, attempting to change the narrative from what was 'good' about the BBI to what was 'bad' about the initiative. His main point of persuasion was that BBI was not about uniting Kenyans or about enhancing peace. It was a "dangerous" proposition likely to plunge the country into "presidential imperialism," he said. With BBI, the president would control the legislature through appointments of MPs to the Executive, and would also control the judiciary, he claimed. "Let us not lie to the people. BBI is dangerous."

The response from Jubilee Alliance Party officials was counter intuitive. They accused the Deputy President of using BBI for his political interests. "If the president of the republic of Kenya said BBI is a good initiative and must pass, who are you as the deputy to come and contradict him," one ODM MP said. The sycophancy of some of the Jubilee stalwarts was beyond the pale. Some of them supported the document without even reading it, prompting some leaders to exhort them to read and understand the report.

But the assault on DP Ruto over his stand on the BBI backfired. More MPs and grassroots leaders flocked to his party: "Four MPs jump to Ruto's UDA," said one headline. "Ruto reaps big in Central as governor and MP join UDA," was the headline in *Capital News*, in announcing the defection of Nyeri Governor Mutahi Kahiga and Tetu MP James Gichuhi. Because of constitutional requirements, the MPs could not officially resign without triggering a by-election. So, they stayed put in Jubilee Alliance Party, but sang UDA songs.

Until the end of 2020, Uhuru did not actively go out of his way to aggressively push the BBI agenda. It was not until February 2021 when he saw the project on the periphery of sinking that he threw himself into the ring. Accompanied by Raila, he toured different parts of the country on a nation-wide campaign to promote the initiative, while dishing out goodies in the form of development projects. He lured MCAs with a KSh.2 million car grant each as 'grease' to pass the BBI bill in the county assemblies.

While on a tour to Kisumu, a Raila stronghold, on May 30, 2021, President Uhuru offered to complete the unfinished Kenyatta stadium in the lakeside city and improve roads in the Nyanza region. In the months that followed, Uhuru orchestrated the removal of some rebel Jubilee MPs who were nominated to parliament or held key house committee positions. One of the victims was nominated Senator Isaack Mwaura. Mwaura was thrown out from Jubilee and lost his seat in May 2021 for opposing BBI, and for associating with Ruto. However, six months later, in November, the High Court nullified the Jubilee's decision saying it was improperly executed. Mwaura was given back his Senate seat.

Uhuru's aggressive lobbying efforts to promote BBI paid off. In May 2021, both the national assembly and the senate approved the Constitution of Kenya Amendment Bill, 2020, by a substantial majority in both houses. The National Assembly passed the bill by 235 against 83 with two abstentions, while the senate voted 51 votes to 11. Forty-four out of the 47 County Assemblies approved it.

DP Ruto saw the passed legislation as a plot to frustrate his match towards the 2022 presidential election. Apart from opposing the role of the President in appointing MPs to the cabinet, he was also against the suggestion that only major political parties would appoint members of the IEBC.

On December 2, 2020, DP Ruto, flanked by about one-hundred legislators, governors, and MCAs, told a press conference that he opposed the idea of a separate BBI referendum to determine the popularity of the initiative as proposed by Uhuru and Raila. Instead, he suggested that the plebiscite be held alongside the 2022 elections to cut costs. However, he was non-committal on whether he would lead a 'No' campaign against the BBI – if there was to be a referendum.

RUTO ANGERED

The new relationship between Uhuru and Raila bothered the DP because of fears of being edged out of the political equation, altogether. While he admitted that Uhuru had informed him about the meetings with Raila, he felt betrayed that in the handshake, Uhuru went beyond what they had agreed on. He said, for example, that they did not agree about amending the Constitution of Kenya, 2010, to create additional executive positions.

Uhuru, on the other hand, felt personally insulted that his number two man would deride the handshake and oppose the BBI. He denied that Ruto was kept in the dark about the impending handshake. In a speech to Mount Kenya leaders at Sagana, Nyeri, in February 2022, Uhuru said: "I briefed him [Ruto], about the planned handshake] until the last minute when I was going to greet my friend [Raila]."[214] The president wondered aloud why his deputy was not being frank.

---

[214] Mwangi, Josphat. "Uhuru: I told Ruto about handshake with Raila, and it was for peace," Capital News, February 23, 2022.

Not wanting to address the matter directly, DP Ruto let his allies fight the Uhuru-Raila alliance at every opportunity available. Ruto's strategy was to attack the BBI using the dynasty-hustler narrative. He called the initiative the "most fraudulent and deceitful agenda" aimed at enriching a few at the top at the expense of the masses.

While Uhuru and Raila are reasonably good public speakers, they don't match Ruto's charisma, eloquence, and bare-knuckle hit-and-run political jabs. "You are a tyrant and a despot," he told Raila in one tweet. "We are not going to allow you [Uhuru] to install a puppet who is going to look after your interests," he told Uhuru at a campaign rally. In calling Raila "a puppet" Ruto, was in effect, calling Uhuru 'a puppet master.'

Raila's broadsides at Ruto centred mainly on widespread allegations of graft that implicated the DP and his instinctive generosity. "Every month he's [Ruto] giving handouts of KSh.100 million. Yet we know that his earnings are about KSh.3 million. Where is he getting the money?"[215] Raila often asked.

With the handshake, Uhuru had managed to corrode and corrupt the opposition the same way Moi did to Raila and his National Development Party (NDP). KANU and NDP had started cooperation in February 1998, where NDP supported KANU in parliament in exchange for appointment of some of its members to influential positions in government. The icing on the cake was in June 2001 when its leader, Raila Odinga, was appointed Minister for Energy. Moi also appointed Raila's colleague Adhu Awiti Minister for Planning and two more NDP MPs assistant ministers.[216] The NDP-KANU alliance culminated in a merger at the Moi International Sports Centre, Kasarani in 2002. At that meeting, in March, Raila dissolved NDP, shook hands with Moi, and accepted to be KANU's Secretary General.

History repeated itself in 2018. Raila shook hands with the same man who torpedoed his ambition in 2002, and later 2013 and

---

[215] Etyang, Hesborn. "Raila hits out at Ruto over donations, pledges to seal graft loopholes if elected," The *Star,* October 14, 2021.
[216] Hornsby, Charles. Ibid.

2017! But with the handshake and the BBI, Raila was back in the corridors of power as President Uhuru's most exuberant partner.

By 'joining' the government, the opposition which Raila – a man chastened and refined by many years of experience in politics – led was now in tatters. It was as if the country had returned to the one-party framework that was in place before 1992. There were no more robust parliamentary debates, and the pursuance of checks and balances slowly vanished. The speaker of the national assembly, Justin Muturi, who was supposed to be impartial, became an enabler of the status quo. The legislative body became a rubber-stamp of the Executive, the same way it was in the 1980s under President Moi.

During Moi's era, top political leaders silently took powers of the national assembly and gave them to the civil service.[217] And the ruling party KANU routinely usurped work which traditionally belonged to parliament. Moi did not need laws to get things done. He made roadside pronouncements which had the force of law, at one time boasting; "I appoint high court judges, provincial commissioners, district commissioners, the vice president, and others. The party is supreme."[218]

Two years before to the end of Uhuru's term, parliament had become so weak that some MPs believed it was no longer effective in exercising its mandate, independently. "Parliament is dead," Senator Kipchumba Murkomen, an ally of DP Ruto said confidently. "It is an extension of [the] Executive, and the opposition is causing a stampede trying to be more government than government itself…. If we continue this way, history will judge us harshly," he added.

But others felt the 'handshake' had enhanced bipartisanship and made parliament stronger. "Legislators are now able to look at things in a bipartisan manner as opposed to what it was before," said MP Junet Mohamed.

The *Africa Confidential* reported on May 13, 2022, that before the handshake, Mama Ngina Kenyatta and her son, Muhoho

---

[217] The *East African Standard*, March 18, 1971, p. 1.
[218] Rule, Sheila. "Power of Kenya's leader is growing," *The New York Times*, December 15, 1986.

Kenyatta, had assured Raila and wife, Ida, that "a role would be created for Raila in government."[219] True to that promise, Raila – following the handshake – was assigned a full contingent of security personnel and chase cars, given an office, and paid a handsome allowance, to promote the BBI agenda around the country.

Raila had at his disposal government choppers and seemed to enjoy every bit of it. Occasionally, Uhuru would dispatch him to official functions to represent him. For example, barely a month after the handshake, Uhuru sent Raila to represent him at the funeral of Winnie Mandela, the estranged former wife of the legendary South African leader, Nelson Mandela. In South Africa, Raila was showered with all the protocol trappings reserved for a state visitor, including private talks with top officials of the ruling African National Congress (ANC). The whole thing was an ingenious trick by Uhuru, but a risky blunder by Raila. Uhuru achieved what he wanted: to keep his nemesis quiet. He claimed the truce would also provide an enabling environment for his government to deliver results to the people. Conversely, Raila became Uhuru's fiddler, "Singing like a parrot," in President Moi's famous phrase.

The handshake achieved one more thing. It hastened the death of NASA. Raila parted ways with Musalia, Musyoka, and Wetang'ula. As the 2022 elections approached, the trio formed another coalition, the One Kenya Alliance (OKA). Just as he had 'destroyed' KANU after his departure, Raila tore NASA into pieces. Paraphrasing writer Curt Gentry, NASA started with a bang in January 2017, but ended not with a whimper, but a yawn, in August 2021.[220]

Similarly, Raila's partnership with Uhuru left Jubilee in a tangle of rival cliques. The party was divided between *Kieleweke* group that supported Uhuru and *Tangatanga*, allied to Ruto. Two groups also went separate ways: Elected and nominated MPs calling themselves 'Team Embrace' supported BBI, while 'Inua Mama' group, made up of parliamentarians affiliated to Ruto, opposed the initiative

---

[219] "Raila Beats Rivals to a New Deal," *Africa Confidential*, Vol. 59, No. 6, March 23, 2018.

[220] Gentry, Curt. J. Edgar Hoover: The Man and the Secrets, W. W. Norton & Company, 1991, p. 103.

As for Uhuru and the Jubilee Alliance Party, the handshake wreaked havoc and made Uhuru's political base of Central Kenya restive. Several elected members from the region soon bolted from the party to join his rival, DP Ruto in his new outfit, UDA. That annoyed Uhuru further. He appeared in Kikuyu vernacular radio and TV stations and poured scorn on Ruto and his allies.

For Raila, however, the handshake bestowed on him a new status: that of a top-tier influencer. Having fallen out with Ruto, the president no longer considered his deputy a worthy partner in government. He isolated him to the extent of not inviting him to cabinet meetings and other important functions at State House.

When President Moi died in early 2020, for example, Ruto was excluded from the team coordinating the funeral arrangements. The task of leading the team was instead given to the Interior CS, Fred Matiang'i. The new development drove Ruto further from the government. It caused internal dissension within the Jubilee leadership and jostling confusion in rank and file. It was a period of bewildering portents. In essence, the Jubilee Alliance Party was in a static paradigm.

It was at that point that Ruto upped the clearly divisive hustler versus dynasty narrative, pitying the "struggling Kenyans of low birth and the alliance of wealthy families, a matter that has monopolised political competition in Kenya for two generations."[221] Ruto projected himself as a modern-day Robin Hood out to save the poor from exploitation by the rich. He showed up at church gatherings and other venues carrying big envelopes with cash which he distributed without care to organisers and hosts.

The introduction of a wheelbarrow as his UDA party's symbol was another attempt to politically separate himself from the mighty and rich Jubilee Alliance Party stalwarts. He promoted UDA as a party of the lowly. To a large extent he succeeded. People flocked to his meetings, some pushing wheelbarrows loaded with mundane merchandise like *Sukuma wiki* vegetables and bananas. They shouted

---

[221] Gathara, Patrick. "Dynasties vs hustlers in Kenya," *Al Jazeera*, September 24, 2019.

Kazi ni Kazi, (work is work) meaning even low-paying jobs were sources of hope and happiness. Soon, opinion polls and projections were showing him as leading in the presidential poll.

In the meantime, eight individual Kenyans and civil society organisations had, in September 2020, petitioned the High Court to stop the BBI bill and block a referendum. The main point of opposition was the applicability of the basic structure doctrine. This is a common law judicial principal safeguarding certain clauses of the constitution from being amended in Kenya.

The petitioners argued that the doctrine limited the amendment power in the constitution under Article 256 and 257. The chief justice constituted a five-judge bench of the High Court sitting as a constitutional court. The court's decision came on May 23, 2021. It ruled that the BBI bill was irregular, illegal, and unconstitutional, because it sought to alter the basic structure of the current constitution.

In a four-hour televised ruling, the court said any proceedings to amend the constitution had to be done either through parliament or through a popular initiative. The court chastised Uhuru for failing to respect, uphold, and safeguard the constitution. It said Uhuru had therefore fallen short of the leadership integrity threshold. Once again, Uhuru's attempt to abuse his presidential powers was thwarted. The BBI was a cataclysmic failure.

Nelson Havi, the president of the Law Society of Kenya, posted on Twitter a picture of himself dancing with a charming caption; *Reggae has been stopped!*

The collapse of the initiative denied a small group of greedy and selfish elite a chance to share power and thus continue with their habit of looting the country. It was an ignominious defeat for Uhuru and a shattering embarrassment for Raila who had spent months seeking support for the initiative. For hardcore BBI enthusiasts waiting for executive positions, the decision left them in an inexplicable imbroglio. The BBI collapse ruined those hopes and frustrated Uhuru's succession plans. Uhuru had hoped to promote a coalition between those leaders and Raila against Ruto. Now, he had to go back to the drawing board to find ways of dealing with his deputy. Some said the BBI crash was "arguably the most significant ruling by Kenyan courts since President Uhuru Kenyatta's election win was nullified in 2017."²²²

In the meantime, Uhuru criticised the court's ruling as "an attempt to stop the will of the people." The government moved to the Court of Appeal to have the ruling vacated. But on August 20, 2021, the president and his government suffered yet another setback when that court agreed with the High Court and dismissed the case. The Court of Appeal declared the BBI steering committee task force "an unlawful entity not recognised by law, and with no legal capacity to initiate any action to change the constitution." The court further said that the involvement of President Uhuru in the process was wrong.

The ruling was lauded by citizens who felt the government had overreached by trying to force a referendum on the people. "Justice has been served," Senator Kiprotich arap Cherargei said in a tweet." Governor Anne Waiguru who had supported the initiative and had not yet moved to Ruto's wing remarked that "Kenya must go on. BBI intended well but we must respect the constitutional authority of the courts and find other legitimate means to achieve Kenya's unity and prosperity."²²³ If the Court of Appeal had embraced the High Court ruling, the country would have gone for a referendum that would have cost the taxpayers millions of shillings.

After the BBI was jettisoned, a dejected Raila announced he would not pursue the matter to the Supreme Court. Instead, he vowed to concentrate on selling his agenda as a 2022 presidential candidate. The government, on the other hand, vowed to continue with the fight through an appeal to the Supreme Court.

One analyst said the "judiciary's rejection of BBI could herald important changes to the unwritten rules of Kenyan politics."²²⁴ That partly came true ahead of the 2022 elections. The registration of new voters was historically low, a sign of voter apathy and fatigue after

---

[222] Omondi, Ferdinand. "Kenya's BBI blocked in scathing court verdict for President Kenyatta," *BBC News*, May 14, 2021.
[223] Maombo, Sharon. "Mixed reactions after Appeals Court halts BBI reggae," Star, August 20, 2021.
[224] Gavin, Michelle. "BBI ruling leaves Kenya at a crossroads," Council on Foreign Relations, August 25, 2021.

years of "exuberant showmanship"[225] by politicians. At every election circle, Kenyans went to the polls to cast votes expecting changes, but those changes never came. Contenders of different parties would give long lists of promises, but once elected, they would disappear not to be seen again, until the next elections.

In the 2022 presidential election campaign, for example, Raila promised to give KSh.6,000 a month to all youths and vulnerable households. He will also employ all jobless teachers and roll-out what he called BabaCare, a universal health insurance plan.

Ruto, the 'wheelbarrow man" said he would reserve KSh.100 billion for youth initiatives and KSh.5 billion for small scale traders under his bottom-up economic plan if he won. He would also allocate 50% of cabinet posts to women and disburse substantial sums of money to counties.

The leader of the Wiper, Kalonzo Musyoka, said he would provide free secondary and university education if elected president.[226]

The most outrageous of the promises came from Alfred Mutua, a third-rate candidate, who pledged to give newly wed couples loans of between KSh.500,000 and KSh.1 million if elected, to be repaid over a 20-year period, to start life. Not one of them explained where the money would come from. Both Musyoka and Mutua eventually dropped their presidential bid to support Raila and Ruto respectively.

---

[225] Haugerud, Angelique. The Culture of Politics in Modern Kenya, Cambridge University Press, 1993, p. 1.
[226]

CHAPTER 16

Uhuru Fallout with Ruto

The Uhuru-Raila handshake was the clearest indicator of relations gone sour; leaving no doubt that President Uhuru and his deputy, Ruto, had reached an inflection point. Uhuru challenged his deputy to quit if he was not happy with the government. "If you are not happy, step aside and allow those who want to move on to do so. You cannot ride on what we have done and talk a different language on the side,"[227] Uhuru said during an interview with senior editors at State House in August 2021. Ruto scoffed at the challenge saying he won't resign.

William Ruto came to be known through his early involvement with the Youth for KANU (YK'92), a group of "especially enterprising young businesspeople eager to accumulate wealth and political power through the state."[228] YK'92 was formed on 16 July 1992 by Ruto, Sam Nyamweya, Cyrus Jirongo, Gerald Bomett, and Michael Kigen. Ruto was the organising secretary while Cyrus Jirongo was the chairman. The vainglorious elite youths were handsomely financed by President Moi, state institutions, and businesspersons such as, Kamlesh Pattni, of the infamous Goldenberg scandal of the 1990s. At that time, Ruto was a student at the University of Nairobi.

---

[227] Mungai, Allan. "Quit if dissatisfied with government you are serving in, Uhuru tells Ruto," *The Saturday Standard,* August 25, 2021.
[228] Kanyinga, Karuti & John Murimi Njoka. "The Role of Youth in Politics, African Journal of Sociology, Vol. V, No. 1, 2002, pp. 89-111.

The group's agenda was to campaign for Moi and the ruling party in the first multi-party elections in 1992. Supported by the provincial administration, the YK'92 founders travelled everywhere in the country falsely promising jobs to youths if they voted for KANU. In return, the "petty bourgeoisie cronies" were incentivised with "state land, most of it already occupied by landless squatters..."[229]

The YK'92 earned a reputation that was more negative than positive. While it delivered votes to Moi, it also earned the wrath of Kenyans for harassing opposition candidates and supporters.[230] It also reportedly recruited "Kalenjin warriors" to attack non-Kalenjin residents in the Rift Valley and engaged in blackmail for personal and political gain.

However, internal feuds led chairman Jirongo to suspend his deputy, Bomett, and treasurer, Sam Nyamweya in November 1992, a month before the polls. Moi disbanded the group immediately after the elections. For Ruto, YK'92 was a steppingstone into elective politics. In 1997, he took his first plunge into elective politics by contesting the Eldoret North constituency seat. He defeated Reuben Chesire, a more established candidate who was close to Moi.

Ruto was the same one who in October 2010 appeared in court together with a fellow MP Sammy Mwaita, and businessperson Joshua Kulei, on fraud charges over the sale of a piece of land in Ngong Forest in January 2009. Ruto had been suspended from office a few days earlier as minister for higher education, science, and technology, pending the outcome of the KSh.272 million fraud case. It was alleged the accused sold the land to the Kenya Pipeline Company, a government parastatal, a decade earlier. It was further alleged that Ruto had pocketed KSh.96 million from the deal as facilitation fee. On April 11, 2011 – soon after Ruto's return from The Hague over the 2007/2008 post-election violence – Chief Magistrate Gilbert

---

[229] Mati, Jacob Mwathi. Emergence of Inter-Identity Alliances in Struggles for Transformation of the Kenya Constitution, The University of South Pacific, *Interdisciplinary Journal*, Vol. 9, No. 1, 2017.

[230] Branch, Daniel. Kenya: Between Hope and Despair, 1963-2011, Yale University Press, 2011.

Mutembei, ruled that there was no sufficient evidence to put the three on their defence. The case was dismissed.

Since the time the two teamed up and throughout the ICC trial and formation of the Jubilee government, Uhuru and Ruto were like conjoined twins. They were inseparable. Together, they campaigned and were victorious, and together they weathered the ICC test. By choosing Ruto as his running mate and deputy president, Uhuru was convinced of Ruto's capabilities as an able assistant. The constitution mandates that a presidential candidate nominates a "person who is qualified for nomination for election as president, as a candidate for deputy president." In essence, therefore, Ruto met the qualifications to be president. The Kenya constitution states that once sworn-in, the deputy president cannot be removed except on grounds of physical and mental incapacity, gross violation of a provision of the constitution, gross misconduct, or unless he commits a crime under national or international law.

Thus, Uhuru could not remove Ruto when the two were no longer in sync. On numerous occasions, Uhuru asked Ruto to resign if he was unhappy in government, but the latter repeatedly refused to leave. Uhuru's main complaint was that Ruto had abandoned his official duties to campaign, and that he was undermining the government he was serving in. But Ruto retorted that he had never failed to execute duties assigned to him by his boss. So, why didn't Uhuru fire him for "gross misconduct" as provided for, in the constitution instead of unceasingly complaining about his work ethics?

From a political point of view, Ruto's frustrations were understandable. He felt double-crossed because Uhuru, a member of the dynasty, had promised to rule for ten years and pass on the baton to him, a hustler, to serve the subsequent ten years. In his political career, Ruto often reminded Kenyans of his poor background and how dynasties often exploited 'hustlers.'

It was therefore difficult to see how Uhuru could work harmoniously with Ruto. At the beginning things worked well. But at the end their friendship was unsalvageable. One writer summed it up by saying that after eight years and two presidential elections later, "the marriage [between Uhuru and Ruto] is broken and we, their children, the ordinary citizens of Kenya, are lost."[231] Relations between the two were never to be the same again. What followed were internecine battles for leadership supremacy between the two former close allies.

To add insult to injury, Uhuru's mother, Mama Ngina, did not trust Ruto. She was concerned about Ruto's growing influence after his acquittal by the ICC in April 2016 and the endorsement he received from Kalenjin elders in June 2017 as the Rift Valley kingpin.

The invasion at Ruto's home in July 2017, only weeks to the polls did not help matters. A man armed with a machete penetrated Ruto's rural home at Sugoi near Eldoret, seriously injuring a police officer manning the gate. There was a gun battle, and both the attacker and a security officer, were killed. Neither Ruto nor his family were in the expansive residence when the attack took place. Luckily, the deputy president had left minutes earlier to attend campaign rallies with Uhuru.

The attack was worrying and raised questions about Ruto's personal safety. Ruto himself said the attack was "aimed at causing tension and disunity among Kenyans."[232] However, there was no evidence that the government was behind the invasion. Ruto's security was beefed up. The attack, horrifying as it was, further lifted Ruto's political stature especially in the Rift Valley, and that too worried Mama Ngina.

There were also strong indications of secret plans aimed at resuscitating the ICC case against Ruto by getting some witnesses to recant testimonies submitted to the court in 2014. If those plans had succeeded, Ruto's case would have been revived, with serious consequences to his presidential ambitions.

After the handshake, plans to torpedo Ruto's ambitions beyond Jubilee's second term were accelerated. And that was done slowly and meticulously. A three-pronged strategy was devised by

---

[231] "Kenyatta, Ruto and Odinga: The true cost of Kenya's political love triangle," *BBC News*, July 11, 2021.

[232] Nduhiu, Dennis. "Attack on my home meant to cause tension – DP Ruto," *Citizen Digital*, July 30, 2017.

Ruto's detractors in Jubilee: get the Ethics and Anti-Corruption Commission (EACC) to harass Ruto on real and/or imaginary corruption allegations, send a cryptic message to the Ruto camp that he was not the automatic choice to succeed President Uhuru, and get former President Moi's favourite but lacklustre son, Gideon Moi, a Kalenjin like Ruto, to work with Uhuru.

On August 22, 2018, a firm published a poll showing that the deputy president was the most corrupt politician in Kenya. Reportedly conducted by the Independent Polling Systems of Society (IPSOS), the poll showed Ruto leading the pack of corrupt officials at 33% while Uhuru came fourth at 11%.

Ruto condemned the poll as 'fake news' saying that, "When my competitors are through with (Monday-Sunday) sponsored headlines, paid opinion polls and fake news, they are welcome to the real contest based on real *mwananchi* issues...." Ruto tweeted the next day. Fake or not, the poll was part of a strategy by the Moi and Kenyatta families to demolish Ruto's political career and portray him as unfit for public office.

As relations between Uhuru and Ruto reached a boiling point, Ruto was a no show at numerous events presided over by the president. He did not attend the commemoration of the first anniversary of the late President Moi on February 5, 2021, was absent when the Tanzania President Samia Suluhu Hassan was received at State House on May 4 and was missing at the Labour Day celebrations on June 1. He however did show up at the National Prayer Breakfast at Parliament Buildings on May 27, 2021.

In 2019, DP William Ruto was shamed when it became known that a hotel he owned in Nairobi, was built on a piece of land allegedly acquired illegally. The land measures 0.773 hectares and sits next to Wilson Airport on a land grabbed from the Kenya Civil Aviation Authority (KCAA). The KCAA confirmed in August 2018 that the land belonged to the organisation which was trying to reclaim it through the courts.

Reports said the land was allocated to a company associated with Ruto on August 30, 2002. At that time, Ruto was President Moi's Minister for Home Affairs. During an interview with BBC's *Hard talk* programme in 2019, Ruto admitted, for the first time, that the said land had been illegally acquired. He stated that when he took possession of the land, he did not know it belonged to someone else. However, in responding to Raila's demands that the hotel be demolished, Ruto reminded him that the hotel was built when he [Raila] was prime minister in Kibaki's grand coalition government and that there were no queries then about the land.

The National Land Commission (NLC) ordered Ruto to pay reparation to KCAA. However, in a High Court ruling in 2020, Judge Bernard Eboso, said that the NLC decision was not binding, meaning that the matter was still in dispute.

The wrangle over the land around Weston Hotel escalated when children at Lang'ata Primary School, next door, abandoned classes to protest the grabbing of their sports field. They were shocked when they returned from their December holidays early in 2015 to find a concrete wall erected around their playground. Someone called the police, and the pupils were tear gassed.

The sight of wailing children, collapsing from the effects of the tear gas infuriated parents and Kenyans at large, with many calling for criminal action against police officers involved. Five children were seriously injured, and several protesters were arrested. The area MP, Kenneth Okoth, pointed a finger at the Deputy President as the one who planned to grab the land which was adjacent to Weston Hotel for use as parking space.

In the meantime, the parliamentary public investments committee (PIC) chaired by MP Adan Keynan, asked the NLC to investigate the circumstances under which the Weston plot fell into the hands of private developers. It recommended that the land revert to KCAA. No action was taken, however, prompting Auditor General Nancy Gathungu, in her review of the 2020 KCAA books, to question the delay in recovering the land.

The troubles facing Ruto continued. In October 2019, the Trusted Society of Human Rights Alliance, an NGO, wrote to the Directorate of Criminal Investigations (DCI) claiming that the Deputy President had grabbed 900-acres in the Masai Mara Game Reserve belonging to former Vice President Joseph Murumbi.

Similar claims were made by one of his opponents in the 2022 presidential elections, Kalonzo Musyoka. The former Vice President alluded to the land grab by Ruto during a press conference in January 2021. Kalonzo asked security agencies to investigate Ruto over the farm located in Narok County.

Murumbi, who was an avid art collector and conservationist, was said to have taken a loan from the Agricultural Finance Corporation (AFC) in the 1960s which he failed to pay in full. After his death, relatives went to court to demand the farm, claiming that the government had written off the loan. However, it was revealed that AFC took the land and auctioned it. A company associated with Ruto allegedly bought it. The Murumbi family has tried for years to get back the land with no success. However, Ruto denied grabbing the land.

As if that was not enough, Ruto was sued in court by a farmer, Adrian Muteshi, for grabbing his land in Uasin Gishu. Muteshi had abandoned the 100-acre farm following the 2007-8 election violence. He left workers on site, but they were chased away by unknown people, and the farm taken over. Ruto argued that he had bought the farm from a third party. The DP lost the case. He was then ordered to vacate the farm and pay Muteshi KSh.5 million in compensation. The case elicited a lot of public interest earning Ruto – a man known for his exuberant self-assurance – the nickname *arap Mashamba*.

In August 2021, Senator, James Orengo, a close Raila ally, questioned Ruto's connection to a foreigner, Harun Aydin, whose presence in Kenya caused consternation. Orengo wanted the DP summoned before the parliamentary security committee to explain his links with the Turkish national. But that did not happen.

Ruto, Aydin, and others, were scheduled to fly to Uganda from Wilson Airport. But that trip aborted seemingly on 'orders from above.' The presence on that trip of the mysterious Turkish businessman was puzzling for the simple reason that he had not previously been seen in Ruto's orbit. So, the question was: who was this person and what kind of association did he have with DP Ruto?

On the day of the flight, Ruto and his group were kept waiting at the airport for five hours before the DP was informed that the trip was put off. The DP and his party were bewildered and stupefied. As for Aydin, the government showed no courtesy. He was taken away and detained. No reason was given.

Aydin had arrived in Kenya on June 24 possessing a work permit issued by Kenya's state department for interior and citizen services, domiciled in the ministry of interior and co-ordination of national government.[233] Ruto and the Turkish Embassy explained that Aydin was a genuine businessman, but the government didn't buy that argument. It branded him a terrorist. Allegations were made that in the past, Aydin was detained at Frankfurt airport, Germany, on suspicion of belonging to a terrorist organisation.

However, this fifty-four-year-old Aydin was mistaken for a man of the same name who was arrested in Germany in 2001 for belonging to Kalifatsstaat (Caliphate State), an extremist organisation. The big difference was that the latter Aydin was much younger, at 24 years. He was a resident of Cologne, Germany, and was preparing to fly to Iran carrying what officials described as a holy war manual.

For Ruto, things got even more convoluted after claiming he had helped Aydin to obtain a KSh.15 billion loan from a local bank to invest in Uganda. Equity Bank denied that it had loaned money to Aydin or his companies. The Turkish, who had been under the custody of the Anti-Terrorism Police Unit (ATPU), was sneaked out of his detention at 4:00 am and deported to his home country.

The puzzling incident left Ruto with an egg on his face. No one believed Ruto's explanation that Aydin was a genuine businessman, nor that he had helped him obtain the huge loan. But even if that was true, one question was, as the number two topmost official in government, was it right for him to negotiate a loan from a Kenyan bank, for a foreigner to invest in another country? After Equity Bank's denial, some tweeps in the social media branded Ruto a "liar."

---

[233] Presidential Executive Order No. 6 of 2019.

Cracks in Governance

The fall-out between Uhuru and his deputy Ruto affected governance throughout Jubilee's second term. The paralysis was evident in several frontiers. The cabinet rarely met especially after the tiff between Uhuru and Ruto. With Ruto "pissing" in from the outside, the government became ruffled and crippled. The DP stopped going to his official office in town and decided instead to work from his government residence and/or his own house in Karen.

To isolate his deputy further, Uhuru appointed the Interior Minister Fred Matiang'I, to chair the national development implementation and communication cabinet committee, a superfluous body whose mandate was to "oversee functions of ministries." In effect, Matiang'i – a man known for disregarding court orders - became Uhuru's *de facto* executive assistant.

In turn, Ruto did not show up at the National Covid-19 Conference convened by Uhuru in September 2020 despite being invited. Among leaders who addressed the conference was Raila.

Ruto was the chairman of the Intergovernmental Budget and Economic Council (IBEC), but when he called a meeting of the council in May 2022, some top government ministers refused to attend. The meeting was called to discuss important economic issues including pending bills and disbursement of funds to counties. Members of the council consisted of cabinet secretaries and county governors.

On several occasions, the President refused to shake Ruto's hand. At his last Madaraka Day celebrations as President on June 1, 2022, Uhuru denied his deputy a chance to address the crowd, a dramatic change in practice for such occasions.

PART V
UHURU SUCCESSION

CHAPTER 17

Ruto Betrayal

On April 13, 2021, President Uhuru sent his brother, Muhoho, and Gideon Moi, for talks with Raila at his Karen home in Nairobi. Details of their discussion were not divulged, but political pundits speculated the meeting had to do with Raila's presidential run.

That meeting was followed by another one on August 5, 2021, between Uhuru and Raila, in Mombasa, to discuss the strategy of endorsing Raila as Uhuru's successor. They met not at State House, Mombasa, but at the president's private residence in North Coast. It was agreed at that meeting that Uhuru should not make a public announcement endorsing Raila yet, but that the Kenyattas would offer tacit approval of his candidature through surrogates.

Not too long after that, Uhuru's trouble-shooter, David Murathe, also the Jubilee Alliance Party vice chairman, made a categorical statement in an interview with the *Sunday Nation* that "it is Baba [Raila] or nothing." Murathe's remarks were troubling because they conjured past images of a loser refusing to accept results and inciting followers to violence.

In December 2021, another Uhuru sycophant, trade unionist Francis Atwoli, made an ominous statement suggesting that Ruto will not be president and "might [even] not be on the ballot come the 2022 General Elections." The prediction was too pregnant to be disregarded. It raised fears in the Ruto circle, in view of the many disappearances and murders of politicians in Kenya's history. A Ruto ally, MP Oscar Sudi, claimed Atwoli's remarks could be part of a "wide scheme to kill or harm the DP." Atwoli had to clarify his remarks. He said he did not wish the Deputy President dead.

On June 4, Uhuru, through Executive Order number 1 of 2020, reorganised his government, renaming the presidency the 'Executive Office of the President.' This meant that President Uhuru no longer needed Ruto's approval over key matters of the State. Ruto himself admitted during an interview on August 4, 2021, that he had been barred from executing the duties of the DP.

Yet, while addressing a Catholic congregation after a mass in a Kiambu church in September, Ruto made a blunder. He told Mama Ngina to her face that: "The first time, you called Uhuru Kenyatta as your first born. Next time, call me as your second born so that I may finish what remains." Ruto said this in his usual mischievous way, while looking straight at the former first lady. It was foolhardy for him to drop a joke at the expense of Mama Ngina. Ruto flopped big time by getting himself entangled in a laughable absurdity.

The joke registered with the congregation. However, it didn't seem to have been appreciated by members of the first family who sat unperturbed on the front row, a few feet from Ruto. The Deputy President had misread the mood of the occasion and blundered. If only he had seized the opportunity to apologise to Mama Ngina personally for the disparaging remarks of his allies, things would probably have turned out differently. Mama Ngina must have left the Church disgusted at the man she so fervently prayed for at Gatundu Stadium, Kiambu.

Ruto's misstep was followed by sensational claims by MP Onesmus Kimani, a Ruto ally that Mama Ngina was among those plotting to stop the DP from succeeding Uhuru in 2022. Ngunjiri talked of a "deep state" conspiracy to bring down Ruto. He linked the Uhuru-Raila handshake to that conspiracy.

The statement was not a bombshell revelation because everyone knew where Uhuru and Mama Ngina stood on the succession issue. But what started as a rough patch with Uhuru congealed into a bigger problem in which Mama Ngina's name was placed at the centre of Ruto's woes. It therefore did not surprise many that earlier on Mashujaa Day celebrated in Kisii on October 20, 2020, Raila Odinga found it necessary to declare Mama Ngina his hero. "Mama Ngina did not just stay home during the independence struggle, but actively participated in the struggle and was detained by British colonialists. She is a hero."

The political coffin of Ruto, the hustler from Sugoi, who had expected to be handed the presidency on a silver platter based on the promise, "*Yangu kumi, yake kumi,*" appeared sealed. But who is this man Raila Odinga?

THE ENIGMA

Raila Odinga is a politician with a fanatical following. He is respected and admired by many in and outside Kenya. His support in the country comes not only from his Luo people but from diverse communities across the country. Raila occupies a position of stature and respectability in the public sector, and his character and disposition, are without a match. He is a man of patriotic moralism who spent three decades defending democracy. He was even singled out by Kenya's *Sunday Standard* of March 14, 2004, as the "central civilian accomplice" of the 1982 bold attempt to overthrow Moi's dictatorial regime. On top of that, he has led some of the biggest political parties in the country's history.

When the Grand Coalition Government led by President Mwai Kibaki was formed in 2008, Raila negotiated and got the prime minister's position. With the March 2018 handshake, Raila appeared ready to risk all that by collaborating once more, with President Uhuru. And for Raila, a man with an overweening ambition for power, that was a gamble he had to take.

But that was not the first time. He had taken political gambles before. He risked everything in 1997 when he resigned his position as Ford-K MP for Lang'ata, and successfully sought a fresh mandate. Raila risked his political career again when he boycotted the October 26, 2017, repeat presidential elections as ordered by the Supreme Court, giving Uhuru a free ride to the presidency.

By collaborating with President Uhuru, Raila had forgotten everything about what had happened after the bungled 2017 elections: the two months of chaos, the killings of innocent people, the stealing of votes, and his own assertion that the manipulation of the polls was "an attack on democracy."

Dozens of Raila's supporters were arrested and tortured during the demonstrations against Uhuru's re-election. Some were killed. Raila had also forgotten the instructions he had given to his supporters to boycott goods manufactured by companies owned by the Kenyattas and those allegedly benefiting from ties to Uhuru's government. He identified three of them as Safaricom, Bidco, and Brookside Dairy.

Raila had forgotten that one morning in November 2017, accompanied by his supporters, he showed up at an Airtel outlet to dramatise his shift from Safaricom to Airtel, its main competitor. There he disowned his Safaricom account and registered as an Airtel customer. Safaricom was one of the mobile telephone companies contracted to transmit most of the 2017 poll results from the polling centres to the IEBC tallying centre in Nairobi.

By agreeing to a handshake with Uhuru, Raila had morphed from being a champion of the oppressed and a defender of democracy to an "apologist of the establishment."[234] The images of the two leaders standing shoulder to shoulder on the steps of the Office of the President, Harambee House, calling each other "brother" depicted two strange and uncomfortable bedfellows trying hard to hide their long-simmering animosity.

It was unimaginable before the handshake to imagine that the previously fearless Jakom (chairman/boss) would act 'cowardly' by abandoning his role as an opposition leader to dine with people he had called 'hyenas.' That was the term Raila himself used when talking about the land grabbing mania by the Kenyattas. During the presidential debate in February 2013 ahead of elections, Uhuru and Raila disagreed on almost everything, from land reform to corruption.

---

[234] "A decade-old assault on the separation of powers has left Kenya a fractious legacy," *The Conversation*, June 24, 2020.

At one time, Raila threw in a bombshell metaphor (some call it a zinger) at his opponent: "You cannot allow a hyena to protect your goats." The meaning of that phrase, meant to hurt both Uhuru and his father, was clear: that the Kenyattas were hyenas and the people goats. Uhuru dismissed the jibe with a blithe wave of his hand.

Nevertheless, the truth was that by joining Uhuru in the 'handshake,' Raila had somersaulted 360 degrees like a daredevil. Either by default or by poor calculation, Raila became the biggest surrogate of the son of Jomo to the extent of being derogatorily referred to in social media circles as Uhuru's 'side-chick.' He ingratiated himself with Uhuru and became a frequent visitor to State House. He even accompanied the president to tour development projects in Nairobi in the dead of the night in 2021 when he was still recovering from Covid-19.

All that for the promise of endorsement as Uhuru's successor. It was also his way of coddling Uhuru's Mt. Kenya region votes. The big basket of Kikuyu votes was crucial for anyone to win the presidency. It has been said that whenever Raila focuses his eyes on the ball, he cannot be swayed. Thus, Raila "can go to bed with anybody so long as there is a chance to win political office."[235]

It had happened before. In 2008, Raila went into negotiations with Kibaki on the formation of the Grand Coalition Government. A close aide who attended some of their closed-door meetings reported how Raila was "cowed" and perhaps hypnotised by Kibaki. "Raila was a different man when he was with us [ODM leaders] from the pitiful wretch he became around Kibaki. With us, he would wail about his stolen election and Kibaki's obtuse arrogance and insolence during their meetings… But once in Kibaki's orbit, his confidence would evaporate. Raila became like a schoolboy before a cruel headmaster, checking himself incessantly, straightening his tie, looking at his suit, fidgeting, and talking incoherently. He couldn't even look Kibaki in the face…."[236] Miguna claimed.

---

[235] Verini, James. The Fall and Rise of Raila Odinga, Foreign Policy, March 2, 2013.

[236] Miguna, Miguna. Peeling Back the Mask: A Quest for Justice in Kenya, Gilgamesh Africa, 2012, p. 250.

However, those remarks must be taken with a grain of salt since they were made after Miguna had broken up with Raila. The bottom line is that Raila used all tricks to negotiate a place in the Grand Coalition Government. The result was that he became prime minister.

In his political career, Raila always kept his eyes on the ball. In some instances, he floundered. In others, he thrived. In 2020, he capitalised on Uhuru's support for his presidential bid, and his political fortunes went many notches higher.

CHAPTER 18

Uhuru's Family Wealth: Innocent Inheritor?

Since Mzee Kenyatta's death, Mama Ngina and her children have been on a shopping spree for new business purchases, investments, buy-outs, and expansions of existing assets. Over the years, Mama Ngina used her comprehensive connections to build a business empire for the family, eventually earning the billionaire status.[237]

In August 2021, the respected international magazine, *Forbes*, named Uhuru among "The richest world leaders of all time," with an estimated net worth of US$500 million, an equivalent of KSh.55 billion. In January 2022, that amount appeared to have jumped to KSh.60 billion, according to a report by the Oxford Committee for Famine Relief (OXFAM). Those amounts, however, represent the total wealth of the Kenyatta family, and do not reflect Uhuru's personal wealth.

The Kenyattas own banks, milk processing plants, agri-businesses, mining and manufacturing concerns, hotels, trading companies, and a media house. The impact of the Kenyatta family

---

[237] Meredith, Martin. The Fortunes of Africa: A 500-Year History of Wealth, Greed, and Endeavour, 2014, *Public Affairs,* pp. 599-600.

in the day-to-day life of Kenyans cannot be underestimated. Imagine the following:

If you are a tea or coffee drinker in Kenya, that tea or coffee, will most likely have come from a Kenyatta estate. The same applies to butter, yoghurt, and milk. In case you have a bank account, or use one of those mobile money transfer platforms, it is possible you are a client of the Kenyatta family. Did you get a Covid-19 test? If so, then the swab they used for your test could as well have been supplied by a Kenyatta. And, yes, if you are a gambler, it is possible that the betting company into which you wagered your money may partly be owned by a Kenyatta.

For those who wear jewellery, the necklace around your neck or the wedding ring on your finger could be from a Kenyatta-owned mine. And if you are endowed enough to go on holiday, either to the coast or to Masai Mara Game Reserve, there is a possibility you will lodge at a facility owned by the Kenyattas. The bed you'll sleep on would belong to a Kenyatta, and the food you would eat would have been bought by a Kenyatta. And even more critically, when you die, your coffin most likely would be made of wood from a Kenyatta-owned company. It is a cradle-to-grave domination of life by one family; at least that is how it looks like.

The Kenyatta family owns at least 500,000 acres of prime farmland in the country, including the 4,000-acre Gicheha farm in Nakuru, the 10,000-acre Gicheha farm in Ruiru, the 30,000-acre ranch in Taita Taveta, the 40,000-acre farm in Endebbes, and the 29,000-acre farm at Kahawa Sukari, among many others.

At the Coast where the Kenyattas and associates own large parcels of land, Uhuru is called "the landlord."[238] A general belief among citizens is that the Kenyattas possess land equivalent to the entire former Nyanza Province, a 12,477 square kilometre region in western Kenya. That, however, has not been verified.

---

[238] Klaus, Kathleen. Land Patron or Landlord? Land Ownership and Political Mobilisation in Kenya, *Institute of African Studies,* Columbia University, March 23, 2013.

Apart from farms, the Kenyattas own or hold shares in a long list of companies. For example, shares of the Kenyatta family at the NBCA Bank Kenya Plc were valued at KSh.6.6 billion at the Nairobi Securities Exchange (NSE) in October 2019. The NBCA Group was established after the merger of the National Industrial Credit (NIC) bank, and the Commercial Bank of Africa (CBA). The NIC Group owns 47% and CBA 53% in the new entity.

Locally, the bank is known as the NBCA Bank Kenya. The involvement of Kenyatta family members in the new bank was kept under wraps until an announcement was made on September 30, 2019. The Kenyattas already owned CBA which, before the merger, was the largest privately-owned bank in Kenya. NIC, on the other hand, belongs to the family of former CBK Governor, Philip Ndegwa.

In 2021, the Kenyatta family added another asset to its land portfolio: a 1,000-acre ranch in Narok County, next to the world renowned Masai Mara Game Reserve. Uhuru acquired the ranch in 2020 from two Maasai groups, the Olerien and the Kengani. The purchase price was not disclosed. The land comprises two parcels; on one side is a luxury safari lodge overlooking the path of the Great Migration, and on the other, a residential mansion.

Was it a coincidence that a year after Uhuru bought the property that an announcement was made to upgrade the Angama airstrip in Masai Mara to an international airport status? The airport will have a very important person(s') (VIPs) lounge, a hint on who is likely to be its most prominent regular visitor.

By settling for Narok, Uhuru is back in the land of his ancestors. His great grandfather, Kungu wa Magana, married a Maasai woman named Susana Musana. They gave birth to Uhuru's grandfather Muigai, father of his father, Jomo Kenyatta. Although Kenyatta was born in Ichaweri in Gatundu, he spent some years in Narok working as a livestock trader.

At home, the Kenyatta family's biggest investment is in milk production. In 1993, the family established Brookside Dairy at their farm in Ruiru, outside Nairobi. Through acquisitions and mergers with companies such as Delamere, Buzeki, Ilara, and Kilifi milk plants, Brookside Dairy grew from a local enterprise serving Nairobi into one of the biggest processors of milk, yoghurt, and butter, in the eastern Africa region – "one of the largest business dynasties in Kenya,"[239] says Kenyan economist David Ndii.

Brookside Dairy processes 500,000 litres of milk per day, making it the largest milk processor in Kenya in terms of installed capacity. The others are New KCC Ltd. and Githunguri Dairy Farmers Cooperative Society. Kenyatta's Brookside controls 40% of the Kenyan milk market, and has tentacles in Uganda, Rwanda, Burundi, Egypt, the Middle East, and the Indian Ocean islands. Visit any supermarket in Kenya today and you will find shelves filled with products from Brookside Dairy and its affiliates.

In 2014, Brookside Dairy sold 40% of its shares to Danone, an international food company, opening the door for the French firm to expand its network in Africa. Danone now has access to 140,000 Kenyan farmers and a distribution network of 200,000 Brookside Dairy-affiliated outlets. In 2015, Brookside acquired the Sameer Africa and Livestock Limited (SALL), a subsidiary of the Sameer Group owned by the late billionaire Naushad Merali, then a long-time friend of the Kenyattas.

The expansion of Brookside into a semi-monopoly was not good news for farmers and consumers. In fact, things went south after Uhuru became president. Since then, according to Ndii, "Brookside has been taking money out of people's pockets." According to Ndii, the company started buying milk from farmers at throw away prices and selling the same to consumers at exorbitant costs. By the end of Uhuru's first term in office in 2017, the consumer price had increased [significantly]…while the producer price had remained unchanged, raising the processors' margin.[240] Neither Brookside nor the Kenyatta family responded to those criticisms.

Enter Covid-19 pandemic in 2020, and the fortunes of everyone, consumers, dairy cooperatives, and smallholder farmers, dropped. The pandemic caused disruptions and messed up production

---

[239] Ndii, David. "Crony capitalism and state capture: The Kenyatta family story," The *Elephant*, July 7, 2018.

[240] Ndii, David. "The economic cost of conflict of interest: The Kenya dairy industry case," The *Elephant*, January 30, 2020,

at Brookside. In late 2021, the company seized the occasion to placate itself from growing consumer complaints of exploitation by increasing producer prices by 17%. That meant suppliers were to be paid KSh.42 per litre compared to the previous price of KSh.36 per litre.

An acute shortage of milk early in 2022 caused shortages as well as increases in retail price from KSh. 45 to KSh. 58 for a 500ml packet.

Similarly, not many people know that Mama Ngina is a top investor in the corruption-ridden Kenya Power, a government-controlled company. She became the fourth largest individual investor. She achieved that feat by boosting her shares to 2.2 million or a 0.11% stake in the electricity distributor. Her stake is valued at KSh.33.7 million. By June 2021, she had earned a dividend of KSh.1.1 million. [241] At Kenya Power, the former first lady shares a platform with key institutional bodies such as the national treasury and the National Social Security Fund (NSSF). The government owns 50% shares.

Ironically, in his heydays as president, Mzee Kenyatta never paid his electricity bills to the company, then known as the Kenya Power and Lighting Limited (KPLC), for consumption in his private businesses. Things got so bad that the Treasury had to dig into the taxpayers' kitty to compensate the company for electricity used by the first family.[242]

Of all its undertakings, the Kenyatta family's dream project remains the KSh.500 billion Northlands City, a mixed-use development of residential, commercial properties, and educational institutions. Northlands City shares the 11,000-acre land with Brookside Dairy. Within the complex is an agricultural farm and a wildlife conservation area.

---

[241] "Mama Ngina listed among Kenya Power's top shareholders," *Business Daily*, May 19, 2013.
[242] Githuku, Nicholas Kariuki. Mau Mau crucible of war: Statehood, national identity, and politics in post-colonial Kenya, Graduate Thesis, and Problem Reports, 5677, West Virginia University, 2014.

The new metropolis is dubbed the largest undertaking of its kind in Kenya. It can also be described as the most advantaged undertaking because President Uhuru ensured it had an easy access to Jomo Kenyatta International Airport (JKIA), the Eastern By-pass, and the Thika superhighway, all critical roads for business success. Uhuru built brand new roads to ensure access.

Pandora Papers ruin Uhuru's mood

As the Kenyattas expanded their businesses and earned billions of shillings in the process, they did not find it safe to keep their money in Kenya, either for secrecy reasons or for tax purposes. Just like President Moi, they shipped some of it to offshore accounts overseas. In 1990s, they were introduced to bankers and financial advisers in Panama and in the British Virgin Islands. Through them, the Kenyattas invested in diverse properties and firms and opened multiple accounts.

The revelations in 2021 by the International Consortium of Investigative Journalists (ICIJ) about the Kenyattas massive offshore accounts awakened Kenyans on where the rich hide their money. The revelations were in the Pandora Papers, a collection of 11.9 million records from 14 law firms based in the UAE, the Seychelles, Panama, Singapore, and other tax havens.

Uhuru was named among 35 former and current world leaders, including Ali Bongo Ondimba of Gabon and Denis Sassou-Nguesso of the Republic of Congo, with secret offshore bank accounts. The Kenyattas, according to the Pandora Papers, had US$30 million (KSh.3.3 billion) stashed in different accounts overseas. It was also reported that they owned a posh flat near Westminster in London, now valued at KSh.150 million. The apartment was once rented by Emma Hardy, a British MP who didn't know the property belonged to the Kenyattas.

For decades, the ICIJ dossier said, Uhuru, his mother, sisters, and brother, had shielded their wealth from public scrutiny through a slew of foundations and companies in tax havens. "*Documents show that the expansion of the Kenyattas' offshore holdings coincided with Uhuru Kenyatta's political rise...even as Uhuru solidified his role as a man of the people."*[243] The Kenyattas are in a class of people author Brett Wilder calls "the quiet millionaires."[244] They are known in offshore banking entities as "Client 13173" a code previously unknown.

One of the foundations registered by the Kenyattas is Varies Foundation, which names Uhuru and Mama Ngina as the beneficiaries of the assets in its name. The foundation is managed by a private wealth management company headquartered in Geneva, Switzerland, Union Bancaire Privee (UBP), which also oversees another entity on behalf of Uhuru's brother, Muhoho. Another foundation in Panama set up by Mama Ngina in 2003, lists Uhuru as the beneficiary of all its assets, in case of the matriarch's death. On paper, therefore, Uhuru is fabulously rich.

The Pandora Papers did not reveal the source of the monies, nor speculate in any way that the loot owned by the Kenyattas emanated from corruption. However, one document referred to a company set up by the Kenyattas in the British Virgin Islands (BVI) as having been established with "savings from their family and their activities."[245]

Uhuru's reaction to the damning dossier was vague and ambiguous. He did not respond directly to the allegations. Instead, he said: "The Pandora Papers and subsequent follow up audits will lift that veil of secrecy and darkness for those who cannot explain their assets or wealth." He then promised to make 'a comprehensive' statement on his return from the US trip he was about to undertake.

Uhuru never made that statement neither did Kenya's shy media make a follow-up. One of the reasons cited by Kenyans for electing Uhuru was that he was too rich to engage in shady activities. But

---

[243] Fitzgibbon, Will. "As Kenyan president mounted anti-corruption comeback, his family's secret fortune expanded offshore," International Consortium of Investigative Journalists, the *Pandora Papers*, October 3, 2021.

[244] Wilder, Brett. The Quiet Millionaire: A Guide for Accumulating and Keeping Your Wealth," FMG Publishing, Inc., 2007.

[245] Mukami, Purity & Simon Bowers. Pandora Papers: The secret offshore world of Kenya's first family, Finance Uncovered, October 3, 2021.

after the Pandora Papers, activist Boniface Mwangi put him in the same class as tax evaders and tax cheats.[246]

LIKE FATHER, LIKE SON

There was no hope that Uhuru would change the *modus operandi* of self-enrichment begun by his father. For example, he could not resist the temptation of using the presidency for self-aggrandisement and to advance the interests of his family members. Reports in November 2021 that the Kenyatta-owned NCBA had negotiated a deal with the government to lease 250 vehicles at a cost of KSh.1.2 billion for use by the National Police Service (NPS) is just one example of how one can exploit their station in society to benefit themselves.

In 2018, 118 vehicles had been delivered under a similar arrangement. The deal was between Toyota Kenya, the NCBA, and the government, which paid quarterly for the lease. NCBA was elated and tweeted: "We are honoured to be providing buses, trucks, and double cabin pick-ups to aid the police in their vital service to the citizens." In normal circumstances, a probe would have been carried out to determine whether there was any conflict of interest in the arrangement. In this case, nothing was done.

The other aspect of this was also how the NCBA clinched the deal. The Cooperative Bank of Kenya (CBK) already had a five-year agreement to lease 412 trucks to the Kenya Police. That agreement worth KSh.2.2 billion had not expired. CBK was financing the lease in an arrangement with RentCo East Africa Limited. CMC Motors and Isuzu East Africa were to supply the vehicles.

The deal signed between NCBA, and the government therefore put the Cooperative Bank of Kenya arrangement in a quandary and led to a clash of interests between the two premier financial institutions.

---

[246] "Nairobi residents react to Pandora leaks on Kenyatta," Africa News with AP, October 5, 2021.

Unsurprisingly, the CBK deal was "brokered by powerful figures in government and a section of the board at Cooperative Bank."[247] In 2018, Uhuru lauded the Cooperative Bank lease arrangement saying, besides increasing the capacity of police service and other agencies, the deal was a boon for leasing companies, financiers, and auto dealers. How the tables turned so spectacularly against CBK is a tale that remains to be told. Its chief executive, Gideon Muriuki, blamed "power brokers" and "traitors" on his board for sabotaging the deal.[248]

In June 2021, NCBA signed an asset finance agreement with Simba Corporation for finance of up to 95% for all commercial and personal vehicles sold by the latter. The partnership was to charge customers an interest rate of 13% per annum on reducing balance over a maximum period of 60 months. Although this was a commercial arrangement, it showed the growing clout of NCBA in penetrating the commercial market.

Since the consolidation of the Kenyatta-owned CBA and NIC to create NCBA, the new entity has seemingly been enjoying favours from the government. In July 2021, the Treasury granted a tax waiver on the transfer of shares between the two ahead of the merger. And then in August, the Treasury selected NCBA, alongside three other banks, to look after approximately KSh.312 billion of civil servants' pension contributions. Without prompts, a Treasury official told the *Business Daily*[249] that the NCBA, Stanbic, and CBK, underwent a competitive exercise, and that they were selected because of experience in handling pension schemes with a value of at least KSh.10 billion.

That explanation was unnecessary because no one had challenged the arrangement. CFC Financial Services Limited is the fund administrator for the Public Service Superannuation Scheme (PSSS). An estimated 350,000 civil servants started contributing 7.5% of their salaries to the scheme as of January 2021.

---

[247] "Co-operative Bank left bitter after losing KSh.2.2 billion deal to NCBA," *Kenya Insights*, November 8, 2021.
[248] "Co-operative Bank left bitter after losing Sh2.2b deal to NCBA," *Kenya Insights*, November 8, 2021.
[249] "NCBA, Stanbic, Co-op bag Sh31 billion pension deal," *Business Daily*, August 30, 2021.

'Professor' Moi

Of all the four Kenyan presidents who have ruled Kenya, President Moi was the most aggressive when it came to cutting deals. He did so with rich tycoons, including convicted criminal Ketan Somaia of the collapsed Delphis Bank, and shady characters like Kamlesh Pattni of the Goldenberg scandal, and Mohamed Aslam of the defunct Pan-African Bank Limited. Through those deals, Moi became a billionaire.

By the time he left office in 2002, President Moi had accumulated wealth worth over KSh.340 billion spread across varied sectors: agribusiness, manufacturing, and banking, in East Africa and abroad. He also had interests in aviation, real estate, transport, hotel industry, and media. He also owned Kabarak University, Sunshine Secondary School, Kabarak High School, Moi Africa Institute (an NGO), and Sacho High School. Most of his wealth was believed to have been acquired during his tenure as president.

As for President Kibaki, his total wealth was put by various sources at between KSh.20 billion and KSh.100 billion by the time of leaving office. His total wealth could not be determined with precision, however. In 2003, he became the first president to declare his wealth, but the contents of his wealth declaration form deposited with the speaker of parliament were not divulged. Kibaki invested largely in farms and real estate. In retirement, he pocketed a monthly pension of KSh.2.86 million. Moi's pension was stopped when he died in February 2020.

CHAPTER 19

Kenyan Dynasties

Throughout his political life, Uhuru had to ward off attacks about his life and dodge questions about how his family acquired its massive fortune. Many Kenyans viewed Uhuru as "the face of wealthy, big business,"[250] "son of a powerful, extraordinarily wealthy family,"[251] who had no clue about the problems and afflictions facing Kenyans. Uhuru sometimes talked of lack of respect for the marginalised groups yet did little to confront the condition which his own father, Mzee Jomo Kenyatta, identified more than a half a century earlier, as one of the biggest challenges facing the country.

Growing up, Uhuru had an easy and comfortable life. In his prepubescent years, he dressed in suits, hand-crafted cardigans, and crisp Kaunda suits, shiny shoes, and knee-high socks. He tagged along with his father whenever he went and mingled with VIPs at State House. Past photos show him, at barely eight years old, socialising with dignitaries including the West German President Heinrich Lubke and Malawi President Kamuzu Banda. In one iconic image, the young Uhuru is seen curiously observing his father signing a visitors' book flanked by Moi and Kibaki. The picture, somehow,

---

[250] Campbell, John. "Raila Odinga sworn in as Kenya's 'Peoples' President,'" Council of Foreign Affairs, January 30, 2018.
[251] Sieff, Kevin. "Who is Kenyatta? A look at the Kenyan president welcoming Obama," The *Washington Post*, July 25, 2015.

portended the future. Jomo Kenyatta was already the president, and those around him were to follow. It is obvious then, that Uhuru was nursed in luxury, and nurtured for leadership from his early years. The family knew the boy was destined for important things ahead.

Once, Mama Ngina described Uhuru as a "model son, the best a mother can hope for." Although Mama Ngina had no direct interest in elective politics, she did have interest in influencing decisions and how those decisions were made. When Mzee Kenyatta's health started failing in the mid-1970s, Mama Ngina was among a small team of confidantes, among them the Minister of State Mbiyu Koinange, AG Charles Njonjo, and Foreign Affairs Minister Dr. Njoroge Mungai, who oversaw the day-to-day running of government and the critical decisions that had to be made for it to function. She also used her position to resolve contentious political issues she felt threatened her family interests.

A de-classified report by the US Central Intelligence Agency (CIA) released in 2019 revealed that "While an increasingly tired and disinterested Kenyatta spends most of his time with his kinsmen and his brother-in-law, Mbiyu Koinange, in Gatundu, oblivious of what is happening, Ngina runs the country plundering it with reckless abandon."[252]

Uhuru admitted he wanted to be like his father. "I would be lying if I told you I did not want to be like my father,"[253] he said, during an interview in June 2019. Another time, he said his dream and ambition were to join the military. Like his father, he almost was. He inherited his father's deep throat laugh, smiled genially when at ease, but displayed a menacing mirthless demeanour when upset. When unsettled, his eyes flashed with fire, just like his father.

However, it was the perception that Uhuru was too affluent and elitist to understand *mwananchi's* problems that irked Uhuru most. As a privileged individual, Uhuru often felt detached from the regular life; perhaps even frustrated. He "always sought to distance himself

---

[252] "A short history of the Mt Kenya mafia, as told by the CIA," Nairobi Law Monthly, April 9, 2019.
[253] Master Card Foundation event, Young Africa Works, *NTV* interview, June 20, 2019.

from his family's privileged position,"²⁵⁴ but that was easier said than done. After returning from the US, Uhuru was a regular visitor at some drinking joints in the Nairobi CBD and in Hurlingham.

As president, Uhuru would sometimes drive himself to private entertainment spots to mingle with old friends. He even ventured into the "low-grade" Kenyatta market in Nairobi in September 2016, sat on a hard bench, and shared *nyama choma* and *ugali* with Senator Mike Sonko, MPs Rachael Shebesh, Johnson Sakaja, and Stephen Kariuki. His surprise presence attracted a huge, curious crowd outside the market. He left the meat seller happy after paying the bill of KSh.21,000 for the delicious meal. Thereafter, he became a regular visitor to the makeshift market named after his father.

And in February 2019, on his way by road from a meeting in Arusha, Tanzania, Uhuru, and his entourage, comprising Ruto and the Burundi Vice President Gaston Sindimwo, stopped at a *nyama choma* joint at Oletepes Kiserian, a small trading centre in Kajiado County, to enjoy roast goat meat. One writer captured the rare scene and narrated how the president "relished every bite with and irresistibly undeniable craving."²⁵⁵

But even his "I-am-only-an-ordinary-folk-like-you" antics, did not stop critics from linking him to affluence. They made dramatic and sensational remarks, some of which had a semblance of truth.

"…the young man has never slept hungry in his lifetime," one said. "He was born in State House, raised in State House, and he does not know what hunger is. Could you advise the president [Moi] to kick that young man out so that things can move?" added MP Patrick Muiruri of Gatundu North. MP Stephen Ndicho agreed: "…it is true Mr. Uhuru Kenyatta was born in State House, and he has never slept hungry."²⁵⁶

---

[254] Mutwol, Abraham. "Great inspiring life lessons from Uhuru Kenyatta," Creative Minds Consultants, 2015.
[255] Omondi, Asher. "Uhuru, Ruto enjoy sumptuous nyama choma as president returns from Tanzania," *Tuko,* February 2, 2019.
[256] Question by Private Notice: Relief Food in Ndaragwa constituency, Hansard, Kenya National Assembly, July 6, 2000, p. 1460.

The two legislators were speaking on the floor of parliament on July 6, 2000, during a debate on hunger. Uhuru was then chairman of the disaster emergency response committee.

"Unajua huyu Uhuru Kenyatta hajawahi lala njaa…" (You know, this Uhuru Kenyatta has never slept hungry), chimed in economist David Ndii in a tweet in October 2019.

It was not just the intellectuals who derided Uhuru's life of opulence and disregard for the disadvantaged. Many ordinary Kenyans were of the same opinion. One citizen identified by the name Christine Wamalwa said in a daring video that went viral on Twitter on October 31, 2019, that: "Uhuru Kenyatta has not slept hungry. He does not know our problems. We ordinary people are suffering. The economy is bad. We have nothing to eat," she said with brittle sarcasm.

Voices against Uhuru grew louder during the Covid-19 pandemic when Uhuru announced, then inordinately prolonged, restrictions against the spread of the pandemic. An estimated 1.2 million Kenyans lost income through job losses soon after the onset of the pandemic early in 2020. Many people slept hungry. Others were evicted from rented houses due to non-payment of rent.

Hit hardest were street children and families who no longer expected to get alms from passersby because of curfew restrictions. Most of the hotels and eateries that normally dished out food to street people were closed. But Uhuru remained adamant, refusing to lift the curfew. Many Kenyans felt that by continually extending the curfew, their president was being dispassionate.

Uhuru also received a backlash for virtually launching internet balloons for 4G network access in July 2020 as the pandemic swept through the country. "People are worried about food, and you call the nation to attention to launch balloons?" asked David Ndii in an open letter to Uhuru. "Many Kenyans have accused you of being a prisoner of your privileged upbringing. Yet you continue to reinforce that perception."[257]

---

[257] Ndii, David. "Open letter to President Uhuru Kenyatta," *The Elephant*, March 25, 2020.

What these people were saying was that Uhuru had lost touch with the ground. Kenyans on Twitter (KOT) were particularly critical and wanted to discredit the president in any way possible. So, they found a way. They questioned Uhuru's level of education by doubting his degree qualification. They bombarded social media platforms with posts asking if he even attended Amherst College at all. Some wrote to the institution for answers. Amherst had to go on Twitter to assure Kenyans that indeed Uhuru was an alumnus of the college.

Nonetheless, despite the above assertions, Uhuru did not "grow" up in State House; neither was he born there. Mzee Kenyatta used State House only as an office space and never spent a single night there. That does not mean Uhuru didn't play on the grounds of the white residence on the hill. The family had three homes at their disposal: their Gatundu residence at Ichaweri village in Kiambu County, a mansion in Muthaiga, and the house on Caledonian Road, next to State House. It was at Muthaiga and in Gatundu, not at the Caledonian Road residence, where Uhuru spent most of his pre-adolescence and adolescence years.

Despite years spent in major cities in England and Russia, Mzee Kenyatta abhorred town life. He particularly didn't like Nairobi city which he viewed as a place of strangers. He made that crystal clear in his book, *Suffering Without Bitterness*. "I work during the day, and then after work, I go home to my *shamba* and have a look at my bananas, potatoes, poultry, and other things. If you elect somebody who spends all his time in Nairobi doing nothing, what good is that?"[258]

That's why he lived in Gatundu and commuted daily to Nairobi for work. Occasionally, he would summon his ministers to Gatundu for a cabinet meeting under a tree. A few times he would lodge at his Muthaiga residence.

The spacious house along Caledonian Road was a gift from Prince Karim Aga Khan IV who offered it to Mzee Kenyatta one week after independence in 1963. The Aga Khans had lived in

---

[258] Kenyatta, Jomo. Suffering Without Bitterness, East African Publishing House, 1968, p. 347.

the premises for years. It was where Prince Karim grew up. In his book, *The Aga Khans*, Willie Frischauer, says the house was set "in a jungle garden full of parakeets and budgerigars, a tennis court, and vast lawns." There is a general belief that in return for the house at Caledonian Road, Mzee Kenyatta in 1975 offered the Aga Khan the prime plot at Central Park for the Ismaili leader to build a hotel.

In 2015, Uhuru demolished the house and began the work of rebuilding it afresh. The work took three years. KSh.700 million of "private money" was spent, according to Manoah Esipisu, the State House spokesman. The modern structure is surrounded by a concrete wall and a high-tech electric fence. The property has living, dining, and kitchen spaces, on the ground floor, and three large bedrooms and other rooms, on the upper floor. It has bullet proof windows and a state-of-the art alarm system for additional security.

KENYATTAS VS ODINGAS

Even though the Odingas do not appear to have the kind of wealth the Kenyattas have, they are fabulously wealthy. The Oginga family owns the Spectre International which manufactures ethanol, methylated spirits, and yeast. Raila, his wife Ida and older brother, Oburu, are the company directors. The Nairobi-headquartered company also produces carbon dioxide gas, a preservative used in the manufacture of beer, wine, and soda.

Spectre International has been on expansion frenzy in recent years. The Odinga family is also into petroleum business and has a significant footing in South Sudan. Raila is said to be close to the once rebel leader, Riek Machar, who is now a member of President Salva Kiir's government in Juba. The Odinga family is also in real estate and is linked to multi-million residences in prime areas such as Runda and Karen in Nairobi. Other properties are in Mombasa and Kisumu. The family also has large tracts of land in Nyanza. There have also been reports that Odinga owns several choppers which he uses during campaigns.

Other than the fact that Uhuru and Raila belong to political dynasties because of their pedigree, the two come from different backgrounds. While the former went to elite private schools in Kenya and the US, the latter attended public schools, and later obtained a scholarship to study engineering in East Berlin in the former communist German Democratic Republic (GDR). The question as to whether he graduated as an engineer in Germany remains a matter of speculation.

After university, Uhuru seamlessly slid into his family businesses, while Raila had to take a junior academic job at the University of Nairobi to survive. He was forced later to sell an old car to start a business, the East Africa Spectre. It was the only firm in Kenya supplying gas cylinders to oil companies.

As a politician, Uhuru had the advantage of wealth and had endowed friends available and ready to bankroll his campaigns. Raila, on the other hand, depended on donations mainly from friends in Europe and the Middle East. Dubai is one of Raila's favourite foreign destinations where he has several oil rich sheikhs as friends. He has travelled there many times.

But Raila has continuously rejected insinuations that the Kenyattas and the Odingas are 'dynasties.' "Jomo Kenyatta was a son of a pauper," Raila said in November 2018, "he struggled, and he was detained by colonialists for all those years. You cannot say there is a Kenyatta dynasty.... Odinga was just another son of a pauper. You can also say he was a hustler; you cannot say Raila is part of a dynasty."[259]

Raila's defence about not belonging to a dynasty was that the Kenyatta and the Odinga families came from simple backgrounds. He said Kenyatta died when Uhuru was 17 years old. If it was a dynasty, he argued, Uhuru would have been crowned a prince. Similarly, he said, Jaramogi came from a poor family, was a teacher,

---

[259] Wanambisi, Laban. "What dynasties? Uhuru and I have struggled, says Raila," *Capital News*, November 2, 2018.

and later a businessman. "We are not political dynasties,"[260] Raila explained painfully.

But their number one enemy, Ruto, disagreed. "The handshake brothers [Uhuru and Raila] have never gone job-hunting. They have never slept hungry even for a day. They don't understand what poverty is," he told a meeting in Nairobi in March 2022. The discourse as to who is and who is not part of a 'dynasty' or 'hustler' threatened to create a class war. Deputy President Ruto identified himself with *mama mboga, mkokoteni* pushers, and hawkers, while portraying Uhuru and Raila as elites.

Dynasties or not, the Kenyatta and Odinga families have dominated politics for most of the country's first six decades of independence. Raila had hoped that his favourite son, Fidel Odinga, would continue with the Odinga legacy, but the young man died in unclear circumstances. The cause of his death has never been made public, despite investigations.

Ahead of the 2022 General Elections, several individuals belonging to the Odinga clan had declared interest in elective offices, among them Raila's brother, Oburu, and sister Ruth. Rumours also circulated that one of the Kenyattas, perhaps Uhuru's brother Muhoho, or his two children Ngina or Muhoho, could enter politics to continue the Kenyatta legacy, after Uhuru departs.

Nevertheless, the question as to whether Uhuru and Raila were descendants of political dynasties dominated public discourse throughout Uhuru's term. Some, like the leader of Thirdway Alliance Kenya (Party), Ekuru Aukot, proposed legislation to prevent the country's leadership from rotating between two or three prominent families. He particularly took issue with the Kenyatta and Moi families who had ruled the country for a total of forty-nine out of the fifty-years of independence. Gideon Moi was made heir to the Moi crown after his father's death and offered himself as a presidential candidate in 2022 on a KANU ticket, but later dropped to favour Raila.

---

[260] Uhuru and I Don't Come from Political Dynasties – Raila, The Free Library, undated.

UHURU KENYATTA

Unlike Raila, Uhuru comes forth as an amiable, warm individual, with *joie de vivre*. His handshake is firm and his face sometimes contorts in a display of anger just like his father's, distracting people from his protruding potbelly and his shifty demeanour.

Though much older, Raila has a stiff personality like an unctuous retired headmaster and bears a smugly confident look on his face. Due to an injury inflicted in detention, he frequently must rub his itchy left eye with the back of his palm. He is not an eloquent public speaker, but he has moments of levity that drive his listeners into a frenzy of laughter especially when he mimics football commentators. During public meetings, he goes into monologues of historical events surrounding the struggle for independence and democracy in which both he and his father were prime players.

The Kenyattas and the Odingas have a long history. Raila's sister, Ruth, once said in interview with the *Daily Nation* that Raila used to carry Uhuru on his back in their childhood.[261] What she didn't explain was precisely "when" that happened and "where." When Raila returned from East Germany in 1970, Uhuru was just nine years old. Mzee Kenyatta and Jaramogi had already parted ways. Raila was 25 years old and worked as a Special Assistant [some records say lecturer] at the University of Nairobi in the 1971/1972 academic year. After that he founded the Standard Processing Equipment Construction Erection Limited, which later became the East African Spectre.

In 1974, he was appointed Group Standards Manager of the Kenya Bureau of Standards (KEBS) rising to the level of Deputy Director. He held the position until 1982 when Moi detained him following the attempted coup by the Kenya Air Force.

Like his father, Raila was politically active and was opposed to Moi's dictatorial rule. Is it possible that Raila could have carried Uhuru in the early 1960s when Uhuru was just a baby? But Ruth was born on February 23, 1963, about a year-and-half after Uhuru. So, her claim that Raila carried Uhuru on his back appears far-fetched.

---

[261] Torchia, Christopher. "Like father, like son: Kenya goes to polls in family affair, *Associated Press*, August 5, 2017.

From his youth, Odinga was known for courage. Before his tribulations as a democracy activist during President Moi's rule, Raila once showed defiance to his own father. At one time, he was expected to join the rest of the family in planting trees. While everyone was busy, Raila was in bed sleeping.

Jaramogi stormed into his room and asked him why he was not out there with others working. Babafemi A. Badejo writes in his book "Raila responded that he was not a slave. Jaramogi floored him and started jumping on him with his gumboots. Raila refused to cry as he took the beatings and kicks, and it was only Mary's [Raila's mother] cries that saved the situation between father and son." He carried that courage as a politician and "protested without fear."[262]

Another example of Raila's bravery that assumed almost heroic proportions was apparent on February 5, 1988. President Moi was about to release all the 23 political prisoners detained on allegations of treason. As a spokesman of the group, Raila had the gumption to face Moi and condemn detention without trial saying it was inhuman. No one ever before had stood up to President Moi and survived to tell the story.

The only encounter that came close to that was in 2001 when MP Martha Karua walked out on Moi while the president was addressing a public meeting. That courageous gesture by the woman legislator bewildered the president and shocked the nation. The 'iron lady' escaped Moi's 'iron fist.' Not so Raila. He was detained two more times by Moi.

Raila's face-up with Moi was an act of courage, a swaggering attitude of bravado. In fact, it was a "dauntless act" that marked the beginning of the Luo peoples' endearment to Raila as a leader of exhaustless energy ready to take bold risks for their interest. Despite a general view that Raila's popularity was due to his father's role in the independence struggle, Raila's credentials, some say, were boosted by the sympathy he got from his detention stints. Raila was also active in

---

[262] Badejo, Babafemi A. Raila Odinga: An Enigma in Kenyan Politics, Yintab Books, 2006, p. 20.

the Gor Mahia football club (named after a Luo legend) which most Luo fanatically identify with."[263]

Although the Kenyatta and Odinga families knew each other, Raila did not know Uhuru well until the former joined parliament as a nominated member in 2001. Both served in the Moi cabinet, Raila as Minister for Energy, and Uhuru as Minister for Local Government. But their relationship was not particularly robust, especially after Moi picked Uhuru as his successor in 2002.

Following that selection, Raila organised a protest outside KANU headquarters at the Kenyatta International Convention Centre (KICC) to oppose Uhuru's nomination. Police chased the demonstrators away, but Raila's strongholds remained tense. Moi however dismissed any assertions that the country was in political turmoil. "There is no crisis in our country," he said.

Uhuru and Raila's relationship got frostier thereafter. Often Uhuru's views were antithetical to Raila's on how the country should be run, or on how the electoral body should be restructured to ensure free and fair elections.

The only time Uhuru and Raila coalesced around a single key issue was when they joined hands to oppose the 2005 constitutional referendum proposed by President Kibaki. Uhuru was then leader of the opposition. Their side won.

But beneath the façade of camaraderie, during the referendum campaign, lurked a major political rift. The two were embroiled in a constant war of words. Their vitriol was so ominously provocative that in a rare front-page editorial on election day on March 4, 2013, the *Daily Nation* appealed for levelheadedness. "If we bungle today's election or go back to killing each other, not only will the world give up on us as a civilised nation, but Kenyans too could lose faith in their own country."[264]

---

[263] Asingo, Patrick O., Cheeseman, Nic, Kanyinga, Karuti & Lynch, Gabrielle, The Oxford Handbook of Kenyan Politics, Oxford University Press, 2020, p. 626.

[264] Benesch, Susan. "The Kenya elections: Peace happened," *The Huffington Post*, March 21, 2013.

The editorial came after Raila's interview with the *Financial Times* of London on March 1, 2013, in which he claimed Uhuru was planning to rig the elections. "I have warned them the consequences may be worse that last time round," adding that "people will not stomach another rigging," he was quoted as saying, referencing the 2007 elections. Although Raila denied saying that, Uhuru was quick to condemn the comments as "dangerous and inflammatory." Uhuru was declared the winner, and their animosity was rekindled. Raila accused both the IEBC and Uhuru of electoral malpractices and demanded a repeat election. Following his loss and failure to convince the Supreme Court to overturn Uhuru's win due to alleged electoral malpractices, Raila called a press conference on March 30 and accepted defeat with the words: "Let us not allow the elections to divide us." That statement ended a tense period brought about by the March 4 elections.

Drama at the airport

However, that was not the end of personal feuds between Uhuru and Raila that played out in public. The standoff between the two deepened when the latter arrived at the JKIA airport on June 3, 2013, to catch a flight to Kisumu and was denied access to the VIP lounge. Airport officials explained that they had received a memo from Cabinet Secretary Francis Kimemia with firm instructions that the opposition leader should not be allowed to use the government facility.

Apparently, Kimemia was acting on 'orders from above' meaning from President Uhuru himself. A few days earlier, Raila's wife, Ida, too had faced the same consequences. It was an incongruous spectacle which was as ridiculous as it was unnecessary. Surprisingly, Kimemia disavowed the memo saying he was not even aware of the correspondence. Raila demanded an apology "from the highest levels of government" for what he called "mistreatment." None was issued. Apparently, it was the same Kimemia who in 2021 turned around and declared that "The whole country, not just Mt. Kenya is safe in Raila's hands."

There was another spectacle at the airport involving Raila. Early in June 2013, while clearing with security at JKIA on his way to South Africa, Raila was ordered to remove his shoes and belt as part of the security screening as he queued with other passengers at the departure unit. He was going to Johannesburg to attend the African Presidential Roundtable.

In defence of the move, the government spokesman, Muthui Kariuki, denied that the former Prime Minister had been humiliated, but could not explain why he was not given the usual VIP treatment, including the use of the airside for his motorcade. A government statement said only the president, visiting heads of state, and the deputy president of Kenya, had access of the airside. As for Raila, the statement said, he did not qualify.

On November 30, 2013, Raila issued a hard-hitting statement accusing Uhuru "of conspiring with MPs to destroy the judiciary, sabotage civil liberties, and entrench repression, by gagging the media."[265] The bone of contention was Uhuru's initial decision to reject the Media Bill and then turning around to inject even more punitive measures, including a proposal to form a tribunal to draw a code of conduct for the media.

Major news organisations in Kenya went on the offensive: "Democracy under attack," the *Standard* headlined its main story. "Dark days: MPs pass law to control media," shouted the *Daily Nation*. Raila said such legislations were found only in "our neighbouring dictatorships." The government, in turn, accused the media of being "unpatriotic" by reporting the alleged looting of goods by soldiers during the Watergate Mall attack.

In 2015, Raila was at it again. He blasted Uhuru's decision to import sugar from Uganda, saying it was bad for Kenyan farmers and bad for the country. He told Uhuru to build factories instead of importing sugar. Raila stopped short of pointing a finger at Uhuru's allies, some of whom were named in illegal sugar importation.

An apoplectic Uhuru responded by saying that Raila was opposing the sale for the sake of it. "I would rather import sugar from Uganda

---

[265] "You've failed Kenya, Raila tells President," *Sunday Nation*, December 1, 2013.

than from Brazil," Uhuru responded with bluster. During a meeting at Chaka, Meru, on November 28, 2016, Uhuru escalated his attacks. He accused Raila of hoodwinking Kenyans on corruption and called the CORD leader a serial liar whose words should be ignored. "Raila has no clear agenda for the nation. The only thing he has been doing throughout his life is to champion propaganda," Uhuru said.

Hostility between the two leaders intensified further when Uhuru blocked Raila's pension unless he retired from politics. Raila was not ready to retire and talked of one bullet remaining in his chamber. Inflamed with rage, he told Uhuru he would not be blackmailed by threats to withdraw his pension. "I deserve to be given the retirement package," he said, but "I wouldn't beg for it." Raila earned the pension when he served as MP and prime minister in the Grand Coalition Government from 2008 to 2013. It was only after the handshake that Uhuru approved the disbursement.

In the meantime, neither Uhuru nor Raila made any effort to ensure a convergence of opinion. Vitriolic attacks between them escalated before and after the 2017 elections, giving Kenyans an unparalleled glimpse of the kind of animosity and division the two harboured. Raila accused Uhuru of being perpetually drunk. Uhuru responded by calling his nemesis a bully, and a project of foreign powers because of his support for the ICC process.

Early in June 2017 – about two months before the August 8 elections – Raila warned his supporters to be alert on election day to stop any infringements of electoral laws. He went further with a bizarre directive which elicited chuckles, especially among women: "All women should deny their husbands conjugal rights on the eve of voting. This will ensure that we wake up early to vote and remain vigilant until the votes are tallied, and the results announced… then you can have sex to celebrate our victory."

The animosity between Uhuru and Raila opened the door to gruesome lawlessness especially during the primaries in April 2017. A Jubilee Party aspirant for the Ruiru parliamentary seat, Isaac Mwaura, reported being shot at allegedly by a rival. He appeared on TV with a heavy bandage on his left ear.

In Isiolo County in northern Kenya, one person was killed during disturbances between rival political groups after a public rally addressed by Uhuru in May 2017. When IEBC's Chris Msando, was found murdered in July, the opposition pointed a finger at Uhuru's Jubilee government. To many Kenyans, Msando's death was a replica of past political assassinations. There was speculation that the government of the day had a hand in his killing. Government officials rubbished the claims. His killers were never found.

One mistake Raila made was to attack the KDF soldiers deployed in Somalia. In November 2015, he accused Kenyan soldiers of engaging in sugar and charcoal smuggling in and around Kismayu. He also blasted Uhuru for 'turning a blind' eye to the smuggling across the Kenya/Somalia border. Uhuru defended the military and accused his foe of spreading falsehoods. "I have never seen such stupidity in my whole life," he said in response to Raila's allegations.

If Raila thought by criticising the military he would shudder Uhuru, he was gravely mistaken. Uhuru's military idolatry was common knowledge. Both Mzee Kenyatta and Uhuru relished wearing the official uniform of the commander-in-chief. In addition, they both enjoyed watching military drills.

No wonder Kenyans quietly jeered and gossiped, when Uhuru appeared in full military uniform to meet King Abdullah II of Jordan on his arrival in Kenya on July 6, 2020, even though the visitor too was wearing army fatigues. "One is a helicopter fighter pilot," tweeted someone by the name Morio, jokingly, "the other wore the uniform in the morning."

Another tweet just told his readers: "Take a look!" tagging both #UKenyatta and #MEsipisu, the State House spokesman. Without doubt Uhuru was a wannabe soldier. He began wearing jungle military fatigue halfway in his term. It was not until 2018, however, when he stepped out in full ceremonial military attire during the Jamhuri Day celebrations. Since then, he has appeared many times on national days wearing the red tunic and blue trousers, and on the side, a sword.

Uhuru did not just love the military; he went further and appointed some uniformed officers into his government. In short, he fetishized the armed forces. Uhuru said he liked the military because of their enviable discipline and integrity. "If all of us had the discipline and integrity of our defence forces," he said during the inauguration of the national youth dialogue at Bomas of Kenya in December 2020, "our country would go far."

Among the top military men Uhuru appointed to positions in his administration were: Major General (Retired) Philip Kameru as director of the National Intelligence Service (NIS); Major General Gordon Kihalang'wa as director of immigration services; and Colonel (Retired) Cyrus Oguna, as government spokesman. Also appointed were former chiefs of general staff, Gen Joseph Kibwana, as chairman of the Kenya Ports Authority, Samson Mwathethe as chairman of the Kenya Electricity Generating Company, and Colonel Alice Mate, a lawyer, who became a director of the Assets Recovery Agency (ARA).

When the Football Kenya Federation was re-constituted in November 2021, one of the members of the caretaker committee was General (Retired) Moses Oyugi. Uhuru appointed more than a dozen officers as ambassadors and chairpersons of government bodies and placed others in strategic economic and administrative positions. His reasoning was that the military were "efficient in delivery, management, and administration."

CHAPTER 20

The Deep State

The idea of a "Deep State" is not a new phenomenon in Kenya. Nor is it a new concept in the world. For as long as there have been nation states, there have been deep states manipulating or undermining them [the states].[266] The concept is believed to have originated in Turkey in the 1990s, but an oligarchic deep state of traditional elites was present in Athens, Ancient Greece, and later in the Roman Empire, many centuries before. There was also a military deep state in the Praetorian Guard, a unit of the Roman Empire. In later years, the military deep state appeared in the General Staff in Imperial Japan.[267] In all cases where the deep state existed, corruption was the driving force.

The definitions of the deep state vary. Some say deep state is a secret government buried deeply within the visible government. Ryan Gingeras, a Turkish organised crime specialist, explains that deep state is a kind of a shadow or parallel system of government in which unofficial or publicly unacknowledged individuals play important roles in defining and implementing state policy. Gingeras argues that the concept is used "to explain why and how agents

---

[266] Fitzgerald, Ian. The Deep State: A History of Secret Agendas and Shadow Governments, Arcturus Publishing Limited, 2020, p. 7.
[267] Asingo, Dr. Patrick O., ISLP Attends Report Launch: "Exposing the Governance Conundrum in Kenya: Deep State, Mega-Corruption," International Lawyers Project, August 7, 2019.

employed by the State execute policies that directly contravene the letter and spirit of the law." And contravening the law often means employing criminals.[268]

As a cabal of people whose main concern is self-preservation, the deep state comprises influential and powerful individuals in government and the corporate world whose intention is to manipulate and control government policy for their good and not for the good of the population at large. Deep states become the vehicles by which they advance their interests. Subsequently, citizens become merely pedestrian bystanders to be knocked down if they get in the way of the deep state.[269]

Dr. Patrick O. Asingo, a political scientist at the University of Nairobi, provides another description of the deep state. He says the deep state refers to "authoritarian, criminal and corrupt segments of the state that function in a democratic regime by exploiting and reproducing its deficiencies." In other words, he says, it is a system of informal institutions operating in the shadows of formal governance institutions. The actors in this informal system, he adds, include politicians, private businesspeople, and corrupt cartels, that use political power and political influence for access to resources and corruption opportunities.

There are many types of deep states: oligarchic deep states, military deep states, corporate deep states, digital deep states, political deep states, bureaucratic deep states, mafia deep states, and many more. The focus of all these deep states is money and power, regardless of how they are obtained; and how they can use collective resources and corrupt means to buy politicians, influence legislation in parliament, change constitutions, manipulate the judiciary, and engage in criminal activities. All this is done to benefit the perpetrators and not the people. Deep states are also known to overthrow governments and install leaders they believe will help their goals by dancing to their (deep state) tunes.

---

[268] Wills, Mathew. The Turkish Origins of the "Deep State," JSTOR Daily, April 10, 2017.
[269] Fitzgerald, Ian, p. 7.

UHURU KENYATTA

In Kenya, deep states emerged during the colonial times. The white settler deep state of the 1920s, 1930s, and 1940s, believed in self-preservation. Although the settlers numbered only 61,000, representing about 1% of the population by 1960, they controlled the economy. They owned everything: agriculture, manufacturing, real estate, and media. They had power to influence the colonial government on political, social, and economic, matters.

The most well-known deep state innovator was Hugh Cholmondeley, the third Baron Delamere, known simply as Lord Delamere, who believed Kenya was a white man's country. He fought vigorously to maintain British supremacy in the colony. The white settler deep state viewed Africans as the enemy who, if given a chance, would extinguish them. "The only way [to self-preserve] …," they felt, was "by standing solidly together, using every endeavour to strengthen and enlarge white settlement, and making room for more of our own people."[270]

So, collectively, the white settler deep state blocked every attempt to advance the cause of African freedoms. In the guise of securing their safety, they manipulated the colonial government into introducing every hurdle to restrict the movement of Africans. One of them was the use of *kipande*, an identification document containing the holder's fingerprint, ethnic group, employment history, and present employment. Africans were forced to wear the metal ID on their necks! Those caught not wearing it were bundled into the dreaded *Black Marias*, taken to court, and charged.

The settler deep state succeeded only because they had the support of the colonial administration deep state and the special branch deep state. Those bodies worked together. The administrative wing, comprising the colonial governor, all the way down to the chief on the ground, set the rules. The Special Branch applied them with the help of the regular police and the army. The law enforcement agencies used all available resources to identify, arrest, humiliate, torture, and detain, those they deemed a threat to white domination.

---

[270] Lord Faringdon. White Settlement in East Africa, UK Parliament, Hansard, February 1, 1944, pp. 1803-2005.

So, when African nationalists like Harry Thuku came along in the 1920s, denounced colonialism, and exhorted Africans to fight for their rights, they were arrested and eventually exiled. Harry Thuku was exiled in northern Kenya for eight years, from 1922 to 1930.

During the Mau Mau rebellion of the 1950s, the special branch deep state went further. It planted informers to spy on the Mau Mau movement and to surveil its activities. The strategy was phenomenally successful and led to the arrest and execution of freedom fighters, among them General Dedan Kimathi, leader of the group.

To stymie the liberation movement, the colonial government elicited the support of the religious deep state in the form of the Moral Rearmament (MRA), a cult-like organisation founded by Rev. Frank Buchman, an American Lutheran pastor. Buchman founded MRA after World War II when he thought the world was in a crisis of morality.

The MRA tenets were honesty, purity, unselfishness, and love. But it also delved into the murky waters of colonial preservation. The organisation later named, Initiatives for Change, used films, songs, and plays to spread its teachings to six continents. In Africa, Kenya was one of the countries that consumed the MRA's "hate-free, fear-free, greed-free world" philosophy, especially in the period during the state of emergency from 1952.

The first known Kenyan MRA deep state operative was a man called Nahashon Ngare Rukenya, a Mau Mau turn-coat detainee. He met the MRA founder Buchman while incarcerated at the Athi River detention camp. Rukenya agreed to abandon the Mau Mau cause for what MRA told him would be "peace, reconciliation, and resettlement of post-war Kenya."[271]

What Rukenya did not fathom was the motive behind MRA's interest in Mau Mau detainees. That motive became known when the colonial government handed over the Athi River camp to MRA,

---

[271] Gathogo, Julius M. Nahashon Ngare Rukenya and the Moral Re-Armament in Kenya: The Turning Point and the Post Mau-Mau War Reconstruction (1959-1970), Kenyatta University, University of South Africa, 2018.

ostensibly for detainee rehabilitation. What happened thereafter is captured by J. M. Kariuki in his book, Mau Mau Detainee.

> *"Soon the bogey of 'confession' appeared. The officials in-charge there did not beat people, but they used many other means, some more subtle than others. Rations were reduced and this forced the weakest to surrender. Joseph [Joseph Kirira, a detainee] told me that prostitutes were brought into camp to speak words of love and to dangle their legs before the detainees to remind them of some of the things they were missing. They were not allowed to taste these joys, though, merely to recall them, before the ladies were taken out."*[272]

MRA was a religious deep state recruited to *manipulate and undermine* the Mau Mau movement. It fitted within the deep state definition, *a kind of a shadow or parallel system of government in which unofficial or publicly unacknowledged individuals play important roles in defining and implementing state policy.*

By July 1954 – two years after the start of the state of emergency – *The Times of London* reported that 270 hard-core detainees at Athi River camp had severed connections with the Mau Mau. The following year, the number went up to 600 detainees, according to MRA. But in his book, Kariuki, said only "three or four people were 'rehabilitated'" or rather, brainwashed, by the MRA.

While MRA was successful in influencing and manipulating the colonial government into being allowed into detention camps ostensibly to "rehabilitate" prisoners, it failed miserably in attempts to infiltrate the trade union movement. The American-backed International Confederation of Free Trade Unions (ICFTU) of which Tom Mboya's Kenya Federation of Labour (KFL) was a member,

---

[272] Kariuki, J. M. Mau Mau Detainee: The Account by a Kenyan African in his Experience in Detention Camps 1953-1960, Oxford University Press, 1963, p. 127.

declined MRA overtures and ordered its affiliate organisations to sever all relations with the religious group.

MRA had plans to form rival unions to counter the ICFTU. If MRA had succeeded in infiltrating the KFL, its influence in the federation would adversely have impacted labour unions in Kenya. It would also have undermined the interests of Kenyan workers and torpedoed the path to independence.

Another person who helped the colonial government to manipulate and undermine the struggle for independence was a man called Stanley Kinga, described only as a "leader of Mau Mau." Kinga was an MRA sympathiser. He even visited the MRA's headquarters in Caux, Switzerland, in 1960. Kinga was one of three people, the others being Nahashon Ngare Rukenya and Leonard Kibuthu-Muturi, also Mau Mau turncoats, who took the MRA film, *Freedom,* to Jomo Kenyatta when he was in detention at Maralal in 1959. In 1968 as President, Mzee Kenyatta appointed Rukenya as the Coast Provincial Settlement Officer.

The film was about a fictional nation of Bokondo under colonial rule and the emergence of a nationalist independence movement there. Earlier, while working at the Githunguri Teachers College, Kenyatta introduced a Kiswahili version of the film to students, teachers, and villagers, during a screening session at the institution.

Kenyan MRA youths also performed a play based on the same theme in different parts of the country. So, the MRA, through Kinga, managed to reach the foremost nationalist leader. It is documented that Mzee Kenyattas clarion call of "let us forget the past and build the nation" was the brainchild of Rukenya and influenced by the MRA.[273]

Independence brought even more deep states to the fore in Kenya. On June 1, 1963, when Kenyatta became Prime Minister, he inherited a security apparatus created and built by the British. The army commander, Major General Ian Freeland, and Police

---

[273] Gathogo, Julius M. Nahashon Ngare Rukenya and the Moral Re-Armament in Kenya: The Turning Point and the Post Mau Mau War Reconstruction (1959-1970), *Studia Historiae Eclesiasticae*, Vol. 44, No. 2, 2018.

Commissioner R. C. Catling were British. The African soldiers were trained by the British. The British Governor-General Malcolm MacDonald was still in place.

As Prime Minister, Jomo Kenyatta had only limited powers to formulate policies. But still, he was partly in charge of running the country with the Governor-General looking over his shoulder. Then on January 24, 1964, men of the 11th Battalion of the Kenya Rifles at Lanet mutinied simultaneously with their counterparts in Tanganyika [now Tanzania] and Uganda, demanding better pay.

Kenyatta panicked. He called on the British forces to help quell the disturbance. There was no indication that the mutiny was an ouster attempt. It was just a genuine protest by disillusioned riflemen. What was disturbing was that the unit had an opportunity to revolt when the colonialists were in power and before Kenyatta was installed, but they didn't.

A day or two before the mutiny, the soldiers had expected Kenyatta to appear on TV and announce a pay increase for them, but he didn't. That infuriated the soldiers. Did the British security deep state instigate the mutiny to warn of risks under an African rule? Or was it the sole work of unhappy junior officers? Two hundred soldiers were dismissed from the force and 70 were court-marshalled. Mzee Kenyatta denounced "acts of disloyalty and destruction." He disbanded the unit and instituted reforms. But the deep state had fired a warning shot to the emerging African state.

Mzee Kenyatta appointed a fellow Kikuyu, Bernard Hinga, to be the first African police commissioner in 1964. He chose Brigadier A. J. Hardy to take over from Major General Freeland as commander of the Kenya Army and retained British Group Captain I. S. Stockwell as the Kenya Air Force (KAF) commander. That was not enough.

Over the years that followed, many Kikuyu were recruited to dilute the armed forces whose soldiers were predominantly Kalenjin and Kamba. The process was done slowly and carefully not to upset the ethnic balance.

In 1973, Kenyatta appointed the first commander of the KAF, a Kikuyu, Major General Dedan Gichuru. Kikuyunisation of the top hierarchy of the army was difficult since all qualified candidates were non-Kikuyu. It was not until 2005 that a Kikuyu, Lieutenant General Agostino Karanu Njoroge, was appointed by President Kibaki to fill the top army position. Before that, all army commanders were non-Kikuyu.

Because of the ethnic composition in the military, there was no room for the emergence of a military deep state during the Kenyatta administration. The presence of British officers on secondment to Kenya for training purposes, guaranteed Jomo Kenyatta stability and peace of mind throughout his rule.

The white officers in the civil service were there to influence policies and implement administrative actions: the hiring and promotion of African elites sympathetic to the colonial thinking and determining legislations. The General Service Unit (GSU), a paramilitary group, was already in place under the command of a British officer. In 1965, Kenyatta established the Anti-Stock Theft Unit (ASTU), an ambiguous and inscrutable brigade of hardcore gun-happy elements, as a back-up force in case he ran into trouble.

While the GSU had specific duties of guarding the president and dealing with rioters and protesters, the ASTU's mandate was unclear. It was camouflaged as cattle-rustling fighting force, but that was not the whole truth. The ASTU was the same unit which, after Kenyatta's death in 1978, plotted to capture and murder Daniel arap Moi to prevent him from taking over government after Jomo Kenyatta's death. The ASTU was headed by a hot-headed assistant police commissioner in the Rift Valley, James Erastus Mungai. Few people knew that one of ASTU's assignments was to assassinate targeted allies of Vice President Moi.

In effect, the ASTU was part of the security deep state working to forcefully overthrow the constitution and install a candidate of its choice to succeed Mzee Kenyatta. Moi was saved only because the ASTU delayed posting a road barrier that was to stop Moi as he rushed to State House Nairobi to be sworn in as acting president. The security deep state had earmarked Dr. Njoroge Mungai, Mzee Kenyatta's first cousin and personal physician, for the position. Dr. Mungai was a leading supporter of the change-the-constitution group which sought to undermine Moi's position as heir to Mzee Kenyatta.

Talking of assassinations, it is not only possible but probable that the security deep state killed J. M. Kariuki (JM) the popular politician. This argument makes sense because the last person to interact with JM was the GSU Commandant Ben Gethi. Gethi was a power-hungry alcoholic who relished in torturing suspects. He was also a major component of the security deep state opposed to Moi. Gethi's name was already tarnished. He had been implicated in the 1982 Kenya Air Force (KAF) coup d'état attempt to oust Moi. Following the attempt, Moi sacked Gethi as police commissioner and detained him for ten months. Bernard Kiarie Njinu took his place.

Jeremiah Kiereini, a long-term civil servant, did not believe that Gethi could have been involved in the 1982 coup attempt. In his autobiography, *A Daunting Journey,* Kiereini insists that Gethi was a loyal public servant, and wonders how he could have been involved in the ouster attempt. "Poor Ben Bethi!" Kiereini shockingly says about the officer's sacking, "I have no idea why Moi sacked Gethi, but the speculation was that Gethi's enemies alleged he was the mastermind of the coup attempt.... He never behaved in any way as a traitor."[274] It is surprising that a top technocrat of Kiereini's calibre was not aware of the existence of a deep state working against Moi.

Two convicted bank robbers, Peter Kinyanjui alias Mark Twist, and Pius Kibathi, had been trailing JM days preceding his murder. But it was the stolid Gethi who took JM to the Special Branch offices on the appointed day. There, JM met four security officers who questioned him about some "missing foreign funds" when he was Mzee's personal secretary and later assistant minister for agriculture.

The officers present at the Special Branch officers were Police Reservist Patrick Shaw, NYS Director and former Mau Mau General Waruhiu Itote, CID boss Ignatius Nderi, and Mzee's head of security, Arthur Wanyoike Thungu, all perceived core members of the security deep state. An argument ensued and Thungu allegedly punched JM in the face. JM attempted to pull out his gun, but Gethi quickly

---

[274] Gitau, Jeremiah Kiereini. *A Daunting Journey*, East African Educational Publishers, 2015, p. 201.

pulled out his pistol and shot JM on the right hand. JM was then bundled into a car and driven to Ngong Forest where he met his fate.[275] From this narrative, it is without doubt that the security deep state participated in Kariuki's brutal murder.

A parliamentary committee of inquiry set up to probe JM's murder recommended that top government officials including the Minister of State in the Office of the President, Koinange, Itote, and Thungu, be investigated further. The report of the committee was released to the public, but names of the suspected chief perpetrators were deleted on orders of Mzee Kenyatta. WikiLeaks later released the full document.[276]

Were Pio Gama Pinto, Tom Mboya, and Robert Ouko, who met their destiny under questionable circumstances also victims of the deep state? When the shocking news of Pinto's death reached parliament, MPs were horrified. Many sobbed. Information Minister Achieng Oneko put hands on his head in disbelief: "No, no, no! Kenyatta must explain," he said. Mzee who was present in Parliament retorted cynically: "Bwana Waziri, do you think it is Kenyatta who killed Pinto." The House went quiet. Not long after that, Vice President Joseph Murumbi resigned "to protest Pinto's murder, [corruption] and subsequent intrigues in Kenyatta's inner circle."

The security deep state had scored its first goal on behalf of the president: to destroy Jaramogi's spirit and scatter his group of insiders. When delivering his judgement against two accused persons for the murder, Chege Thuo and Kisilu Mutua, Chief Justice John Ainley said that "the case wears an unfinished aspect… we may not have all who were involved in the crime before us."[277] Who were the others? Thuo was freed for lack of evidence. Mutua was given a life sentence.

Mboya's murder took an almost similar pattern. The difference was that the alleged attacker was a man known to Mboya. Mboya had helped the young man to secure a scholarship to Bulgaria. But he was

---

[275] Ngotho, Kamau. *Daily Nation*, March 2, 2000.
[276] Kariuki Murder Report, WikiLeaks, June 4, 1975.
[277] Aiyar, Sana. Indians in Kenya: The Politics of Diaspora, Harvard University Press, 2015, p. 272.

a hatchet man because when he was asked whether the gun found in his house belonged to him, he responded with precision: "Why don't you ask the big man?"[278] Who was that big man? The answer to that question went to the grave with Nahashon Njenga who was executed at the Kamiti maximum prison on November 8, 1969.

In the case of Robert Ouko, his burnt body was found in a thicket ten kilometres from his rural home in Koru, Kisumu. One of those arrested as a suspect was no other than the loyal Moi man, Biwott, who was then minister for industry. Biwott, who wore a perpetually worried expression, was one of the richest Kenyans during Moi's rule. He called himself the "Total Man" because he lived high on the hog from corruption and illicit deals.

In 1991 when he was earning a paltry monthly salary of KSh.21,033 as energy minister, Biwott was already worth "hundreds of millions of dollars," money that was held mainly in offshore accounts, according to the British high commission in Nairobi.[279] Also detained for two weeks for Ouko's murder was Hezekiah Oyugi, the powerful permanent secretary (PS) for internal security and head of a clandestine group of deep state functionaries called "Special DOs [District Officers]." The DOs were some of the most feared officials in government.

The 'special DOs' were members of a parallel, opaque, intelligence group, reporting directly to Oyugi who then passed the information to President Moi. Also in the clandestine group were a prominent Nairobi lawyer, and two DOs. Oyugi died in 1992 from poisoning (the security deep state was suspected), and Biwott in 2017 supposedly from natural causes.

More than 100 people who could have appeared as witnesses in the Ouko murder investigation died under suspicious circumstances. John Troon, a Scotland Yard detective who investigated the murder, had this conclusion: 'Hezekiah Oyugi was the mastermind of the

---

[278] *Daily Nation*, September 3, 1969.
[279] Perlez, Jane. "Citing corruption by Kenyan officials, Western nations are cancelling aid," *The New York Times*, October 21, 1991.

minister's death. He was the trigger man; the PS was not working alone.'

That conclusion left many questions unanswered. If the PS was not working alone, then who was, or who were the other characters? Why were they not named? Evidence was presented to the parliamentary committee of inquiry investigating the murder that Ouko was duped into going to State House Nakuru where he was killed[280] and his body dumped on a hill where it was found. Everyone knew who the official occupant of the State House Nakuru was, but no one dared question Moi about that report. He was not called to testify in any inquiry.

A comprehensive and abstruse investigation was conducted by Kenyan and UK detectives, but no one was prosecuted for Ouko's murder. It was a typical operation conducted by the administrative deep state in cahoots with the security deep state.

Mbai's assassination

Assassinations of prominent people also occurred during President Kibaki's government. Dr. Crispin Odhiambo Mbai was a constitutional law expert who was advising the Constitution of Kenya Review Commission (CKRC). He was a professor at the University of Nairobi. On September 14, 2003, Mbai, who was closely allied to ODM leader Raila, was murdered. A group of unknown people stormed into his house and shot him on the head and chest causing brain contusion haemorrhage, lung collapse, and hemothorax. Nothing was stolen and no one else was injured or killed.

Mbai's murder stirred up anger among University of Nairobi students who demonstrated on the streets for almost a week. Police raided university hostels and assaulted female students. Ten western nations expressed concern and called for "a thorough, speedy, and effective investigation." Three people were arrested: Collins Ketore, a guard at Mbai's home, Ramadhan Otieno, and Moses Mbuthi.

---

[280] Robert Ouko "Killed in Kenya State House," *BBC News*, December 9, 2010.

They were in remand for eighteen months, but due to "lack of evidence," High Court Judge Kalpana Rawal freed them. It appeared the investigations were not conducted with alacrity or thoroughness expected of such a high-profile case.

Some analysts pointed fingers at the political establishment of Kibaki. That point of view was underscored by a witness's confession that an MP close to the president was involved. No evidence was raised to prove that connection. The only motive left was that the killing had something to do with the constitutional review process. Mbai was chairperson of the Committee on Devolution of Power at the CKRC. Many believed Mbai was killed by the security deep state to undermine the constitution-making exercise which was already mired in ethnic and political divisions. The deep state feared the devolution – if achieved – would eat into the president's immense powers.

The deep state also played havoc in Kenyan elections. Take, for example, the KANU nominations in February 1988. On August 20, 1986, the KANU delegates' conference at the KICC resolved that from thereon, primaries would be conducted using the queuing system popularly known as *mlolongo*. The candidates were to stand in front of a line and their supporters were to queue behind them. The person with the longest line would be the winner.

That strange system of selecting candidates gave the deep state and those with deep state dispositions an opportunity to rig elections. KANU mandarins who supervised the nominations with assistance from the administrative and security deep states made sure that only establishment candidates won, regardless of how long or short their lines were. Dozens of politically correct candidates with short lines "won" over those with longer lines.

Among the "losers" were political heavyweights known to be Moi's critics including Vice President Kibaki, Martin Shikuku, Kimani wa Nyoike, and Charles Rubia. After the 'defeat' Kibaki was stripped of the number two position and moved to the health docket. KANU, the administrative, and the security deep states, had accomplished their mission: ridding the party of Moi detractors, at least for the time being.

Governor Francis Kimemia might have been right when he said on Citizen TV on September 21, 2021, that it is the deep state that decides who wins or loses an election. "Yes, the deep state exists…," he said. "If you have two candidates – let's, say – at 50-50, the deep state backs one, you can be sure that one will win the election…."[281]

That explanation fitted tightly with what transpired in 2007. The deep state backed Kibaki, so he 'won'. Former State House spokesman Alfred Mutua agreed with Kimemia that there were people in government and in institutions "with instruments of power who can influence results [and] they can control events…," but he fell short of confirming that the deep state indeed influenced Kibaki's election win in 2007.

As a former Head of Civil Service and Secretary to the Cabinet, Kimemia knew what he was talking about. He was a key member of the inner circle in Kibaki's government. He is one of the officials who chaperoned the transition from Kibaki to Uhuru and continued as Secretary to the Cabinet in the new regime.

If there is someone who knows how a deep state operates in government, it is the ever-smiling governor. His remarks raised eyebrows, and some MPs even called for an investigation. "Did the so-called deep state have any influence on the election of Kenyatta and Ruto in 2013 and 2017?"[282] asked one analyst.

Uhuru's deep states

During Uhuru's term there existed numerous deep states all scrambling to influence policies and advance individual or group gains. There was of course the Gatundu Mafia consisting of mostly Kenyatta kins and close associates. This was a deep state, controlled and managed by Uhuru's mother, Mama Ngina. All major pronouncements by Uhuru that could impact the interests of the

---

[281] "Omondi, Ian. Governor Francis Kimemia reveals how 'deep state' influences elections in Kenya," Citizen Digital, September 21, 2021.
[282] Gatitu, Son. "Is Kenya's 'deep state' a reality or scarecrow in its democracy?" *The Africa Report*, October 5, 2021.

Kenyattas had to get her approval. She managed the president and the presidency by remote control.

Her youngest son, Muhoho, was the equivalent of the 'Underboss" in a Mafia family structure. He was the contact man between the family and the outside world. He was the 'implementer.' It was his job to follow up on his mother's approvals to ensure they were implemented to the fullest advantage of the interests.

During the Uhuru administration, the intelligence deep state was intimately engaged in fighting corruption, terror groups, and political opponents. It paid close attention to politicians and other elements opposed to Uhuru, as well as terror groups like Al-Shabaab and other urban guerrilla militias like *Mungiki*.

The head of the NIS for most of Uhuru's term, Major-General Philip Wachira Kameru, was a close family friend though his home district is Nyeri. He could therefore be considered as an adopted member of the Gatundu deep state given his high security position. Kameru took over from Major General Michael Gichangi who resigned in the wake of the Westgate Mall terror attack.

The National Intelligence Service (NIS) is one of the most powerful organisations in the country. It is also perhaps the most secretive and misunderstood government department. The Organisation's 'real' budget is unknown, and its expenditure is not scrutinised by the auditor general like other government departments.

The NIS, by its designation, is also an active participant of the security deep state. The security deep state is composed of all security agencies as well as some key members of the cabinet. It operates under the umbrella of the National Security Council, a tight elite group chaired by the President. Also in the group is the attorney general, the chief of defence forces, the inspector general of National Police Service, and the interior minister.

The saga that played out in Nairobi prior to the 2022 elections involving Johnson Sakaja, a Ruto aspirant for the governorship of the capital city, was created and orchestrated by the security deep state. It was executed with the connivance of the executive deep state and its sole intention was to sink Sakaja's candidature. The deep states did not want Sakaja, an anti-establishment politician, to be the one to manage the most important city in the country. The hullabaloo over his educational credentials was purposefully engineered to get him out of the race to make it easier for the compliant deep states' favourite, Polycarp Igathe, to win the elections. The deep states used money, intrigues, subterfuge, and power, to ensure 'their' city did not fall into the hands of an erratic and sometimes irritating man. They had learnt their lesson from Sonko, the previous governor.

The NIS works closely with the State-controlled Communications Authority (CA) and internet service providers and monitors incoming and outgoing internet traffic. It also intercepts personal telephone conversations and tracks an individual or group of individuals without requiring a court warrant. Similarly, the CA has powers to force telephone and internet providers to release any information gathered online for use by security agencies.[283]

In the second term of Uhuru's administration, several politicians opposed to Uhuru found themselves in trouble. The politicians, mainly allied to DP Ruto were routinely harassed. They were summoned to appear before the directorate of criminal investigations (DCI) or the EACC and subjected to questioning about their finances and/or tax records. Some were arrested and charged in court on criminal counts dating back years ago. The NIS also enhanced its telephone surveillance against Ruto's allies and carefully monitored hate speech by opposing politicians. It passed that information to other government agencies like the DCI, the EACC, and the National Cohesion and Integration Commission (NCIC), for action. All those agencies represented the security deep state intent on protecting the status quo.

At one time, ten MPs and senators supporting Ruto's UDA were reported to and summoned by NCIC to answer questions over hate speech. The NCIC chairman, Samuel Kobia, warned purveyors [read Ruto supporters] of hate speech that they would be jailed, "and as they await to go to jail, we will put them out of the leadership of this country and ensure they never run again [for political office] in

---

[283] Track, Capture, Kill: Inside Communications Surveillance and Counterterrorism in Kenya, Privacy International, March 2017.

this country."[284] (*A deep state is a kind of a shadow or parallel system of government in which unofficial or publicly unacknowledged individuals play important roles in defining and implementing state policy.*)

Ruto called it political witch-hunt and insinuated that Uhuru who "grew up as a child of the deep state," [285] could be behind his woes. "Everyone knows this," he said. "If you visit or are seen as a friend of the Deputy President, the next day, you will get a visit from the DCI," Ruto claimed in an interview with *Radio Jambo*. "Not because you have stolen anything."

Under Uhuru, the NIS posted over 300 officers across all the 47 counties to bolster surveillance.

In September 2021, a few days after the Kirinyaga County Governor Anne Waiguru, announced plans to leave the ruling Jubilee Alliance Party and defend his seat on Ruto's UDA ticket in the 2022 elections, she got a call from EACC. The anti-corruption body grilled her for hours about a KSh.52 million pending land transaction which she signed as the county boss. The land was formerly held by the defunct Kirinyaga County Council in 1965. After her election, she arranged to have the land sub-divided for different uses. Geo-acre Surveyors was contracted to do the job for KSh.74 million. The council had paid KSh.21 million leaving a balance of KSh.52 million which Waiguru approved for payment. The governor said the money was not paid and therefore no money was lost. She described the EACC move as "politically instigated."

That was not the end of Waiguru's woes. For weeks, the former CS kept Kenyans guessing about her plans in the political matrix of the day. She had to decide whether to abandon Jubilee and its Project Raila or cross over to join the UDA bandwagon. Finally in October 2021, she announced her decision to dump Jubilee and support Ruto. Barely forty-eight hours later, she was summoned by the EACC.

---

[284] Gladys Wanga, Cleophas Malala, among 10 lawmakers summoned by NCIC, The Free Library, undated.
[285] Nyakagwa, *The Nairobian*, June 29, 2021.

The agency announced it had completed its investigation and planned to charge Waiguru. The stipulated charges included conspiracy to commit an economic crime, abuse of office, false accounting, deception, and forgery, relating to the KSh.52 million fraud allegations. She spent hours at Integrity House answering questions from detectives. She emerged to denounce the EACC claiming its action was an attempt at engineering the succession politics. "It wouldn't work. Kenyans are not stupid," she lamented. Once again, the security deep state was at work.

Politician Jimmy Wanjigi was also a victim of state intimidation. Wanjigi was a member of ODM and had shown interest in his party's presidential nomination against his boss, Raila. Because Raila had the support of Uhuru and the Jubilee Alliance Party, Wanjigi was seen as a spoiler out to torpedo Raila's chances. One night in January 2022, a contingent of security officers went to his offices to arrest him. They broke the main door of the office, but they could not reach Wanjigi who was hiding deep in an underground bunker.

Hours later, however, Wanjigi emerged from his hideout and gave himself up. He was arrested, spent the night in police cell, and was arraigned in court the following day on charges of forging a title document. Many saw the police action as a revenge plot by the security deep state to punish Wanjigi for getting Kinoti, the DCI director sentenced to four months in jail for contempt of court. Wanjigi was released without being charged following a High Court order barring the State from arresting and charging him.

With Raila as Uhuru's project, there was no way the deep state would have allowed Wanjigi to challenge the ODM leader in the nomination process. The former had to be stopped, and stopped he was. As he made his way to his party's national delegate's convention at Kasarani gymnasium, a group of Raila supporters pounced on him and frog matched him out of the venue. There is no reason to doubt that the move was a deep state manoeuvre. After all, a senior police officer was captured on video taking instructions from an ODM party official to have Wanjigi ejected. A law enforcement officer can only take instructions from his seniors, not from a party functionary who is not even in the ruling establishment.

Eventually, Wanjigi left Jubilee Alliance Party and joined Safina Party to contest the presidency. But he was disqualified by the electoral body because he lacked a degree.

And in early April, when Raila and his team were stoned by a rowdy crowd after a funeral in Ruto's Rift Valley stronghold, three leaders allied to Ruto, MPs Caleb Kositany, Oscar Sudi, and the speaker of the Uasin Gishu county assembly, David Kiplagat, were the first ones to be summoned to the DCI to write statements.

Private sector deep state

During the Moi, Kibaki and Uhuru administrations, there existed active private sector deep states geared at protecting business and/or individual interests. Take the case of the late Chris Kirubi, a multi-billionaire businessman, industrialist, and entrepreneur. Kirubi was a private sector deep state influencer. He was a significant player in the election and re-election of the three leaders.

Kirubi was an unknown entity before Mzee Kenyatta appointed him to manage the Kenya National Transport Company (KENATCO), a government-owned transportation company. Kenatco was one of the largest and most profitable public enterprises in the 1960s and 1970s. It operated taxies, mini-buses, and heavy transport. But Kirubi and other senior managers ran it down. It went into receivership in October 1983 after defaulting on loans amounting to KSh.22 million advanced to it by the Industrial and Commercial Development Corporation (ICDC), another government parastatal. By the time Kenatco collapsed, Kirubi was already a wealthy man having committed the organisation to heavy debts.

As he established new companies and bought into others, Kirubi became a major influencer in political circles and government. He used his media company, Capital FM, to flaunt his wealth and build his brand of interest as a DJ. He was the largest shareholder in the Nairobi Security Exchange-listed company, Centum, and numerous other firms. He courted friendship with the mighty and the powerful both inside and outside the country. Armed with useful contacts,

Kirubi bid and won multi-million-shilling public sector tenders. He also accompanied Uhuru on most of his foreign trips, and in the process, secured deals with Chinese, French, and Arab investors, other entrepreneurs could not.

One of the tenders was for the KSh.174 billion coal power project in Lamu. Centum was part of a consortium of Kenyan companies under the umbrella of Amu Power. Apart from having coal-handling facilities, the 1,050-megawatts project had plans for a jetty and associated infrastructure. The capital for the project was raised by Centum in partnership with Gulf Energy.

The flamboyant high lifer had a penchant for political wheeler-dealing. He led a group of business influencers to a KSh.1 million per-plate dinner in 2017 to raise money for Uhuru's re-election. Within minutes, the group had raised KSh.1 billion. Known as the Mount Kenya Foundation (MKF), the group had all dispositions of a deep state. The group's true colours came out during the period preceding the 2022 elections. Seeing no possibility of another Kikuyu succeeding Uhuru, the MKF had to find another best person to shield them from hostile business forces. They conducted what was akin to employment panels with leading contenders appearing before them for interviews. It was a charade that convinced Raila he had the support of Mt. Kenya voters.

The millionaires and billionaires, including media mogul, S. K. Macharia, Mama Ngina's brother George Muhoho, former bank magnate Peter Munga, former top civil servant Michael Waweru, and coffee mills guru Pius Ngugi, among others, met to impose conditions on a candidates seen to be favourable to their agenda. By doing that they were trying to influence the elections, a standard deep state phenomenon.

From the beginning of their deliberations, the MKF appeared to prefer Raila for the presidency, one, because Raila was closest to Uhuru, their fellow Kikuyu, thanks to the handshake. And two, the MKF considered him amenable to persuasion and manipulation given his long, missed, presidential ambitions. Raila was in his sunset years and desperate for the presidency. Failure to win in 2022 could mark the end of his chequered career defined by many political successes and failures.

During the Grand Coalition Government of Kibaki and Raila, Kirubi regularly convened what came to be known as the Prime Minister's Roundtable, a convergence of prominent politicians and businesspeople who met to exchange views on the direction of the country. An honorary consul of Mauritius, Kirubi was also responsible for KSh.5 billion worth of investment brought into Kenya by Mauritian investors, including the acquisition of the stock-broker Apex Africa Capital Limited. He was also credited for attracting the 51% shares in Transmara Sugar Company which operates sugar mills in Kisii, western Kenya.

In his quest to fight corruption, Uhuru turned to this group of blue-chip company leaders to draft a code of conduct which eventually led to the passing of the Bribery Act in 2017. Operating under the guidance of the Kenya Private Sector Alliance (KEPSA), the top businesspeople also helped to map up corruption risk areas in the private sector and drafted guidelines to enhance compliance of the Bribery legislation. The Bribery Act became useless as soon as it was enacted as corruption continued to ravage the private sector.

Whether those business influencers represented a private sector deep state out to manipulate the government and thus benefit their enterprises is difficult to know. But they fitted into the description of a deep state: *"influential and powerful individuals in government and the corporate world whose intention is to manipulate and control government policy for their good and not for the good of the State."*

On September 14, 2020, Deputy President William Ruto explained that Kenyans had passed the politics of ethnicity and asked his UDA followers not to bow down to intimidation and coercion from Jubilee Alliance Party leaders. "The so-called deep state and system," he said, "is hot air. It is a cocktail of criminals." Ruto was right. As Gingeras surmised, deep states are vehicles for criminal activities. They undermine governments and overthrow legitimate constitutions. But Ruto was wrong when he initially claimed that deep state does not exist. As the 2022 election day approached, Ruto appeared to have changed his mind. He admitted that indeed the deep state existed, but "we will defeat it hands down."

The Youth for KANU 1992 (YK'92) outfit of which Ruto was a member was a deep state wing of the ruling party. It spent millions of shillings influencing elections for President Moi, bribing voters, intimidating opponents, and even engaging in fraudulent and violent activities. Opposition leaders claimed YK'92 was a cover for a paramilitary organisation, trained to disrupt opposition meetings and create inter-communal violence to justify a ban on opposition activities.[286] YK'92 functions were certainly not above board. "It turned out much of YK activities included not so much campaigning for KANU but using strategic positioning to grab public land and loot state institutions… under the guise of raising funds for President Moi's re-election."[287]

The pretentiousness of YK'92 leaders was by itself scary. They were shadowed by security officers whenever they went. Formed a year before the first multi-party elections in 1992, the YK'92 also participated in vote rigging. KANU paid the body to engage in illegalities for the sole purpose of manipulating the elections in favour of Moi, a typical deep state role.

The *nyayo* deep state was known by the notoriously sounding moniker, the Rift Valley Mafia. This group comprised people from Moi's Rift Valley region, among them Nicholas Biwott, Ezekiel Barng'etuny, Mark Too, Abraham Kiptanui, and Joshua Kulei, among others. Those were Moi's closest allies who had the last word about most of the policy issues. They also influenced many of the decisions in government. Apart from Biwott and Kiptanui, the others were semi-illiterates who danced to Moi's tune like a flower in the wind.

It was not only individuals who manipulated the government. Companies were formed purposely to exploit the State in a truly corporate deep state fashion. Goldenberg International Limited we

---

[286] Throup, David W. & Hornsby, Charles. *Multi-Party Politics in Kenya: The Kenyatta & Moi States & the Triumph of the System in the 1992 Election*, James Currey, 1998, p. 193.

[287] Gaitho, Macharia. "How hustler Ruto broke into exclusive club to launch career," *Daily Nation*, May 29, 2016.

saw earlier was one of them. It received millions of shillings from the exchequer as payment for gold exports that did not exist. It was a conspiracy of the bureaucratic deep state and the private deep state to exploit the country for their own good. The scandal caused an uproar in the country. Three years later, Goldenberg was closed with a KSh.60 billion loss to the taxpayer. An estimated 10% of the country's GDP ended up in the bank accounts of a small group of politicians, influencers, and investors.

PART V
THE INTRIGUES

CHAPTER 21

Who next?

Ruto began his presidential campaign nonchalantly in 2018 with appearances in Churches on Sundays. One of his early visits was in Kisii in May where he expressed interest in vying for the presidency. He commissioned roads in Kwale in June and presented a bus to Joy Valley Special School in Bumula, western Kenya in July.

His residence in Karen became a hive of activity. Soon, he was convening public rallies across the country. Apart from short intermittent pauses in between, Ruto held rallies throughout 2020 and 2021, amid Covid-19 restrictions imposed by his own government. Until he officially announced his interest for the seat at a rally in Eldoret on January 8, 2022, Ruto coated his forays around the country as "meet the people tours," and "inspecting government projects." But he was clearly setting the ground for the 2022 elections.

By the beginning of 2022, opinion polls were showing Ruto way ahead of Raila who had officially announced his bid in December 2021. A poll by the Radio Africa Group on January 19, showed 46.1% of Kenyans preferred Ruto against 35.1% for Raila. That was a slight decline for Ruto who had polled 45.6% in November 2021, and an impressive jump for Raila's perevious number of 28.6%. But a month later, on February 17, the same poll showed Ruto had increased his lead to 47.1% against Raila's 35.1%.

Raila's poll was impressive, thanks to Uhuru's efforts in persuading his Central Kenya home people to support his 'project.' When Radio Africa Group did another poll in March, the trend had changed. Raila had overtaken Ruto. Among those polled, 47.4% of Kenyans said they would vote for Raila against 43.4% for Ruto. A poll released by the *Nation* on May 12, 2022, showed the two candidates were in a dead heat at 42% each. Six days later, on May 18, Tifa Research showed Raila had overtaken Ruto. The firm put Raila at 39% against Ruto's 35%. Fourteen percent were undecided and 9% did not indicate their preference. It was still too early though to predict the winner with three months to the August 9 elections, but everything pointed to a tight race.

* * *

The Odinga name is known throughout Africa and the world. His father, Jaramogi, was a well-respected nationalist and vice president under Mzee Kenyatta. As prime minister, Raila attended and addressed numerous conferences in Africa and abroad, among them the 21st World Economic Forum on Africa, in Cape Town, South Africa, in April 2011, and the 2nd Session of the Global Platform for Disaster Risk Reduction in Geneva, Switzerland, in June 2009. In the process, he made contacts with many heads of state and governments. One of the leaders he met in February 2022 was Prime Minister Narendra Modi during the former's visit to India in February 2022. He also visited the US and UK in March and met with senior government officials.

Ruto did not get such opportunities. His name went global only after his appearance at the ICC in 2014. So, who is Ruto?

The man from Sugoi

Compared to Uhuru and Raila, DP Ruto hails from a humble family. He was born on December 21, 1966, in Kamagut, Uasin Gishu, to peasant farmers, Daniel Cheruiyot and Sarah Cheruiyot. He went to local schools, sold chickens, and later joined the University of Nairobi, graduating in zoology in 1990. Two years later, he registered as a member of KANU and became the MP for Eldoret North in 1997. He served briefly as assistant minister and then as minister for home affairs.

In January 2005 when Uhuru was elected KANU chairman, Ruto became its secretary general. He resigned from KANU in October 2007 to join Raila in ODM. When the Grand Coalition Government was formed in 2008, he was appointed agriculture minister. In 2009, he was implicated in a maize scandal and left ODM. After a short stint in the United Democratic Party (UDM), he left to join the United Republican Party (URP). He teamed up with Uhuru in 2016 to form Jubilee Alliance Party. In 2020, frustrated by Uhuru's dalliance with Raila, he engineered the formation of UDA which became his presidential vehicle for 2022.

Along the way Ruto accumulated wealth the way a squirrel accumulates nuts. In fact, the story is that he also sold groundnuts during his earlier days. He established an insurance company, started his own chicken farm then moved to dairy. He bought a 395-acre farm in Trans Mara, Narok, and acquired a ranch in Taita Taveta. He also built the Weston Hotel in Nairobi and the Dolphin Hotel outside Mombasa city. He said he was making KSh.1.5 million daily from the chicken farm of 200,000 birds. He had 400,000 shares in Safaricom and 80,000 in Kenya Airways. He also reportedly owned five helicopters and a gas company. By ordinary standards, Ruto is a billionaire who masquerades as a 'hustler.' In 2021, some estimates put Ruto's wealth at KSh.30 billion.[288]

During the 2022 campaign, Ruto used the hustler epithet effectively, earning much political capital from the less fortunate Kenyans in slums and around rural trading centres. He won hearts of many by associating himself with the struggles of the ordinary people all over the country. Where other presidential contenders, like Raila, Musyoka, and Mudavadi, feared to go, like Mt Kenya,

---

[288] "Rich people: "DP Ruto net worth 2021 – house, choppers, sources of wealth," *Diaspora Messenger*, September 15, 2021.

Ruto went periodically, made his case, and gathered support. His opponents followed that path much later when the early bird had already gathered the worms.

One of the biggest embarrassments for Ruto was when the Interior Cabinet Secretary Fred Matiang'i – a man with a strong assumption of superiority – appeared before a parliamentary committee in August 2021 and released a list of properties he said belonged to Ruto. For a long period of time, Ruto had kept his wealth secret.

However, Matiang'i's expose` laid the hustler-man bare in what was a scripted act of unspeakable humiliation for Ruto. Testifying before the parliamentary national security and administration committee, Matiang'i revealed that 257 armed officers were assigned to guard Ruto's properties around the country. The message was that Ruto had "a lot of property" hence the large security contingent. According to the cabinet secretary, that was the highest number of guards assigned to anyone other than the president, whose security personnel numbered around 3,000.

The intended exposure by Matiang'i followed demands by Ruto allies for the government to explain why it had withdrawn the elite General Service Unit (GSU) security officers from Ruto's properties. The GSU officers had been removed and replaced by the low-graded Administration Police officers. Authorities said the move was a normal re-assignment of duties, but Ruto allies smelt mischief. Ruto himself said the move was a political vendetta to endanger his life.

In his political career, Ruto has faced numerous challenges questioning his integrity. One scandal of 2009 almost ended his future dreams. At that time, he was serving in the Kibaki government as minister for agriculture. An audit report by the PricewaterhouseCoopers alleged Ruto had asked his personal assistant to write a letter requesting an allocation of 1,000 bags of maize from the National Cereals and Produce Board (NCPB).

Ruto was among several officials cited in the scandal, among them the then permanent secretary, Romano Kiome, and two officials in the Prime Minister Raila's office. The report alleged that the officials bought maize cheaply from government stores for sale to millers at exorbitant profits. One was accused of buying as much as 10,000 bags of maize from the NCPB.

Ruto denied responsibility and shifted the blame to other officials and agencies in government. However, he admitted writing the letter to assist a disabled person though the grains were not supplied. "I don't see a crime in that." MPs wanted Ruto impeached. Others called for his resignation. Ruto said he was innocent and insisted he would not resign. The chairman of the Public Accounts Committee (PAC), Bonny Khalwale, tabled a motion in parliament to censure Ruto, but the Speaker rejected the evidence.

In October 2010, Ruto appeared in court together with a fellow MP, Sammy Mwaita, and businessperson Joshua Kulei, on fraud charges over the sale of a piece of land in Ngong Forest in January 2009. Ruto had been suspended a few days earlier as minister for higher education, science, and technology, pending the outcome of the KSh.272 million fraud case. It was alleged the accused sold the land to the Kenya Pipeline Company, a government parastatal, a decade earlier. It was further alleged that Ruto had pocketed KSh.96 million from the deal as facilitation fee. On April 11, 2011 – soon after Ruto's return from The Hague over the 2007/2008 post-election violence, Chief Magistrate Gilbert Mutembei, ruled that there was no sufficient evidence to put the three on their defence. The case was thrown out.

In January 2020, the government reopened investigations into the forest land deal. That was after Deputy President Ruto had broken up politically with President Uhuru over the 2018 "handshake" between Uhuru and Raila. No one knows why the government decided to reopen the case nine years after the accused had been acquitted. But investigators said they wanted to know how the KSh.272 million was distributed and who benefited from the loot. By the time of the 2022 elections, the matter was still in the hands of the directorate of criminal investigations (DCI).

Another matter which discomfited Ruto happened early in 2020. It revolved around an ally who was also a former cabinet secretary and a meeting which took place in the boardroom of his official office. CTTV footage showed the former ally accessing Ruto's Harambee House Annex office on February 13, 2000, accompanied by two white foreigners. The foreigners were reportedly executives of an American company who were made to understand that they were in the building to meet the DP to discuss a KSh.39 billion arms sale for the MOD.

It turned out that the former official had allegedly intended to defraud the foreigners by pretending he could help them secure a tender involving the supply of military equipment to MOD. The foreigners were identified as Mustafa Lofty and Stanley Kozlowski Bruno, directors of a company called Eco Advanced Technologies.

Ruto did not deny that the meeting took place in his official office but explained that he was neither present nor knew of the arrangement. In a tweet, Ruto said his office did not procure for government ministries and departments and wondered whether the involved individuals had also visited the MOD. And if so, who did they meet? Ruto asked in sheer amazement. He further claimed the whole issue was a "choreographed smear campaign" by his political enemies. Investigators later said that a fictitious tender document in the possession of the former Cabinet Secretary had the signature of the Defence Cabinet Secretary Ambassador Monica Juma. It turned out Juma had nothing to do with the letter which could have been a forgery.

Four uniformed officers who were on duty on the day of the incident were suspended. A few days later, Richard Echesa, who was once a cabinet secretary for sports, was arrested and charged along with three others, Daniel Otieno Omondi, Kennedy Oyoo, and Clifford Okoth. They were arraigned on six counts of conspiracy to defraud and obtaining KSh.11.5 million from Bruno by false pretences. Echesa pleaded not guilty. The accused were eventually let free for lack of evidence.

A man of overwhelming charisma and political savvy, Ruto is also a devoted Christian who often likes to quote from the Bible. He even dreams of being a preacher after leaving politics. During the ten years as DP, Ruto became the enemy of most of the people in the government he helped to construct. He was hounded by the executive, summoned by parliament, bashed for his bottom-up economic model, accused of grand corruption, set up for an arms scam, deluded of his crack security unit, punished by the courts, and humiliated, as he tried to fly out to Uganda. He was even threatened with eviction from his official residence in Karen by Jubilee stalwarts. All in all, it was a turbulent decade for a man whose mantra was: no surrender no retreat.

Ruto lost friends as fast as he found new friends. Uhuru and Raila, his erstwhile friends, drifted away so did Kalonzo Musyoka, and for a while Musalia Mudavadi and Moses Wetang'ula, but he won new ones, mostly young, ambitious, and determined, leaders in all the counties including Uhuru's and Raila's Central and Nyanza strongholds. Old alliances morphed into new ones until 2021 when Ruto said enough was enough. He pledged to proceed without the entanglements of coalitions and personalities in alliances. He aligned himself with UDA, a vehicle for his 2022 presidential bid.

Initially, Ruto refused to allow other parties to join him as equal partners in UDA. But as Raila's campaign gained momentum, he changed his mind and agreed to work with others in a coalition. His biggest catch was Musalia Mudavadi, leader of ANC and partner in OKA with Musyoka, Wetang'ula, and Gideon Moi. During his party's national delegates conference (NDC) at Bomas of Kenya on January 23, 2022, Mudavadi made the much anticipated 'earthquake' announcement. He declared he was dumping the nascent coalition for an association with Ruto and his UDA. The move was a big blow to Raila and his cohorts in Jubilee and prompted Uhuru to admit he was "disappointed" with Mudavadi. They had tried for months to lure him into their camp, but at the end Mudavadi saw UDA as the best option for his political survival.

By that time, Ruto's short-term lone ranger crusade had already plunged the country into further ethnic divisions, threatening to return the country to the ethnic conundrum of 2007/2008. The populous western Kenya once a Raila stronghold was split between various small parties, so was the coast, central Kenya, eastern and northern Kenya. Ruto's own Rift Valley region broke up in two large pieces, one controlled by Ruto and the other by Gideon Moi. Even clan elders were divided over who to bestow the leadership of the vote-rich region. In central Kenya, Kikuyu elders allied to the Kiama

Kia-Ma group complained that Ruto was dividing the region by putting a wedge between the various Kikuyu leaders. While Uhuru described Ruto as "dishonest and unsuitable to lead," others like MP Moses Kuria, claimed the UDA leader had "liberated Mt. Kenya from political repression" [of the Kenyattas] and deserved the presidency.

Studies have shown that polarisation breeds violence. In Kenya, violence, based on ethnic lines, had occurred around almost every general election since the 1990s. Jennifer McCoy, Tahmina Rahman, and Murat Somer, in their paper titled "Polarisation and the Global Crisis of Democracy," believe that polarisation occurs whenever a country's politics revolve around an axis of personal charisma and authority, as it does in Kenya.

Analysts have warned of political instability should the ruling class of the Kenyattas and Odingas leave. The departure of the two families could create a vacuum of violence as seen in the pass and degrade democracy,[289] they aver.

That is to be seen. But the unequivocal truth is that Kenya will survive as a nation beyond the Kenyattas and the Odingas.

---

[289] Montesano, Tad. Dynasty Politics in Democracy: Kenyattas, Odinga, and Democratic Erosion in Kenya, 9 December 2020.

CHAPTER 22

Uhuru's Scorecard

"President Uhuru has turned to a dictator;" "Sonko: President Uhuru is a dictator;" "Justin Muturi accuses Uhuru of dictatorship," "Is President Uhuru Kenyatta a dictator?" "Kenya – Does Uhuru want to be a dictator?" "Shock as Ruto says Uhuru is turning into a dictator." These are just a few newspapers headlines that dominated the subject during Uhuru's term.

Truth be told, Uhuru was no Idi Amin of Uganda, nor was he Jean-Bedel Bokassa of the Central African Republic, two of Africa's most brutal dictators. Nor was Uhuru his father, Mzee Jomo Kenyatta, or Daniel arap Moi, who oppressed and detained opponents, embraced single party systems, and ruled by iron fist.

As he left office after the August 9, 2022, elections, President Uhuru was no longer the "callow young man with skinny legs," portrayed in my earlier work, *The Politics of Betrayal*. He was "beefy, chubby-cheeked, and pot-bellied," emblematic of a decade of privileged, stately life, at the seat of power. He was also a more seasoned politician and, like his father, an internationally recognised leader.

In many ways though, Uhuru was closer to Mzee Kenyatta and President Moi in terms of governance style, than to President Kibaki. The former was cut from the same cloth of imperiousness and haughtiness. Unlike Mzee Kenyatta and Moi, however, Uhuru did not detain anyone nor operate the Nyayo House-like torture chambers. But he did suppress and intimidate the media, passed some draconian laws, harboured dynastic insolence, and abused the rule of law.

It is therefore safe to say that Uhuru's presidency was in part a return to his father's "assuming to oneself the state's capacity for domination."[290] Was that enough to classify him a dictator? Some say yes! Others disagreed, yet some dismissed Uhuru as a passive dictator simply because he used proxies, such as parliament, to fight his unscrupulous war for him.[291]

Like his father and President Moi, Uhuru encouraged the suppression of press freedom and free expressions. The arrest of journalists attested to that. In November 2015, the *Daily Nation* group editor, John Ngirachu, was arrested and detained for a night for writing an article about corruption in the interior ministry. Ngirachu had queried why the ministry had spent KSh.3.8 billion in a single day. The government said the information in the article was "confidential" and thus aimed at igniting mass action against Uhuru's government.

But Tom Mshindi, the editor-in-chief of the publication called the arrest a "strong-arm tactic" to intimidate journalists. Also arrested on the same issue was a parliamentary reporter of the *Standard*, Alphonse Shiundu. No charges were filed against the two. In December 2016, Jerome Starkley of *The Times*, was arrested at the JKIA after arriving from the UK. He was deported. The government did not give reasons for his expulsion.

Uhuru also clamped down on opponents and applied 'Big Man' tactics of deflating the judiciary and parliament to give himself more powers. He also allowed law enforcement bodies to kill people extra-judicially, thus threatening to turn the country into a "police state." So, did that make him a dictator? Under Uhuru, independent media still enjoyed some freedoms. Television programmes such as *The News Gang* on *Citizen* occasionally criticised Uhuru and his government,

---

[290] Burbidge, Dominic. The Shadow of Kenyan Democracy: Widespread Expectations of Widespread Corruption, Taylor & Francis, 2016, p. 45.
[291] Githinji, George. "Is President Uhuru Kenyatta a dictator," *The Saturday Standard*, May 1, 2016.

and writers sometimes got away with harsh critiques of the system. But only to a certain level.

Similarly, both the judiciary and parliament were seemingly independent, notwithstanding a spattering of negative rhetoric occasionally coming from the executive. But Uhuru didn't command absolute power nor oppose political pluralism. Based on that, it can be concluded that Uhuru was not a dictator like Mzee Kenyatta and Moi. But he did possess dictatorial tendencies.

There is a Swahili proverb which says: *Siku njema huonekana asubuhi* (A good day manifests itself in the morning). And it did that just four months after Uhuru took over in 2013. A group of demonstrators converged outside parliament to protest the enactment of the Security Laws (Amendment) Bill 2014. The bill was passed amid yelling and near fistfights, as a section of MPs dismissed it as draconian and likely to turn the country into a police state. The opposers complained that the drafters of the legislation disregarded provisions of the Bill of Rights which guaranteed free expression. The police used teargas and dispersed the crowd.

The bill, signed into law by Uhuru on December 19, 2024, had 109 new provisions and 21 amendments to the existing provisions. The Security Laws Amendment Act gives the NIS more power to surveil online communications as a security precaution. It also restricts press freedom because it requires journalists to obtain permission from authorities before publishing stories on domestic terrorism and other security matters. The government explained the law was necessary to give the president additional powers to deal with militants. But the Act also has disdainful provisions like the one providing a ten-year jail term for anyone who intentionally "insulted the modesty of any other person by forcibly stripping such a person," which was seen to be politically motivated.

Opposition MPs and the International Press Institute (IPI) claimed the changes were only another move to entrench 'executive dictatorship' in the country. "If you ever needed proof that the country is relapsing into dictatorship,' said Senate Minority Leader Moses Wetang'ula, 'this is it." *The Daily Nation* nailed it with the question: So, Uhuru Wants to be a Dictator? Then went on to say:

"Kenyatta should not sneak dictatorship in through the back door. If he wants to be an authoritarian like Moi or Kenyatta Senior, the paper added, "Let him call a referendum on a new constitution. Shredding the current one and trying to rule by executive fiat is dishonest and deceitful."[292] Uhuru allies like MP Moses Kuria, rubbished the dictatorship tag saying, "The issue about dictatorship is an argument without any proof."[293]

A television journalist, Larry Madowo, claimed Uhuru aspired to become another African strongman. "When peaceful protesters are violently dispersed or demonstrations outlawed entirely… when journalists are too scared to keep the people in power accountable, and the opposition is harassed, and the rights of ordinary citizens infringed upon, what is that if not autocracy?[294] Another commentator likened Uhuru to Mzee Kenyatta and President Moi. [He] "… is slowly embodying the image of a dictator through a combination of co-opting Kenya's wealthy economic and political class, and brute force."[295]

Moreover, Uhuru's official speeches were full of imperious commands: "I direct…," "I order…," "I have instructed…" Sometimes those commands came not from him personally but from his trusted advisers including top civil servants and political appointees.

Ruto too denounced Uhuru's "dictatorial tendencies" in May 2020 when the president's Jubilee Alliance Party ousted Ruto allies from key positions in parliament and the senate. Sixteen MPs who had expressed support for Ruto were removed from parliamentary committees. Senators Kipchumba Murkomen and Susan Kihika were kicked out as senate Majority Leader and Majority Whip,

---

[292] Mutiga, Murithi. "Kenya – Does Uhuru Kenyatta want to be a dictator?" *Daily Nation*, December 8, 2013.
[293] Ayaga, Wilfred. "Dictatorial tendencies' tag stalks Uhuru Kenyatta's regime to 2015," Pan African Visions, December 30, 2014.
[294] Madowo, Larry. "Opinion: Kenya is sliding into a dictatorship," *The Washington Post*, February 7, 2018.
[295] "How Kenyatta has gone about stifling the free press in Kenya," *The Conversation*, February 7, 2018.

respectively. Kithure Kindiki, the deputy speaker in the senate was also ejected, so were the Majority Leader Benjamin Washiali, and his deputy, Cecily Mbarire, among others. Early in 2022, Uhuru's Jubilee decided to remove from committee positions more MPs allied to Ruto. The Jubilee Alliance Party's slogan, *Tuko Pamoja*, (We are together), was thrown out of the window. It was replaced with another similar fuzzy slogan, *Mbele Pamoja* (Ahead together).

Following the president's remarks in June 2020; that his successor would only be a person who valued his legacy, an ally of DP Ruto, MP Soy Kositany, called Uhuru the "worst dictator ever." Uhuru's legacy suffered immeasurable damage when he chose and then vigorously campaigned for Raila to be his preferred successor. By choosing his successor, Uhuru was repeating history. In 2002, Moi did the same thing. He dumped his vice president, George Saitoti, in favour of Uhuru.

"No no no!" shouted Ruto. "Stop insulting us by imposing Raila on us." Moses Wetang'ula his colleague in the Kenya Kwanza coalition had similar advice. "Uhuru, don't soil your legacy by imposing Raila on us."

During his ten-year rule, Uhuru did not hide his admiration for President Moi. He followed his *nyayo* philosophy religiously and, when he was alive, consulted him regularly. Like his predecessor who wanted people to 'sing' like Moi, Uhuru expected his subordinates and surrogates to do exactly what he said. Some in Jubilee known for their scrupulous and chivalrous loyalty to Uhuru, even prayed that their leader would find a way of manipulating the constitution and go for a third five-year term either as president or prime minister. "Uhuru is too young to retire from politics," a sycophantic Francis Atwoli, kept on repeating. Uhuru himself ruled out 'complete' exit from the political arena. He said as chairman of Jubilee he would continue to comment on political issues. Raila, on the other hand, promised to appoint Uhuru as his economic adviser if elected.

Uhuru also followed his father's norms when it came to treating colleagues in politics, some in his own party, Jubilee. During his time, Mzee Kenyatta treated his ministers and senior officials like "junior schoolboys' occasionally using his cane to drive his point home. At one time, he threatened to beat up his vice president, Murumbi, after a disagreement, according to Murumbi's own admission in his book, *A Path Not Taken: The Story of Joseph Murumbi*. Although Uhuru was not as excessive, he did not shy away from berating his men in public. Angry at losing a by-election in his home ground of Juja in May 2021, for example, Uhuru chased everyone away, including government officials, from State House, "telling them he never wanted to see them in the next coming days."[296]

He also went ballistic at a State House summit in October 2016 attended by top law enforcement and administrative officials. For "19 minutes and 15 seconds, the president lamented about the lacklustre performance of the judiciary, the director of public prosecutions, the AG, the auditor general, and the directorate of criminal investigation,"[297] for their inaction in tackling corruption. He exonerated himself from blame but did not spare his officials "It is you who have slept on the job," he told the bewildered officials.

Like his father, Uhuru was quick to anger. At the Madaraka Day celebrations in 2022, Uhuru harangued, raised his voice, and appeared emotionally agitated at his deputy and those who didn't appreciate his achievements.

Signs of the continuation of Mzee Kenyatta and President Moi dictatorships were clear when Uhuru's portrait went up in all public institutions and businesses soon after his inauguration. Many had expected their 'modern' leader to discard that archaic, colonial, legacy, but no, he opted to follow his predecessors. When at the height of a clash between Uhuru and Raila in 2016, the Siaya governor, Cornel Rasanga, told traders to display Raila's portrait instead of Uhuru's on their premises, the interior ministry hit back. It threatened to impose fines against traders who failed to display Uhuru's picture. The same thing happened in 1968. Mzee Kenyatta's government warned of unspecified penalties against those who didn't display the president's portrait. And in 1973, Mzee Kenyatta went further and ordered

---

[296] Mbati, John. "Uhuru Kicks Out Officials from State House After Mt Kenya Losses," *Kenyans.co.ke*, May 20, 2021.

[297] Nyamori, Moses. "President Uhuru roasts top officers over holes in corruption war," *Standard*, October 19, 2016.

"business, sports, political and ethnic associations, to stop using the title 'president.'" All those were signs of dictatorial tendencies.

Mzee Kenyatta's image also flashed like an imperial king on currency notes. On top of that, his statue outside Kenyatta International Convention Centre (KICC) "sits like a golem on the humongous compound... One has to wonder if Jomo Kenyatta's wasn't strategically, and ironically, placed, to show that his concrete will would rule over Kenya, forever, like a giant shadow,"[298] Tom Mochama wrote poetically.

In October 2020, Uhuru's cabinet approved measures to force politicians to seek approval from the police before holding public meetings. The measures were recommended by the National Security Advisory Committee (NSAC) which he formed to clamp down on gatherings. Under the directive, politicians were required to obey orders of the Officer Commanding [Police] Stations (OCS), in a move intended to tame political incitement and violence in political rallies, social media, and the mainstream media.

Those attending such meetings were also required to be peaceful and not to be in possession of any weapons. Attendees were also to respect freedom of expression of other people, and not abuse, exclude, or demean, other people. The measures, again taken directly from President Moi's playbook, were unnecessary, given the fact that the constitution already guaranteed freedom of expression and movement and approved peaceful protests and gatherings. There were also laws already governing the activities. The sad part of that directive was that it was only one person, the OCS, or his representative, who had the final say on whether a meeting took place or not. Such directives were common in dictatorships. Uhuru also appointed a high-powered multi-agency team to monitor compliance. The team comprised representatives from the interior ministry, the AG's office, the NIS, the National Police, and the Communications Authority of Kenya (CAK).

---

[298] Mochama, Tony A. Political Parties after Political Parties: The Changing Nature and Reality of Political Power in Kenya, Konrad Adenauer Stiftung, 2021.

Here is another example of Uhuru's dictatorial tendencies. In June 2021, a political analyst in the *Star* newspaper, Henry Makori, wrote a biting commentary, accusing Uhuru of having turned into a dictator. That he had violated the oath of office, betrayed public trust, and abused his authority. Makori said Uhuru should resign or be forced out through civil disobedience. The stinging article immediately caused a stir in official circles. Some expressed shock at the writer's apparent dauntless courage. Following pressure from the top, the *Star* withdrew the article barely eight hours after it appeared online. Although Uhuru was persuaded to keep his cool, thus debunking the common perception of an arm-twisting dictator, the very fact that he got the newspaper to withdraw the article showed the level of intolerance by his government.

A prominent lawyer, Dr. John Khaminwa, who was himself a victim of detention under President Moi, did not have any kind words for Uhuru when he stood before the Court of Appeal in July 2021. He was making submissions on whether the Kenya constitution should be amended as per BBI. He inveighed against Uhuru's regime and oligarchs and tribal demagogues supporting the regime. Short of calling Uhuru a dictator, Khaminwa said Uhuru and his cronies stood for "nothing… and simply seek power to enrich themselves." He claimed that through the amendments Uhuru planned to extend his term in office by trickery.

Former justice minister in President Kibaki's government, Martha Karua, called Uhuru a "modern dictator" because, she said, he used 'modern methods of changing the constitution,' through unconstitutional means. Conversely, both David Kipkorir, a prominent lawyer, and David Murathe, a close Uhuru ally, urged Uhuru to apply 'benevolent dictatorship' to make things work for him. "Our age-mates; Malaysia, Thailand, South Korea and Singapore, developed because they were led by benevolent dictators," Kipkorir averred. The two wanted Uhuru to be like Presidents Paul Kagame of Rwanda and Yoweri Museveni of Uganda who changed laws to strike out age limits for the president, so that Uhuru could rule 'for life.'

In January 2008, the Uhuru government shut down three local television stations, NTV, KTN, Citizen TV, for ignoring a government directive against live coverage of the sham swearing-in of Raila as the "peoples' president." They did that after Uhuru summoned and warned senior editors that he would shut down their stations and revoke their licences if they aired Raila's swearing-in event. The four independent stations ignored the warning and broadcast the event live. The following day, security officers camped at *Nation* House to arrest three senior journalists, Linus Kaikai, Larry Madowo, and Ken Mijungu. The journalists had to spend the night at the NTV newsroom for fear of arrest. The following day, lawyers went to court and obtained anticipatory bail to bar the police from arresting them. The stations remained closed for several days.

After Raila's mock 'swearing in,' the government launched a major crackdown on members of the opposition. Security officers raided their houses, arrested, and prosecuted them. They also withdrew their bodyguards, official cars, and guns. Some MPs allied to Raila spent nights at parliament buildings fearing arrest. "The younger Kenyatta's tough stance has gotten some pundits pondering whether the Jomo [Kenyatta] in Uhuru has woken up...."[299]

From early during his rule, Uhuru had tried to coax the media by inviting them to tea and lunch parties at State House in the hope of stopping them from bashing his regime. It began with a breakfast meeting with top editors and journalists of mainstream media on July 11, 2013. In his brief remarks, Uhuru said the meeting marked the "opening of a new chapter in press-state relations" and "an outreach to various stakeholders in our economic, political, and social scene." He talked of a free press and expressed a commitment to ensure "the media can effectively support our democracy by promoting prudent governance." The State House meeting received disparaging criticisms in the social media. But the meeting produced what Uhuru had wanted all along: positive coverage of the government in the wake of the ICC indictment.

In addition, Uhuru dangled a sweet potato in front of the media by appointing a handful of journalists to government positions.

---

[299] Obonyo, Oscar. "Uhuru ruthlessness in silencing critics a replica of Jomo's style," Sunday Nation, February 18, 2018.

Radio broadcaster Caroline Mutoko was appointed to the board of the Kenya Institute of Mass Communication. Also appointed to that board was a journalist working for *Citizen TV*, Farida Karonney. She was later elevated to Cabinet Secretary Lands and Physical Planning. Another beneficiary was TV anchor Julie Gichuru who joined the board of Brand Kenya.

The breakfast meeting was followed by dinner at Norfolk Hotel in November 2013. In that invites-only affair, only journalists considered sympathetic to the Jubilee Alliance Party were invited. The friendship between the state and the media did not last long, however. In December, angered by government attempts to push through the Information and Communication (Amendment) Bill, 2013, hundreds of journalists across the country came out to demonstrate on the streets. They sealed their mouths with tape to illustrate media gagging and carried placards denouncing the legislation.

In Nairobi, members of the Kenya Union of Journalists (KUJ) and the Kenya Editors Guild (KEG) handed over a petition to officials at the Office of the President. By the beginning of Uhuru's second term in 2017, the Kenya media had become so toxic against the government that officials were threatening journalists. Justus Wanga, a journalist at the *Nation* Media wrote a story about a split between Uhuru and Ruto over the appointment of the cabinet which was not viewed favourably by the executive.

"*Unataka kufutwa kazi? Ukitaka kufutwa kazi utafutwa, utafutwa, sikudanganyi, utafutwa…* (Do you want to lose your job? If you want to be sacked, you will be sacked, sacked, I am not lying, you will be sacked). Ruto's spokesman, David Mugonyi, reportedly told the journalist through texts.

"I am telling you for free," he told Wanga, "there are people who have crossed that path before…you are not the first journalist my friend,"

No one censored Mugonyi, a former journalist, for that unbecoming behaviour.

The most egregious 'dictatorial tendency' on Uhuru's part was his efforts to change the constitution through the BBI to create positions for a select group of elites. That move was meant to burnish his image and cement his legacy. It had zero benefit for the wider population. That move appeared to comply with what the former Nigerian President General Olusegun Obasanjo (himself a creation of a military dictatorship) stated: that the anti-colonialism struggles in Africa were "waged as much to end foreign rule, racial bigotry, and the associated indignities as to extirpate illiteracy and all manner of backwardness. Yet, no soon had colonial rule ended that our new rulers set about converting the revolution into one of fire and thunder against their own population."[300] Indeed, the BBI was an anti-Wanjiku initiative meant to fatten a few and impoverish many.

* * *

The table below shows President Uhuru and Ruto's promises and an assessment of whether they were achieved or not. Not all the promises were fulfilled partly because of money crunch and the effects of Covid-19. But Kenyans saw fulfilment of some of those promises.

PROMISE	SCORECARD
1. Corruption	*Not delivered*. Remember Uhuru promising some of the toughest anti-graft laws? In 2016, he signed the Bribery Bill aimed at criminalising corruption in the private sector. He also took measures to make it easier for the judiciary to deal with corruption cases. Those moves, and others, did not amount to much. Corruption remains a monumental challenge for the country.

---

[300] Assensoh, A. B. & Alex-Assensoh, M. Corrupt and Dictatorial Tendencies: The Tacit Invitation for Military Intervention, African Military History and Politics, 2001, pp. 61-79.

2.	Health	*Largely Delivery.* Uhuru promised that "Within the first 100 days we will ensure that maternity fees are abolished, and that all citizens of Kenya are able to access government dispensaries and health centres free of charge."
3.	Food Security	*Not delivered.* Food security was one of the promises Uhuru made to the people of Kenya. That "We become a food-secure nation by investing in and modernizing the agricultural sector by equipping it with the relevant information and technology it needs to grow." Thus in 2013, the Uhuru administration identified the Galana-Kulalu project at the coast as one that would propel food production in the country. That project has floundered. In short, the food situation at the end of Jubilee government was as dire as it was before the Uhuru administration assumed office. As the prices of maize meal, sugar, cooking oil, and other necessities surged, Kenyans resorted to the social media to blame Uhuru and the Jubilee government. By January 2022, food prices had risen by 8.89%, according to the Kenya National Bureau of Statistics. Saddled with election campaign pressures, politicians maintained an uneasy silence.

4.	Affordable housing	*Partly delivered.* Uhuru announced in November 2021, that 186,000 housing units had been built during the previous four years. That was still far too short of the 500,000 units Uhuru had promised to deliver. However, construction was still ongoing in mid-2022. The finished houses were sold to Kenyans at a reasonable price. For example, a 30 sq m one-bedroom flat was sold at KSh.1.5 million, a 2-bedroom 40 sqm flat at KSh.2 million and a 3-bedroom unit of 80 sqm at KSh.4 million.
5.	Infrastructure development	*Delivered.* (See below)
6.	Laptop in Schools	Not delivered. One of the biggest failures of the Uhuru government was the much-touted school laptop project. It was part of the main Jubilee election promises.
7.	Coordination in government	*Partially delivered.* Problems in governance was caused by the schism between the President and his deputy emanating from the handshake. The incessant wrangles between the executive and the judiciary threatened a constitutional crisis.
8.	Poverty reduction	*Not delivered.* In 2022, an estimated 8.9 million Kenyans, especially in rural areas, lived in extreme poverty.
9.	Free Wi-Fi in major towns	*Partly delivered.* Only Nakuru city managed to install free Wi-Fi for its citizens. The city is the third in Africa to enjoy free digital services. The others are Kigali in Rwanda and Tshwana in South Africa.

10. Dams	*Partly delivered.* Some dams such as the KSh. 11 billion Thiba dam and the KSh. 28 billion Karimenu dam in Gatundu were completed. But others like the Arror and Kimwarer in the Rift Valley, and the High Grand Falls Dam in River Tana, stalled for a variety of reasons including corruption. Construction at Itare dam also stopped due to tendering disputes.
11. The Gender Rule	*Not delivered.*
12. Insecurity	*Partly delivered.* Threats of attacks from the terrorist group Al-Shabaab lingered throughout Uhuru's term. Efforts by the government to stop serious attacks by terrorists on soft targets appear to be paying off. However, at 61.71%, the rate of violent crime was classified as 'high' in November 2021, but much lower than the rate of corruption and bribery which was 'very high' at 84.39%.[301] Cases of killings, kidnappings, suicides, rape, and violent robberies were rampant.
13. Title Deeds	*Partially delivered.* Five-point-one million title deeds were issued by the end of 2021. Thousands more title deeds were issued by Uhuru in 2022. However, millions of Kenyans still live as squatters in many parts of the country, especially at the coast and the Rift Valley. Hundreds of displaced persons, victims of past political violence, were still homeless when Uhuru left office.

---

[301] Safety in Kenya, Numbeo, 2021.

14. One million three hundred thousand jobs	*Not delivered.*
15. Rebuilding Kenya's image regionally and globally	*Partially delivered.*
16. National unity	*Not delivered.* The 2022 elections and tribal politics polarised Kenyans. Years of mistrust between the Kikuyu and Kalenjin continued. The 'handshake' alliance between Uhuru and Raila helped to reduce tensions, but divisions between Uhuru and Ruto re-opened new wounds. One only needs to scan social media to see the hatred, vitriol, and utter divisions in the country.
17. Accountability and inclusiveness	*Not delivered.* Public servants continued to loot taxpayers' money through corruption and fraud despite efforts to close loopholes in procurement of government stores.
18. Stadiums	*Partly delivered.* Work on new stadiums continued months before the end of Uhuru's term. It had been expected that one new stadium would be ready in each of the 47 counties by August 2022, but progress was hampered by financial constraints and tendering disputes.
19. Enhanced manufacturing capability	*Not delivered.*
20. Comprehensive statement on his family's wealth	*Not delivered.* Uhuru promised to issue a comprehensive statement on his family's wealth stashed in overseas account. He never did.

21. Life-style audit	*Not fulfilled*. Uhuru promised to subject himself, his deputy, and all civil servants, to personal audits as evidence of his commitment towards eradicating corruption. That never happened.
22. Contract Kenya signed with China	*Not fulfilled*. Uhuru promised to release the contract Kenya signed with China on the construction and maintenance of the SGR. He never did.
23. Standards of living	*Not fulfilled*. Uhuru's promise in 2017 to reduce the cost of living by stabilizing the cost of basic foodstuffs, energy, and transport, was not met. Prices of foods and fuel skyrocketed in 2021, pushed high by supply chain issues resulting from the Covid-19 pandemic. The war in Ukraine was also blamed for shortages and high consumer prices. That trend continued into 2022, thanks to increased fuel costs. Kenyans' complaints about exorbitant food prices fell on deaf years.
24. Reduced cost of electricity	*Partly fulfilled*. During the Jamhuri Day celebrations in 2021, Uhuru promised cheaper electricity. He vowed to cut down the cost of electricity for domestic and commercial consumers by 30% by the beginning of 2022. He did it. But for many Kenyans, the cost of electricity is still prohibitive.
25. Economic crimes	*Partly Fulfilled*. Uhuru promised to increase penalties for economic crimes. That was achieved as seen in the large penalties meted out by courts. But still pending were dozens of corruption-related cases, most of which involved prominent citizens. The courts were unable to cope.

| 26. Free maternity services | *Delivered.* |

They also promised a lean, rationalised, and well-coordinated government, the rule of law, reinvigorating the private sector and national unity. Below are further comments on the promises.

Economy

Kenya's economy is on a downward spiral. Experts predicted a deceleration of growth caused by increase in food and fuel import costs. It is projected to hit 5.9% in 2022 but will decline in 2023 to 5.7%. Gains were achieved after recovery from Covid-19 in 2021, propelling the country's economic growth to 7.5%.

The depreciation of the Kenya shilling meant higher prices for imported goods such as farm inputs, electronics, cars, and others. The decline was caused largely by dollar shortage. In May 2022, the shilling was at the high rate of 116 per dollar.

During his eighth State of the Union address in parliament on December 1, 2021, Uhuru boasted that the GDP had grown from KSh.4.74 trillion when he took over to KSh.11 trillion.

Health

More than 1.2 million mothers up from 600,000 mothers can now access prenatal and natal care in health facilities. More modern hospital equipment such as radiology, and imaging machines, ICU beds, and ultrasound machines, were purchased, substantially increasing the capacity in public health facilities. Six hundred and three dialysis machines were acquired and distributed to all 47 counties. In 2013, there were only 26 dialysis machines.

Overall, the government supplied 1,241 pieces of specialised medical equipment to 113 hospitals. Uhuru's government also built 25 new hospitals in Nairobi, installed six renal units, bringing the total units to 54. When he took over government, the bed capacity in public health facilities was 56,069 hospital beds. By 2020, according to Uhuru, the capacity had gone up by 47% to 82,291 beds.

Some of Uhuru's legacy projects in the health sector such as the universal health coverage, and the nationwide mental health initiative, were suspended. Months ahead of his departure, it was announced the administration had signed an agreement with the pharmaceutical company, Moderna, to build a state-of-the-art facility in Kenya to produce vaccines. That was a major medical coup for the Jubilee government that would most likely be one of Uhuru's biggest legacies. The KSh.57 billion plant will produce up to 500 million doses per year of the mRNA vaccine when in operation.

Food security

In 2014, a contract was given to an Israeli company, Green Arava Limited, for the implementation of a 10,000-acre model farm at Galana-Kulalu Irrigation Scheme. However, the contract was faulty. It was single-sourced and gave the company an advantage in the "competitive bidding, pricing, capacity and competence," said the Auditor General Edward Ouko. This meant Green Avara Limited would manage the proceeds from production leaving the government at its mercy. There was another problem. The designing firm was associated with the contractor. Ouko feared the conflict of interest could lead to poor designs.

After spending KSh.5.9 billion of taxpayers' money, or 80% of the total cost, the project in Kilifi and Tana River counties was abandoned in July 2019, after a dispute over payments between the government and the Israeli contractor. The Israeli Ambassador to Kenya, Noah Gal, blamed what he called "people with vested interests who have fought the project from day one."[302] He did not elaborate. By that time, 85% of the model farm had been completed.

In December 2020, the government commissioned a new contractor, Irrico Kenya, and tasked it to complete the first phase

---

[302] Kibii, Eliud & Ngotho, Agatha. "Drought Exposes Collapse of Galana Kulalu Project," *The Star*, 2 April 2019.

of the project for KSh.797 million by June 2021. The company was to install additional pumps and rehabilitate the water intake at the farm. Irrigation was to be used for production of maize, bananas, and mangoes. The fate of that phase could not be determined.

Kenya has faced serious food shortages over the years due to inadequate rains and desert locust invasions. The growth of the population by 32% when Uhuru assumed office to over 56 million people, and the Covid-19 pandemic worsened the food situation. Rural areas where most of the food was produced suffered from increased transportation costs due to fuel increases and market supply chain slowdowns caused by Covid-19 and shutdowns.

There were a series of increases of prices of petroleum products. In June, the government hiked the price of a litre of super petrol to KSh. 159.12 and diesel KSh. 140. Users of kerosene were to pay KSh. 127.94 per litre, a record high.

Infrastructure development

Uhuru's pride was the construction of the Standard Gauge Railway (SGR) from Nairobi to Mombasa which has not only eased transportation to the coast by road but also cut down to almost half the duration of travel time. The only downside about the SGR was the massive corruption that accompanied the project.

Eleven thousand kilometres of roads were built, including the 17-kilometre Dongo Kundu Bypass Highway, connecting Mombasa mainland west to Mombasa mainland south. The Bypass left taxpayers KSh.24 billion poorer, but it has greatly supported tourism and trade between Kenya and Tanzania through the Lunga Lunga border crossing.

Also to Uhuru's credit were the first tarmac roads since independence, in Wajir, Lamu, and Samburu counties. The flagship project of the infrastructure initiative is the KSh.73.5 billion 27-kilometre Nairobi Expressway running from Mlolongo to James Gichuru Road. Each one of the counties got at least one road project. The Jubilee government promised to deliver 10,000 kilometres of paved road during the eight-year period. It exceeded that limit.

The Uhuru administration also built more airstrips, and a new port at Lamu - the second seaport in the country at a cost of KSh.310 billion. The Kisumu port was also revived. The government also installed a KSh.1.9 billion floating bridge at Likoni, connecting Mombasa and Lamu counties.

Laptops in Schools

In partnership with Microsoft, Kenya was to provide more than 400,000 free laptops to first graders. The choice of Microsoft to pilot this programme was mysterious, and even shady. There was no consultation with the people over the matter and no tendering. So how was Microsoft chosen? By Uhuru Kenyatta himself!

On June 4, 2013, Uhuru held a closed-door meeting with the president of Microsoft International, Jean-Philippe Courtois, at State House. Courtois had flown into Kenya to assure Kenya that his company was ready to supply the laptops and support the government in the training of primary school teachers. It was also to offer technical support in hardware, connectivity, and software. Each laptop was to cost KSh.30,000.

Microsoft's involvement was opposed by some technology institutions. Evans Iku of the Linux Professional Institute in Kenya, for example, said having Microsoft as the sole implementer was detrimental to the country. "... locking our children to one vendor's software platform is not only self-defeating but also immoral." While it could not be concluded that corruption played a role, the way the deal was concluded raised eyebrows among Kenyans.

The distribution process was scheduled to start in January 2017. Six thousand schools had been earmarked to pilot the project. In total 1.1 million pupils in 23,000 primary schools were to benefit.

What Uhuru did not take into consideration was the environment in which most schools operated. Many were not connected to electricity. In some schools, children were still learning under trees. Many schools did not have desks and pupils were sitting on stones. In addition, the majority of first grade teachers were computer illiterate. It was difficult from the beginning to fathom how the school laptop project would work. Critics like Wilson Sossion of the Kenya National Union of Teachers (KNUT) called the project 'illogical' and asked the government instead to build better schools, provide desks, and provide enough textbooks to schools.

The laptop project, described by government officials, as "complex and transformational," was in jeopardy because it was capricious and unreasonable. The government could not accommodate it in its budgets however much it tried. Cartels battled for tenders in and outside courts as they tried to elbow each other over the KSh.24.6 billion bounty.

Finally, in 2019, the government announced it was suspending it, putting to death one of the most ambitions legacy projects of the Uhuru presidency. The let-down was huge. By the time Uhuru left office in 2022, the children who would have benefited from the project were already in high school, some in college.

School development

Education, important as it is for any country's sustainable development, is one of the better budgeted sectors in Kenya. Expenditure on education has ranged from 13% in 1993 to 26% of the KSh.3.66 trillion 2021 budget. But even then, there were still hundreds of schools that were in deplorable conditions during Uhuru's term. Overcrowding and underfunding meant that many school did not have enough qualified teachers, had unmotivated teachers, had insufficient desks, had poorly constructed and inadequate latrines, and lacked recreational and other facilities.

So, when in 2017, the World Bank (WB) approved a project to improve school infrastructure, President Uhuru scored a major achievement. The WB through the International Development Association (IDA) was to pump in US$22 billion in credit into the Kenya Secondary Education Quality Improvement Project (KSEQIP). The credit was for a thirty-year duration with a grace period of five years, but the project itself was to be completed by 2023.

The ambitious project was intended to improve student learning in secondary schools and aid transition from primary to secondary education in targeted areas. It was also to improve quality of teaching, provide scholarships to the needy, and address the supply and demand issues constraining schools.

However, in January 2021 Uhuru suspended the project and refused to release the necessary funds needed for the project. Instead, the government ordered a fresh procurement process. Uhuru did not explain the reasons behind his decision to halt the project, but speculation pointed to infighting within government over tenders. The WB warned delay in signing contracts with construction companies would halt the project.

By the end of 2021, taxpayers were staring at the risk of losing tens of thousands of shillings in compensation by twenty-one companies that had been identified to construct dormitories, toilets, classrooms, and other facilities in schools. No formal contracts had been signed, but the government had issued letters of tender awards to the companies in 2020. When the Ministry of Education went to court to terminate contracts of four companies worth KSh.4 billion, the High Court stopped it. High Court Justice James Makau turned down the ministry's petition and ordered that no adverse action be taken by the government until the suit was determined.

CBC

To reform the educational sector, the Uhuru administration in 2017 introduced a new system of education called the Competency-Based Curriculum (CBC). Instead of pupils spending eight years in primary schools, four in secondary, and four at the university (8-4-4), they are now to spend two years in nursery, six years in primary school (lower and upper), three years junior secondary and three years in senior secondary, that is (2-6-3-3).

The changes were necessitated by myriad problems in the 8-4-4 system introduced in the 1980s that prompted parents to move children from public to private schools hoping to get better grades for entry into universities. There were also problems of corruption in ranking and placement in the old system. In some cases, admission letters were being sold for as much as KSh.100,000, making some school principals millionaires.[303]

However, as revolutionary as the new system may be, CBC has generated a mixed reaction from parents. Because the system calls for innovative creations from pupils like making paper scarecrows, vehicles, and wheelbarrow, among other things, parents must find time to assist in making those gadgets. Some of the assignments require the use of computers and internet, thus disadvantaging students from remote and poor areas of the country.

Others saw the changes as "noble." President Uhuru emphasised that the CBC was there to stay. But the shortages of teachers and classrooms, and lack of relevant equipment, could be detrimental to the future of the initiative.

"The 8-4-4 was a teacher-based system, where the teacher was at the centre of learning. This will not be the case anymore," one analyst said. He explained that the CBC was a student-based system giving the student the ability to self-learn and develop relevant skills for their future use."[304] With time, it will be seen whether the new system of education is tenable. The authenticity of the new CBC curriculum has been challenged in court.

Finance

Poverty and disease, two of the three challenges Mzee Kenyatta posed in 1964 – the other being illiteracy - remained troublesome during Uhuru's term. A survey by FinAccess in 2016 showed 17% of Kenyans had no access to financial services, meaning they did not operate a bank account, or use other services such as mobile money. The survey also revealed that 80% of the rural folk were excluded from financial services, so were 38% of the elderly over the age of 45,

---

[303] Amutabi, Maurice. Competency-Based on Curriculum (CBC) and the End of an Era in Kenya's Education Sector and Implications for Development: Some Empirical Reflections," *Journal of Popular Music Education*, Vol. 3, No. 10, March 2021, pp. 45-66.

[304] Dinda, Gabriel. "What is the philosophy of the new education curriculum in Kenya," Strathmore University, undated.

and 55% for females. The basic reason why such a large population of Kenyans shunned financial institutions was poverty. More than 40% of youths are jobless and therefore do not need financial services.

Without a steady income, many informal sector workers were unable to meet the usually restrictive requirements to open a bank account. Thus, a large population of Kenyans survived on loans from mobile providers. Nineteen million Kenyans have active mobile loans with 40% of that having at least six mobile lending accounts.[305] An estimated 400,000 Kenyans are defaulters with a stained record at the Credit Reference Bureau (CRB). To ease their burden, Uhuru ordered that loan defaulters of amounts up to KSh.5 million would not be blacklisted by the CRB. That moratorium was to last until September 2022.

1,300,000 jobs

Unemployment generally increased. Out of the approximately 50 million Kenyans only about 16 million were fully employed. Among the jobless were university graduates and high school leavers. The situation worsened at the height of Covid-19 in 2020. The much-anticipated expansion of new investments in manufacturing did not materialise.

One of the biggest failures of Uhuru's administration was its inability to control labour migration from Kenya to countries in the Arabia. The administration opened floodgates for employment agents to exploit desperate, jobless, Kenyans, for opportunities that often turned tragic. Thousands of young men and women travelled to Saudi Arabia, the UAE, Qatar, Bahrain, and Oman, in search of what they thought were greener pastures. While some survived the tough conditions subjected to them by employers, some did not. They were returned home in coffins.

In Saudi Arabia alone, more than 100 Kenyans, mostly domestic workers, died during Uhuru's term. Saudi Arabia officials claimed

---

[305] CyproGuru. 19 million Kenyans have active mobile loans with 40% being multiple mobile lenders, BitcoinKE, March 14, 2019.

most of them died of cardiac arrest, but former workers testified that deaths were often caused by physical abuse by employers. Employers confiscated the workers' passports and phones upon arrival in the new land, leaving them disadvantaged. Some were denied pay, and girls were subjected to rape and sexual abuse. In September 2021, the Kenya Ministry of Foreign Affairs imposed a temporary ban on recruitment of workers for jobs in Saudi Arabia. Local agents ignored the ban and continued to sneak Kenyans out of the country without proper contracts.

The Kenya embassy in Saudi Arabia and missions in the other Arab countries failed their nationals by ignoring their calls for help and refusing to take diplomatic action against offending employers. Bilateral agreements signed between Kenya and the various countries aimed at protecting the workers from exploitation have not helped. Kenyans there are on their own.

Similarly, the Kenya Central Organisation of Trade Unions (COTU), which should have been at the forefront of defending workers' rights did nothing to help because its head, a pouty voluble man with small pitiless eyes, was busy politicking than working for his employers.

Rebuilding Kenya's image regionally and globally

Apart from Somalia, Kenya existed peacefully with its neighbours. The internal war in Ethiopia between government forces and the Tigray Defence Forces (TDF) in northern Tigray region did not seriously affect Kenya. Uhuru tried to play a mediator in the conflict and managed in a small way to calm the situation. Additional diplomatic intervention came from the AU and the international community.

Enhanced manufacturing capability

Kenya faced several challenges in fulfilling Uhuru's promise to bolster the manufacturing sector. Higher unit costs of producing locally made products made it difficult for the country to compete with foreign companies. Another big challenge was the lack of stable and reliable energy. As explained earlier, electricity generating, and distribution agencies failed consumers in ensuring quality service. Kenya Electricity Transmission Company (Ketraco) promised in 2021 to invest heavily on more 400 kilovolts (KV) transmission lines to improve delivery. The first such line in the whole of East Africa covering the 482 km Mombasa-Nairobi-Suswa-Isinya stretch was launched in Mombasa by President Uhuru in 2017. Since then, nothing much seems to have been done. The Kenya Association of Manufacturers (KAM) listed corruption as a major hindrance to the development of the sector.

In the meantime, Uhuru scored one landmark manufacturing achievement. Kenya no longer must import certain types of weapons. In July 2021, the president launched a weapons factory at Dedan Kimathi University of Technology in Nyeri, which will save taxpayers millions of shillings every year.

CHAPTER 20

The Last Word

The term 'lame duck' describes a politician, especially a president, whose term in office is coming to an end and what remains is only to hand over power to a successor. A year before his term ended, Uhuru Kenyatta talked, acted, and behaved like a 'lame duck' president. According to the Brewer's Dictionary of Phrases and Fable, the term originated in the world of finance in London. It was first used to describe an out-of-luck broker who didn't pay his debts and had to "waddle out of the alley like a lame duck."

Over time, the term became a common expression in political science. Some describe the 'lame duck' period as "the last gaps of a dying giant."[306] For President Uhuru, the last year of his presidency was as electrifying as it was distressing. His influence waned. He became angry and unpredictable, often unleashing undesirable epithets. Three cabinet secretaries, Charles Keter, Devolution; John Munyes, Petroleum; and Adan Mohamed, East African Community Affairs, were among 30 State officials, including principal secretaries (PS) and chief administrative secretaries (CASs) who left government for elective positions in the 2022 elections. For two years, major

---

[306] Johnson, Karen S. "The Portrayal of Lame duck Presidents by the National Print Media," Presidential Studies Quarterly, Vol. 16, No.1, The Media and the Presidency, Winter 1986, pp. 50-65.

policy issues stalled because the cabinet, which was supposed to give direction, failed to meet.

Uhuru watched as his political strongholds, especially Mt. Kenya, slip away into the hands of his friend-turned-foe, Ruto. His Jubilee Alliance Party (JAP), the behemoth that propelled him to two terms in office as president, first as a coalition then as a party, was reduced to a hollow shell. Members rebelled, joined other parties, or formed their own in protest, to compete for re-election.

"Uhuru is a lame duck president," declared MP Rigathi Gachagua, his erstwhile Personal Assistant and ally turned DP Ruto's point man in Mount Kenya.

In the process, Uhuru chose Raila Odinga as his preferred presidential candidate in the 2022 election. During the Jubilee Parliamentary Group meeting at State House on February 4, 2022, Uhuru announced his intention to actively participate in the 2022 campaigns to get Raila elected. He denied that the ODM leader was a "State project," but all optics pointed to the fact that indeed he was. Raila enjoyed State resources including the use of military choppers, contrary to the provisions in the Election Offences Act of 2016. Some of the vehicles Raila used in his campaign for the presidency were government property. He was accorded prime time space in the State media and had unlimited access to Uhuru's media empire.

This is the man Uhuru described as muguruki, a mad man, during the 2013 and 2017 election campaigns. At that time, he described his deputy as a brilliant strategist, and the best candidate to succeed him. By 2020, all those praises had evaporated. Raila was now a "good man" and Ruto "a bad man" for Kenya and "incapable of reviving the economy."

In the spirit of the handshake, Uhuru did apologise for his characterisation of Raila in a bad way, admitting he "lied." "Yes, it's true I used to insult that man. But I am now growing old. I have no energy to insult anyone."[307]

---

[307] Kaguora, Joseph. "Yes, I insulted Raila, but that is in the past – Uhuru tells Mt. Kenya," *The Star*, February 23, 2022.

UHURU KENYATTA

With months remaining before relinquishing office, President Uhuru spent a lot of time worrying about his legacy projects.[308] He inspected the Nairobi Expressway, visited construction works at Uhuru Park, and opened the Uhuru Gardens National Monument and Museum. He graced Raila's 77th birthday bash at the latter's residence in Karen and hosted a meeting of frenzied youths at State House singing *Yote Yawezekana bila Ruto* (All is possible without Ruto). It is the same political song (with a name change) which escorted Moi into retirement after his 'Project Uhuru' lost elections in 2002. He also received numerous delegations at State House and accepted to work as chairperson of the Azimio la Umoja-One Kenya Coalition after leaving office.

Was Uhuru a great president? No! Did he have a vision for Kenya? Yes! Did he inspire the people? No! Did he engage in strategic and critical thinking? No! How was his interpersonal communication? Good! Was he self-aware enough to understand his strengths and flaws? No! Was he responsible and dependable? No! Did he have patience and tenacity? No!

Based on the qualities of "great" leadership as espoused by Sonya Krakoff of Champlain College,[309] Uhuru performed averagely as a president. His public rating at home ranged from "the worst president," to "a tribal king," to "the best president Kenya has ever had." While some praised him for initiating mega infrastructure projects, others blamed him for perpetuating "mega corruption scandals, entrenching ethnic politics, reducing democratic space, and accumulating massive debt."[310]

A Survey by a non-partisan firm, Pew Research Centre, identified corruption, lack of employment, poverty, and crime, as the biggest problems Uhuru inherited from previous administrations. Uhuru could not solve those problems. Under his watch, 'mafia-style' cartels

---

[308] The Big 4 Agenda comprises of food security, affordable housing, manufacturing, and affordable healthcare.

[309] Krakoff, Sonya. "The top ten qualities of a great leader," Champlain College Online, undated.

[310] Kodero, Cliff. "What do Kenyans think of Uhuru presidency so far?" Quora, undated.

of organised criminals worked within the confines of government – doing business with politicians and high-ranking civil servants and manipulating the system for their own benefit. Uhuru knew about the cartels and periodically castigated them as the country's greatest enemies. But he did nothing to confront them.

Uhuru also watched helplessly as the cartels grabbed pieces of prime land in Nairobi and elsewhere, manipulated prices of petroleum products and consumer items, sabotaged electricity, and water supply, engaged in illicit imports of goods, and stole billions of shillings from government coffers. Such activities not only shook investor confidence, but also distorted the economy.

The Competition Authority of Kenya (CAK), which is charged with enforcing rules against businesses and entities engaged in Restrictive Trade Practices (RTP), cartel behaviour, and abuse of dominance, was unable to put a lid on cartelism, despite stiff penalties provided for in the 2017 amendments of the Competition Act (No. 12 of 2010). Without serious government intervention, cartelists roamed government offices cutting deals that resulted in the loss of billions of public funds.

Meanwhile, investors worried about the exorbitant costs of doing business in Kenya, high taxation, insecurity, inconsistencies in government policy, electricity cost, and of course, corruption. To attract more foreign investment, Uhuru initiated a broad range of business reforms especially in the areas of company registration, electricity supply and cost, and land allocation, but investor worries persisted. Numerous companies left the country to set up operations elsewhere in the continent due to bureaucratic hurdles and corruption in government, especially in the departments of land, registration, and taxes. The good news is that the introduction of a single business permit did help to ease the burden for businesspersons and investors.

One of the major failures of Uhuru's administration was his inability to control what went on in his government. Knowing that, he had to remind Kenyans on several occasions that he was in charge and in control of the government. His frequent absences from the country gave civil servants room to stay away from offices instead of serving the nation. Many engaged in private businesses to earn extra money.

When in January 2019 Uhuru ordered his AG to draft a bill to bar civil servants from setting up private businesses, the suggestion was hamstrung by government officials. The bill would have repealed the 1971 recommendation of the Duncan Ndegwa Commission which allowed civil servants to run businesses. But for some reason, Uhuru did not press further.

Another example of the weakness of President Uhuru's government was seen in the first two years of Covid-19 (2020-2021). First, there was the KEMSA scandal, which saw billions of shillings lost as he watched. If he had been serious about stemming corruption at KEMSA, billions of shillings would have been saved. Some of the criminals were within his own Jubilee Party. So, the looting continued.

Second, there was what he didn't do to stem the rising cases of Covid-19. If he had acted more stringently to stop mega-spreaders in the form of political gatherings, perhaps the 5,651 who had died by June 2022, would have been saved. But he sat quietly, and even participated in political rallies, thus spreading the pandemic to many more poor Kenyans. The rally organisers failed to adhere to the Covid-19 protocols outlined by his own government.

Many people also feel that President Uhuru scored high on some areas and deserved commendation. Uhuru is credited with transforming the country's landscape for the better. The Nairobi Expressway is aesthetically awesome, so are the numerous highways, over-passes, and bypasses, stretching for miles all over the country.

In addition to the SGR from Mombasa to Naivasha, train services were introduced or improved in some areas of Kenya. Now trains connect cities and major towns such as Mombasa-Nairobi-Nakuru-Kisumu. There are also local passenger train services leading into Nairobi, which allow Kenyans to conduct business and move goods and services quickly and easily.

Commuters can also now walk leisurely from Mombasa Island to the southern mainland without having to wait for the crowded and accident-prone ferries. Transportation to the tourist areas of

Diani was improved, thanks to the Dongo Kundu bypass and other links like the Mombasa Causeway.

The question is, at what cost? Almost all the major infrastructure projects completed during Uhuru's reign were built on borrowed money.

That was partly the reason why in 2022, the Standard Bank Group Limited named Kenya as among the five African countries expected to face debt risk in the subsequent two years because of ballooning public debt. President Uhuru Kenyatta, alongside his handshake partner Raila Odinga, Deputy President William Ruto, and the Jubilee Alliance Party government in general, must take responsibility for these failures, including the huge public debt.

On another level, there were those like COTU secretary general Atwoli, and Jubilee Alliance Party Vice Chairman Murathe, who believed Uhuru, at 61-years, was too young to retire. His predecessors were in their old age when they left office: Mzee Kenyatta died of natural causes, and Moi and Kibaki, retired. After leaving office, Moi and Kibaki, had no influence on matters of State. Kibaki appointed his predecessor as special peace envoy to Sudan, and when his time came, Kibaki himself lived quietly at his Muthaiga and Nyeri residences.

Thus, Kenyans and people around the world would be watching to see if Uhuru, as chairman of the Azimio la Umoja-One Kenya Coalition, would use his position to influence policies and governance. Or he would play the role of an elder statesman like what Nelson Mandela, Julius Nyerere, Kenneth Kaunda, and a host of other African leaders, did. The three leaders assumed the role of 'elder statesmen' after leaving office. They worked to drive globalisation, peace, and conflict resolution, in the region and the world.

Choosing to run the government by proxy would be unprecedented and dangerous. Uhuru's successor must be accorded the independence to run the government in the best possible way without interference. Undoubtedly, if given a chance, Uhuru would want to continue to influence the continuation of some of his failed Agenda Four items. He would also want to pursue the collapsed

BBI and make changes to the 2010 constitution. He once talked of a "constitutional moment," a concept many thought, was meant to allow him to succeed himself. There was a lot of talk of Uhuru wanting to be prime minister in the BBI arrangement. That talk had not subsided by the time he left office.

Then there is the matter of leadership in the key Mt. Kenya region. After Uhuru, who will take the mantle of leadership in the region? The Kenyattas dominated Kikuyu politics for years. Was Uhuru 'the last' in the Kenyatta political dynasty? Or would someone else emerge? So far, no one in the family has shown interest in pursuing the path followed by Mzee Kenyatta and Uhuru.

It would also be interesting to see whether future governments would want to probe the Kenyattas over their accumulation of wealth. President Kibaki refused to prosecute Moi for the sake of unity and peace in the country.

Even then, Moi was thrust into an awkward dilemma after leaving office. Some parcels of land he had acquired during his rule were contested in court and ended reverting to their rightful owners. For example, a 53-acre piece of land in Uasin Gishu in the Rift Valley which Moi grabbed in 2007 was returned to Susan Cheburet Chelugui. She lost it in 1993. In 2007, the land was transferred to Moi. High Court Judge Anthony Ombwayo ruled against the former president. He said Moi had behaved in a way that was "unconstitutional, irregular, unprocedural, and tainted." He ordered Moi to pay a compensation of KSh.1.06 billion to Chelugui.

Another person who took Moi to court to recover land was Malcolm Bell who accused President Moi of snatching one-hundred acres belonging to him. The land is adjacent to the president's home in Kabarak. Kabarak High School which Moi built is on that land. Bell, a farmer in Nakuru, won the case on appeal after the High Court had ruled in favour of Moi in mid-1990s.

In 2016, media reports claimed President Moi was paid KSh.500 million by a private developer for a disputed piece of land in Nairobi, also claimed by the United States International University (USIU-A). There was a public scene at the site when hundreds of people protested the grab of the 20-acre land. Drama escalated when a third party, Dr. George Kiongera, a Kenyan resident in the US, emerged to claim the property, a claim the USIU-A rejected. Kiongera claimed he bought the land from President Moi and had documents to prove it. The piece of land was among numerous parcels of land President Moi had acquired dubiously.

In the early 2000s, President Moi and leading politicians were named in a scandal to grab tens of thousands of acres of land in the Mau Forest. It turned out the whole idea was to benefit people like Moi, Environment Minister Joseph Kamotho, and Mama Ngina. President Moi later admitted that he owned land in the area but added that the said land was on the edge of the Mau Forest and not inside the water tower.

In June 2021, President Moi's family was ordered by a court to leave a prime beach plot in Mombasa. A three-judge bench ruled that the title of the land had been obtained illegally and without due process. The land was eventually returned to the Mombasa County government.

What happened to Moi could happen to future presidents and certainly to the Kenyattas. Uhuru's successor must also release the full report, without reductions, of the Truth, Justice, and Reconciliation Commission (TJRC), for Kenyans to know the full extent of land grabbing during Kenyatta and Moi eras.

In the meantime, Uhuru went home leaving behind a country beset by multiple problems: biting debt, runaway inflation, chronic joblessness, abject poverty, rampant corruption, ethnic polarisation, and numerous other challenges.

THE END

SELECTED BIBLIOGRAPHY

BOOKS

Aiyar, Sana. Indians in Kenya: *The Politics of Diaspora,* Harvard University Press, 2015.

Angelo, Anais. *Introduction in Power and the Presidency in Kenya: Jomo Kenyatta Years,* (Cambridge University Press), 2019.

Archer, Jules. *African Firebrand: Kenyatta of Kenya,* Julian Messner, 1969.

Arnold, Guy. *Kenyatta and the Politics of Kenya,* J. M. Dent & Sons, 1974.

Asingo, Patrick O., Nic Cheeseman, Karuti Kanyinga, & Gabrielle Lynch, *The Oxford Handbook of Kenyan Politics,* Oxford University Press, 2020.

Badejo, Babafemi, A. *Raila Odinga: An Enigma in Kenyan Politics,* Yintab Books, 2006.v

Burbidge, Dominic. *The Shadow of Kenyan Democracy: Widespread Expectations of Widespread Corruption,* Taylor & Francis, 2016.

Cullen, Poppy. *Kenya and Britain After Independence: Beyond Neo-Colonialism,* Palgrave MacMillan, 2017.

Dudziak, Mary L. *Thurgood Marshall's Bill of Rights for Kenya: Exporting American Dreams,* Oxford University Press, 2008.

Fitzgerald, Ian. *The Deep State: A History of Secret Agendas and Shadow Governments,* Arcturus Publishing Ltd., 2020.

Gentry, Curt. *J. Edgar Hoover: The Man and the Secrets,* W. W. Norton & Company, 1991.

Gimode, Edwin. *The Role of the Police in Kenya's Democratisation Process in Kenya, 2007.* See, *The Struggle for Democracy,* Godwin G. Murunga & Shadrack W. Nasongo, Godesria Book, 2007.

Gitau, Jeremiah Kiereini. *A Daunting Journey,* East African Educational Publishers, 2015.

Githuku, Nicholas K. *Mau Mau Crucibles of War: Statehood, National Identity, and Politics of Post-Colonial Kenya,* Lexington Books, 2015.

Haugerud, Angelique. *The Culture of Politics in Modern Kenya,* Cambridge University Press, 1993.

Hornsby, Charles. *Kenya: A History Since Independence,* I. B. Tauris & Company, 2013.

Huxley, Elspeth. *White Man's Country: Lord Delamere and the Making of Kenya,* Frederick A. Praeger, 1935.

Kariuki, G. G. *The Illusions of Power: Reflections on Fifty Years in Kenya Politics,* East African Publishers Ltd., 2001.

Kariuki, J. M. *Mau Mau Detainee: The Account by a Kenyan African in his Experience in Detention Camps, 1953-1960,* Oxford University Press, 1963.

Kenyatta, Jomo. *Suffering Without Bitterness,* East African Publishing House, 1968.

Khamisi, Joe. Land Redistribution: Rich Bastards from the City, in, *Looters and Grabbers,* Jodey Book Publishers, 2018.

Kyle, Keith. The Politics of the Independence of Kenya, McMillan Press Ltd., 1999.

Meredith, Martin. *The Fortune of Africa: A 500-Year History of Wealth, Greed, and Endeavour,* Public Affairs, 2014.

Miguna, Miguna. *Peeling Back the Mask: A Quest for Justice in Kenya,* Gilgamesh Africa, 2012.

Murray-Brown, Jeremy. *Kenyatta,* E. P. Dutton & Co., In., 1973.

Murunga, Godwin R. & Shadrack W. Nasongo, *Kenya: The Struggle for Democracy,* Godesria Books.

Okumu, John J. Some Thoughts on Kenya's Foreign Policy, *The African Review,* 1973.

Throup, David W. & Hornsby, Charles. *Multi-Party Politics in Kenya: The Kenyatta & Moi States & the Triumph of the System in the 1992 Election,* James Currey, 1998.

RESEARCH JOURNALS AND ARTICLES

A Decade-Old Assault on the Separation of Powers Has Left Kenya a Fractious Legacy, *The Conversation,* June 24, 2020.

Abdication of Responsibility: The Commonwealth and Human Rights, *Human Rights Watch*, 1991.

Africa Watch, Kenya. Taking Liberties, *An African Watch Report,* July 1991.

African Research Bulletin (Political, Social, and Cultural Series), 1978, pp. 4947-4948.

Akech, Migai. Abuse of Power and Corruption in Kenya: Will the New Constitution Enhance Government Accountability? *Indiana Journal of Global Legal Studies,* 2011.

Angelo, Anais. Becoming President: A Political Biography of Jomo Kenyatta, *European University Institute*, November 21, 2016.

Anthony Duff to the Secretary of State for Foreign and Commonwealth Affairs, "Kenya: The Future Prospect, December 10, 1974.

A short history of the Mt Kenya mafia, as told by the CIA," Nairobi Law Monthly, April 9, 2019.

Assensoh, A. B. & Alex-Assensoh, M. Corrupt and Dictatorial Tendencies: The Tacit Invitation for Military Intervention, *African Military History and Politics,* 2001.

Asingo, Dr. Patrick O. ISLP Attends Report Launch: Exposing the Governance Conundrum in Kenya: Deep State, Mega-Corruption, *International Lawyers Project,* August 7, 2019.

Asingo, Patrick O., Nic Cheeseman, Karuti Kanyinga, & Gabrielle Lynch, The Oxford Handbook of Kenyan Politics, Oxford University Press, 2020, p. 626.

Ayaga, Wilfred. Dictatorial Tendencies' Tag Stalks Uhuru Kenyatta's Regime to 2015, *Pan African Visions,* December 30, 2014.

Brief on Memorandum by the Meru People, March 23, 1969.

Calabresi G. & Berghausen E. The Rise and Fall of the Separation of Powers, *Northwestern University Law Review,* 2012.

Campbell, John. Raila Odinga Sworn in as Kenya's 'Peoples' President, *Council of Foreign Relations,* January 30, 2018.

Campbell, John. Kenya's Big Men are Failing Her, *Council of Foreign Relations*, September 27, 2017.

Chome, Ngala. The Kenyan Elite and the Constitution, *Heinrich Boll Stiftung*, July 5, 2021.
Confidential. Anthony Duff to the Right Honourable Sir Alex Douglas-Home, October 18, 1972.
Confidential. Diplomatic Report. *Kenya Annual Review for 1970*, January 12, 1971.
Confidential. Inward Telegram No. 508, Land Settlement: Parliamentary Question, March 9, 1964.
Colins, Robert. The Ilemi Triangle, *Annales d'Ethiopie*, 2005.
Craig, Lori. Thurgood Marshall and Kenyan Independence, *USC Gould School of Law*, December 12, 2008.
D'Arcy, Michelle & Agnes Cornell. Devolution and Corruption in Kenya: Everyone's Turn to Eat, *African Affairs*, March 2016.
Chilungu, Simeon W. "Kenya- Recent developments and challenges," *Cultural Survival Quarterly Magazine*, September 1985.
Dinda, Gabriel. "What is the philosophy of the new education curriculum in Kenya," Strathmore University, undated.
Dok, Akol Nyok Akol, & Bradley A. Thayer. Takeover Trap: Why Imperialism China is Invading Africa, *The National Interest*, July 10, 2019.
Duerr, Benjamin. Not Guilty, Not Acquitted: Kenya Ruling a Major Setback for ICC, *IPI Global Observatory*, April 11, 2016.
Duff, Record of Conversation, December 2, 1974.
Final Report – TJRC Report, *I. Core TJRC Related Documents*, 2013.
Fitzgibbon, Will. As Kenyan President Mounted Anti-Corruption Comeback, His Family's Secret Fortune Expanded Offshore, *The Pandora Papers*, October 3, 2021.
Gathogo, Julius M: Nahashon Ngare Rukenya, and the Moral Re-Armament in Kenya (1959-1970): The Turning Point and the Post Mau-Mau War Reconstruction, *Institute for Theology and Religion*, University of South Africa, 2018.
Gavin, Michelle. BBI Ruling Leaves Kenya at a Crossroads, *Council on Foreign Relations*, August 25, 2021.
Githuku, Nicholas Kariuki. Mau Mau Crucible of War: Statehood, National Identity, and Politics in Post-Colonial Kenya, *Graduate Thesis*, 2015.

Goldbert, T. Simon, Daniel L. Aharonson, D. Leykin, & B. Adini. Twitter in the Crossfire: The Use of social media in the Westgate Mall Terror Attack in Kenya, *PLos One,* 2014.

Harton, Helene. Jomo Kenyatta and Kenyan Independence: The Twists and Turns of Memory, *HAL Archives,* January 8, 2020.

Hidalgo, Paul. Kenya Divided, *Foreign Affairs,* July 9, 2014.

"ICC: Kenya deputy president's case ends," Human Rights Watch, April 5, 2016.

Independence Without Freedom: The legitimization of Repressive Laws and Practices in Kenya, *A Kenya Human Rights Commission Report,* February 1994.

Jensenius, Francesca R. & Abby K. Wood. Caught in the Act but Not Punished: On Elite Rule of Law and Deterrence, *Penn State Journal of Law, and International Affairs,* 2016.

Kariuki Murder Report, *WikiLeaks,* June 4, 1975.

Kenya: One Year in Office for Uhuru Kenyatta and William Ruto, *Kenya Human Rights Commission,* undated.

Kenya After Elections: Working to Prevent Conflict Worldwide, *International Crisis Group Africa Briefing,* No. 94, May 15, 2013.

Kiai, Mugambi. Extrajudicial Killings in Kenya, *Open Society Foundation,* January 30, 2011.

Kibet, Kibet Emanuel & Kimberly Wangeci. A Perspective on the Doctrine of the Separation of Powers Based on the Response to Court Orders in Kenya, *Strathmore Law Review,* January 2016.

Koinange, Jeff. Collaborator and/or Nationalist? Koinange-wa-Mbiyu: Mau Mau's Misunderstood

La, Minh-Ha. 10 Facts About Corruption in Kenya, *The Borgen Project,* March 3, 2020.

Lashitew, Additsu & Majune K. Socrates. How Have Lockdown Policies Affected International Trade? *Brookings Institution,* March 9, 2021.

Lang'at, Patrick. What Exactly is BBI? An A-Z Breakdown of Kenya's Handshake Initiative and Why You Should Care, *Vox,* November 30, 2020.

Leader, *Journal of African History,* 2001.

Levitt, Steven & James Snyder. Political Parties and the Distribution of Federal Outlays, *American Journal of Political Economy*, 1995.

Lord Faringdon. White Settlement in East Africa, UK Parliament, *Hansard*, February 1, 1944.

Maina, Grace. Opportunity or Treat: The Engagement of Youth in African Societies, *Africa Dialogue Monograph Series*.

Mair, David. Westgate: A Case Study: How Al Shaabab Used Twitter During an Ongoing Attack, Conflict Terrorism, *Studies in Conflict and Terrorism*, Routledge, April 2016.

Makali, David. Tweet, September 18, 2021.

Mati, Jacob Mwathi. Emergence of Inter-Identity Alliances in Struggles for Transformation of the Kenya Constitution, *Interdisciplinary Journal*, 2017.

Mochama, Tony A. Political Parties After Political Parties: The Changing Nature and Reality of Political Power in Kenya, *Konrad Adenauer Stiftung*, 2021.

Montesano, Tads. Dynasty Politics in Democracy: Kenyatta, Odinga, and Democratic Erosion in Kenya, *Williams College*, December 9, 2020.

Muhammad, Farooq Sabil. Kenya and the 21st Century Maritime Silk Road, *World Scientific*, March 6, 2020.

Mukami, Purity & Simon Bowers. Pandora Papers: The Secret Offshore World of Kenya's First Family, Finance Uncovered, October 3, 2021.

Mutua, Makau. Justice Under Siege: The Rule of Law and Judicial Subservience in Kenya, *Human Rights Quarterly*, 2001.

Mutwol, Abraham. Great Inspiring Life Lessons from Uhuru Kenyatta, *Creative Minds Consultants*, 2015.

Navigating the Pandemic, Kenya Economic Update, *World Bank*, November 2020.

New African Development (NAD), March 1977.

Norris to Secretary of State, Kenya Annual Review for 1970, January 12, 1971.

Onsumo, Eldar, Boaz Munga & Violet Nyabaro. The Impact of Covid-19 on Industries Without Smokestacks in Kenya: The Case of Horticulture, July 28, 2021.

Personal Communication with James George, See, Jeroen Cuvelier, *International Peace Information Service*, April 2011.

Pickard, Carmel. Challenging Culture of Impunity in Kenya, *Africa LII*, March 6, 2019.

Preliminary Reaction to Government's Aggressive Campaign Against Mau Mau, *Consul General at Nairobi to the Department of State, Foreign Relations of the United States,* October 24, 1952.

Private and Confidential. Report on Kenya, September 1974.

Regeru, Njoroge & Company. High Court Rules Judiciary is Not Under Parliament's Control, *Lexology,* July 1, 2014.

S. Makinda. Kenya's Role in the Somalia-Ethiopia Conflict, Working Paper, *Strategic and Defence Studies Centre* (Australia), 1982.

Shilaho, Western Kwatemba. Old Wines in New Skins: Kenya's 2013 Elections and the Triumph of the Ancien Regime, *Journal of African Elections*, 2013.

Shiundu, Alphonce. Railway to Nowhere, *Development and Cooperation*, December 22, 2019.

The Arrest and Mistrial of Jomo Kenyatta and Five Other Nationalists, *Memory of the World Register,* Ref. No. 2010/55 (Summer).

Thomas, B. Donald & Paul J. Nugent. *Walter Martin, Friends Visit Jomo Kenyatta at Maralal, Quaker History,* 2010.

Thuku, Henry Ng'ang'a. Factors Contributing to Crime Among Juveniles: A Case of Majengo, July 2017.

Torchia, Christopher. Like Father, Like Son: Kenya Goes to Polls in Family Affair, *Associated Press,* August 5, 2017.

Translations on Sub-Saharan Africa: *United States Joint Publication Research Service,* 1978.

Trap, Capture, Kill: Inside Communications Surveillance and Counterterrorism in Kenya, *Privacy International,* March 2017.

Uhuru Barks but Cannot Bite, Civil Society says, AfriCog, May 24, 2019.

Verini, James. The Fall and Rise of Raila Odinga, *Foreign Policy,* March 2, 2013.

Warah, Rasna. Covid, Debt, and Taxes are Plunging Millions of Kenyans into Poverty, *Aftershocks One Campaign,* July 26, 2021.

Wills, Mathew. The Turkish Origins of the "Deep-State," *JSTOR Daily*, April 10, 2017.

Wolf, Thomas P. International Justice vs Public Opinion? The ICC and Ethnic Polarisation in the 2013 Kenyan Elections, *Journal of African Elections*, June 2013.

MEDIA

A Handshake that Shook the Whole Country, The *Standard,* March 10, 2020.
A brief history of the Mt Kenya mafia, as told by the CIA," *Nairobi Law Monthly*, April 9, 2019
Achuka, Vincent. Unease in Jubilee as Graft War Splits UhuRuto Allies, The *Standard*, June 23, 2018.
Aglionby, John. "De La Rue's contract to print Kenya's banknotes cancelled," *The Financial Times*, January 8, 2018.
Atellah, Juliet. "Toa Kitambulisho!" Evolution of Registration of Persons in Kenya, The *Elephant*, June 14, 2019.
Benesch, Sudan. The Kenya Elections: Peace Happened, The *Huffington Post*, March 2, 2013.
Blunder or Sabotage? Uhuru's New Headache, The *Daily Nation*, May 25, 2009.
Brown, Douglas. Kenya Facing Threat of Red Take-Over, The *Sunday Telegraph*, November 29, 1964.
Cheronoc, Stella. Computer Guru in Sh4bn Hacking Case Lives Large and Brags Big, *Nairobinews.nation.co.ke*, March 23, 2017.
Clarke, David. Kenya Steps in to Rescue Shilling, Economic Data Worsen, *Reuters*, September 29, 2011.
Cooperative Bank Left Bitter After Losing Sh2.2bn Deal to NCBA, *Kenya Insights*, November 8, 2021.
Corona Virus Update in Africa: Nigeria Confirms First Case, Kenya Bans Flights from China, The *Guardian*, February 28, 2020.
Editorial: Crack down on nepotism in public institutions," *Business Daily*, January 28, 2019.
Gatitu, Son. "Is Kenya's 'deep state' a reality or scarecrow in its democracy?" The *Africa Report*, October 5, 2021.

Etyang, Hesborn. "Raila hits out at Ruto over donations, pledges to seal graft loopholes if elected," The *Star*, October 14, 2021.

Eulich, Whitney. Kenyan Court Clears Kenyatta for Presidential Bid, Despite War Crime Charges, The *Christian Science Monitor*, February 15, 2013.

Gachuri, Francis. "Uhuru on the spot as corruption scandals rock the country," *Citizen Digital*, May 26, 2018.

Gaitho, Macharia. How Hustler Ruto Broke into Exclusive Club to Launch Career, The *Nation*, May 29, 2016.

Gatitu, Son. "Is Kenya's 'deep state' a reality or scarecrow in its democracy?" The *Africa Report*, October 5, 2021.

Gathara, Patrick. Dynasties vs Hustlers in Kenya, *Al Jazeera*, September 24, 2019.

Ghai, Yash Pal. "A scorecard on Uhuru's presidency," The *Elephant*, September 17, 2020.

Gibbons-Neff, Thomas, Eric Schmidt, Charlie Savage & Helen Cooper. Chaos as Militants Overran Airfield Killing 3 Americans in Kenya, The *New York Times*, January 22, 2020.

Githinji, George. Is President Uhuru Kenyatta a Dictator? The *Saturday Standard*, May 1, 2016.

Githongo, John. Kenya's Rampant Corruption is Eating Away at the Very Fabric of Democracy, The *Guardian*, August 6, 2015.

Gitonga, Nancy. "AG on the spot after series of case losses," *People Daily*, June 14, 2021.

Goldstein, Joseph. Kenyans Say Chinese Investment Brings Racism and Discrimination, The *New York Times*, October 15, 2018.

Jomo Kenyatta: A Giant of the 20thj Century, The *Baltimore Afro-American*, August 29, 1978.

Kaberia, Judie. Kathleen Kihanya Speaks Out on Health Ministry "Scandal," *Capital News*, October 29, 2016.

Kabukuru, Wanjohi. Kenya's Lady of Grace, *New African*, January 25, 2012.

Kamadi, Geoffrey. Who Should Care for the Forests? In Kenya, the Question Sparks Violence, The *Christian Science Monitor*, October 14, 2020.

Kamau, Macharia. Kenya Power Bounces Back to Post Profit of Sh1.5bn, The *Standard*, October 31, 2021.

Kamau, Richard. Raila Says Kenyans are Concerned About His Stance on Corruption, *Nairobiwire.com*, July 9, 2021.

Karuti, Kanyinga. From Jomo to Uhuru: How Roadside Declaration Replaced Research as the Basis for National Policies, The *Daily Nation*, November 22, 2015.

Kenya Denies Scandal in Ivory: Deplores Reports on Kenyattas, The *New York Times,* June 14, 1975.

Wilson, Tom. "Handshake ends crisis and leads to signs of progress in Kenya," The *Financial Times*, November 2019.

"Kenya is run by mafia-style cartels, says chief justice," The *Guardian*, January 13, 2016.

Kenyatta of Kenya, *LIFE* magazine, Vol. 61, No. 6, August 5, 1966.

Kenyatta, Ruto, and Odinga Leaves Kenyan Opposition Reeling with Decision to Bury the Hatchet, The *Business Day,* March 12, 2018.

Kenyatta's Statue Unveiled in Kenya, The *New York Times,* August 30, 2019.

Key Role for Obure as Moi Reshuffles Cabinet, The *New Humanitarian*, November 21, 2001.

Kibii, Eliud & Agatha Ngotho. Drought Exposes Collapse of Galana Kulalu Project, The *Star,* April 2, 2019.

Kiplagat, Sam. Kenya: Defiant Uhuru Kenyatta Reopens Kenya Meat Commission Plant Despite Court Ruling, The *Nation,* May 25, 2021.

Krakoff, Sonya. "The top ten qualities of a great leader," Champlain College Online, undated.

Krippahl, Cristina. "Kenya: A 'sweet' deal gone sour," *Deutsche Welle*, September 13, 2018.

Lough, Richard. Analysis: Kenyatta's Bid for Kenya Presidency a Diplomatic Headache, *Reuters,* February 14, 2013.

Madowo, Larry. Opinion: Kenya is Sliding into a Dictatorship, The *Washington Post,* February 7, 2018.

Maharaj, Davan. Terror-Related Travel Advisories Harming Tourism Trade in Kenya, The *Baltimore Sun,* June 22, 2003.

Maina, Anthony. "David Ndii hits Uhuru hard with claims of drinking in the office," *Pulse*, November 22, 2018.

Mageka, Hillary. Senators Raise Alarm Over 'Militarisation' of Public Institutions, The *People Daily,* September 20, 2020.

Maina Anthony. Uhuru Nearly Insulted Us with the Word ku** - Jubilee MP, *Pulse*, November 14, 2018.

Maombo, Sharon. "Mixed reactions after Appeals Court halts BBI reggae," The *Star,* August 20, 2021.

Master Card Foundation Event, Young Africa Works, The *Nation TV,* June 20, 2019.

McConnell, Tristan. Uhuru Kenyatta: From Millionaire Playboy to Kenyan President, *AFP,* August 4, 2017.

McKenzie, David. Kenya Intelligence Warned of Al-Shabaab Threat Before Mall Attack, *CNN,* September 30, 2013.

Miriri, Duncan. Third of Kenyan Budget Lost to Corruption: Anti-Graft Chief, *Reuters,* March 10, 2016.

Muchira, Njiraini. Kenya Moves to Tame Rising Wage Bill with Three-Year-Contracts, The *East African,* June 25, 2019.

Mugendi, Jacob. Corruption and Inefficiencies at Kenya Power are the Enemies, *iAfrican,* February 15, 2021.

Musalia Slams Raila Over Alliance with Governors, *Tuko* November 5, 2019.

Mutai, Edwin. Muhoho Kenyatta in List of Sugar Importers, The *Business Daily,* June 26, 2018.

Mutiga, Murithi & David Smith. "Discovery of witness's mutilated body feeds accusations of state killings," The *Guardian*, January 5, 2015.

Mutiga, Murithi. Kenya – Does Uhuru Kenyatta Want to be a Dictator? The *Daily Nation,* December 8, 2013.

Mutua, John. Kenya Spends Sh1.7bn to Secure Foreign Loans, The *Business Daily,* September 17, 2021.

Mwakideu, Crispin. Uhuru Kenyatta's War on Graft: A Turning Point or Just Scoring Points? *Deutsche Welle,* July 31. 2019.

Mwalimu, Mandela. Mother of the Nation, undated.

Mwangale, Alex. Uhuru's Frequent Trips are a Burden to the Taxpayer, The *Saturday Standard*, March 9, 2016.

Mwanza, Eddy. Details of Mama Ngina's First Interview, *Kenyans.co.ke*, September 8, 2020.

Mwere, David & Justus Mwanga. IEBC Chiefs Expose Fault Lines as Feud Over Tenders Escalates, The *Nation*, June 28, 2020.

Namaswa, Mark. How Corruption Rings Run in Kenya, *This is Africa*, September 22, 2015.

Ndii, David. Crony Capitalism and State Capture: The Kenyatta Family Story, The *Elephant*, July 7, 2018. Ndurya, M. 'Uhuru predicts 20-year run for Jubilee," The *Daily Nation*, September 21, 2013.

Ndurya, M. 'Uhuru predicts 20-year run for Jubilee," The *Daily Nation*, September 21, 2013.

Ngetich, Jacob. NHIF Loses Sh10 Billion Through Fake Claims from Health Facilities, The *Standard*, September 13, 2021.

Ngotho, Kamau. Kenya: The Day Uhuru Was Thrown Out of Government Building, The *Daily Nation*, September 13, 2020.

Njoka, Lewis. Roadside Orders: Expensive Burden That Baffled Many, The *People Daily*, February 7, 2020.

Nyakagwa, Eric. "'Deep state' will win State House race and it will not be by chance," The *Nairobian*, June 29, 2021.

Nyaringo, Joseph Lister. "Has Raila been outfoxed by the handshake? The *Standard*, April 20, 2019.

Nyawira, Lydia. DP Ruto Tells Off Financial Analysts, Says Jubilee Regime is Transparent, The *Saturday Standard*, February 24, 2018.

Odero, Norbert. "Accept and Move On": The Handshake's Hollow Cure for Decades of Communal Loss and Grief, The *Elephant*, March 8, 2019.

Odongo, David * Solomon Koko. Controversial City Man Clears Bis Name from 2.5 Gold Saga, The *Sunday Standard*, August 20, 2013.

Odula, Tom. In Kenya, Police Kill Suspects with Near-Impunity, *Associated Press*, December 5, 2014.

Ogemba, Paul. Firm in Dams Scam Seeks Sh80bn Compensation, The *Standard*, November 24, 2021.
Okoye, Uju. Kenya's Latest Scandal Reveals the Bitter Taste of Corruption, The *Diplomatic Courier*, June 27, 2018.
Ombati, Cyrus & Roselyne Obala. Over Sh10 Billion Lost in New NHIF Pay Scandal, The *Standard*, February 25, 2019.
Omondi, Ashe. Uhuru, Ruto Enjoy Sumptuous Nyama Choma as President Returns from Tanzania, *Tuko*, February 2, 2019.
Omondi, Ferdinand. Kenya's BBI Blocked in Scathing Court Verdict for President Kenyatta, *BBC News*, May 14, 2021.
Omondi, George. Uhuru's Naivasha Dry Ports Deal Triggers Debate, The *Business Daily*, July 14, 2019.
Onyango, Protus. Kenya's Karura Forest: Symbol of Greenbelt Movement, Suffering Death by 1,000 Cuts, *Mongabay*, April 29, 2015.
Perlez, Jane. Citing Corruption by Kenyan Officials, Western Nations are Cancelling Aid, The *New York Times*, October 21, 1991.
Prince Charming: Here are all President Uhuru's Women, The *Standard*, undated.
Raila Beats Rivals to a New Deal, *Africa Confidential*, March 23, 2018.
Ritter, John. America's 25 Most Awkward Allies: How Obama Has Curried Favour with a Rogue Gallery of Tyrants and Autocrats, *Politico Magazine*, March/April 2014.
Robert Ouko "Killed in Kenya State House," *BBC News*, December 9, 2010.
Rule, Sheila. Power of Kenya's Leader is Growing, The *New York Times*, December 15, 1986.
Ruto Denies Bid to Halt ICC Trial, The *Sunday Nation*, May 9, 2013.
Sanga, Bernard. I Had No Time for Uhuru, I Was Busy Lighting Christmas Tree – Governor Joho, *The Standard*, undated.
Samora, Mwaura. "Mutahi Ngunyi: Uhuru is a political greenhorn," The *Standard*, January 17, 2014.
Seii, Jerotich. Power Struggles: Unmasking the Thieves Behind the KPLC Heist, The *Elephant*, May 31, 2018.

Sieff, Kevin. Who is Kenyatta? A Look at the Kenyan President Welcoming Obama, The *Washington Post,* July 25, 2015.

Shoumatoff, Alex. Agony and Ivory, *Vanity Fair,* August 2011.

Some, Kipchumba. Amherst College Humbled Uhuru Despite High Life Back Home, The *Daily Nation,* February 18, 2017.

Thiong'o, Josphat. IEBC Tender Wars a Big Tinder in the Next Polls, The *Standard* 12, 2021.

Tubei, George. "Mama Ngina Kenyatta worried Uhuru may lose the presidential election," *Pulse,* March 18, 2017.

Uhuru Blocks Pay Rise for MPs, *Insurance Newsnet,* July 5, 2010.b

Wadhams, Nick. Kenya Outrage After Leaders Ditch Mercedes, *Time,* November 18, 2009.

Waiguru Accuses Dr. Ruto of Hypocrisy After Allies' Insults to the President, *Kenyan News.co.ke,* September 9, 2020.

Wainaina, Ndung'u. No, Uhuru Kenyatta, You Cannot Change Constitution While in Office, The *Star,* December 5, 2019.

Wafula, Benjamin. Blame President Uhuru for Mumias sugar financial crisis – Raila, *Citizen Digital,* July 22, 2016.

Wafula, Paul. Exclusive: Behind the SGR Walls, *The Standard,* July 8, 2018.

Wambui, Mary. Mama Ngina Recounts Her Pain During Uhuru's ICC Trial, *Nairobi News,* November 22, 2016.

Wanambisi, Laban. How Mark Too Kick-Started My Political Career – Uhuru, *Capital News,* January 9, 2017.

Warah, Rasna. Let It Never Be Said That Kenyans Went to War Over Mammary Glands, The *Elephant,* September 18, 2020.

Weaver, Maurice. Kenyatta and Wife at Centre of Scandal Over Corruption, The *Daily Telegraph,* November 18, 1974.

Wilson, Tom. "Handshake ends crisis and leads to signs of progress in Kenya," The *Financial Times,* November 2019.

Yusuf, Mohammed. Kenya's Judiciary Puts Executive on the Spot Over Appointment of Judges, *VOA,* June 8, 2020.

INDEX

A

Abaja, Joseph 132
Abdalla, Amina 230
Abdisamad, Dr. Abdiwahab Sheikh 138, 139
Abdullahi, Ahmednasir 167, 187
Abey, Isaac Hassan 253
Abrahams, Peter 4,
Achieng Lencer 132
Aga Khan, Prince Karim 303, 304
Ahmed, Abiy 231, 240
Ahmed, Abubakar Shariff 'Makaburi' 137
Ainley, Justice John 324
Akello, Boaz 211
Akombe, Dr. Roselyn 254
Ali, Mohamed 137
Ali, Mohamed Hussein 56, 80
Amin, President Idi 29, 349
Amolo, Otiende 100
Annan, Kofi 47, 55
Angaine, Jackson 22
Armitage, John Stuart 170
Asingo, Dr. Patrick O. 316
Atwoli, Francis 52, 284, 353, 380

Aukot, Ekuru 253, 306
Awiti, Adhu 265
Awori, Moody 44
Aydin, Harun 278, 279

B

Badeyo, Babafemi A. 308
Badi, Major General Mohamed Abdalla 103, 108
Balala, Najib 71, 244
Banda, Kamuzu 299
Barasa, Daniel 211
Boinnet, Joseph 102
Bensouda, Fatou 77, 80
Berng'etuny, Ezekiel 336
Berset, Alain 217
Biden, Joe 90, 238, 239, 240, 244
Biwott, Nicholas 59, 325
Bokassa, President Jean-Bedel 349
Bomett, Gerald 272, 273
Buchman, Rev. Frank 318
Bush, George W. 238
Bwayo, Job

C

Cameron, David 74, 237
Carson, Johnnie 78
Carter, Jimmy 6, 238
Catling, R. C. 321
Chao, Mary 176
Chebukati, Wafula 200
Cheburet, Stephen 140
Cheeseman, Nic 122
Cherargei, Kiprotich arap 270
Cheruiyot, Daniel 342
Cheruiyot, Sarah 342
Cholmondeley, Thomas Patrick Gilbert 317
Chomba, Mary 211
Chesoli, Kennedy 258
Correa, Assel 90
Criticos, Basil 24
Criticos, George 24
Crumpton, Henry 136

D

Dida, Mohamed 253
Diggs, Charles 14
Dolan, Father Gabriel 122
Duale, Aden 77, 98, 171
Dullo, Fatuma 105

E

Eboso, Justice Bernard 277
Echesa, Rashid 346
Elachi, Beatrice 107
Esipisu, Manoah 230

F

Farell, Chief Justice Dennis 95
Foot, Sir Dingle 33
Freeland, Major General Ian 320
Frischauer, Willie 304

G

Gachagua, Rigathi 27, 376
Gaitho, Macharia 139, 226
Gal, Noah 366
Galgalo, Tiya 127
Gakuo, Dr. Ephantus Njuguna 11
Gakuo, Magdalena 11
Gakuo, Margaret 11, 17
Gakuya, James Mwangi 194
Gathecha, Chief Muhoho wa 7
Gathungu, Nancy 104, 179, 195, 207, 210
Garang, John de Mabior 235
Gecaga, Jomo 229
Gecaga, Nana 15, 180
Gecaga, Soiya 15
Getonga, Alfred 39
Gethi, Commandant Ben 323
Gicheru, Justice Lucy 35
Gingeras, Ryan 315, 335
Githanga, Brigadier James 103
Githongo, John 44, 182
Gathecha, Chief Muhoho wa 7, 8, 9
Gathecha, Kinyua 9
Ghurair, Aziz al 201
Ghurair, Majid al 199
Gichangi, Major General Michael 85, 329
Gichuhi, James 263
Gichuru, Major General Dedan 321
Gichuru, Julie 358
Githinji, Nelson 192
Gondi, James 78

Grammaticas, Romi 33
Guda, John 116

H

Haji, Noordin 177
Haji, Yusuf 259
Hancox, Justice Alan Robin 96
Hardy, Brigadier A. J. 321
Havi, Nelson 269
Hernandez, Landy Rodriquez 90
Hinga, Bernard 321
Husbands, Geoffrey 11, 12
Hussein, Yassin 140

I

Igathe, Polycarp 330
Imanyara, Gitobu 78
Isaak, Ibrahim Haji 104
Iria, Mwangi wa 198
Itote, General Waruhiu 323, 324
Itumbi, Dennis 139

J

James, C. L. R., 12
Jensenius, Francesca R. 110
Jiis, Yusuf 90
Jinping, Xi 160, 247
Jirongo, Cyrus 253, 272
Juma, Elizabeth 219
Juma, Monica 346
Jumwa, Aisha 196

K

Kabaiku, William 36
Kabura, Josephine Irungu 191
Kaggia, Bildad 4, 19, 95
Kaguthi, Joseph 124
Kagwanja, Peter 259
Kagwe, Mutahi 109, 110, 175, 176
Kaikai, Lunus 357
Kaluyu, Japhet 253
Kairu, Justice Gatembu 128
Kajwang, Otieno 50
Kamau, Damaris Wambui 125
Kamau, Johnstone 16
Kamau, Macharia 76, 77
Kameru, Philip Major General (Rtd) 258, 314, 329
Kamotho, Joseph 382
Kandie, Phyllis 72
Kanyinga, Karuti 125
Kariuki, J. M. 319, 323, 324
Kariuki, Kihara 35, 106, 107, 129
Kariuki, Stephen 301
Karonney, Farida 124, 358
Karua, Martha 61, 105, 253, 308, 356
Karuga, J. M. 180
Karumba, Kungu 4
Karume, Njenga 31
Kaunda, Kenneth 6, 380
Kay, Steve 79
Kega, Kanini 170
Kegoro, George 44, 78, 122
Keino, Irene 195
Keino, Kipchoge 220
Kenyatta, Anna Nyokabi 15
Kenyatta, Christine Wambui xx, 5, 15, 33
Kenyatta, Edna Clarke 8, 9, 11
Kenyatta, Grace Wanjiku 9, 15
Kenyatta, Jane 'Jeni' Makena 8, 15

Kenyatta, President Jomo xix, xx, xxi, 3-23, 26-32, 34, 42-43, 47, 59, 95-96, 114, 124, 132, 140-142, 191, 229, 234, 241, 245, 287, 289, 290-291, 293-294, 299-300, 303-305, 307, 309, 313, 320-322, 324, 329, 333, 342, 348-349, 351-355, 381

Kenyatta, Mama Ngina xx, 6-10, 17, 19, 23-26, 28, 29, 30-36, 40, 42, 56-58, 79, 258, 266, 275-276, 284-285, 289, 293, 295, 300, 328, 334, 382

Kenyatta, Margaret 11, 30, 66, 232

Kenyatta, Margaret Wambui 4, 5, 8, 42

Kenyatta, Muhoho xx, 10, 15, 169, 170, 171, 201, 266, 283, 306, 329

Kenyatta, Muhoho, Jr. 306

Kenyatta, Ngina 306

Kenyatta, Nyokabi Anna 10

Kenyatta, Peter Magana 8, 11

Kenyatta, Peter Muigai 8

Kenyatta, President Uhuru Muigai xix, 3, 9, 10-11, 15-16, 23-27, 29-30, 32, 39, 40-42, 44-67, 71-74, 77-81, 87, 89, 92, 96, 101, 103, 104-105, 107-109, 115, 117, 118, 120, 123, 125-132, 135, 137-138, 141, 147-149, 153-155, 157, 158-160, 162-163, 166, 169, 172-175, 178, 180-182, 185, 188-189, 191, 201-203, 205, 210, 217-218, 222-223, 226-233, 237-239, 240-242, 244, 247, 251, 253, 255-265, 267-270, 272-275, 280, 283-284, 286-288, 291, 294, 295, 297-307, 309-314, 328-335, 345, 347-354, 356-381

Kenyatta, Wahu 4, 8, 9

Kerry, John 74

Keynan, Adan 277

Khalif, Abdulkadir 100

Khalwale, Bonny 345

Khaminwa, Dr. John 113, 356

Khasinah, Beryl Aluoch

Kiai, Maina 122

Kiama, Mutemi wa 163

Kiaraho, David 195

Kibaki, David 10

Kibaki, Lucy 31

Kibaki, President Mwai xix, 24, 31, 40, 43-44, 46, 47, 52, 56, 58, 64, 67, 96, 99-100, 104, 115, 123, 125, 132, 188, 213, 222, 228, 237, 241, 277, 287, 298-299, 322, 326-328, 333, 335, 349, 356, 380

Kibaki, Tony 10

Kibara, Gichara 42

Kibathi, Pius 323

Kibicho, Karanja 106, 107, 170, 260

Kiboro, Winfred 122

Kibwana, General (Rtd) Joseph 314

Kiereini, Jeremiah 323

Kigen, Michael 272

Kihalang'wa, Major General (Rtd) Gordon 314
Kihanya, Kathleen 178
Kihika, Susan 352
Kiir, President Salva 304
Kimani, Willie 140
Kimathi, General Dedan 318
Kimemia, Francis 310, 328
Kimunya, Amos 47
Kinditi, Kithure 353
Kinga, Stanley 319
Kinoti, George 105, 106
Kinyanjui, Peter 323
Kinyua, Jane Nduta 172
Kiome, Romano 344
Kiongera, Dr. George 382
Kipkorir, Donald 356
Kiplagat, David 333
Kiptanui, Abraham 336
Kirira, Joseph 319
Kirubi, Chris 333, 334, 335
Kirubi, Dr. Isaac 35, 36
Kiunjuri, Mwangi 171
Kobia, Samuel 330
Kodhek, Argwings 39
Koech, Nelson 201
Koinange, Jean Njeri 7
Koinange, Paul 26
Koinange, Peter Mbiyu 7, 8, 300, 324
Konyimbih, Tomiik 100
Koome, Chief Justice Martha 99, 128, 129, 130,
Korir, Justice Weldon 129
Korir, Welsely 220
Krakoff, Susan 377
Kositany, Caleb 333, 353
Kosgey, Henry 56, 80
Kubai, Fred 4
Kulei, Joshua 273, 336, 345
Kungu, Ngengi 34
Kung'u, Chief Waruhiu wa 6
Kuria, Edward Ng'ang'a 106
Kuria, Moses 112, 348, 352

L

Leliman, Frederick 140
Lenachuru, Clement 100
Lenku, Joseph Ole 84
Lenolkulal, Moses 197
Lenaola, Justice Isaac 96
Lesit, Justice Jessie 131
Lubke, Heinrich 299
Lynch, Gabrielle 122

M

Ma, Jack 173
Maathai, Professor Wangari 222
MacDonald, Malcolm 321
McCoy, Jennifer 348
Machage, Wilfred 253
Machar, Riek 304
Macharia, S. K. 334
Madowo, Larry 352, 357
Magana, Kungu wa 291
Mahamat, Moussa Faki 257
Mahamoud, Bashir Mohamed 90
Maina, Atanas Kariuki 221
Makau, Justice James 128
Makhtoum, Sheikh Mohammed al 223
Makokha, Kwamchetsi 122
Makone, Hellen 102
Makori, Eunice 102
Makori, Henry 356
Makori, Justice Evans 129
Mandela, Nelson 267, 380

Mandela, Winnie 267
Mangiti, Peter 192
Maore, Maoka 54
Maraga, Justice David 99, 129, 130, 131, 254
Marshall, Thurgood 12, 13, 14, 15,
Mate, Colonel Alice 314
Mati, Mwalimu 49
Matiang'i, Fred 122, 142, 170, 171, 174, 268, 280, 344
Matiba, Kenneth 40
Mathenge, Isaiah 31
Matonda, Samuel 212
Mbai, Crispine Odhiambo 326, 327
Mbagaya, Abigael 100
Mbarire, Cecily 353
Mbiyu, Chief Koinange wa 7, 8
Mbogholi, Justice Msagha 61
Mboya, Peter 39
Mboya, Tom 13, 14, 15, 319, 324
Mbugua, Simon 54
Mburu, Jonah 196
Mbuthia, Benson 142
Melle, Wilbert Le 14
Merali, Naushad 186, 188, 292
Mijungu, Ken 357
Miguna Miguna 112, 113, 288
Mochama, Tom 355
Mohamed, Adan 72, 183
Mohamed, Amina 72
Mohamed, Rashid Echesa 182
Mohamed, Junet 266
Mohamed, Kassim 137
Mohammed, Jamila 128
Moi, President Daniel arap xix, 17, 31-32, 39, 40-43, 67, 95, 96, 101, 114, 123-124, 132, 140, 151, 188, 222, 238-239, 265-267, 272-273, 294, 298-299, 308-309, 322-323, 326, 333, 336
Moi, Gideon 10, 253, 283, 306, 347, 349-351, 353, 354-356, 381, 382.
Moi, Philip 10
Monario, Ombori 28
Mongo, Chimwaga 126
Monson, Alexander 144
Moose, George 14
Morsi, President Mohamed 75
Mrima, Justice Antony 103, 106, 108
Msando, Chris Chege 134, 254, 313
Muchelule, Justice Aggrey 129
Mucheru, Joe 120
Mudavadi, Musalia xx, 41, 43, 58, 200, 228, 252-253, 257, 267, 343, 347
Mugambi, Riungu Nicholas 97
Mugo, Beth 15, 40
Mugonyi, David 358
Muigai, Githu 181
Muhoho, Anne Nyokabi 7, 8
Muhoho, George Kamau xix, 7, 31, 40, 334
Mshindi, Tom 350
Muia, Julius 174
Muigai, Githu 23
Muigai, James Ngengi 15
Muigai, Ngengi 15, 17, 31, 40, 57
Muigai, Kamau wa 3,
Muiruri, Daniel 34
Muiruri, Dr. John Njoroge 34

Muiruri, Joseph 140
Muiruri, Patrick 301
Muite, Paul 187
Mukio, Cynthia Mwakali 133
Mulyungi, Gideon 28
Munga, Peter 334
Mungai, Dr. Njoroge 300, 322
Munia, Sam 137
Manoti, Stephen 118
Murathe, David 172, 283, 356
Muriithi, Silas 100
Murkomen, Kipchumba 266, 352
Murumbi, Joseph 13, 277, 278, 324, 354
Murungaru, Christopher 44
Murugi, Esther 127
Murungi, Kiraitu 44
Museveni, Yoweri 66
Musyoka, Rose 100
Musyoka, Stephen Kalonzo xx, 41, 43, 59, 228, 252-253, 257, 267, 271, 278, 343, 347
Mutai, Abraham 25
Mutembei, Gilbert 274, 345
Mutoko, Caroline 358
Muthaura, Francis 56, 80
Mutua, Alfred 328
Mutua, Kisilu 324
Mutunga, Justice Willy 65, 98
Muturi, Justin 266, 349
Musana, Susana 291
Muthama, Samantha Ngina 172
Muthoni, Fridah
Mutyambai, Hillary 106
Mwaita, Sammy 273, 345
Mwaliko, Sylvester 45
Mwangala, Juma Mwatata 214

Mwangi, Boniface 187, 188
Mwangi, Leonard 140
Mwathethe, General (Rtd) Samson 91, 314
Mwatsumiro, Mohamed 'Modi' 136
Mwaura, Isaack 263, 312
Mwaura, Michael 253
Mwenda, Josephat 140
Mwendwa, Chief Justice Kitili 95
Mwiraria, David 44
Mwita, Justice Chacha 106, 131

N

Namu, John-Allan 137
Namuye, Catherine 214
Namwamba, Ababu 253
Nassir, Abdulswamad 176
Nassir, Shariff 41
Ndereba, Catherine 115
Nderi, Ignatius 323
Ndicho, Stephen 301
Ndiema, Duncan 141
Ndii, David 126, 154, 292, 302
Ndwiga, Benson Njiru 141
Ngala, Katana 41, 43
Ngala, Ronald 10
Ndumbu, Maryanne Carol 134
Ng'ang'a, Lucy Nduta 106
Ngei, Paul 4
Ngengi, Peter Mungai 34
Ng'eno, Johanna 25, 26
Ngilu, Charity 71
Ngirachu, John 350
Nguesso, Denis Sassou 294
Ngugi, Justice Joel 129
Ngugi, Justice Mumbi 197
Ngugi, Pius 334
Ngunjiri, Kimani 29

Ngunyi, Mutahi 26
Njeri, Lucy 34
Njogu, Emma 100
Njonjo, Charles 20, 49, 300
Njonjo, Paramount Chief Josiah 20
Njoroge, Esther Nyokabi 34
Njoroge, Lieutenant General Agostino Karanu 322
Njoroge, Nahashon Isaac Njenga 14, 325
Njoroge, Patrick 165
Njoroge, Virginia Wairimu 34
Njuguna, Justice Lucy 131
Njuki, Muthomi 199
Nkaiserry, Joseph 87
Nkrumah, Kwame 4, 8,
Nyagah, Jeremiah 22
Nyagah, Joseph 253
Nyandemo, Samuel 171
Nyakang'o, Margaret 152
Nyamweya, Sam 272, 273
Nyerere, Julius 8, 380
Nyoike, Kimani wa 327
Nyong'o, Peter Anyang' 77, 132

O

Obado, Zachary Okoth 197
Obama, President Barack 73, 238, 242
Obama, Barack Snr 73
Obasanjo, President General Olusegun 359
Ocampo, Luis Moreno- 56, 57, 79, 81
Obwayo, Justice Anthony 381
Ochoi, Bernard 112
Odhiambo, Bruce 214
Odhiambo, Morris, 119
Odinga, Ida 258, 267, 304
Odinga, Fidel 306
Odinga, Jaramogi Oginga xix, xx, 13, 14, 21, 40, 95, 305-306, 308, 324, 342
Odinga, Mary 308
Odinga, Oburu, 304, 306
Odinga, Raila Amolo xix, 29, 32, 43, 46-47, 55-56, 59, 60, 62-63, 65, 74, 79, 107, 109, 127, 130, 188, 193, 200, 203, 206, 228, 252, 254-256, 258, 259-262, 265, 267-268, 270-271, 277, 283, 285-288, 304-313, 326, 331-332, 334-335, 341, 342-345, 347-348, 353, 357, 363, 376, 380
Odinga, Ruth 306
Odunga, Justice George 97, 98, 113, 129, 211
Ogeto, Kennedy 174
Ogola, Justice Eric 107
Ogoti, Douglas 214
Oguna, Colonel (Rtd) Cyrus 218, 314
Okengo, Ali Wadi 27
Okoth, Kenneth 277
Okoyo, Philip 27
O'Loughlin, James Aloysius 36
Omange, Justice Judith 129
Omar, Sheikh Ibrahim 137
Ombeta, Cliff 187
Ombija, Trevor 212
Omtatah, Okiya 75, 99, 122, 149
Ondimba, Ali Bongo 294
Ongili, Paul 27
Onkwami, Samuel Aboko 27

Oneko, Achieng 4, 324
Onyango, Ibrahim 140
Onyiego, Justice John 104
Onyonka, Richard 195
Oparanya, Wycliffe 174
Orengo, James 113, 278
Orinda, Felix 112
Otunga, Cardinal Maurice 114
Ouko, Edward 153, 224, 366
Ouko, Robert 324, 325, 326
Owino, Babu 112
Oyugi, Hezekiah 325
Oyugi, General (Rtd) Moses 314

P

Padmore, George 4, 12
Pattni, Kamlesh 208, 272
Pendo, Samantha 132
Pinto, Pio Gama 324
Pouncey, Peter 16

Q

Queen Elizabeth 11

R

Rahman, Tahmina 348
Ramaphosa, Cyril 233
Rasanga, Cornel 354
Rawal, Justice Kalpana 327
Reagan, Ronald 238
Rege, James 53
Rogo, Sheikh Aboud 137
Rotich, Henry 171, 178, 209
Rubia, Charles 32, 327
Rukenya, Nahashon Ngare 318, 320
Ruto, Isaac 252, 253

Ruto, William Samoei xix, 24-27, 29, 56-61, 65, 71, 73, 76, 77-78, 80-81, 109, 118, 123, 126, 133, 139, 152, 166, 178, 201-202, 230, 241, 251, 257, 262-266, 268-269, 271, 272, 273-280, 284, 301, 329-331, 335-336, 341-346, 349, 353, 358-359, 376, 380

S

Sagar, Abdulhakim 138, 139
Saitoti, George 39, 43, 353
Sakaja, Johnson 59, 301, 329
Sang, Joshua arap 56, 80, 81
Savani, Suri A. 33, 34
Seii, Major John 259, 260
Selassie, Emperor Haile
Semelang'o, Evans Gor 214
Serem, Cornelius 169, 170, 171
Sergon, Justice Joseph 102
Shaw, Patrick 323
Shaw, Robert 48
Shebesh, Rachael 301
Shiels, Dr. Drummond 3,
Shikuku, Martin 327
Shiundu, Alphonse 350
Sio, Stephen 219
Somaia, Ketan 208
Sindimwo, Gaston 301
Somer, Murat 348
Sonko, Mike 107, 108, 118, 301, 330, 349
Starkley, Jerome 350
Stock, Dina 11
Stockwell, Captain I. S. 321
Sudi, Oscar 25, 26, 222, 284, 333

Swazuri, Mohammed Abdalla 100, 221

T

Taib Ali Taib 210
Thacker, Ransley 5
Thani, HE Sheikh Tamin bin Hamad al 227
Thugge, Kamau 209
Thungu, Arthur Wanyoike 323, 324
Thuo, Chege 324
Tillerson, Rex 258
Too, Mark 41, 336
Torerei, Samuel 100
Torome, Saitoti 102
Troon, John 325
Trump, Donald 93, 239
Tsvangirai, Morgan 113
Tuju, Raphael 27
Turner, Christian 74

W

Wahome, Alice 108
Wakhungu, Judy 218, 219
Waki, Justice Philip 55
Walingo, Mary 221
Waluke, John 218, 219
Waiguru, Anne 26, 72, 191, 192, 193, 270, 331
Wainaina, Ndungu 261
Waititu, Ferdinand 118
Wamalwa, Christine 302
Wamalwa, Eugene 211
Wambua, Enoch 152
Wambua, Jennifer 134
Wamuchomba, Gathoni 26
Wanga, Julius 358
Wangari, Sarah 141
Wanjigi, Jimmy 105, 106, 113, 332
Wanjiku, Silvia 140
Wanyeki, Muthoni 122
Wamalwa, Eugene 59
Wandayi, Opiyo 224, 225
Warah, Rasna 25, 122, 234
Wario, Umuro 213, 214, 219, 220
Washiali, Benjamin 353
Wasilwa, Justice Helen 127, 128
Waweru, Michael 334
Wetangula, Moses 252, 253, 257, 267, 347, 351, 353
Wood, Abby K. 110

Y

Yatani, Ukur 161, 168
Yebei, Meshack 133
Young, Andrew 14

Z

Zandi, Ali 223, 224
Zayed, Sheikh Abdullah bin 228

www.ingramcontent.com/pod-product-compliance
Lightning Source LLC
Chambersburg PA
CBHW071733150426
43191CB00010B/1554